ROUGHDRAFTS

ROUGHDRAFTS

The Process of Writing

Alice Heim Calderonello
Bowling Green State University

Bruce L. Edwards, Jr.
Bowling Green State University

Houghton Mifflin Company   Boston

Dallas   Geneva, Illinois
Lawrenceville, New Jersey   Palo Alto

To John and Josh, and to Joan and Matthew, Mary, Justin and Michael: our definition of love, patience, encouragement and hope

Acknowledgments

Book and Cover Design: DANIEL EARL THAXTON

Advertisement for Mercedes-Benz 300 SD Turbodiesel. Reprinted by permission.

Andy Rooney, "When Death Comes, We Each Weep For Our Own," Reprinted by permission: Tribune Media Services.

Katharine Brush, "Birthday Party." Reprinted by permission of Thomas S. Brush. Originally published March 16, 1946, in *The New Yorker*.

Carolyn Reed, "Contempt for Females Can Be Taught." From the Cleveland *Plain Dealer*, December 19, 1983. Reprinted by permission.

Frederick Buechner, "Once Upon a Time." From pp. 34–43 of THE SACRED JOURNEY by Frederick Buechner. Copyright © 1982 by Frederick Buechner. Reprinted by permission of Harper & Row, Publishers, Inc.

Russell Baker, "Summer Beyond Wish." Copyright © 1978 by The New York Times Company. Reprinted by permission.

From I KNOW WHY THE CAGED BIRD SINGS, by Maya Angelou. Copyright © 1969 by Maya Angelou. Reprinted by permission of Random House, Inc.

Peter Elbow, "Freewriting." from *Writing Without Teachers* by Peter Elbow. Copyright © 1973 by Oxford University Press, Inc. Reprinted by permission.

"When Camping Out, Do It Right" by Ernest Hemingway from the compilation *Dateline: Toronto*. (Originally appeared in the Toronto Star, 1920). Reprinted with the permission of Charles Scribner's Sons.

Copyright page continued on page 540.

Library of Congress Catalog Card Number: 85-80767

ISBN: 0-395-35501-X

ABCDEFGHIJ-H-89876

Contents

About this book

Current research in composition has taught us that writing is, at heart, a process of revision and rewriting. As we have sought to apply the insights of modern composition theory, particularly the work of Linda Flower, we have created a pedagogy that helps students see writing as a *continuous* process of revising and rewriting as they invent, plan, and draft their texts.

Roughdrafts is the fruit of our extensive classroom teaching experience; it places revision at the center of the writing process, demonstrating that successful writers revise—i.e., rethink, restate, rearrange, reformulate— their prose at every juncture in their writing processes. To enable apprentice writers to acquire strategies for rethinking and reformulating their texts, revision is presented as a two-step process. First, the writer is trained to evaluate a text objectively and recognize ineffective text-, sentence-, and word-level features. Second, the writer learns which revising strategies will be most helpful in addressing the problems found in a close textual analysis. Our method teaches students—in concrete terms—how to evaluate their own drafts and plan and execute revision strategies according to their individual intention and audience.

Linda Flower's concept of writer-based prose has proved to be a break-through concept because it explains concretely the difference between a text that communicates primarily to the writer and one that is accessible to a reader other than the writer. *Roughdrafts* extends Flower's work by introducing the concepts "predraft" and "rough draft" to distinguish primarily writer-based drafts from primarily reader-based drafts. The predraft is a draft whose thesis and intention are still ambiguous, whose organizational structure is inappropriately narrative, whose sentence structure may be convoluted, and/or whose word choice is marred by code words that communicate mainly to the writer. A predraft cannot be easily revised by adding, deleting, substituting, and rearranging materials; an entirely new draft is in order, though ideas and patterns of thought should be harvested from the earlier draft. In contrast, a rough draft has a discernible thesis and intention, an appropriate structure, and relatively fewer problems in sentence structure and word choice. Revising a rough draft is thus more a matter of reworking the draft through adding, deleting, substituting and rearranging materials.

Editing is seen not as the central focus of revision, but as the final stage of preparing a text for a reader. Further, it is not an end in itself nor should it be of paramount concern to the writer in the early stages of his or her draft.

Roughdrafts recognizes that writing and revising are best learned as students look over the shoulders of successful writers as these writers think, plan, write, and rewrite, moving from draft to draft in response to a writing task. Consequently, we use the work of our students to illustrate the writing and revising strategies introduced and discussed in Part One. *Roughdrafts* contains abundant exercises, writing tasks, and writing assignments throughout the text, each designed to help students recognize, practice, and master a particular component of the writing process, from inventing and planning to drafting and revising. We believe that by learning from others' strategies and by developing their own, apprentice writers can become confident, effective writers who can capably face any writing task during their college years and after.

Roughdrafts is divided into three parts. Part One (Chapters 1–5) presents the inventing, planning, drafting, and revising components of the writing process, illustrating them with practical, clear examples of students at work. Here apprentice writers receive practical instruction in how to (1) generate ideas; (2) discover their intention; (3) plan the basic organization of their texts; (4) survey their intended audience; (5) move through the drafting process; (6) evaluate their drafts; and (7) proceed with appropriate revision strategies.

Chapter 1 presents an overview of the writing process and discusses its recursive nature. Chapter 2 provides inventing and planning strategies to prepare the writer for drafting. Chapter 3 illustrates the drafting process, following the evolution of essays about graffiti by two student writers with radically different composing strategies. Chapters 4 and 5 examine intensely the common text-, sentence-, and word-level features of predrafts and rough drafts, showing students both how to recognize and distinguish the two kinds of drafts and how to revise them effectively.

Part Two (Chapters 6–10) is the core of the book, presenting the work of five student writers as each completes a different kind of writing task: the personal experience essay, the process essay, the informative essay, the evaluative essay, and the persuasive essay. The chapters in Part Two initially explain and illustrate with professional examples a particular kind of essay. Then three of the chapters (6–8) offer extended analyses of the inventing, planning, and drafting processes of the student writers; two of the chapters (9 and 10) offer incisive summaries of the students' writing processes and present their final drafts. All five chapters include a writing task that enables students to work alongside the student writer in each chapter.

Part Three (Chapters 11–13) focuses on the last component of the writing process, editing—the process of readying the final copy for the reader. It contains three chapters, each focusing on a different aspect of editing: sentence structure, word choice, grammar/usage/mechanics. This section treats editing as a two-step process, involving strategies for locating and identifying specific kinds of errors as well as strategies for correcting these errors. Part Three is thus designed as a resource section for students with particular needs and problems.

Adaptable to a wide range of classroom applications, *Roughdrafts* may be used alone as a comprehensive rhetoric, since its extensive use of student texts and many professional essays make a separate reader unnecessary. Other instructors may choose to use *Roughdrafts* as a supplemental text, to teach students how to revise. *Roughdrafts* is especially useful to the instructor who uses peer editing groups or who teaches with extensive conferencing, since it focuses directly on acquisition of reading and revising skills.

In the writing of any textbook there are many colleagues, mentors, editors, and reviewers to thank. In addition, there are countless others who deserve recognition, not the least of whom are our students at Bowling Green State University. Deserving special thanks are our students whose work appears in this textbook: Pati, Charlene, Brenda, Joe, Anita, Beth, and Jeff. Thus, the following list is not exhaustive, only representative of those who regularly—and significantly—provided invaluable help in the conception and birth of *Roughdrafts*. First, our thanks to those who have typed various portions of the textbook, especially Joan Edwards who typed the first draft and later helped piece together revisions by hand, and also Joanne Lohr, who provided encouragement along with clean copy. Thanks also to Suzanne Andrews, departmental administrator, who helped us clear some time on the departmental printers at crucial moments in the evolution of the text.

No textbook can be written without influences from the profession we serve in and are served by. We are especially indebted to the work of Linda Flower, whose pioneering inquiries into the writing process and the textual features that mark writer-based prose have served us so fruitfully in the writing of this book. In addition, such theorists and researchers as James

Kinneavy, Winston Weathers, Donald Stewart, Nancy Sommers, and Ken Macrorie have inspired much of the foundation of this textbook. Those authors, colleagues, and confidants who have also exerted an influence over the way we conceive of the writing and reading process include: Walter Ong, Jim Karpen, C. S. Lewis, Flannery O'Connor, and Tom Klein.

We must thank, of course, our reviewers, early and late, who helped us rethink our ideas and recast them in ways accessible to teachers and students, making *Roughdrafts* an exemplification of what it seeks to teach students about revising. These reviewers include:

- Jay Balderson, Western Illinois University
- Rick A. Eden, The Rand Corporation
- John P. Ferré, University of Louisville
- Sandra Hanson, LaGuardia Community College
- Thomas M. Johnson, Riverside College
- Malcolm Kiniry, University of California–Los Angeles
- Emily Meyer, University of Massachusetts–Boston
- James S. Mullican, Indiana State University
- Twila Yates Papay, Rollins College
- Peggy Irene Paulisin, Lincoln Land Community College
- Evan Rivers, Skidmore College
- Paul Schlueter
- David E. Schwalm, University of Texas–El Paso
- Eric C. Walker, Florida State University

We thank, as well, the staff of editors at Houghton Mifflin who believed in our textbook and its platform of ideas and who provided expert assistance in rewriting, designing, and editing.

A.H.C., B.L.E

ROUGHDRAFTS

Part One

The Writing Process

This first section of *Roughdrafts* will introduce some basic composition strategies and terminology that will assist you in becoming a more effective writer.

Chapter 1 will help you discover how writers write, that is, how successful writers think about the task of writing and how they go about the process of crafting a text for specific audiences. At the end of Chapter 1 is a writing questionnaire that will help you become aware of yourself as a writer: your attitudes, your strengths and weaknesses, your typical behavior as an apprentice writer. This chapter thus presents an overview of the writing process that will prepare you for practicing the components of writing discussed in Chapters 2 through 5.

Chapter 2 presents inventing and planning strategies. Inventing and planning include any activities that writers use to help them prepare for and move successfully through the drafting of a text—like brainstorming, outlining, answering specific questions about a topic, finding a thesis, and considering one's audience. Throughout this chapter, you will follow the efforts of Frank Day, one of our students, as he works through these strategies and activities toward the completion of a draft of his essay on the Cleveland Indians.

Chapter 3 discusses various ways that writers draft their texts. In this chapter you will be presented with an intensive examination of the drafting processes of two students, Pati and Charlene, who have greatly contrasting writing behaviors but who both successfully complete a writing task about graffiti.

Chapters 4 and 5 explore means of examining a draft in order to evaluate it and determine an appropriate revision strategy. Chapter 4 focuses on the *predraft*, an exploratory draft that a writer writes to discover what he or she wants to say. Chapter 5 focuses on the *rough draft*, a more finished reader-directed draft, and on how to proceed in revising it to make it better suited for its intended audience.

Part One sets the stage for Part Two, where you will watch students' works-in-process as well as gain experience in writing different kinds of texts.

1 *How Writers Write*

Writing as a
Recursive Process

One way a writer can learn to write more effectively is to study the composing process of successful writers. That is, he or she can study how successful writers start writing, develop their ideas, and move toward a final draft. This textbook is based on our conviction that apprentice writers can learn more about how to write by looking over the shoulders of writers at work than by following rules and prescriptions. In Part One of *Roughdrafts* you will learn about the different strategies that writers employ to create satisfying, successful drafts. In Part Two you will get the opportunity to observe five student writers working their way through five different writing tasks. In Part Three you will be given some helpful strategies for recognizing and correcting common problems in grammar, word choice, and mechanics.

The composing processes of individual writers vary greatly, and it is difficult to draw a uniform picture of how a successful writer writes. But even though no two texts come to their final form in exactly the same way, it is possible to generalize about the most important aspects of successful writing behavior. Here are three important generalizations about the writing process:

Writing is a process of **revising**.

Successful writers know that revision is not just correcting errors or cleaning up a manuscript, not just an activity confined to the very end of the writing process. These writers make changes throughout the composing process. They add, delete, substitute, and rearrange material in their texts to make their meaning clear to their readers.

Writing is a **recursive** process.

Successful writers do not merely begin at the beginning and write until they run out of things to say; writing is not simply a matter of putting words together. Writers behave recursively; that is, a writer must often double back while writing—altering content, making changes in organization and wording, rethinking a text at every level—in order to communicate his thesis and intention to the reader. The word "text" indicates writing that is deliberately planned and structured by a writer to communicate to a reader other than the writer himself. A writer's "thesis" is the point or points he wants to express. His "intention" refers to what he wants his text to accomplish (e.g., inform, persuade, amuse, etc.).

Writing is a **drafting** process.

While in the process of developing a final text, a writer may produce a series of drafts: a *predraft,* which is basically the writer talking to himself, finding his thesis and a direction for organizing and developing his text; one or more *rough drafts,* drafts that emerge as clearer, more developed texts, directly addressed to a reader other than the writer himself; and a *final draft,* a text that expresses the writer's meaning and intention to his readers as fully as possible.

The Writing Process

It may seem contradictory to refer to the writing process as *recursive* and then discuss writing as a linear evolution of drafts. But, to write effectively, writers inevitably must deal with their own drafts, the concrete texts in front of them. And to learn how to generate, evaluate, and revise these drafts, it is helpful for an apprentice writer to recognize and practice five common components of the writing process: inventing, planning, drafting, revising, and editing.

It is important not to make the mistake of thinking that these components must occur separately or always in the same sequence. Although some writers go through somewhat discrete stages in a particular order, every writer goes *back and forth* among these five components to some extent. For example, after a writer has begun drafting, he may discover that he needs to generate more information, or he may discover that he needs to redefine his main idea. All five components are crucial to effective writing, regardless of the sequence in which they occur in your writing process.

Inventing

Inventing is any activity that involves the writer in discovering and generating what he wants to say. It can take place at any time, even during drafting. Reading, talking, thinking, brainstorming, doodling, going over notes, and using a specific inventing method (such as a set of questions) to examine a topic are some examples of inventing activities. Some writers engage in these procedures extensively before they write so that they know—as much as possible—what they are going to say before they begin drafting. Other writers insist that it is impossible for them to know what they are going to say until after they have said it. These writers, then, begin drafting immediately with no clear notion of what they will say, discovering the content as they work through a draft of their text.

Exercise

Chapter 2 will introduce you to several inventing techniques, but to give you an idea of how some writers get ideas or "invent," try your hand at these short writing tasks.

1.   Sit in a large public place (such as a cafeteria or one of the lounges in the Student Union) and observe the persons around you. Write a description of the physical features of a particular individual; or describe an interaction between two or more persons; or describe the expression on someone's face. If you are particularly intrigued by what someone does or by an interaction between some individuals or by the expression on someone's face, write about it. Speculate as to what really happened, or what caused _____ to happen, or why _____ looks so _____. You may wish to write a story about a particular individual or incident. Use your imagination.

2. Record any reactions you have to the reading or work you are required to do for other classes: "I never thought of that; I wonder _____"; "This is ridiculous because _____"; "I don't understand _____ because _____." Or you may wish to write out questions related to or summaries of what you read.

3. Record any reactions you have to what you read in a magazine or newspaper, or to what you see on television or in a movie. You might, especially, like to try writing a mini-review of a television series or movie that you really like or dislike.

4. Whenever you get in a discussion or debate with your friends, try to record, as soon as possible, your emotional responses, your opinions and attitudes, and your reasons for these responses/opinions/attitudes. Such a discussion or debate might concern, for example, whether a particular grade is fair, a particular campus incident, a campus activity such as sorority/fraternity rush, or a campus tradition like homecoming.

5. Record what Ken Macrorie refers to as "short fabulous realities."

FOR EXAMPLE:

Two adjacent signs in a bank: One says, "Keep America strong; open a savings account." The other says, "Let us loan you money; we've got the best rates."
Or, a man and a woman walk into a restaurant together. She is 4'11", petite, with dark hair and eyes. He is at least 6'5", large-boned, heavy-set, and fair.

Describe these "realities" as vividly as you can. You also might like to write commentary or, perhaps, brief stories on some of them.

6. Select someone you know and interview him or her. Determine your questions before you conduct the interview—selecting an orientation like "I'm collecting attitudes about grading practices here at Foo U; are they fair?" or "I'm trying to determine why people are attending Foo U rather than working." Write a narrative describing the interview, or write a summary of the interview, or write your reactions to being an interviewer, or write a piece not directly related to the interview but somehow inspired by it.

Planning

Planning is the activity by which a writer tries to determine *how* to say what he wants to say. It involves answering such questions as:

☐   What is my thesis and intention in this text?

☐   Who is my audience for this text?

☐   How much information is relevant to the task? How will it be presented, in what form and in what order?

☐   What tone (humorous, serious, ironic) is best?

Individual writers do plan differently. Some plan as they invent; some plan largely after they invent; some plan as they draft and revise. However, every writer must determine in some way the form that his final text will take. Chapter 2 will cover these matters in some depth, but we want to highlight two areas of planning here.

CONSIDERING AUDIENCE

One of the most important elements in planning is the writer's consideration of his *audience*. A text is usually addressed to a particular reader or readers, and audiences vary in specific ways that are worth considering. Suppose, for example, that a writer wishes to argue in favor of tax credits for parents of children who attend private schools. Whether the writer's audience is a group of parents whose children attend private schools or a group of public school teachers is a crucial consideration that will affect the way the writer develops and organizes his text. How a writer approaches the drafting of a text will depend upon how well he knows his audience. For example, how well educated are they? What occupations do they hold? What are their values? How old are they? What do they know about the writer's topic? What is their attitude toward the topic?

The characteristics of a particular audience are an important consideration for just about every skilled writer. Although many writers think about these matters almost immediately, some prefer to consider them most extensively as they focus their attention on the shape and structure of their draft. On the other hand, some considerations that apply to any audience and every reader include:

1.   Every reader needs a reason to begin and keep reading a text.

2.   Every reader needs to be cued to the principle of organization so that he or she can anticipate and follow the text's development without guesswork.

3.   Every reader needs more than the writer's assertion that something is true in order to accept his meaning.

4.   Every reader prefers to be *shown* rather than *told* the meaning of a text. Avoid editorializing.

5.   Every reader needs a sense of closure, an appropriate and meaningful conclusion that is neither abrupt nor superficial.

6.   Every reader needs a legible, clean manuscript.

As you work through this textbook, you will gain experience in addressing all these needs as they arise during the drafting of a text. This list suggests many of the questions involved in planning.

PRODUCING A TEXT

One other essential element of planning is considering how to produce the text itself. Along with questions about the characteristics of an audience or the intention for writing, a writer may ask himself these kinds of questions:

☐   Would it be better to read some essays for ideas about how to begin the piece? Or would it be better to compose a list of possible first sentences?

☐   Would it be better to think about the audience during the development of a general idea or a means of structuring? Or would it be better to postpone thinking about the audience until after the drafting begins?

☐   Would it be better to begin with general information and eventually become more specific? Or would it be better to get to the point immediately?

Planning, whether for the text itself or for the best strategies for producing the text, is often stimulated by what has already been written. Successful writers frequently alter their plans after they have produced a draft or part of a draft. Sometimes the only way to determine that a plan is poor is to produce a draft and *see* that it is poor. Sometimes the only way to determine that a strategy is not working well is to examine the results of its use.

Exercise

The following list of items about the Mercedes-Benz 300 SD Turbodiesel appeared in an advertisement:

☐   the 300 SD is one of the "least extravagant corporate automobiles"

☐   over the last 3 years, the resale value of the 300 SD has averaged 90%

☐   "no fewer than 120 safety features" are standard

☐   five adults will fit comfortably

☐   the EPA highway mileage figure is 33 mpg

☐   the 300 SD comes with a 36-month or 36,000-mile warranty

☐   the 300 SD is "deeply pleasurable" to drive

☐   the efficient 3-liter diesel engine is powerful

☐   the interior trimming is in "genuine hand-finished woods"

☐   "passengers are hardly ignored"—provided with reading lamps and a separate ventilation console

☐   the 300 SD serves as a "fine advertisement"

☐   the 300 SD costs $38,000

   This advertisement clearly presupposes certain things about its readers and potential buyers. You may or may not feel yourself a part of the audience to which the advertisement is directed, but suppose you were a consultant who was being paid to advise a Mercedes-Benz dealer who intends to send a letter that describes the 300 SD to prospective buyers in the locality. You may pick the location—Chicago, Illinois; Akron, Ohio; Cheyenne, Wyoming; etc. Do some inventing about that letter—brainstorming, jotting down ideas, arranging the items of information in certain groupings, asking yourself about the potential buyers of such a car.

   Now look over the inventing you did in preparation for advising the car dealer. What ways of organizing the letter occur to you? How much are you thinking of the audience? Which of the items in the list of information do you consider most significant? Continue working on planning the piece by answering the following questions:

1.   Describe the audience. How much money do they have to spend on a car? What are their occupations? If they own businesses, are these businesses large or small? How might they use the Mercedes: to entertain out-of-town customers? for business travel? to impress potential customers?

2.   List the facts about the 300 SD that you would incorporate in such a letter. Group them together and identify larger organizing principles, where appropriate. For example, you might cluster the information about the 3-liter engine, the standard safety features, and the 3-year warranty into a larger category entitled "quality engineering." Jot down any ideas you have for ordering the information that should be included in the letter.

3.   How might you begin the letter? What factors should you consider in determining how to begin it? Write a first sentence or several first sentences.

4.   How would you end the letter? What are some good strategies for ending it? Why are these strategies good ones?

Drafting

In order to produce a first draft, all writers, whether skilled or not, require certain implements: pencil and paper; a typewriter and paper; or a word processor and printer. Imagine two writers at roughly the same stage of the writing process. They both have done enough preliminary inventing and planning to have a fairly detailed conception of what they want to say and how they think they want to say it. They are both writing first drafts that will, eventually, become finished texts. While drafting, these two writers will go back and forth between inventing and planning, drafting, and even editing—that is, they *revise* as they write, when and if it is necessary to do so. There the similarity may end.

Other generalizations about what writers do when they are drafting probably are not very useful. The amount of time a writer stops, gets stuck, takes a break, becomes frustrated, or becomes elated during a drafting session varies with every writer and with every session. What a writer does when he gets stuck also varies tremendously. One reads some material, rereads what he has already written, or reads an earlier, successful piece of his own. Another takes a break, eats, talks to a friend, starts all over on another part of the text. But all experienced writers have a repertoire of strategies, which they are constantly adding to and refining, that work for them. Again, in Part Two of this textbook you will get a firsthand look at the drafting process.

Exercise

Refer to the exercise on pages 9–10. Look over the results of your inventing and planning. Assuming that you will provide the Mercedes dealer with a sample letter, use the first sentence(s) you have already written and write a first draft of a letter describing the Mercedes-Benz 300 SD.

Revising

Revising is *not* the same as proofreading or editing. It involves rethinking and changing the text—possibly changing the introduction, or a paragraph, or several paragraphs, or part of a paragraph, or a major argument. Revising involves adding new writing, or cutting out writing, or rearranging what is written, or substituting another way of saying something. It is something a skilled writer is willing and able to do, but skilled writers do not always revise extensively every time they write. The amount of revising varies according to the writing patterns of the individual writer and according to the requirements of the particular writing task and the context in which that task is presented to the writer. For example, how much time is available? How demanding does the writer perceive the audience to be? These kinds of questions affect a writer's revising strategies.

Revision may be defined as any activity that involves a change in a text. Suppose, though, that you have generally conceived of revision as something a person does when just about finished writing. You do not recall having done much revision, except for making small changes, such as correcting a spelling error, changing a verb form, or substituting one word for another. If a teacher required you to revise, you inserted a sentence or two in response to such marginal notes from your teacher as "Your meaning isn't clear; are you talking about _____ or _____?" or "Provide some specific examples of _____." Then you recopied or retyped your essay, making any other changes in spelling, grammar, and/or mechanics that your teacher required, and handed it in again.

We may have just described what you think you do when you revise: You make changes, most often at the word level, *after* a writing task is largely finished. Word-level changes are those that involve single words, such as changes in spelling, in grammatical form, and of one word to another. These changes, however, do not begin to include everything that is involved in revision. Writing is a process that involves many choices. You must make choices about both *external,* contextual matters, such as audience, and about *internal,* textual matters, such as organization, content, sentence structure, word choice, and usage. You must make choices about which ideas to use and which to save for another time; choices about which means of structuring to attempt; choices regarding word selection.

A writer who sees revision as an unimportant part of the writing process, a part that occurs at or near the end, severely limits his choices. He gives up the opportunity to monitor important decisions *throughout* the writing process. In a sense, this limited notion of revision encourages the writer to make every important decision quite early in the process. These decisions include: What is my intention in writing? How will I view my audience? How will I structure my text? But every decision may not work out once drafting begins. "This means of organizing isn't working"; "my purpose seems to have changed"; "I can't think of much to say about _____." The writer then has little recourse but to proceed and hope that, if the piece is tidy and there are no errors in spelling, punctuation, grammar, and the like, the reader will not notice any major problem.

On the other hand, a writer may see revision as an ongoing process that involves changes in ideas, in strategies for proceeding, in methods of organization, in the structuring of sentences at any time during the construction of a piece of writing. Then he provides himself with choices, with a range of options. If he runs out of ideas in the middle of a draft, he has a variety of responses to try. If he discovers, while writing, that his purpose in writing seems to have changed, he knows what to do. He will try one technique, and if it does not work, he will try another. If that one does not work either, he may decide that his purpose was probably not as clear to him as he thought it was, and so he will begin again by inventing once more. And so on.

Revision includes two main activities: *evaluation* and *rewriting*. It effectively involves evaluating what has been written and determining what kind of revising strategy is appropriate. It also involves learning to recognize *writer-based* features in one's writing. These are text, sentence, and word-level features that are meaningful only to the writer himself. They must be revised to make the text more *reader-based,* more accessible and clear to the reader to whom it is addressed. Through revising, a writer learns how to determine whether a first draft is a *predraft,* addressed primarily to the writer himself, that cannot be revised merely by adding, deleting, substituting, or rearranging, or a *rough draft,* which can be revised successfully through such operations. Once he has become experienced in evaluating his text, he can learn strategies for reconceptualizing, reorganizing, or rephrasing it. He can learn how to *rewrite* ineffective sections to make the text more effective as he moves toward a final draft.

Revision, then, can be seen as the primary activity whereby a writer makes *choices.* The first step in learning how to write well is to conceive of revision as an ongoing process that begins the moment a writer begins writing and continues until he has finished. If you adopt such a view of revision, you will see the process of writing differently. You will become interested in learning strategies for making choices. You will begin to wonder about things like, "What are good questions to ask?" "When should I ask them?" "What should I look for in a text in order to determine what I should do next?" "What are some techniques I can use to accomplish _____?" "How do I know whether a strategy I've chosen is producing the desired results?" This textbook will address these questions as it explores the writing process and examines texts that others have written.

Exercise

Examine the two versions of the same letter that follow. The second version is a revision of the first.

To: Director of Parking and Traffic

Every semester it gets harder and harder to find a place to park. The university is obligated to provide ample parking, but they fail to do so. The lots are all congested. This is especially true at the beginning of the semester. I happen to know that the Speech and Hearing Clinic doesn't open until the second week of classes so I don't understand why it is necessary for them to have reserved spaces before then.

I request that you do something regarding this matter.

To: Director of Parking and Traffic

The beginning of each semester is a particularly hectic time for everyone—new classes and all of the accompanying mania! It is especially difficult for us all, therefore, to find the parking lots especially congested at that time—although this is perfectly understandable.

I have noticed that quite a few parking spaces in several parking lots are reserved for customers of the Speech and Hearing Clinic. However, it is my understanding that the Clinic doesn't schedule clients until the middle of the second week of classes. I must confess that I have been tempted several times to park in one of the reserved spaces—only the threat of a ten-dollar fine has deterred me.

Would it be possible for restricted lots/spaces to be available to the public when and if they are not being used for designated purposes—especially if these lots/spaces are not being used at the beginning of the semester?

I appreciate your concern regarding this matter.

What problems did you find in the first draft of the letter? Were there problems with focus? organization? tone? sentence structure? word choice? mechanics/usage? What suggestions for revision would you make? Did the second draft correct all the difficulties? Why or why not? What additional suggestions would you make? Write your own revised version of the first draft of the letter.

Writing Task

Think about what you did when you revised the "Parking" letter. How did you determine what was wrong with the first version? With the second? How did you decide how to correct these problems? Using these revision skills, revise your Mercedes letter. Evaluate your draft to determine what needs to be changed, then make those changes. You may need to revise the letter several times before you are satisfied with it.

Editing

Editing means polishing a piece of writing by making word-level changes: in *spelling* ("I've misspelled 'apparent' again"), *mechanics* ("I need to use a comma here"), *usage* ("I'd better check the past tense of 'lie' "), *word choice* ("I've used 'justify' three times in two sentences; maybe I can substitute another word"), and so on. Most often, writers edit a piece of writing at the end of the writing process, after the piece is finished in all other respects. This gives them one last opportunity to inspect the piece and to determine whether it meets their standards. However, some writers edit throughout the composing process. They find that attending to small word-level errors as they compose is not a distraction, but a means of gaining additional time to think about what they are writing as they write. Writers who edit a great deal as they write still prefer to do so again when the piece is finished, however. No matter how skillfully a text is written, errors can have a number of undesirable effects. Careless errors can affect the meaning of a piece of writing, can give the readers a negative impression of the writer, and can cause readers to read less carefully than they would otherwise.

Exercise

Examine the following sentences. Each sentence contains an error that would have been corrected if the writer had edited carefully. Correct the error and explain why it might confuse the reader or give the reader a bad impression of the writer.

1. In response to expressions of concern from personnel, a special service telephone number is being established on a trail basis.

2.   Formally, the Summer Dean of each college received a budget, which was apportioned among their departments.

3.   Dear Sir: I have requested an application for employment twice, but I haven't yet recieved one. Thank you for your consideration.

4.   Preparation of this paper was supported by a grant fom the National Institution of Education.

5.   In the spring time flew by at an alarming rate.

Writing Task

Proofread your Mercedes letter. When you have finished, the letter should be ready to send to potential customers. Make sure you examine it carefully.

Discovering Your Own Writing Behavior

Although all writers must devote a great deal of time to inventing, planning, and revising, as well as to drafting, the behavior of individual writers differs considerably. Chapter 3 will explore the actual writing processes of two students to illustrate kinds of writing behavior that are typical of apprentice writers. Here, however, we want to preview that section by generally describing the way each of these students proceeded through the drafting of a text.

Writer 1 behaved pretty much the way that writers are expected to behave. First, she engaged in inventing by reading, thinking, and brainstorming in order to narrow and focus her topic. Then she decided on a thesis for her essay, and eventually crafted a detailed plan. She then used this plan to write a rough draft, which she rewrote several times, focusing on smaller, less significant changes each time.

Writer 2, on the other hand, started by reading and gathering information, but she wrote a first draft rather quickly. Then she used this predraft as a repository of ideas, which she manipulated in another lengthy inventing session. Following that, she produced a rough draft that did not need extensive rewriting. She reworked this draft several times, making all changes, both larger ones and smaller ones, at the same time.

The differences between what the two writers did to produce an essay are instructive. Not every piece of writing can or should be written *after* the writer has devoted considerable time to determining what she wishes to write about and how she should go about it. When writing is preceded by extensive inventing and planning (as in writer 1's case), it is not unusual for a writer to produce a first draft that has a thesis and is quite structured. However, if writer 2 had mistakenly identified her earliest draft as a piece of writing with a definite thesis and a recognizable structure, she might have tried to revise it by adding something here and rewording something there, and she might have had considerable difficulty. Writer 2's first draft was a *predraft,* a repository of ideas. It was a piece of writing addressed to herself that she wrote in order to figure out what she was going to write. She knew enough about her behavior as a writer, however, to recognize that she often wrote a first draft to sort things out and come up with ideas for a thesis. Thus she knew what to expect from her first draft and did not attempt to rewrite it. Rather, she looked at it as a communication to *herself,* not as a completed text for another reader. In it, she asked herself, "What does this draft tell me about what I want to write?"

Like writer 2, any writer may find it useful to be conscious of how he behaves when he writes. Given a particular kind of writing task, does he tend to think about the topic, narrow it, compose an outline, write a rough draft, and so on? Or does he need to begin writing almost immediately, producing a predraft or a succession of predrafts, one of which is eventually shaped into a rough draft and then a finished piece? There are various ways in which writers can discover what they do when they write, and some are more practical than others. You can determine which ones appeal to you.

Sometimes engaging in self-observation can be interesting and instructive. This does not require much, just some paper (perhaps a notepad) other than that you are using for your essay. Whenever you notice something about what you are doing as you write, write it down: "Got stuck in the second paragraph as I was trying to explain _____. Reread what I had already written up to this point. Didn't work. Still stuck. Reread the notes I took on _____, which made me think of _____, which I used to explain _____." Sometimes you might want to make brief notes to yourself, such as "changed 'ideal' to 'value,'" in the margins of or within the text of your essay. Examining the scratchouts, insertions, and other changes you have made can also be instructive, especially if you try to recall *when* you made them. And, of course, always save several drafts of the same essay, at least for a time. You can examine and reexamine these, or compare them with the drafts of other essays.

Writing Task

In a brief paragraph, try to describe what you think you do when you write an essay. Do you always behave in the same way, or does your behavior differ, depending upon the writing task? It may help you to write this paragraph if you consider whether you write more like writer 1 or writer 2.

Another, more elaborate, way to discover your writing behavior is to take a personal inventory by filling out a questionnaire. Before continuing to the next chapter, answer the following questions. This will help you determine the place of the five writing components we have discussed in this chapter—inventing, planning, drafting, revising, and editing—in your writing process. Answer the questions as honestly as possible.

WRITING QUESTIONNAIRE

A. Inventing and Planning
1. What do you do, if anything, to avoid writing?

_____ do other homework   _____ visit a friend or phone someone

_____ clean   _____ write letter(s)

_____ arrange desk   _____ other: _____

2. What do you do to begin a writing task?

_____ think about it (without   _____ write notes/make lists/
      making notes)   make outlines

_____ read (in general)   _____ begin writing

_____ read (in relevant   _____ a combination (explain):
      materials)   _____

_____ talk to friends/class-   _____
      mates/teacher

_____ depends (explain): _____   _____ other: _____

_____   _____

3. How do you discover what your main idea or thesis will be?

_____ brainstorm/jot down   _____ read
      notes or ideas   _____ read and take notes

_____ talk to people   _____ write

_____ think about it   _____ depends: _____

_____ combination: _____   _____

_____   _____

_____ other: _____   _____

_____   _____

4. When do you do most of your inventing?
   _____ at the beginning of a writing task
   _____ once at the beginning and once more if I get stuck
   _____ throughout the entire process
   _____ occasionally   _____ not at all
   _____ other: _____

5. Do you "know" what you are going to say before you begin writing?
   _____ always   _____ most often   _____ rarely   _____ never
   _____ depends (explain): _____
   _____ other: _____

6. When do you plan what you are going to write?
   _____ before I begin writing, as I am inventing
   _____ before I begin writing, after I have done some inventing
   _____ as I write
   _____ combination: _____
   _____ depends: _____

7. How do you plan?
   _____ with a detailed outline
   _____ with a sketchy, informal outline
   _____ with notes   _____ with a list   _____ with a chart or diagram
   _____ by thinking about it   _____ while writing (as I go)
   _____ combination: _____
   _____ depends: _____
   _____ other: _____

B. Drafting
   1. Which statements describe what you do when you write?
      a. I usually begin writing:
         _____ after I have invented and planned extensively
         _____ after I have done some inventing and planning
         _____ after I have done some inventing
         _____ right away
         _____ depends: _____
         _____ other: _____
      b. Once I begin writing I feel:
         _____ relieved   _____ worried   _____ bored   _____ anxious to finish
         _____ upset   _____ excited   _____ confident   _____ unsure
         _____ combination: _____
         _____ depends: _____
         _____ other: _____

2. Which statements describe what you do when you write?
   a. When I get stuck while writing I:
      _____ panic _____ reread what I have already written
      _____ look over my notes
      _____ read some books or essays _____ talk to someone
      _____ take a break
      _____ brainstorm or jot notes _____ read over my outline
      _____ repeat earlier composing strategies
      _____ other: _____

   b. When I finish writing my first draft:
      _____ I am done
      _____ I copy it over (or type it), correcting spelling, etc.; then
            I am done
      _____ I put it aside; then I look at it later and decide if it is
            done
      _____ I read it and mark things I need to fix, then fix them
      _____ I put it aside and begin a second draft, referring to
            the first now and then
      _____ I give it to a friend to read and ask what needs to be
            fixed, then I fix it
      _____ I try to fix major problems first, without paying attention
            to individual words or sentences, then I correct smaller
            errors
      _____ I go back and correct everything, big or little, all at
            the same time

C. Revising
   1. Which statements describe what you do when you write?
      a. When I change what I write, I:
         _____ add things _____ cross things out _____ rearrange
         things
         _____ reword things _____ other:_____
      b. The changes I make most often have to do with:
         _____ spelling and punctuation _____ grammar
         _____ words _____ sentences _____ information I left out
         _____ ordering (changing sequence of words, sentences)
         _____ reducing wordiness _____ clearing up transitions
      c. When I discover problems with a draft, I am willing to write it
         over:
         _____ always _____ usually _____ sometimes
         _____ rarely _____ never
         _____ other: _____

    d. My preoccupation with correct spelling, grammar, and usage interferes with my ability to rewrite:

      _____ always   _____ usually   _____ sometimes   _____ rarely   _____ never

      _____ other: _____

    e. I usually write a draft over:

      _____ once   _____ twice   _____ as many times as it takes

      _____ only if required   _____ never

      _____ other: _____

    f. The main thing that prevents me from rewriting is:

      _____ I don't know how   _____ It's too tedious

      _____ I don't have time   _____ I get too upset

      _____ other: _____

2. Check the parts of an essay you most frequently examine and, if necessary, change when you rewrite:

    _____ introduction   _____ conclusion   _____ topic sentences in paragraphs

    _____ major arguments and explanations   _____ transitions within paragraphs

    _____ transitions between paragraphs

    _____ other: _____

3. Check the statements that describe what you usually do when you write:

    _____ I change major problems with structure and ideas first, before I make small changes

    _____ I make changes regarding each problem I find, no matter what it is

    _____ To me, rewriting means making major changes

    _____ When I rewrite, I produce several different drafts

    _____ When I rewrite, I keep working with the same draft; I never start a new one

    _____ other: _____

D. Editing

1. Check the statements which apply to you:

    _____ I always devote a separate reading to my draft *after* have finished rewriting, just for proofreading and editing.

    _____ I always read my essay out loud at least once.

    _____ I proofread several times for different kinds of problems.

    _____ If I find a major problem, I am willing to fix it, even though I thought my draft was finished.

_____ If I find a major problem, I ignore it and hope no one notices it.

_____ I proofread each time, even if I know I'm going to rewrite.

_____ I proofread several times, but I always look for "everything" each time.

_____ I only proofread at the very end of a writing task.

_____ I constantly proofread as I'm writing, even if I'm just doing inventing.

_____ I proofread while I am typing the final draft of a piece of writing.

Getting Started: 2 Using Inventing and Planning Strategies

The Importance of Inventing and Planning

Few writers sit down with a perfectly detailed idea of what they want to say. Therefore, all writers must learn how to begin to write and how to proceed through the drafting of a text. They must learn how to recognize the elements of an unfinished draft and develop strategies for molding that draft into an appropriate text for their readers. Two activities that must precede or accompany the drafting of a text, as discussed in Chapter 1, are *inventing* and *planning*. These are the processes by which a writer discovers both what she wants to say and the best way of saying it. Writers use diverse strategies—some mental, some graphic, some free-wheeling, some highly structured—to explore possibilities and ideas and to plan the final form of their texts.

Inventing is a kind of idea juggling or mind-doodling that allows the writer to try out notions without feeling committed or bound to them.

During inventing, the writer temporarily ignores the potential reader while she discovers what she wants to say. Some writers invent and plan in their heads and commit little to paper before drafting a text. Others must do all their idea juggling on paper or on a word processor, whether in short snippets, notes to themselves, or large chunks of freewriting. Every writer discovers useful ways of bringing her ideas and the relationships among them onto paper, where they can be shaped into a form that is appropriate for presentation to a reader.

Inventing often leads to *planning*. After a period of inventing, during which she generates the raw material from which she will draft her text, the writer may start to plan the rest of the writing effort. In planning, a writer begins to consider the audience, how to group and order her ideas, and her voice, stance, and tone. Together, inventing and planning comprise a series of activities that writers typically perform *before* they begin to draft a text. But, because writing is a dynamic, recursive process, writers frequently revise their expectations and goals *during* the drafting process itself, and they engage in further inventing and planning as they gain greater control of their emerging text.

In responding to the writing questionnaire in Chapter 1, you may have discovered something you did not know about the way you compose. Specifically, you may have discovered that when you begin a writing task, you have no particular method or methods for discovering *what* you have to say or *how* to say it. In the following sections, you will be introduced to several inventing and planning procedures that will help you get started and help you gain control of the text when you draft.

Inventing: Finding and Exploring a Topic

How to discover a topic to explore may seem mysterious, sometimes even impossible. Even if an instructor has specified a subject area, the writer still faces a blank page, often wondering where and how to begin. There are, however, ways of acquiring a topic and, subsequently, ways of exploring and shaping a thesis derived from it. We are distinguishing between *topic* and *thesis* in this way: A *topic* is a broad subject area that gives the writer some general boundaries. A *thesis* grows out of a topic and becomes the point or series of points about that topic that the writer wants to make. For example, "Problems in Introductory Writing Courses" is a topic. "The main problems that freshman writers reveal in introductory writing courses include sentence fragments, incoherence in organization, and lack of development in paragraphs" is a thesis derived from that topic. This section introduces four inventing strategies.

Freewriting

Many people sit down to write and do not know where to begin. Freewriting is a perfect strategy for getting started in the most literal sense. Freewriting, as its name implies, is writing freely, starting with a blank sheet and a pen and letting your thoughts flow without regard to connections or direction. It is a way of releasing and stimulating the powers of thought and imagination.

Determine to write without stopping for a specified period of time, say ten minutes. There is only one rule: Don't stop writing. Write whatever comes to mind. Whenever nothing seems to come to mind, just repeat what you've already written, or write "I can't think of anything else to say." Your first attempts may be halting or short, but remember, your only purpose in freewriting is to get something down on paper, to empty the "data banks" while you search for something to say. Here is an example from one student, Frank Day, who was asked to freewrite for ten minutes:

> The Indians. Man, why can't they ever win a pennant? year after year, the same old thing. Lose Lose Lose. Ugh. They change managers every other year. They never stay with their rookies. They never get into a pennant race. Just once in my life I'd like to see the Indians featured on the game of the week. Joe Garagiola interviewing one of our Indians. Indians. Indians. They give real Indians a bad name. So why do I feel so strongly about them? Am I worse than a Cubs fan? Baseball season. I can't wait for it to start in the Spring. Or be over in the fall, after the Indians fall on their face again.

Writing Task

Freewrite for ten minutes. Remember: Don't stop. If you get stuck, repeat the last word you wrote, or write "I can't think of anything else." Let your imagination flow over whatever comes to mind.

Brainstorming

Brainstorming is a process of focusing the mind on a particular idea and recording the results. It is a general term for an unstructured activity that uses association of ideas rather than a rigid examination of relationships. It is like freewriting in that its effectiveness lies in the quick, free jotting down of any word, phrase, or full-formed sentence that uncovers potentially useful content. Unlike freewriting, it usually involves a topic that the writer has been given or has chosen in advance.

Consider this situation. An instructor assigned a writing class an "explanatory" writing task—one in which the writers were required to explain a phenomenon to an audience by considering its origin, present features, component parts, effect on individuals, future status, and so on. Some possible choices might be the debate between evolutionists and creationists, or the sources of the opposition to the Equal Rights Amendment. After several freewriting sessions, the class members were asked to choose a topic from their initial freewriting and to brainstorm for five to seven minutes. Frank Day decided to use his freewriting about the Cleveland Indians as the starting place for his paper. His brainstorming led him to jot down, along with other less useful items, these ideas and associations:

--Frequent manager changes
--No one wants to play in Cleveland
--They have the wrong idea about Cleveland, the city
--The stadium is old; but it has character
--The financial backing of the club is suspect
--The uniforms stink
--No free agents
--Tough division
--Baltimore always wins
--Baltimore has stability
--Cold
--Only one newspaper in Cleveland
--Sportswriters enjoy predicting failure in spring training

As you can see, Frank's list is wide-ranging. There is no particular order to these jottings, although some items seem to be related. Some items on the list are only fragments of a thought, such as "No free agents," or a mere sensory image, like "Cold"; others are more developed and suggestive ("The stadium is old; but it has character"; "Baltimore always wins").

For the moment Frank will ignore some of his jottings in order to focus on those that seem to fit together. When he begins to consider *why* the Indians have not been as successful in recent years, he begins to uncover what may be a thesis and an organizing principle for his explanatory paper. He can begin to group ideas from this list, groping toward a possible thesis:

> The Indians are in the toughest division, play in the oldest stadium, have poor financial backing, change managers too frequently.

Writing Task

1.   Suppose you have been asked to write an explanatory text similar to the one just described. From the freewriting you generated in the previous exercise or in other classroom freewriting sessions, select a topic or idea for further brainstorming. Jot down whatever comes to mind without worrying about immediate connections or relationships. Brainstorm without stopping for five to seven minutes.

2.   Take your jottings and search for emerging relationships, especially noting similarities and differences among the various items, just as Frank Day did with his Cleveland Indians brainstorming.

3.   Choose another topic of your own, something you have been concerned about or bothered by, and brainstorm about it. You might choose a campus problem that needs resolution or a situation in your community.

Treeing a Topic

Although freewriting and brainstorming are helpful for dredging ideas out of a writer's head in a general, undifferentiated way, eventually the writer must begin to structure the ideas that emerge into groups of related items. If ideas remain discrete and unconnected bits of thinking in a list, the writer cannot hope to create a coherent text.

One simple way to begin grouping ideas is to "tree" them out on paper, *graphically* exploring apparent relationships. Look at how Frank Day might have treed his brainstorming list:

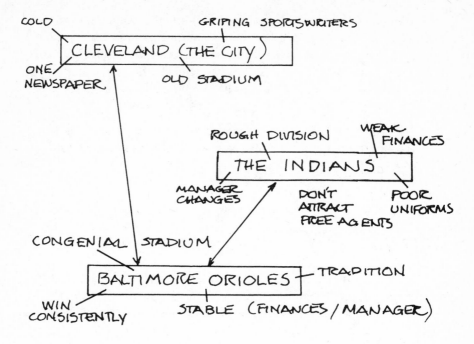

You can see how Frank's ideas have begun to come together as he *discovers* and *creates* relationships among the items on his brainstorming list. It is important to keep the distinction between discovering and creating relationships in mind as you begin to look for an organizing principle for your raw "data." Although some relationships between ideas are apparent upon even a superficial examination, a writer may ultimately order her data by perceiving links between items that at first seemed unrelated. In ordering, the writer uses not only the jottings themselves but also any linking or contrastive words or phrases that express relationships between them.

For instance, Frank undoubtedly had only the Indians in mind as he began his brainstorming, but another team, the Orioles, began to creep into his consciousness. There was no necessary connection between Cleveland and Baltimore, but in *choosing* to explore how the Indians contrasted with the Orioles, Frank began to understand better the possible reasons why the Indians were consistently unsuccessful. This contrast yielded some new information about his topic and thesis that he began to work into his inventing activity.

Exercise

1. Using your brainstorming material from the writing task on page 27, try to tree the notions that appear related.

2. The items below came from a student's freewriting and brainstorming about dieting. How would you begin to tree these items?

☐ I struggle with my weight
☐ diet pills harmful to metabolism
☐ pictures of me trim and energetic in high school
☐ awkward and unattractive to the opposite sex
☐ my friends, Ron and Kathe, have similar concerns
☐ optimum weight for my size is 110 lbs.
☐ I've grown to hate physical exercise
☐ talk shows full of diet plans and schemes
☐ what about those powdered diet supplements?
☐ how much of this is genetically determined?
☐ clothes don't fit well
☐ peer pressure, date Saturday night

5W+: Six Journalistic Questions

The stock in trade of any journalist is the ability to ask provocative and revealing questions of interviewees or situations. The journalist wants to be able to walk away from an interview or scene with answers to the "five W's plus one": *who–what–where–when–why–how*.

Each of these questions implies a range of relationships and interconnections involving the topic under consideration. Together, they help you to determine both what you know and what you would like to know about your topic. Not only can the 5W+ procedure help you generate useful information for drafting a text, it may also help you discover and articulate a thesis and a reason for presenting that thesis to a particular audience. It may thus also serve as a checklist of your eventual reader's needs.

Consider how Frank Day might use the 5W+ procedure to further explore his topic:

Who:	Cleveland Indians	or	Baltimore Orioles
What:	Failure to win consistently		Consistently win playoffs
Where:	Decrepit stadium		Memorial Stadium
When:	Last World Series 1954		Year after year
Why:	Change managers too often		Stability in management
How:	Mid-season/off-season		Front office secure

By placing the Cleveland Indians in the *who* slot, Frank considers certain relationships in his emerging thesis:

1. *What* about the Indians? They fail to win consistently.

2. *Where* does this occur? In aging, decrepit Municipal Stadium.

3. *When* did the Indians last perform well? In 1954, when they won the American League pennant with the most wins ever in one season.

4. *Why* don't they win? They change managers too often and thus lack stability.

5. *How* do they make these changes in management? At the worst possible times during the season; they rarely spend enough time to carefully consider the kind of manager they need.

As you can see, the questions are quite open-ended. They are designed to provoke and to jog the mind of the questioner. Any one of the questions might have gone in a different direction, depending upon the writer's inclination. Likewise, the same questions might be asked regarding another team, the Orioles, to provide a contrast. The more questions the writer asks, the more data she generates that she may include in her text.

A different item might be placed in the *who* slot, yielding other kinds of information:

Who:	Free agents	or	Free agents
What:	Rarely choose Indians		Attracted to Orioles
Where:	Cleveland the city		Baltimore the city
When:	End-of-season draft		End-of-season draft
Why:	Indians perceived as losers by press, baseball experts		Orioles use all players resourcefully
How:	Consistent losses		Consistent successes

Literally any item can be placed in the *who* slot, making the 5W+ procedure a versatile invention activity, limited only by the writer's imagination. A writer who uses this procedure probingly and with an earnest interest in discovery may focus and frame the kind of information she needs to formulate and support a convincing thesis.

In addition, this technique can help the writer in these ways:

1. Some of the data gathered are refocused in new ways. For instance, when he places "free agents" (baseball players who are free to sign with any club they wish) in the *who* slot, Frank must ask questions about the Indians and, by contrast, about the Orioles *from the perspective of the free agents*. Previously, in brainstorming and treeing, Frank was basically looking at emerging theses from only one perspective and with only one intention in mind, an analysis of the management and performance of the Cleveland Indians.

2. Although some information from the initial brainstorming and treeing activity is duplicated, such as "the Indians usually do not go to the World Series," and Frank does not always discover new data with the 5W+ procedure, the questions detail or spotlight information that a reader who knows very little about major league baseball might need to make sense of the eventual thesis. An example might be, "What is a free agent?" This leads the writer to consider the reader early in the writing process.

3. Although some of the questions seem awkward, each of them forces the writer to look for underlying relationships, and this may uncover potentially useful information. For instance, *where* does not always seem to have an obvious or direct relevance to the data one is compiling. However, having to answer the question, even though it does not at first seem germane, compels the writer to explore her subject matter more intently.

4. Indirectly, the 5W+ procedure may help to ground the writer in the *concrete* world of experience. That is, when she has to answer specific, yet open-ended, questions about her topic and any emerging theses, the writer is called upon, with a journalist's tenacity, to answer without generality and vagueness. When Frank asks himself, "Why don't free agents usually take the Indians' offer seriously?" he cannot merely answer, "They don't *like* the Indians." He must go further and supply a concrete response, such as, "They perceive the Indians as losers."

The 5W+ procedure thus yields a set of subjects, actions, and objects that a writer can explore in drafting a text.

Exercise

1. Using your freewriting and brainstorming from previous exercises, use the 5W+ procedure to explore the same ground. Begin by placing at least five different items in the *what* slot this time.

2. Using the brainstorming/treeing material about dieting, page 38, generate new data and new combinations of data by placing different diet-related items in the *who* or *what* slots. Use at least five different items.

EXAMPLE:

Who:	Writers of diet books
What:	Motives—to make money
Where:	On talk shows/interviews
When:	Afternoon shows/Donahue, Hour Magazine
Why:	Housewives watching, the major consumers
How:	Play on fears of public, especially women, about looks and health

Discovering and Evaluating a Thesis

Although some apprentice writers plunge into the drafting of their texts without inventing or planning, you will find that these activities will enable you to gain control of your writing process much sooner and more naturally than you would without them. Once a writer has chosen (or been assigned) a topic and has engaged in enough inventing to generate information, relationships, and ideas and to uncover one or more possible theses based on that topic, she is ready to do some planning. Planning involves making a number of choices. This section is designed to help you understand and make the choices that are necessary if you are to draft a coherent text. Here are some of the choices a writer makes as she plans or drafts a text:

1. What specific *thesis* do I want to communicate to my reader?

    This is how to tune a V-6 engine; the Lions need a new quarterback; all drivers should wear seat belts, etc.

2.   What is my *intention* in writing; that is, what do I want my text to do?

   Defend, explain, debate, entertain, analyze, etc.

3.   Who is my *audience* for the text, both generally and specifically?

   A group of my peers/18-year-olds who must register for the draft; older adults/adults over 65 with fixed incomes; a general audience of educated people/those with college degrees

4.   What *information* will my readers need, and what is the best *form* or *structure* for arranging that information?

   Narration; exposition; argumentation; question-and-answer, etc.

5.   What *point of view*, *voice*, and *tone* are best for the kind of text I want to create?

   First person/third person; objective/personal; sober, sardonic, playful, wistful, etc.

Of course, a writer cannot make all these choices at once, and some of them depend on each other to such an extent that the writer can at first make only tentative decisions. But this brief list suggests the range of decisions that a writer must eventually make as she drafts a text.

Discovering Useful Theses

Inventing does not automatically guarantee a writer a thesis. A useful, workable thesis is often not readily discovered. A writer may mistake the listing of a few good ideas for the discovery of a thesis. Or, she may have to choose between several possibilities.

   Consider the data Frank Day assembled when he treed his brainstorming list. Although he started with only a vague idea of what he wanted to write about, the Indians' dismal record, his inventing actually uncovered some interesting information and relationships:

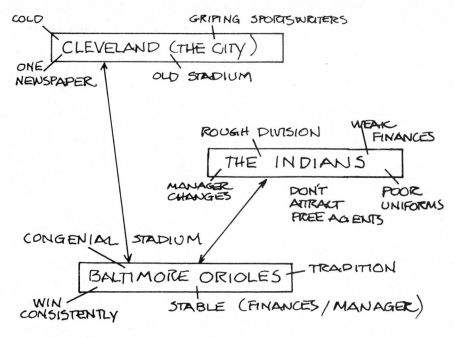

Examining these data reveals several leads to a possible thesis that are worth pursuing. For instance, notice these items clustered around "Cleveland (the city)": "one newspaper, cold, old stadium, griping sportswriters." This suggests a possible thesis:

> Cleveland is a poor location for a baseball team because of a number of factors (one newspaper; cold; old stadium; griping sportswriters).

Frank was interested in pursuing this particular thesis, so he began to think of a possible *intention* for writing (what he wants his text to do):

> I intend to convince my readers that the Indians' poor record is not entirely the fault of the players because their home, Cleveland, is a poor location for a baseball team. Cleveland has only one newspaper; it's cold; it has an old crummy stadium; it's the home of the grumpiest, griping bunch of sportswriters I've ever seen.

Having progressed this far, Frank decided to engage in additional brainstorming in order to generate information to support his points about Cleveland:

One Newspaper	Cold	Old Stadium	Griping Sportswriters
biased	hard to play	poorly kept bad field home runs hard to hit	never give rookies a chance fawn over visiting teams pounce on every mistake

Now Frank began to discover a problem with this thesis. He could not think of much to say about two of his four points. He discovered this problem when he attempted to generate the additional information that he knew he would need to include in his essay if he was to fulfill his intention for writing. He decided, therefore, to reexamine his initial tree for further ideas:

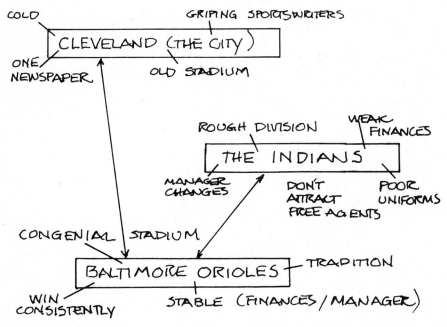

It occurred to Frank that he had several options. Here are a few:

1. He could abandon his budding thesis altogether and explore a different

portion of his tree. For example, he could start to brainstorm with regard to managerial changes and how they affect the Indians.

2. He could think about ways of generating more information about the two difficult subareas (one newspaper; cold) of his original thesis. He could go to the library or talk to friends, and then possibly generate more information.

3. He could drop the two subareas entirely and concentrate on the *stadium* and the *sportswriters* only.

4. He could think about modifying his thesis in ways suggested by his tree. For example, he could contrast the stadiums of Cleveland and Baltimore.

5. He could begin inventing all over again, using another method—the 5W+ method, for example.

Let us leave Frank with his dilemma momentarily and reexamine what he did to discover a possible thesis in the material he generated as a result of inventing. Frank scanned his data for a particular aspect or portion upon which he could focus his attention: Cleveland (the city). The aspect he selected was one about which related information already seemed to cluster (one newspaper; cold; old stadium; griping sportswriters).

In general, then, to identify a possible thesis from generated information, it is helpful to look for a small portion of that information *that seems to be related to additional information.* This is especially useful if your inventing has begun to reveal the nature of the relationship between the portion of the information you chose and the information that is related to it. But sometimes inventing, especially those types that *do not* create visual displays, does not reveal these relationships. Or it may reveal them insufficiently, so that it does not help in the development of a thesis. When this happens, one or more devices that sort and/or display information can be useful.[1]

Suppose that, as a result of brainstorming, you have generated the following data related to losing weight:

☐   eat only certain foods and nothing else (popcorn diet)

☐   cut out certain foods (no cakes or candy)

☐   cut down on certain types of food (restrict fats and/or carbohydrates)

☐   eat at certain times during the day (not at night)

☐   eat more small meals

---

[1]This method for sorting and displaying information was suggested in Irvin Hashimoto, "Helping Students Sort and Display Information," *College English* 45(1983):277–287.

☐ exercise certain parts of body for muscle tone (sit-ups)

☐ fast on some days

☐ restrict caloric intake every day (1,000 calories/day)

☐ vigorous exercise every day (jogging or swimming)

☐ become more active (walk, don't sit; go bowling instead of to the movies; use stairs, not elevators

☐ diet pills (suppress appetite)

☐ certain foods that I crave (cut down on?)

Of course, this information can be divided into lists, but this is not always simple. Some items might belong in two or more categories:

DIETING

☐ eat only certain foods and nothing else

☐ cut out certain foods

☐ cut down on certain types (fats, carbohydrates)

☐ fast

☐ restrict daily caloric intake (1,000)

☐ eat more small meals??

☐ restrict foods I crave

DRUGS

☐ diet pills

BEHAVIOR MODIFICATION

☐ eat at certain times

☐ eat more *small* meals (less food?)

☐ cut down on certain types (fats, carbohydrates)

☐ restrict daily caloric intake (1,000)??

☐ restrict foods I crave

☐ become more active generally

☐ cut out certain foods

EXERCISE

☐ certain parts of body (muscle tone)

☐ jogging or swimming

☐ become more active generally

Notice the interesting relationships that begin to emerge, however, if the data is placed in circles, rather than in lists:

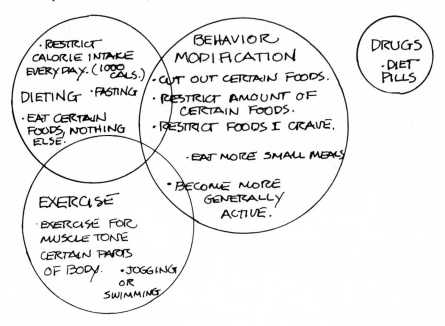

These circles categorize the data, help the writer focus on a particular aspect or aspects, and provide information about various relationships. For example, it can be seen that cutting out certain types of food, such as cakes and candy, is a type of diet, but it is also a form of behavior modification. Indeed, the circles themselves begin to suggest a possible thesis:

> The best way to lose weight is to modify one's eating habits, both *how* and *what* one eats, and to alter one's daily activities so as to become more active.

Other methods of sorting and/or displaying information are frequently used. Some writers prefer to use treeing as the primary method of illustrating relationships among already generated data. Other writers use outlining to reveal relationships. Still others prefer to devise their own graphic representations, which are specifically designed to fit a collection of data. The important point to remember is that, at the least, you must focus on an *aspect* of the generated data, such as Cleveland, home of the Indians, and perceive its relationship to some of the other generated data (one newspaper; cold; old stadium; griping sportswriters) in order to discover a possible thesis or theses.

Evaluating a Possible Thesis

Once the writer has discovered one or more tentative theses, she must evaluate each of them, preferably one at a time. She needs to discover whether she wishes to proceed with a particular possibility, whether she must modify it, or whether she wishes to scrap it altogether. To begin this process, a writer should anticipate some of the crucial choices she will eventually need to make as she plans and drafts her text. Here again (from pages 32–33) are some of these choices:

1. What specific *thesis* do I want to communicate to my reader?
2. What is my *intention* in writing; that is, what do I want my text to do?
3. Who is my *audience* for the text, both generally speaking and specifically?
4. What *information* will my readers need, and what is the best *form* or *structure* for arranging that information?
5. What *point of view*, *voice*, and *tone* are best for the kind of text I want to create?

At the very least, one or two of the first four items should guide the writer as she begins to evaluate a thesis in terms of the information she has generated.

As you recall, Frank used questions 1, 2, and (in part) 4 to evaluate his thesis:

1. What specific thesis do I want to communicate to my reader?

    Cleveland is a poor location for a baseball team because of a number of factors (one newspaper; cold; old stadium; griping sportswriters).

2. What is my intention in writing?

    I intend to convince my readers that the Indians' poor record is not entirely the fault of the players because their home, Cleveland, has only one newspaper; it's cold; it has an old crummy stadium; it's the home of the grumpiest, griping bunch of sportswriters I've ever seen.

3. What information will my readers need, and what is the best form or structure for arranging that information?

> I will need to provide information about Cleveland's one
> newspaper; the cold there; the old stadium; the griping
> sportswriters. I will also need somehow to relate this
> information to the Indians' poor record.

Of course, Frank began to have problems with his thesis when he started
to evaluate it and probe it in terms of item 4. He needed to modify it or
to begin again and seek a new thesis. But let us suppose that Frank had
generated a thesis that did not cause him problems initially. What would
happen next? When and how does a writer feel reasonably satisfied that
she has discovered a usable thesis that will, ultimately, be well defined for
a reader?

   Again, there are no iron-clad rules; a writer must eventually, with practice,
develop an inner sense of propriety and usability. But there are some
general questions to ask about a potential thesis.

IS MY THESIS PROPERLY NARROWED?

A common problem for an apprentice writer is choosing a thesis that is
too broad to be addressed adequately in a short text. Consider the following
theses Frank might have developed from his inventing.

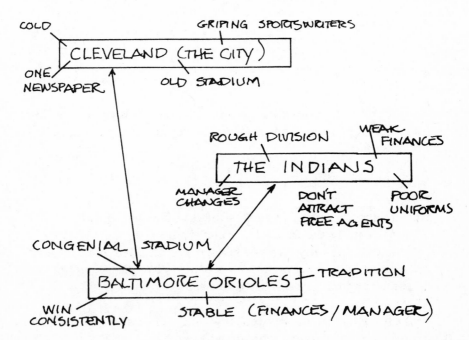

1. Baltimore has a better team than Cleveland.
2. No free agent likes the Indians.
3. The Indians are neither well coached nor well managed.

All these theses are inadequate because they are too broadly conceived to be fully addressed in a short essay. Frank has, indeed, focused on an aspect of the information he generated, and these theses do allude in some way to the relationship he uncovered during treeing. Nevertheless, a careful look at these theses reveals that they will give him little help in focusing his text. What, specifically, makes Baltimore a better team? Exactly what discourages free agents from considering the Indians?

Consider the following general example in which a thesis is successively narrowed until it is usable:

1. World War II was fought for many reasons.

    Yes, it was, but this is not a helpful thesis unless the writer plans to execute a multi-volume work on the causes of World War II. The thesis is too vague and open-ended, and would undoubtedly lead the writer to be equally vague in his development.

2. World War II was fundamentally a war based on economics.

    The writer has begun to narrow her focus somewhat, but it is still too broad for a short text. Likewise, the term *economics* is quite ambiguous.

3. Germany's participation in the war was based on economics.

    Better, but still vague in conception—what does it mean for Germany's participation in World War II to be "based on economics"?

4. The aggression that led Germany into war resulted from its economic collapse after World War I.

    This is improved. It demonstrates that the writer has begun to carefully analyze the data that her inventing has actually yielded.

IS MY THESIS SUPPORTABLE OR EXPLAINABLE WITH REASONABLE, CONCRETE EVIDENCE, CONVINCING TO MY INTENDED AUDIENCE?

Consider this possible thesis for Frank: "The solution to the Indians' on-the-field woes is the building of a new, domed stadium." This version, while certainly novel and intriguing, does not present much opportunity for further development. It would inevitably lead Frank to ill-founded speculation and an extravagantly opinionated text, since little in his inventing (consider again his tree) really prepares him to discuss it. Certainly, if Frank examines this thesis in terms of the *information* he needs (question 4, page 39), he will discover that he needs to scrap his thesis or do more inventing.

IS MY THESIS CREDIBLE TO MY READERS GIVEN MY SCOPE OF EXPERIENCE, READING KNOWLEDGE, OR RESEARCH?

The following thesis would encourage Frank's readers to dismiss his text as immature or merely silly: "A return to the uniforms of the 1920s would increase the chances that the Indians would return to the World Series in the near future." Although Frank's inventing includes a reference to poor uniforms, there is no other information in it that is related to this thesis. Even if Frank should decide to do additional inventing to yield more data about this thesis, he must anticipate that his readers will find it rather implausible. This sense of audience should guide him in selecting a focus for his inventing. Likewise, a writer who chose any of the following theses would be stretching the credibility of his text unless he provided his readers with overwhelming support for the thesis.

1. There is probably life on Mars.
2. The removal of all government restraints on our educational institutions would lead to a more enlightened electorate.
3. The most important invention of our times has been the microwave oven.
4. An increase in tornadoes is attributable, in part, to reduced agricultural activity in the Gulf States of the United States.

IS MY THESIS, AS MUCH AS POSSIBLE, TRULY INFORMATIVE TO MY INTENDED AUDIENCE?

Unless your text is being written primarily to record what you know about a subject for a specific audience (for example, an exam for your history or chemistry professor), you owe your audience a text that is truly informative. That is, a text should offer your reader (1) something relevant (worth knowing) about your thesis and (2) something that is not merely a repetition of conventional wisdom about your thesis, presented without fresh insights on your part.

Again, a possible thesis for Frank's text is: "The Indians have been playing in an old stadium for a long time." True, but so what? Can this statement form the basis for a text that is informative for a reader? Consider the following theses and their effectiveness according to the two criteria mentioned above, *relevance* and *insightfulness:*

1.   The eagle is an endangered species.

     So what? What *about* the eagle? The thesis does not relay any
     new information as such and does not call upon the reader to
     do anything about the situation.

2.   The computer has had a great effect on the way businesses do their
     work.

     This is a truism, but what *kind* of effects has it had, and are
     these effects helpful, hurtful, novel, etc.?

3.   When Jackie Robinson broke baseball's color barrier, it paved the way
     for blacks to play professional sports.

     Again, true—but does the writer wish to stress anything more
     specific or important about this particular event, about Robinson
     himself, about the social consequences for the Dodgers, etc.?

4.   Edgar Allan Poe is an acknowledged master of the macabre tale.

     If so, where does this lead? Will the writer try to debate the
     issue or try to compare "a master of the macabre tale" with
     others who are not? This statement reveals little of the writer's

intentions and will not be a helpful guide to her text's later development.

Of course, how informative a text is depends on its perceived audience, and this quality should not be confused with *interestingness* or *debatability*. The fact that a reader does not find a writer's thesis interesting does not mean that it is not informative, full of fresh insight. Likewise, the fact that a reader questions or disagrees with the thesis of a text does not necessarily determine how informative the text actually is.

Exercise

Evaluate the following thesis statements that Frank might have developed from his inventing activity according to these criteria: (a) proper narrowness and focus, (b) supportability with the promise of reasonable evidence, (c) credibility with an audience, and (d) informativeness for an audience. If you find a statement to be inadequate according to any of these criteria, write a revised version that presents the thesis more effectively. You may wish to refer to Frank's inventing material to form your judgment.

☐ The Indians are unsuccessful because of their lack of financial stability compared with other teams.

☐ The Orioles have the most successful franchise in the American League because of the stability of their management.

☐ Free agents aren't attracted to the Indians because of the city of Cleveland, the stadium the Indians play in, and the lack of enthusiasm among their fans.

☐ The Cleveland sportswriters are essentially responsible for the failure of the professional teams in the area because they are bad losers who wish they could move to another city.

Exercise

Examine the following two sets of inventing materials. In each set, (a) identify possible theses available to the writer; (b) use the four criteria mentioned in the previous exercise to determine which of the possible theses is the most useful; (c) craft a thesis that you think best suits the material that has been generated; and (d) write the kind of text that is appropriate, based upon your thesis.

The Problem with the Sports Pass

Justin Edwards had had enough; this was the second time in two weeks that he had gone to Memorial Hall to get a ticket to the hockey game, only to find that there were no more student tickets left. "You can buy a regular general admission ticket for $4.50, if you want," the office clerk had told him. "But that's why I bought an All-Sports Pass," Justin argued, "so that I would be guaranteed a ticket to every game at a student discount!" Why should I have to pay general admission for a *guaranteed* ticket? he muttered to himself as he walked away. He decided to vent his rage by writing a letter to the school paper. Here are his brainstorming notes.

☐ I bought a sports pass to get guaranteed entry to all events.

☐ The university obviously oversells these tickets, thinking not everyone will go to the same event.

☐ Hockey has just caught on here with the public; the students are the ones to suffer for it.

☐ Dishonest, a cheat, the rec director's deceit.

☐ The sports pass costs $85.00 for the year; I'm not rich.

☐ The students at Northern Michigan get a better deal than this.

☐ Nobody at the basketball games here; I deserve a refund or a ticket.

☐ When my sister went here the students were first, public second.

☐ Dear Editor: The sports program here is a menace to the students and I blame the rec director.

☐ How many other people has this happened to? A hundred? Something has to be done.

The City Council Election

June Benedict, Ward 3 Council candidate, had worked hard to gain student support for her election drive, but the incumbent, Dr. Kevin Vance, a University administrator, had campaigned hard on the fact that Benedict herself was not a college graduate and could not serve student interests as well as he could. The day before the election, the Student Caucus invited each candidate to appear on a platform to discuss the live campus issues. Each candidate was permitted a five-minute opening speech. Here are the notes Candidate Benedict jotted down in order to craft her speech:

☐   Not a college graduate, but well-read, informed, interested in student welfare. Worked to put three children through college in the early 70s.

☐   I care about the town and the university and how each affects the quality of the other.

☐   The issue here isn't education but dedication and interest; Dr. Vance has fine academic credentials, but his voting record is inconsistent—he rides the fence on many issues, including the recent Anti-Noise law passed by the last city council. Many students thought it was discriminatory against students—I disagree. Yet I sympathize with your age and musical tastes. (I even like Culture Club.)

☐   Students have rights—so do townspeople; there are young children in university neighborhoods as well as elderly.

☐   We can work together; having a housewife, mother, and self-employed seamstress as your council representative is not such a bad thing.

☐   I will be accessible to everyone in my ward, student and nonstudent alike.

☐   Vote intelligently; vote on the basis of the issues and not on the number of degrees beside a person's name.

Planning a Text: Discovering Intentions

Using the four criteria identified in the previous section—proper focus, supportability, credibility, and informativeness—the writer may examine her inventing notes to determine her *intention*. By "intention" we mean what the writer wants her text to *do*. In the exercise on page 44, you may have noticed that when you tried to create a thesis from the inventing material you were given, you inevitably had to focus on intention as well as thesis. It is not enough for your text merely to express a point; a text must also manifest a specific intention. Your reader must be cued to the reason why you have written your text.

Here are some of the intentions a writer may have in drafting a text:

1. explain the nature of something for a reader
2. persuade a reader of the validity of something
3. instruct a reader in a process
4. move a reader to act in a certain way
5. tell a story to entertain
6. analyze the consequences of an event
7. provide information to an audience so that it can make a decision

Once a writer has settled on a thesis and an intention, she can plan a draft of her text with her reader in mind. She can begin to move away from her preoccupation with her own need; it may have enabled her to begin writing, but it may not be useful to a reader.

Consider Frank Day's inventing activity again. He ultimately may have determined that his thesis was something like this:

> The Indians team has been unsuccessful in the past two decades basically because (1) they have lacked solid financial backing; (2) they have rarely maintained a stable coaching staff; (3) the city's and the club's "loser image" has discouraged quality players from joining the team.

Even though in many ways this is a model thesis statement, clearly focused, supportable, credible, and informative, Frank still must decide what kind of text he wants to create. That is, he must decide what his intention is in writing the text. Here are some of his options:

1. Discuss the Indians' failure simply in order to *explain the phenomenon* and to place it in perspective in the local and/or national sports scene.
2. Discuss the Indians' failure in order to *praise another baseball club*, e.g., the Baltimore Orioles.
3. Discuss the Indians' failure in order *to express his personal frustration and anxiety* over this state of affairs.
4. Discuss the Indians' failure in order to *argue for* a possible remedy.

In the course of drafting his text, Frank may reveal a little of each of these intentions, but he should choose one as his primary concern.

Of course, a writer's intention is never pure. One can hardly explain without attempting to persuade, and one cannot present a convincing argument for a particular action without doing a great deal of analysis. However, choosing a primary intention lets the writer plan her text much more efficiently, using her announced thesis and intention as a guide in drafting her text—or altering her thesis and intention if, in the process of writing, she discovers a more compelling and useful approach.

Here is a revised version of Frank's thesis that now includes a stated intention. Together they form a thesis statement:

> In my text I plan to identify and analyze the main reasons for the Cleveland Indians' recent failure on the field: (1) the club's lack of financial stability; (2) the continued instability of the club's coaching staff; and (3) the inability of the club to overcome the "loser image" of the city and the club. My analysis will attempt to place the club and its operation in the context of other American League clubs and to suggest possible remedies for the club's shortcomings.

Intentions and Modes of Development

In determining her intention in drafting a text, a writer is also implicitly making choices about the structure of a text, since what the writer wishes a text to do will affect how that text is structured. Traditionally, writing teachers have talked about text form or structure as *modes of development*: narration, description, exposition, and argumentation. A *mode* may be thought of as a *means of expression*, the *form* a particular text may take. Although no text ever reflects a purely narrative or descriptive or expository or argumentative form, a writer usually employs one primary mode in drafting her text.

NARRATION

The *narrative* mode, as its name indicates, is used by a writer basically to narrate or relate a series of events, usually in chronological order. The narrative mode moves from event to event, pausing for description or elaboration, but following a sequence of events toward a conclusion. Here are two sample narrative paragraphs:

. . . All that afternoon I had carefully gone over my wardrobe to select the proper symphony of sartorial brilliance. That night I set out wearing my magnificent electric blue sport coat, whose shoulders were so wide that they hung out over my frame like vast, drooping eaves, so wide I had difficulty going through an ordinary door head-on. . . . I had spent fully two hours carefully arranging and rearranging my great mop of wavy hair, into which I had rubbed fully a pound of Greasy Kid Stuff. . . .[1]

. . . Back home, I knew that what I must write, really, was our black saga, where any individual's past is the essence of the millions'. Now flat broke, I went to some editors I knew, describing the Gambian miracle, and my desire to pursue the research; Doubleday contracted to publish, and Reader's Digest to condense the projected book; then I had advances to travel further. . . .[2]

In these two examples, the purpose of the paragraph is to get the reader from one event to another, to move the text from one point in the past to another point nearer the present. Typically, the narrative mode presents *past* events in order, and a writer using this mode should be careful to keep the tense of her verbs consistent. Likewise, she should keep the point of view (first person or third person) consistent, lest the reader become confused as to where the writer intends to locate him in the narrative sequence of the text.

Exercise

Refer to Justin Edwards's unfortunate experience with the sports pass (page 45). Write a narrative paragraph, pretending that *you* are Justin. Your intention in writing should be to help your readers (your peers) understand the frustrating experience you have had.

DESCRIPTION

The *descriptive* mode is a method of development that stresses the vivid depiction of something: perhaps a place, an object, a person, or a mood.

[1]Jean Shepherd, "The Endless Streetcar into the Night and the Tinfoil Noose," *In God We Trust: All Others Pay Cash* (New York: Doubleday & Company, Inc., 1966).
[2]Alex Haley, "My Furtherest-Back Person: The African," *The New York Times Magazine* (1972).

Its hallmark is the choice of concrete and specific words that allow a reader to see, hear, feel, smell, and taste the subject of the description.

As a mode of development, description is closely allied to narration. A writer can hardly present a series of events without including appropriate descriptions of the participants, the setting, the action, and so on. The writer does not merely wish to report what she experiences, she wants the reader to stand alongside her and experience it for himself. Thus the writer must show the reader what she has experienced, rather than telling him.

The most common way to suggest the difference between effective and ineffective description is to contrast description that is *concrete* and *specific* with that which is *abstract* and *general*. Concrete language appeals to the senses. It presents the reader with vivid visual, aural, and tactile images: "Harry lifts 100-lb barbells effortlessly, like some men lift a cup of coffee" rather than the abstract, "Harry is strong." Specific language avoids generality and vagueness. It doesn't merely approximate the description of a phenomenon, it captures it as graphically as possible—"The delegates interrupted the Chrysler Corporation chairman more than a dozen times with deafening applause," not "The crowd gave the chairman an enthusiastic reception."

Here are two sample descriptive paragraphs:

> . . . Yellowstone, it seemed to me, was the top of the world, a region of deep lakes and dark timber, canyons and waterfalls. But, beautiful as it is, one might have the sense of confinement there. The skyline in all directions is close at hand, the high wall of the woods and deep cleavages of shade. There is a perfect freedom in the mountains, but it belongs to the eagle and the elk, the badger and the bear. The Kiowas reckoned their stature by the distance they see, and they were bent and blind in the wilderness. . . .[3]

> . . . New York is a town of 3,000 bootblacks whose brushes and rhythmic rag-snaps can be heard up and down Manhattan from midmorning to midnight. They dodge cops, survive rainstorms, and thrive in the Empire State Building as well as on the Staten Island Ferry. They usually wear dirty shoes. . . .[4]

[3]N. Scott Momaday, *The Way to Rainy Mountain* (Albuquerque: University of New Mexico Press, 1969).

[4]Gay Talese, "New York is a City of Things Unnoticed," *Esquire* (1960).

Exercise

Return again to Justin Edwards's experience (page 45). Write a descriptive paragraph as if you were he. Your intention is to help your readers (your peers) experience the sense of frustration you felt when you tried to get a hockey ticket. Use concrete, vivid detail.

EXPOSITION

Exposition is a mode of development used primarily to explain something to a reader. The following kinds of operations are characteristic of expository writing:

- ☐ defining one's terms
- ☐ classifying items under discussion into categories that will help the reader understand the writer's point
- ☐ illustrating and supporting statements of fact with specific evidence and detail
- ☐ comparing and contrasting differing elements within a discussion
- ☐ analyzing a process or the causes and effects of certain phenomena.

A writer using exposition is concerned with conveying her information in the clearest and most accurate way, since her intention is usually to inform an audience. Here are three examples of effective expository writing, with some explanatory commentary:

> . . . In discussing Chesterton's novels it is valuable to use the discarded term "romance." As a literary genre, a romance is neither fantasy nor escape; it is defined by its particular assumptions about reality. Two forms popular today are the western and the detective story, both usually considered second-rate, even if, as was true in Chesterton's day, it is these popular writers who are widely read. Romantic fiction either creates a world that is simpler than reality, or escapes into another time or place; the unpleasant aspects of either love or money are ignored. Dickens was a romancer, and Chesterton was his disciple, writing in allegorical terms about his own time and its controversies. . . .[5]

[5]Alzina Stone Dale, *The Outline of Sanity* (Grand Rapids: William B. Eerdmans, 1982) 116.

In this extended definition of a romance, not only is the term classified ("literary genre") and differentiated ("neither fantasy nor escape"), but it is carefully *illustrated* with examples ("the western and the detective story"), and its functions are discussed ("creates a world that is simpler than reality, or escapes into another time or place"). Notice how smoothly the definition has been worked into the larger discussion. The paragraph would have been abrupt and awkward had the writer written it this way: "*The American Heritage Dictionary* defines 'romance' as 'any long fictitious tale of heroes and extraordinary or mysterious events.' It is important to discuss Chesterton's novel using the term 'romance.'"

> . . . "Women's language" is that pleasant (dainty?), euphemistic, never-aggressive way of talking we learned as little girls. Cultural bias was built into the language we were allowed to speak, the subjects we were allowed to speak about, and the ways we were spoken of. Having learned our linguistic lesson well, we go out in the world, only to discover that we are communicative cripples—damned if we do, and damned if we don't.
>
> If we refuse to talk "like a lady," we are ridiculed and criticized for being unfeminine. ("She thinks like a man" is, at best, a left-handed compliment.) If we do learn all the fuzzy-headed, unassertive language of our sex, we are ridiculed for being unable to think clearly, unable to take part in a serious discussion, and therefore unfit to hold a position of power. . . .[6]

In the first paragraph of this passage, Robin Lakoff declares that women are "communicative cripples . . . damned if we do, and damned if we don't" who lack the linguistic freedom that men possess. Without further illustration, this paragraph would seem to be more of a harangue or diatribe than a thoughtful reflection on a social problem. The follow-up paragraph, however, further illustrates and elaborates the author's perspective on this dilemma: "If we refuse to talk 'like a lady,' we are ridiculed . . . If we do learn . . . we are ridiculed." Illustration is a key element in expository writing. Lack of illustration in a text gives a sense of incompleteness, insincerity, and immaturity. The writer who wants to be taken seriously strives to support her statements with carefully chosen examples and relevant details.

[6]Robin Lakoff, "You Are What You Say," *Ms* (July 1974).

. . . TB is often imagined as a disease of poverty and deprivation—of thin garments, thin bodies, unheated rooms, poor hygiene, inadequate food. . . . In contrast, cancer is a disease of middle-class life, a disease associated with affluence, with excess. Rich countries have the highest cancer rates, and the rising incidence of the disease is seen as resulting, in part, from a diet rich in fat and proteins and from the toxic effluvia of the industrial economy that creates affluence. The treatment of TB is identified with the stimulation of appetite, cancer treatment with nausea and the loss of appetite. The undernourished nourishing themselves—alas, to no avail. The overnourished, unable to eat. . . .[7]

In this comparison and contrast paragraph, Sontag skillfully draws a contrast between the way the public generally responds to two different diseases. One has become associated with poverty and loss, the other with affluence and success. She presents this contrast in order to explain why cancer has come to be feared and dreaded in our culture. The important thing to remember about comparison and contrast is that they are not in themselves a kind of text. They are a means to an end, not an end in themselves. A writer must compare and contrast something for a *specific purpose;* no one wants to read about the similarities and differences between two items unless the writer has a larger reason for making the comparison.

Exercise

Refer to the data Frank Day generated in his treeing and 5W+ inventing activity (pages 28 and 30), and write an expository paragraph explaining to a general audience why the Indians are unsuccessful and the Orioles are successful.

ARGUMENTATION

The fourth mode of development is *argumentation,* a mode that writers use to articulate and defend a thesis that may be controversial or unusual. Argumentation is used primarily in texts in which a writer intends to be *persuasive,* but there is an element of argumentation in every text in which a writer attempts to convince a reader of her text's validity. Even the writer of a simple narrative text wants the reader to believe that her personal

[7]Susan Sontag, *Illness as a Metaphor* (New York: Vintage, 1979) 14.

experience or story is true. Every writer, at least implicitly, is "arguing" for acceptance of her text's information and point of view.

In the argumentative mode, however, the argument is brought to the surface of the text; nothing can be left to mere implication. *Evidence* (facts, figures, and authority) is marshalled and expressed explicitly. Unlike the illustration called for by the expository mode, evidence is chosen specifically to support and to *prove* the writer's thesis, not merely to provide examples. The writer purposely engages the reader with a series of declarative statements that lead him through the writer's reasoning process to the proper conclusion, i.e., the conclusion that the writer wants the reader to accept and make his own.

We could discuss this mode for dozens of pages without exhausting the many components of effective argumentation. Just listing the kinds of reasoning fallacies a writer should avoid, let alone the kinds of reasoning strategies she should use, would fill a good-sized book. However, our goal here is to suggest the major requirements of effective argumentation and to show you an example of an argumentative text that employs them.

Argumentation is the most abstract of the modes we have considered. An argumentative text asks its reader to come to *agree* with the stance the writer has taken, not merely to listen to a story or see what the writer sees or understand what the writer has explained. The writer is asking her reader to adopt, so to speak, her reasoning strategies, accept her evidence, come to her conclusions. No other mode is so inextricably intertwined with the writer's intention. Because of this, this mode is the most difficult for the apprentice writer to master; since she feels strongly about her thesis, she may not provide enough clear, relevant evidence to support her contentions. Her own conviction may undermine her textual responsibility to her readers. What one feels most committed to is often the hardest to write about convincingly.

Here are five principles to guide your use of the argumentative mode:

1. State your thesis prominently and unambiguously.

2. Define key words and acknowledge the existence of opposing viewpoints.

3. Anticipate the most effective counterarguments to your thesis, planning your refutation or your strategy for explaining why these are irrelevant to the point you are making.

4. Marshall the strongest and most compelling evidence available to support your thesis, avoiding repetitious or irrelevant information.

5. Maintain a dispassionate tone, avoiding blatant appeals to prejudice, sentiment, or questionable authority.

Examples of effective argumentation are not as easy to excerpt as are effective expository texts. Nevertheless, the following text by Thomas Jefferson, the main author of the Declaration of Independence, illustrates well the elements that an effective argumentative text must have. In this famous document, Jefferson articulates the reasons why the Continental Congress has decided to seek independence from King George of Great Britain and climaxes his argument by announcing the Colonies' momentous decision.

Declaration of Independence
Thomas Jefferson

In CONGRESS, July 4, 1776

When in the Course of human events, it becomes necessary for one people to dissolve the political bands which have connected them with another, and to assume among the powers of the earth, the separate and equal station to which the Laws of Nature and of Nature's God entitle them, a decent respect to the opinions of mankind requires that they should declare the causes which impel them to the separation.

We hold these truths to be self-evident, that all men are created equal, that they are endowed by their Creator with certain unalienable Rights, that among these are Life, Liberty and the pursuit of Happiness.

That to secure these rights, Governments are instituted among Men, deriving their just powers from the consent of the governed.

That whenever any Form of Government becomes destructive of these ends, it is the Right of the People to alter or to abolish it, and to institute new Government, laying its foundation on such principles and organizing its powers in such form, as to them shall seem most likely to effect their Safety and Happiness. Prudence, indeed, will dictate that Governments long established should not be changed for light and transient causes; and accordingly all experience hath shewn, that mankind are more disposed to suffer, while evils are sufferable, than to right themselves by abolishing the forms to which they are accustomed. But when a long train of abuses and usurpations, pursuing invariably the same Object evinces a design to reduce them under absolute Despotism, it is their right, it is their duty, to throw off such Government, and to provide new Guards for their future security.

Such has been the patient sufferance of these Colonies; and such is now the necessity which constrains them to alter their former Systems of Government. The history of the present King of Great Britain is a history of repeated injuries and usurpations, all having in direct object the establishment of an absolute Tyranny over these States. To prove this, let Facts be submitted to a candid world.

He has refused his Assent to Laws, the most wholesome and necessary for the public good.

He has forbidden his Governors to pass Laws of immediate and pressing importance, unless suspended in their operation till his Assent should be obtained; and when so suspended, he has utterly neglected to attend to them.

He has refused to pass other Laws for the accommodation of large districts of people, unless those people would relinquish the right of Representation in the Legislature, a right inestimable to them and formidable to tyrants only.

He has called together legislative bodies at places unusual, uncomfortable, and distant from the depository of their public Records, for the sole purpose of fatiguing them into compliance with his measures.

He has dissolved Representative Houses repeatedly, for opposing with manly firmness his invasions on the rights of people.

He has refused for a long time, after such dissolutions, to cause others to be elected; whereby the Legislative powers, incapable of Annihilation, have returned to the People at large for their exercise; the State remaining in the mean time exposed to all the dangers of invasion from without, and convulsions within.

He has endeavoured to prevent the population of these States; for that purpose obstructing the Laws for Naturalization of Foreigners; refusing to pass others to encourage their migrations hither, and raising the conditions of new Appropriations of Lands.

He has obstructed the Administration of Justice, by refusing his Assent to Laws for establishing Judiciary powers.

He has made Judges dependent on his Will alone, for the tenure of their offices, and the amount and payment of their salaries.

He has erected a multitude of New Offices, and sent hither swarms of Officers to harass our people, and eat out their substance.

He has kept among us, in times of peace, Standing Armies without the Consent of our legislatures.

He has affected to render the Military independent of and superior to the Civil power.

He has combined with others to subject us to a jurisdiction foreign to our constitution, and unacknowledged by our laws; giving his Assent to their Acts of pretended Legislation:

For Quartering large bodies of armed troops among us:

For protecting them, by a mock Trial, from punishment for any Murders which they should commit on the Inhabitants of these States:

For cutting off our Trade with all parts of the world:

For imposing Taxes on us without our Consent:

For depriving us in many cases, of the benefits of Trial by Jury:

For transporting us beyond Seas to be tried for pretended offenses:

For abolishing the free System of English Laws in a neighbouring Province, establishing therein an Arbitrary government, and enlarging its Boundaries so as to render it at once an example and fit instrument for introducing the same absolute rule into these Colonies:

For taking away our Charters, abolishing our most valuable Laws, and altering fundamentally the Forms of our Governments:

For suspending our own Legislatures, and declaring themselves invested with power to legislate for us in all cases whatsoever.

He has abdicated Government here, by declaring us out of his Protection and waging War against us:

He has plundered our seas, ravaged our Coasts, burnt our towns, and destroyed the lives of our people.

He is at this time transporting large Armies of foreign Mercenaries to compleat the works of death, desolation and tyranny, already begun with circumstances of Cruelty & perfidy scarcely paralleled in the most barbarous ages, and totally unworthy the Head of a civilized nation.

He has constrained our fellow Citizens taken Captive on the high Seas to bear Arms against their Country, to become the executioners of their friends and Brethren, or to fall themselves by their Hands.

He has excited domestic insurrections amongst us, and has endeavoured to bring on the inhabitants of our frontiers, the merciless Indian Savages, whose known rule of warfare, is an undistinguished destruction of all ages, sexes and conditions. In every stage of these Oppressions We have Petitioned for Redress in the most humble terms: Our repeated Petitions have been answered only by repeated injury. A Prince, whose character is thus marked by every act which may define a Tyrant, is unfit to be the ruler of a free people. Nor have We been wanting in attentions to our British brethren. We have warned them from time to time of attempts by their legislature to extend an unwarrantable jurisdiction over us. We have reminded them of the circumstances of our emigration and settlement here. We have appealed to their native justice and magnanimity, and we have conjured them by the ties of our common kindred to disavow these usurpations, which, would inevitably interrupt our connections and correspondence. They too have been deaf to the voice of justice and of consanguinity. We must, therefore, acquiesce in the necessity, which denounces our Separation, and hold them, as we hold the rest of mankind, Enemies in War, in Peace Friends.

WE, THEREFORE, the Representatives of the UNITED STATES OF AMERICA, in General Congress Assembled, appealing to the Supreme Judge of the world for the rectitude of our intentions, do, in the Name and by Authority of the good People of these Colonies, solemnly publish and declare, That these United Colonies are, and of Right ought to be FREE AND INDEPENDENT STATES; that they are Absolved from all Allegiance to the British Crown, and that all political connection between them and the State of Great Britain, is and ought to be totally dissolved; and that as Free and Independent States, they have full Power to levy War, conclude Peace, contract Alliances, establish Commerce, and to do all other Acts and Things which Independent States may of right do.

And for the support of this Declaration, with a firm reliance on the protection of divine Providence, we mutually pledge to each other our Lives, our Fortunes and our sacred Honor.

Exercise

Refer to the City Council election described on page 45, and write a paragraph in which you argue to an audience of student voters why they should or should not vote for June Benedict.

Planning a Text:
Considering Your Audience

Except for our private diaries and such things as laundry and shopping lists, we do not write solely for ourselves. In those writing tasks that we face in our households, in our schooling, and in our jobs, we must consider the *audience* for which we are writing. The easiest audiences to write for are, of course, those that are carefully circumscribed by the writing situation itself. The more we know about the persons to whom we are writing, the better able we are to draft a text that will communicate what we want and need to say to them.

Imagining an audience for the practice writing one does in composition courses, however, is not an easy thing to do. Furthermore, many writers find it distracting to try to think of their audience during the initial stages of drafting a text. Nevertheless, awareness of the audience can increase the writer's control of her subject matter and its development. By thinking about her audience at various points in the drafting process, she will be able to anticipate her readers' needs and adjust the content, format, diction, and tone of her text to best address those readers. In planning your text, you should ask yourself these questions:

1.   What do I know about my readers in terms of their (a) age, (b) sex, and (c) educational and cultural background?

2.   What do my readers know about the subject matter of my text?

3.   What might my readers want and need to know about the subject matter of my text?

4.   How will my readers react to the thesis of my text?

5.   What do I want to happen after my text has been read?

Consider how Frank Day answered these questions concerning his potential audience:

1.   What do I know about my readers' age, sex, and educational and cultural background?

> Since I am writing to my peers, they are generally my age. About half of them are male and half female. They are freshmen in college, mainly from an urban environment. Quite a few of them are business majors, with a few majoring in phys ed, biology, and elementary education. There are two English majors and one journalism major.

2.   What do my readers know about my subject matter?

> Most of them know baseball as a game, although they are probably not Indians fans. Most of the baseball talk around here is about the Detroit Tigers. Probably few of them read *The Sporting News*, as I do, and none of them are as aware of the factors involved in running a baseball team as I am. Most of my classmates seem to be football and basketball fans. Baseball seems to be a minor sport to them.

3. What might my readers want or need to know about my subject matter?

> Since most of them do not seem to be baseball fans, they may not want to know anything. However, most of them do know about the Indians' failures and probably have heard enough Cleveland jokes to be curious about why the Indians are not a classier team. I imagine I will have to explain some of the details of how teams build their clubs, defining terms like *general manager* and *free agent*, and providing a context for comparing the Indians with other major league teams.

4. How will my readers react to the thesis of my text?

> I do not think they will find it too controversial, although the few baseball fans among them may take issue with my evaluation of some of the other teams. Since I know my readers are not rabid baseball fans, I will need to catch and maintain their interest early—probably with another version of a Cleveland joke.

5. What do I want to happen after my text has been read?

> I want my readers to be better informed about the status of the Indians, and about the way sports teams in general overcome failure and become successful. I also hope that a few of them become interested enough in baseball to read about the game and attend a few games.

Because Frank ultimately chose to write an explanatory paper, his emphasis would be on the clear presentation of relevant information, rather than on the advocacy of a position his audience should take. His intention was to *explain,* although he obviously hoped that his evidence would be persuasive enough to prove his point. In considering his audience, he realized that he had to attract their attention to a subject that was not necessarily interesting to them. He would be careful, therefore, not to overload his text with intricacies and technicalities. And he would define clearly those terms that are peculiar to the baseball world he was trying to evoke.

Exercise

Here are two scenarios, each of which suggests a certain writing task for a certain audience.

Examine the brainstorming notes of each writer. For each set of notes, (1) identify possible theses available to the writer; (2) craft a thesis and intention that you think best suits the material that has been generated; (3) answer the five questions about audience on page 59; and (4) write the indicated text based upon your thesis statement and consideration of the audience.

The Unexpected Phone Call

Pam Yates had been studying for her chemistry exam for several hours when she received a phone call from her mom: Jeffy, her five-year-old nephew, had become very ill and had been rushed to a hospital. That was all she knew. Her mom pleaded with her to come home. She decided to write her professor a note explaining the circumstances and hoping for understanding. Here are her inventing notes:

- ☐ hope the professor cancelled the class
- ☐ I can't afford to miss another exam
- ☐ Mom said that my nephew was very ill
- ☐ there's no one else to take care of Aunt Jill's other kids but me
- ☐ but I've already missed four classes
- ☐ student excuses are always so lame
- ☐ who'd believe my reason?
- ☐ must take the consequences whatever they are
- ☐ she's really stern in class about tardiness and absences
- ☐ the exam is today; I could get a ride with Sandi
- ☐ I've got to leave; couldn't do well on the test anyway

The Broken Stereo Receiver

Dan Underwood eagerly opened the package from home, knowing it was his birthday present: a Sansound Deluxe #100, 80 watt-per-channel stereo receiver with digital tuning, the perfect complement for his turntable and cassette deck. He ripped open the box and, without reading the instructions, lifted the receiver out of its packaging and plugged it into his system. As he anxiously awaited the welcome sound of his favorite FM station, KXYZ, he fiddled with the various buttons and dials on the front of the receiver. But nothing came out. He checked everything: the wiring to the speakers, the lead from the cassette deck and turntable; the LED lights were on, so it wasn't the electricity. What could be wrong? After working through the accompanying manual for several hours, trying to find the cause, he gave up and decided to box up the stereo and ship it back to his mom for exchange. Exhausted from the ordeal, he finally opened the card that accompanied the receiver. His eyes fell to the P.S. at the bottom of the card: "We bought the receiver on close-out, Dan; if there are any problems, you'll have to contact the Consumer Relations agent at the manufacturer." Frustrated and disappointed, Dan generated this list for his letter to Sansound, Inc.:

☐   I opened the box and nothing worked

☐   a birthday present from my mom purchased at Daily's Electronics store in Brideshead, Ohio

☐   Sansound is a respected name in receivers and turntables

☐   I own a Sansound turntable and cassette deck

☐   I suspect it's the unit's power supply

☐   Daily's will not accept a return or exchange

☐   It is a discontinued model/replaced by the new Special deluxe model #105

☐   should I request a refund/repair/replacement unit?

☐   should I be cordial, angry, upset?

☐   should I have the company direct their reply here or to mom?

☐   I know a little about electronics; I know when something is my fault or the machine's

☐   the invoice doesn't list a specific consumer relations mgr., so who should I address the letter to?

Writing Assignment

The following is a personal experience essay written by a student who has done little inventing and planning. As a result, the text is incoherent, often filled with clichés, and not directed at a particular audience. Despite these problems, the writer thinks of the text as complete and, of course, as an accurate, even compelling depiction of a personal experience. Read it carefully and answer the questions that follow it.

Working at the Laundry

Like many, many freshmen, I have to support myself to get through school. I hope that through my career choice, I can become a productive, respectable United States citizen. While at college, I am working at a local laundry to earn my way.   1

It is sometimes an interesting job. You meet all kinds of people when you work at a laundry, including the employer. My employer is a very considerate man. He lets me work the hours I want. Sometimes he even lets me off for dates.   2

Some of the things I do at the laundry are: scrubbing the floors, emptying the garbage, and making change for the patrons. At this laundry there is no automatic change machine so someone has to be there all the time with change. This requires someone with responsibility, someone the employer can trust with large sums of money.   3

I hope that my job at the laundry will help me in becoming more mature as a person. By interacting with people you can learn a lot. I know I have. Not only does this job give an income with which I can go to school, it provides me with the kind of experience that my future employers will be looking for.   4

Those who have a "free ride" through college with scholarships and wealthy parents don't know what they are missing by not having to work. The only way to get the kind of experience that I am getting is by working at a job while you are going to school.   5

I'm glad that I have to work. If more Americans would feel this way, our country would not be in the trouble that it is in.   6

DISCUSSION QUESTIONS

1. What does the writer seem to be writing *about*, i.e., what seems to be his thesis? What appears to be his intention in writing this text?

2. In each short paragraph the writer seems to shift focus for no apparent reason. For instance, he moves freely from his "career choice" in paragraph 1 to the cliché "meeting all kinds of people" in paragraph 2. What other shifts of focus do you find?

3. The writer uses a lot of "code words," word choices that mean something specific or peculiar to the writer but that actually conceal the meaning from

the reader. In paragraph 1, the writer speaks of becoming "a productive, respectable American citizen"; what do you think he means by this? Likewise, in paragraph 4, he speaks of "becoming more mature as a person" and "interacting with people," two equally puzzling and inarticulate expressions. What other code words do you find in the text?

4.   The conclusion comes rather abruptly and seems to introduce a topic that the writer had not previously considered. How do you account for this? What thesis or intention that potentially contains the actual text the writer wants to create may be lurking in paragraph 6?

Write a note to this writer (call him Dave), suggesting a revision strategy that would address the following components of his writing process:

1.   What ideas and/or theses that are apparent in Dave's text can be explored further and focused more sharply using the inventing procedures you have learned in this chapter? Be sure to give Dave some good examples from his own text that he might explore using freewriting, brainstorming, treeing, or 5W+.

2.   What primary thesis do you think Dave should isolate and make the center of his text? Make sure you discuss this important matter in terms of the four criteria addressed on pages 40–43.

3.   What seems to be Dave's intention in writing his text? How can he sharpen that intention and reveal it to his readers more directly? Should his personal experience essay explain, argue, vent frustration, or do something else?

4.   Dave's implicit audience is his fellow college students. How can he be more sensitive to the outlooks, financial status, and information needs of this audience? Discuss the characteristics of his audience in your note.

5.   How can Dave "unpack" his code words to reveal and not conceal his meaning?

Writing Assignment

Read the following personal narrative by Andy Rooney, the well-known CBS commentator. In it, Rooney takes an intensely personal experience and produces a text that speaks universally. As you read Rooney's narrative and answer the discussion questions, contrast it with Dave's text. Which piece expresses the writer's intention more clearly? Which text seems more vivid and concrete? Which is structured more effectively? Which evidences more detailed inventing and planning?

When Death Comes, We Each Weep For Our Own
Andy Rooney

My mother died today. She was a great Mom and I am typing with tears in my eyes. There were a lot of things she wasn't so good at but no one was ever better at being a mother.

She never wanted to be anything BUT a good mother. It would not satisfy many women today. If I were a woman it would not satisfy me but there was something good about her being one that exceeded any good I will ever do.

I think I know why she was a world champion mother. She had unlimited love and forgiveness in her heart for those close to her. Neither my sister nor I ever did anything so wrong in her eyes that she couldn't explain it in terms of right. She assumed our goodness and no amount of badness in either of us could change her mind. It made us better.

Mother gave the same love to our four children and even had enough left for our family bulldog, Gifford. One summer afternoon at her cottage in a wooded area with a lot of wildlife, some food was left on the table on the front patio. When we came back later part of it had been eaten and everyone but Mother suspected our bulldog.

"It couldn't have been Gifford," Mother said. "It must have been some animal."

From the day she went into the hospital there was never any question about her living. The doctor treated her as though she might recover but he knew she would not. I hope he is treated as well on his death bed.

Something has to be done about the way we die, though. Too often it is not good enough. Some of the people who have heard of Mother's death at age 93 and knew of her protracted illness said, "It's a blessing" but there was nothing blessed about it.

For seven terrible weeks after a stroke, Mother held on to life with a determination she would not have had if she hadn't wanted to live.

Visiting her, at first, I was pleased that she seemed unaware of anything and was not suffering. I would bend over, stroke her hair and whisper in her ear, "It's Andrew, Mom." It would not seem as though she heard but her hand, which had been picking at the blanket in a manner distinctively her own, groped for mine. She did hear. She did know. She was in a terrible half-dream from which she could not arouse herself. She was suffering and in fear of death and I could not console myself that she was not.

My wife stood on the other side of the bed. They got along during the 20 years Mother lived with us. Mother lifted her other hand vaguely toward her. Dying, she wished to include my wife, who had been so good to her, in her affection.

Something is wrong, though. She has something in her throat or one of her legs is caught in an uncomfortable position. You don't dare touch anything for fear of disconnecting one of the tubes leading from the bottles hanging overhead into her. The nurses are busy with their bookwork or they are down the hall working routinely toward Mother's room. Other patients there are caught or choking, too. The nurses know Mother will probably not choke before they get there.

The nurses are very good but without apparent compassion and you realize it has to be that way. They could not possibly work as nurses without some protective coating against tragedy. We all have it. In those seven weeks Mother lay dying, I visited the hospital 50 times but when I left, it was impossible not to lose some of the sense of her suffering. I knew she was still lying there picking vaguely at the blankets in that sad, familiar way but it didn't hurt as much as when I was there, watching.

I wondered if she was the president of the United States, what extraordinary measure would they be taking for her? How could I get them for her? She is not president, she is only my mother. The doctors and nurses cannot know that this frail, dying old woman did a million kindnesses for me. They wouldn't know or care that she was girls' high jump champion of Ballston Spa in 1902 or that she often got up early Sunday morning to make hot popovers for us or that she drove her old Packard too fast and too close to the righthand side of the road. No stranger would have guessed any of those things looking at her there and perhaps would not have cared.

There is no time for each of us to weep for the whole world. We each weep for our own.

DISCUSSION QUESTIONS

1. Even though Rooney speaks very personally about his mother's death, he communicates something beyond that very poignant experience. What would you say is his intention in this text? What do you think he wants readers to reflect upon after they have finished reading it? Who do you think was Rooney's intended audience for this compelling text?

2. An important component in this text's effectiveness is its concrete images. Rooney uses few, if any, code words and vividly evokes his mother's

hospital room, her relationship to him and his sister, and his memories of her. Point out specific instances of this showing of his experience that avoids mere telling.

3. How does Rooney avoid mere sentimentality, the kind of emotion that manipulates the reader awkwardly and may evoke an opposite reaction?

4. Why is his abrupt, two-sentence concluding paragraph an effective means of ending his text?

Choose a personal experience from your own life that has led you to reflect on a deeply felt relationship. Craft a text that: (1) proceeds from one or more of the inventing strategies discussed in this chapter; (2) contains a clearly focused thesis and intention; (3) addresses a particular audience whose characteristics you have carefully explored; (4) avoids the use of code words; and (5) is expressed in vivid, concrete terms.

3 *Drafting a Text*

The Drafting Process

At some point, a writer must sit down and attempt to shape the material he has generated into a text. Through drafting, a writer gives his raw material textual form. Although some writers may produce only one draft, a draft that is nearly finished and that requires few alterations, most writers need to produce more than one. Each successive draft helps a writer develop his thesis and intention. The goal of the drafting process is a final text whose form and content express the author's ideas and communicate those ideas to a reader.

As with all aspects of the writing process, the drafting behavior of writers varies. Some writers draft on a typewriter or word processor; others use a pen or pencil and paper. Writers frequently use one medium, perhaps pen or pencil, to produce early drafts and another medium, perhaps a typewriter, to produce later, more final drafts.

Some writers use two mediums simultaneously while drafting. They may draft their actual text on, say, $8\frac{1}{2} \times 11$ lined paper, but as they continuously reread their draft, they record ideas or commentary in a lined notebook, which they keep handy. Some writers find this a useful strategy, since it enables them to jot down ideas for revision without disturbing their stream of thought.

How writers pace themselves when drafting also varies significantly. Some need to produce a draft in one sitting, if at all possible. Others produce a draft in stages, over a period of time. Some writers feel compelled to move forward as rapidly as possible so that they do not lose their momentum. They will often leave blank spaces within sentences if they can't think of the right word. Or they will move past sentences that they know are poorly written because revising these sentences might disrupt their flow of thought. Other writers, on the other hand, find it absolutely necessary to ponder every word. The reflection they engage in to select the best word for a particular context is a vital part of their drafting process, helping to move them on toward a finished text.

Whatever their drafting behavior, however, all writers constantly reread what they have already written as they draft. This enables them to move forward and write more. It diverts their attention from the narrow concern of putting thoughts into separate, grammatical sentences toward more global concerns, such as developing intention. Rereading also shapes a draft because words and sentences set off chains of thought, which, in turn, influence what is written. As writers reread, they make textual changes. They may, for example, add or delete information, reorder the sequence of presentation, recast sentences, substitute one word for another, and so forth. This recursive behavior is characteristic of all writers, and revision— making changes—is at the heart of the drafting process for all successful writers.

Aside from these few brief generalizations about drafting, there is not much to be said. The best instruction in drafting is to show you how it is done. Most of this chapter is a case study involving two of our student writers, Pati and Charlene, who were given the same writing task, but who moved through the drafting process in radically different ways. We will look over Pati's and Charlene's shoulders as they draft, after a preliminary discussion about a drafting strategy that some writers use.

Exercise

Think about what you did when you drafted your personal experience essay (Chapter 2, page 67), and answer the following questions:

1. Did you do a great deal of inventing and planning *before* you began to draft? If so, describe what you did; for example, did you write out a plan? If not, explain what you did and why you began drafting almost immediately.

2. Did you prefer to draft in one sitting (if possible) or in several sessions? Explain and describe what you did.

3. Did you often leave blank spaces for words or portions of sentences as you drafted, or did you often stop to think of the right word or the best way to structure a sentence? Explain.

4. Did you draft on a typewriter or word processor, or did you *have* to use a pen or pencil, at least for early drafts? Explain.

5. Overall, how did you feel while you were drafting? Relieved? Frustrated? Totally engaged? Explain.

Predrafts and Rough Drafts

A draft is shaped and influenced by many factors, such as the writer's intention, the audience being addressed, and decisions regarding organization, word choice, and sentence structure. These factors are related to one another and influence one another. Drafting also involves language use, motor skills and hand-eye coordination, reading, thinking, and reasoning. Although the precise method of drafting varies from writer to writer, revision is at the heart of drafting, whether the writer makes significant changes in the text on paper, on the screen of a word processor, or in his mind, or whether he makes changes within a single draft or throughout a series of drafts.

Writers, whether experienced or not, frequently respond to the challenge of a writing task by writing their first draft to and for themselves. Such a draft is a *predraft*. Writing a predraft is useful for several reasons. It lets a writer explore a topic freely, generating information and exploring relationships, without being concerned about the structure or thesis of the text. Drafting to and for oneself is perfectly reasonable in an early stage of writing. However, a predraft is likely to be structureless, incoherent, unfocused, and useful only to the writer who created it. Predrafts are a kind of *writer-based prose*, writing that is composed for the benefit of the writer, not a reader. *Reader-based prose*, on the other hand, is writing that communicates successfully to a reader.

Although it is theoretically possible for a writer to have engaged in such extensive, successful inventing and planning that his first draft is perfectly constructed, conveying his thesis and intention to the reader exactly as he intended, this rarely happens. Successful writers must usually either make significant alterations in their first drafts after they complete it or write several successive drafts. Those writers who create predrafts produce additional drafts, since predrafts are usually not well enough focused or structured to be reworked.

A draft that is substantial in development and structure and that has begun to reveal the writer's intention and thesis to a reader successfully is a *rough draft*. Rough drafts are more reader-based than predrafts; thus, they may often be reshaped by adding, deleting, rearranging, and so forth. Since the aim of drafting is to produce a final text whose form and content skillfully reveal thesis and intention to a reader, drafting can be seen as a process whereby writer-based prose is transformed into reader-based prose.

WRITER-BASED   READER-BASED
            PROSE ————————————————————→ PROSE
(written for the   (written for the
            writer)   reader)

Most drafts—other than final drafts—may be classified as either primarily reader-based or primarily writer-based. A writer-based text may include elements that attempt to communicate with a reader, such as a carefully constructed introduction. Likewise, a reader-based text may have elements that are addressed to the writer and that may confuse or irritate a reader, such as an unsupported assertion or an unfocused, incoherent paragraph. A predraft is *very writer-based*, since it contains little that is addressed to the reader; the author has made almost no attempt to communicate with the reader. As we have said, unless a writer produces a very reader-based initial text, which requires few alterations, drafting involves the production of several drafts, each of which is successively more reader-based.

Exercise

Read the following text, which is a first draft of a letter that will be sent to the Director of Freshman Writing:

Dear Dr. Marcus:

Last week I took the English Proficiency Exam and I failed it. Now my teacher says I can't pass the course. I spent about two hours arguing with her, saying that all semester long I did the work. I wrote eight papers and I got C's on two and a B on one. The Proficiency Exam is an essay exam graded by someone who doesn't even know you. How can a person who doesn't even know you decide if you should pass a course or whether you shouldn't pass a course especially if you worked hard and did all the assignments? Not only that, it's true that we knew the topics for the Proficiency Exam beforehand and it's also true that we discussed them in class but I had the flu. Also, yes, you get to take the exam again and I didn't do so well the second time, but still I don't understand, if I did the work and got 2 C's and a B and also rewrote some papers which eventually were passing, why shouldn't I pass the course?

The Proficiency Exam system is unfair to all students. It makes their whole grade depend on one test instead of depending on a semester of work. Also, effort should count and also why should a stranger (not even your teacher) be in charge of deciding whether you pass or fail? The Proficiency Exam system should be studied carefully and then gotten rid of.

I appreciate your time and your consideration of this important matter.

Yours sincerely,

Bob Smithson

Bob Smithson

Examine Bob Smithson's draft and answer the following questions:

1. What, exactly, does Bob want Dr. Marcus to do? Is Bob appealing his failing grade or complaining about an unfair system?

2. How would you expect Dr. Marcus to react if he received Bob's first draft? Explain why.

3. Does the draft seem to be well structured? Explain.

4. What does Bob need to do *before* he sends his letter to Dr. Marcus? Be as specific as you can.

From First Drafts to Final Drafts: A Case Study of Two Writers

Up until now we have been talking about the drafting process somewhat abstractly, using such terms as predraft and rough draft. Having laid the conceptual groundwork, we are ready to show you the actual drafting processes of two of our students. As you read this section and work through the exercises based upon Charlene's and Pati's texts, keep in mind the distinctions between writer-based and reader-based texts that we have been making.

We think you will see dramatic differences between Charlene's and Pati's drafts, although each of them ended up with a satisfactory final draft. Both writers had been asked to write an expository essay about "the function of graffiti" that would be interesting to and informative for a group of their peers. Although both women went to the library and read a number of works about graffiti, and both gathered various samples of graffiti in and around the university and the nearby downtown area, their behavior, including drafting methods, differed markedly.

Inventing and Planning

Pati began by gathering graffiti from a variety of sources, including bathroom walls. One particular source of graffiti, the restroom walls of a popular college bar, captured her attention and imagination. This was especially true because she was able to get graffiti from both the men's room and the women's room—her boyfriend went into the men's room and gathered graffiti for her. The graffiti written by the women were very different from those written by the men, and Pati began to wonder whether there was anything special about the graffiti that women wrote. She decided to look for information about graffiti written by and for women, and so in a sense, this question led her to narrow the scope of the library sources to which she referred. Pati was able to locate appropriate sources, including an article about feminist graffiti. After examining these sources, she began to think about a tentative topic. She wasn't sure, but she thought that writing about women as members of an "oppressed social group" who wrote graffiti might be interesting. Pati thought that, "maybe, underneath the exaggerated humor found in many of the graffiti, there were some truths" to be discovered and written about.

Charlene began by gathering graffiti from a variety of places and by reading a number of essays about the function of graffiti. From this, she sensed that "there were lots of varieties of graffiti" and that graffiti functioned in many different ways, depending upon the writer and the circumstances. At this point, Charlene recognized that she needed to narrow her topic. She decided that reading more about graffiti would help her to see how the material tied together and to discover a number of focused, narrowed topics within the more general topic of graffiti.

Exercise

Review Pati's and Charlene's inventing and planning and answer the following questions:

1. Charlene read a number of essays before she started to narrow her topic; Pati narrowed her topic before she read any essays. Which strategy appeals to you more? Which would you consider more effective, and under what circumstances?
2. How did the strategy of gathering graffiti from *both* men's and women's bathrooms help Pati shape a more specific writing topic?

Writing Task

Strategy A: Pick one of the following topics and spend about five to ten minutes writing about it, either freewriting or brainstorming. Then discuss the topic with one of your classmates for ten minutes. Put together what you wrote initially with what you discovered as a result of your discussion with your classmate.

1. obedience to authority
2. grades
3. foreign aid
4. housework
5. experimentation with animals

Strategy B: Now pick another of the topics and discuss it with one of your classmates for ten minutes. Then write for five to ten minutes on the topic. Put together what you discovered as a result of your discussion with your classmate with what you produced on your own.

   Compare the two strategies. Which did you find easier? What advantages or disadvantages do you see with each of these strategies?

Moving Toward a Goal

After Charlene read additional sources about graffiti and took notes, she decided to focus on "an age group or locality." She soon decided to write about adolescents. Perhaps graffiti writing helped some adolescents cope with the problems they faced during "this period of change" (adolescence). As she thought more about this possible approach to her essay, Charlene speculated about some of the seemingly contradictory needs that are often ascribed to adolescents: the need to form a unique identity; the need to feel self-worth; the need to belong; the need to be independent. Perhaps writing graffiti allowed some adolescents to express their frustration, confusion, and/or anxiety; perhaps writing graffiti afforded some adolescents the opportunity to assert themselves, to feel unique.

As a result of her thinking, Charlene tentatively decided to use this strategy: "The procedure I will follow . . . in my paper will be to discuss adolescents and the problems they face. Then I will explain how writing/drawing graffiti may function as a device for helping adolescents cope." She also wrote a rather detailed plan for the essay, which she would later use to write the rough draft.

Here is the plan Charlene devised:

Graffiti and Adolescents

Purpose: to explain how graffiti can help some young people
           cope with the problems of adolescence
Audience: sociologists (sociology teacher)

-- Graffiti is commonly done by adolescents
-- By far the most potent crisis is that of attaining a sense of ego
   - identity while overcoming identify confusion.
   - Person w/identity knows what is expected of him and what to expect of others
-- Effort to assert a unique original self--often encounters demoralizing and frustrating experiences from the adult society. Glaring adult double standards aggravate the sad conflicts of adolescents' self-doubts
-- Variations exist in modern society in the strategies being employed to ease the situation in each setting

-- Much of the handwriting on today's walls (1972) is nothing more than names and cryptic numbers, which psychologists attribute to crude youthful efforts to express personal identity
-- Graffiti fulfill several of our needs as individuals:
   - A graffito enables one to communicate w/others.
   - A person reaching out to anyone who will read the graffito is apparent in the plea, "I am anonymous, help."
   - A graffito serves as an outlet for self-expression.
   - A graffito allows one to achieve some small semblance of immortality (to leave one's mark on the world)
-- Unlike spoken communications, graffiti provide safety from direct rebuttal, are more permanent than the spoken word, and reach larger audiences over a period of time.
-- Graffiti are much more than doodles or vandalism. They are the written thoughts, wishes, hopes, and dreams of individuals.
-- The writing of graffiti is gaining more recognition as a legitimate means of communication than it ever has before
-- Because the intent of graffiti is self-expression, in a restrained, repressive society the addition of more restraints (laws) in actuality encourages the graffitist to commit the act
-- The most common graffiti among adolescents are those of sexual desire:
   - sexual <u>activity</u> most common graffiti of boys
   - sexual <u>desire</u> most common graffiti of girls
-- Self-identity is the second largest category for adolescents
   - this suggests the individual's preoccupation with his sense of self in relation to others and to the world
-- Many of the graffiti deal w/the "new" self and the "new" body
   - the most prevalent subcategory was "who am I?"
-- Graffiti writers are usu. adolescents
   - artists feel a kinship (belonging)
   - indicates life cycle needs of adolescents & ability of society to meet needs
-- Adolescent personality: sexual maturity, self-identity, idealism, iconoclasm, and rebellion
-- Graffiti (singular graffito) derived fr/Italian verb <u>graffore</u>, meaning "to scratch"
-- Specific groups of people produce specific types of graffiti

-- To inscribe a message on a public wall is to attempt communication; even to invite response

-- Graffiti give the writer a sense of achievement and a positive self-concept

-- The writing seems to be linked w/a sense of belonging, since the graffitists run in cliques and have names that are known by other clique members

-- Adolescence is a subculture representing the transition from child-hood to adult life that usually occurs between the ages of 12 and 18 years

Pati's behavior differed dramatically from Charlene's. Here are some excerpts from her inventing and planning notes:

Well, I'm just about ready to panic. I went to every bar in town last night, looking for graffiti and I didn't find a darn thing. But I did get some ideas about other places to look on campus, which is what I'm going to do right after class.

I have a book on "the history of ideas about women," which is a series of essays. The one by Betty Friedan looks like it may be helpful, and I'm sure there are other articles that deal w/what women need to express. By comparing what I read to the graffiti I find, I hope to come up with some good ideas for this paper. I hope. I almost wish I could go home this weekend; I know that there are some excellent graffiti at Oberlin College. B.G. women don't write as much as I thought they would. I may have to modify my topic—well, I guess I'll find that out in the next couple of hours.

I'm not sure where to focus my thoughts on this yet. The idea of repressed social groups appeals to me, so I may concentrate on feminist graffiti. I find that the writings in bathrooms and at bars are especially interesting because the alcohol and the privacy tend to release in-hibitions. I think women are writing things on bathroom walls that they don't dare to express to anyone.

Much of the writings seem like there is no truth or seriousness involved (especially about sex), but I would not be surprised to find that under the exaggeration and humor lies some truth.

In contrast to the relative ease with which Charlene focused her raw material and identified a series of points, Pati felt "ready to panic." She thought she might even have to modify her topic if she did not come up with anything "in the next couple of hours." Although she was confused and uncertain of what she would write, Pati decided to plunge in and write a first draft anyway. She wanted to see what she would come up with.

The First Draft

Charlene and Pati both wrote drafts of their essays. As you read through them, remember how each of them invented and planned and consider how their different preparation has affected the draft each has produced.

CHARLENE'S FIRST DRAFT

1   Graffitists are commonly adolescents. Graffiti serves a useful function for people in this age group. Adolescence, a period of change and challenge for young people, poses many problems and new situations which the young people never before encountered. Graffiti can serve as an outlet for adolescents to express their feelings and thoughts. To see the relationship between adolescence and graffiti, let us first look more closely at adolescence.

2   Adolescence is an entire subculture of our society which represents the transition from childhood to adult life. It usually occurs between the ages of 12–18 years. During adolescence, young people experience physical, emotional and menta social changes that can be confusing and frustrating. In the midst of all these changes an adolescent must form a sense of identity and a personal set of values.

3   Since adolescence brings on confused emotions confusion about values and identity, a need exists for an expressive outlet. For many adolescents, writing graffiti helps-to-relieve-the-confu-pressure-and-confusion is a useful means of expressing their frustrations, confusion and anxieties, as well as asserting personal identity. Therefore, Particularly for youths who have no one to even talk to about their/feelings, writing graffiti is the best way of getting someone to "listen." In an effort to assert a unique original self many adolescents often encounter demoralizing and frustrating experiences from the adult world society.

4   According to an article by Spann, graffiti fulfill several of our needs as individuals: (1) "A graffito enables one to communicate with others." One can infer the message "I am reaching out to anyone who will read the graffito." (2) A graffito serves as an outlet for self-expression. (3) A graffito allows one to achieve some small semblance of immortality;

to leave one's mark on the world. These ~~needs~~ Graffiti fulfill these needs in particular for adolescents who are seeking to establish a sense of identity and to prove to others that they are, indeed, significant individuals.

Now that we have examined the adolescence, let us ~~turn to~~ focus on specific ways ~~that~~ graffiti ~~itself~~ function in helping adolescents cope.

The most common graffiti among adolescents ~~of~~ are that of sexual desire, probably because this is a new feeling for them to experience. Graffiti on the topic of sex ~~is~~ are important for young people as they struggle to form a personal set of values dealing with sex.

Self identity is the second largest category for adolescent graffitists. As stated in <u>Adolescence</u>, this suggests the individual's preoccupation with his sense of self in relation to others and to the world. Much of the graffiti, therefore, deal with the "new" self and the "new" body with a prevalent subcategory of "Who am I?" This graffiti demonstrate the adolescent search for identity. A great deal of the handwriting on walls is simply names and cryptic numbers which psychologists attribute to crude youthful efforts to express personal identity. Graffiti gives the writer a sense of achievement and a positive self concept, particularly when he has written his own name. He can then feel important because people will read ~~his~~ HIS name.

~~Graffiti~~ A graffito has certain advantages over spoken communication. It provides safety from direct rebuttal. Therefore, the youth feels free to say what he ~~fee~~ thinks--proving that he can be his own person. Also, ~~gr~~ a graffito is more permanent than the spoken word and reaches a larger audience over a period of time. Because of this permanence, the graffito has a greater impact than spoken word. If the graffito is a name, the person can *actually* feel famous because of his large audience.

Since graffiti are generally not acceptable means of expression, the writing of graffiti is an act of rebellion. Rebellion, for adolescents, is a way of asserting their independence, which is a part of being one's own person with an identity. *Therefore,* When laws are passed or become stiffer, it serves only to encourage adolescent graffitists because they feel compelled to rebel, to be independent.

As Stern wrote in her article in the <u>New York Times Magazine</u>, graffiti writing "seems to be linked with a sense of belonging since the graffitists run in cliques who have names known by other clique members." Adolescents have a strong need to belong and to be accepted by a peer group. Belonging and acceptance strengthen an individual's self concept and reinforce his sense of identity. By writing an name that is known to other group members, as well as belonging to the group itself, a graffitist is able to assert his identity as someone unique and significant.

11   In conclusion, we can see that an adolescent through graffiti can deal with the many of the problems that he encounters during this period of change. The individual is able to express his feelings about his new body, his new self and new desires without fear of direct rebuttal. He is able to express his new independence and assert his self identity. For Therefore, for many adolescents who have no other means of self-expression, writing graffiti helps them to deal with their lives.

Let us examine Charlene's draft. It is quite long and seems to be structured in the manner that she intended. The essay begins with an introductory paragraph that includes the thesis, "Graffiti can serve as an outlet for adolescents to express their feelings and thoughts." This introduction is followed by a section discussing relevant aspects of adolescence. The following section explains several ways in which graffiti may function for adolescents. The essay concludes with a summative paragraph that reiterates what has been said.

Charlene was pleased with her first draft because, although it was not finished, it was definitely a *rough* draft. That meant she would be able to rewrite it by adding, deleting, rearranging, and restating. She was particularly concerned with refining the structure of her essay, since she felt that in parts of the essay her purpose was not clear to the reader, and she was not certain that the reader could easily follow her arguments or the connections between one part of the essay and another. Of course, she was also concerned about such matters as sentence structure, word choice, and the "artfulness" of her piece, but she decided to focus on structure initially.

Exercise

Examine Charlene's rough draft and answer these questions.

1. Write down specific words and phrases that call the reader's attention

to the *structure* of the essay—the way the author intends to proceed in the text and its order, arrangement, and sectioning.

2.   Paragraph 8 begins with the sentence, "A graffito has certain advantages over spoken communication." How many such advantages are mentioned? Do you think the paragraph covers them adequately? Why or why not? Also, is the connection between these advantages and the function of graffiti made clear?

3.   Paragraph 7 begins with the sentence, "Self identity is the second largest category for adolescent graffitists." Is this a good beginning sentence for the paragraph? Can you locate specific words within the sentence that are problematical? Why is this sentence a particularly important one?

4.   Paragraph 10 begins with the sentence, "As Stern wrote in her article in the *New York Times Magazine*. . . ." Does this sentence provide an effective transition from the preceding paragraph to this one? Why or why not?

5.   Suppose you had written Charlene's first draft. How would you go about revising it? Would you first read through it several times and make notes to yourself about what to change and how to change it? Would you just begin to read and revise immediately, going back and forth to various parts of the essay again and again? Describe in some detail what you would do; refer to specific portions of the draft if you can.

PATI'S FIRST DRAFT

My generation must learn well. We learned to respect property above ideas. We learned not to sqwack about social issues; all that noise never did any good anyhow. And we learned that women don't have it so bad after all. Turns out, things are just fine the way they are.   1

True, there are still a few bleeding hearts clilnging to the idea of equality between the sexes. But these are the same type of people that write on bathroom walls. Luckily for B.G. this handful of blatantly liberal women has reduced itself to an anonymous shrinking feeling that no one wants to represent.   2

I looked to BG's graffiti on campus and off, particularly in bars' restrooms to see what women are feeling about themselves. I expected to find the writings of repressed, frustrated women trying to identify w/a group. I expected to find women trying to help each other deal w/their role in society. MS. Magazine told me that all I had to do was look--feminist graffiti is everywhere. Well, I looked and judging from   3

what I found it appears that the women's movement barely exists in
B.G.

4   For the most part, women just don't write on walls anymore. And
when they do write they tend to write about men and sex. While this
may reflect our recently gained sexual freedom I don't think it does
much toward raising women's consciousness level. That type of graffiti
occurred for the most part in only one place--Howard's Club H.

5   Of course Howard's has some inane graffiti also, but mingled among
it are some truly heartening words. Repressed social groups need an
outlet to express themselves and vent frustrations. The privacy of a
bathroom stall provides an opportunity for anonymous uncensored
communication. People can ask for and give advice, express their
personal feelings, or write messages as simple as ♀   Women Unite.

6   People can write things on bathroom walls that they wouldn't dare
talk about. Many others seek advice about love and sex. Often these
problems are answered by other women, whose recommendations
usually get strong rebuttals. One girl in Mosely Hall actually tried to
mediate between two feuding women. Another of my sources points
out that women must unite and not let men drive them apart.

7   Simple self-expression can be therapeutic for both writer and reader.
One young women at Howard's left an original poem.

        Continuing--
        Each one had defenses, they said
        the sheets were full of static
        Sometimes, when they went to bed
        He biting drunk, she swollen with silences
        They pulled the blankets to shreds
        and wrapped themselves separate as shrouds.
        In the museum, sand held skeletons
        nothing could pry the fingers from the clench
        and the round spine reminded them all humans are alone
        In time they must uncurl, combine, beg
        and forgive one another. It is nearly impossible
        to live under one roof w/o speech
        or that slow growing into something they needed
        to name love, for want of another way
        to say how lonely it is here on earth
        and how the nights are cold.

original

But graffiti such as this is alarmingly rare. Many of the ~~slogans~~ 8
messages are familiar slogans such as A woman w/o a man is like a
fish w/o a bicycle. Perhaps the most encouraging message was a door
size drawing at Howard's of a modern girl saying "What do you mean
its not that bad?" I can understand her exasperation, because as far
as the general attitudes of the masses goes, things aren't that bad.
They're worse.

Now let us examine Pati's draft, which is quite different from Charlene's.
Pati was anxious to write something down, even though she didn't have
a particularly clear idea of what she was going to write. Therefore, Pati
wasn't necessarily expecting to produce a rough draft. In fact, she figured
that that was pretty unlikely. Indeed, when Pati finished her first effort—
two and a half scrawled pages—she knew that what she had written was
definitely a predraft.

This meant that Pati's first draft was *not* something that she could easily
rewrite by adding to it, deleting from it, and so on. Nevertheless, she was
quite interested in what her predraft might reveal to her about potentially
better focused topics, theses, or writing strategies.

Exercise

Examine Pati's predraft and answer the following questions.

1. Write the first seven words of the sentence that first gives you the
sensation that Pati has gone off the track.
2. Why might Pati's use of the term "feminist" in paragraph 3 cause
problems for the reader? For Pati?
3. Is the first sentence of the predraft, "My generation must learn well,"
misleading? Why or why not?
4. Describe the structure of Pati's predraft. What does the essay do first,
next, and so on? Is the structure effective? Why or why not?
5. List some possible theses that can be gleaned from Pati's predraft.
Does the predraft suggest any strategies for planning and/or organizing a
next draft? Does the predraft suggest a next step or stage in the production
of a completed essay?

PATI'S SECOND INVENTING SESSION

As you remember, Pati had expected to produce a predraft, given the rather perfunctory nature of her first inventing and planning session. And she did. Therefore, rather than attempting to rewrite her draft, which was largely an unstructured "dump" of ideas and thoughts, Pati read through it and identified quite a few leads. She then engaged in another inventing session. From the results of this second session, you can see that Pati is beginning to get control of her drafting process.

Women's restrooms

personal   self-expression/fantasy   free, uncensored
                                                     unedited
                therapy/conversation   anonymous

social   group identity/consc. raising   excess energy

        SEX

women   are a repressed group so they   deface
tend to write more   I am somebody

Top subjects--MS

sex   love   Marriage

Sexuality   Abortion   Politics   Fem. Messages

        DISMEMBER RAPISTS   NYC

Women Unite

                                                        Eva Peron

FAMOUS LIES

(You won't get pregnant, etc.)

Continueing   (poem)
        humiliated
I   ∧   Myself.

I AM DEAD

   Women use graffiti to express a dissatisfaction with their life &
role which they do not feel comfortable expressing publicly.

Sex - advice - who's good, bad   Disappointment - Mark, You
              herpes etc.   don't as well as you think -
                                         Kathleen

Lots of ♀♀ Ashes to Ashes
             Dust to Dust
             There's no man a woman can trust
             So have no man & have no   I am Dead
             sin & have no sorrow   I humiliated myself
             Gone tomorrow
                       Kim & Michelle

Famous Lies -

   You won't get pregnant
   I'll respect you in the morning

RELATIONSHIPS -
   Continueing - bad relationship

I'm so jaded

Oh my Love, I have one thing to say to you
          "Get a Grip!"

                                        Marriage is prostitution w/one man

          Divorce today - pleasure tomorrow

As a culture we appear satisfied but we aren't.
          Why are we so passive?
               learned behavior
               easier to be less

Graf. reflects changes in society   70's lots of feminist
                                                    soc/political

Social - What do you mean it's not   now very little
          so bad?   now personal
     EVA PERON

Prying fingers from the clench

SEX   Advice - who's good, bad;   who has herpes,

Disappointment - Mark - you don't as well as you think - Kathleen

ANGER - Famous Lies - You won't get pregnant
                         I'll respect you in the morning

          I'm sick of reading it.
          No one cares.
          I humiliated myself
          I am dead.

CONFUSION - Lend your Love to me tonight. Don't ask me who or
               what is right ... I have no strength I cannot fight. Just
               flood my darkness with your light.

PAIN -

    I've got a problem. Maybe someone can help me.   Mosely

ANGER AT ROLE - Marriage is prostitution w/one man   NYC

    Divorce today--pleasure tomorrow
                NYC

RELATIONSHIPS
I'm so jaded.   Oh my Love I have one thing to say to you
                          "Get a Grip"
I'm tired of men who think they
own me.
               Continuing - end of a relationship
                    all humans are alone

SOCIAL -
EVA PERON
  ♀   Women Unite
What do you mean it's not so bad!?
Dismember Rapists   NYC

WOMEN UNITE

Ashes to Ashes   Dust to dust
There's no man a woman can trust
So have no man & have no sin
And have no sorrow for gone tomorrow
          Kim & Michelle

You'd be surprised   You'd be surprised
How much better you   How much
do in Life   MOSELY   better you'd
w/out GUYS!   do in college
                      w/out guys!

Sorry but I need guys for
my sex life.

Life at school can be tolerated

But life w/o men or life w/o alcohol
Cannot be a life worth living

Stay
ignorent → You've got a great deal
            ↗ to learn of life

It'll get you nowhere

Why?   To express disatisfactions about our role as women—primarily
       as it pertains to sex and relationships—Anger we won't express
       publicly. Graffiti is anonymous, uncensored, private yet public
       defacement of property = release of energy/frustration

Howard's - Drunk, uninhibited women in a setting designed to pair
           up males and females - escape from men in one place only.

self-expression is therapeutic - release
    Leaving a mark, esp. a creative one builds self-esteem
    Some women sought a response, advice
    Others offered advice w/o being asked.

Feeling of bitterness, disillusionment - defeat, dismay
Not many fighting words   lots of lamentations

Graffiti reflects changes in society. In 1970s women's social/political
graffiti was way up. Now (here anyway) it seems to have disappeared.
We are bummed out as individuals. No group cohesiveness.

Women will write messages to men in women's bathrooms. Gets it
off her chest w/o telling him

To express publicly that things suck is unfeminine and unattractive.
Everybody wants to get married, thus we must be as pretty as possible.
We shave, we tweeze, we paint on smiles and we don't complain.

Me - too young when women's lib was big

Mother - too old, taught old sex roles and values

Now - apathy

As a result of inventing again after she wrote an initial predraft, Pati drew some interesting conclusions (p. 88) from which she crafted a thesis: "Women are trying to live up to commonly held role expectations without believing in them wholeheartedly. This has caused many women to feel dissatisfaction, which they express in many of the graffiti they write." Pati now felt ready to write a second draft, and she was confident that it would be a rought draft this time.

Exercise

1.   Examine the results of Pati's second round of inventing. Do any aspects of it seem to have been influenced by her predraft? What are they? Does the form of Pati's second batch of raw material seem to have been influenced by her predraft? Explain.

2.   Have you begun to suspect that you sometimes (frequently? always?) write to yourself first, even though this never occurred to you before? List some of the things that make you suspect this. For example, have you ever had an essay returned to you with a summative comment such as this: "This essay has no purpose and no recognizable structure. It meanders from _____ to _____. Decide what you want to write about; either _____ or _____ or _____ or _____. Then . . ."

The Second Draft

Both Charlene and Pati produced several drafts before they were satisfied. As she had anticipated, the draft Pati wrote after her second attempt at inventing was a rough draft. It was quite good, and she did not need to do much extensive rewriting. She wrote one more draft and was satisfied with it. Charlene reworked her initial rough draft several times, producing three additional drafts. Then she, too, was satisfied with her work.

Reproducing each intermediate draft that Charlene and Pati produced would probably not be instructive, but Pati's second draft is interesting, especially compared to her predraft. Here, then, are two further drafts: Charlene's second rough draft and Pati's second draft, her first rough draft.

CHARLENE'S SECOND DRAFT

The Function of Adolescent Graffiti

Graffiti, commonly written by adolescents, serve a useful function for people in this age group. Adolescence is a period of change and challenge. It poses many problems for the young individuals because they are exposed to situations and experiences which they have never before encountered. Adolescents must develop ways of handling themselves, or codes of behavior, for each situation. Developing suitable and acceptable codes of behavior can be a trying challenge that results in mixed-up feelings. Graffiti can serve as an outlet for adolescents to express their feelings and thoughts. To see the relationships between adolescence and graffiti, let us first look more closely at adolescence.

Adolescence, which represents the transition from childhood to adult life, is an entire subculture of our society. It usually occurs between the ages of 12–18 years. During adolescence, a young person experiences physical, emotional and social changes that can be confusing and frustrating. But to complicate things further, in the midst of all these changes an adolescent must form a sense of identity and a personal set of values.

Since adolescence brings on confusion about values and identity, the youths need outlets for self-expression. For many adolescents, writing graffiti is a useful means of expressing their frustrations, confusion and anxieties, as well as asserting their personal identity. In an effort to assert a unique original self, adolescents often encounter demoralizing and frustrating experiences from the adult society. Therefore, particularly for youths who have no one to talk to about their feelings, writing graffiti is the best way of getting someone to "listen."

Now that we have examined adolescence, let us look at specific ways that graffiti function in helping adolescents cope. The most common graffiti among adolescents are those which express sexual desire, probably because this is a new feeling for them to experience. Also, because talking openly about sexual desire and activity is taboo, adolescents may feel free to express their sex-related thoughts only through graffiti. Graffiti on the topic of sex are important for young people as they struggle to form a personal set of values dealing with sex.

Self identity is the second most common topic of adolescent graffiti. The frequency of graffiti on this topic suggests the individual's preoccupation with his sense of self in relation to others and to the world.

Much of the graffiti, therefore, deals with the "new" self and the "new" body. This self-oriented graffiti demonstrates the adolescent search for identity. In addition to graffiti that openly explores questions like "Who am I?" there is a great deal of handwriting on walls that is simply names and cryptic numbers. The numbers are usually part of the graffitist's nickname. Psychologists attribute the writing of names to crude youthful efforts to express personal identity. Name writing gives the writer a sense of achievement and a positive self concept. The writer can feel important because people will read HIS name.

Graffiti can function to help adolescents meet their growing need for independence. Since graffiti is generally not an acceptable means of expression, the writing of graffiti is an act of rebellion. Rebellion, for adolescents, is an assertion of independence. As young people mature they need to become more independent, which is part of establishing their own unique identities. Thus, for some adolescents, writing graffiti is a means of asserting independence. Because of the way graffiti functions to prove independence, stiffer laws concerning graffiti serve only to encourage adolescent graffitists.

Another function that graffiti serves for young people is to give them a sense of belonging. As Stern wrote in her article in the New York Times Magazine, graffiti writing "seems to be linked with a sense of belonging since the graffitists run in cliques who have names known by other members." Adolescents have a strong need to belong and to be accepted by a peer group. Belonging and acceptance strengthen an individual's self concept and reinforce his sense of identity. By writing a name that is known to other group members, proving acceptance into the group, a graffitist is able to satisfy his need to belong.

In conclusion, we can see that an adolescent, through graffiti, can deal with many of the problems that he encounters during his transition from childhood to adulthood. The individual is able to express his feelings about his new body, new self and new desires without fear of direct rebuttal. He is able to express his independence and assert his self identify. Therefore, for many adolescents who have no other or no better means of self-expression, writing graffiti helps them to deal with their changing lives.

Exercise

1. What changes in structure do you notice between Charlene's first and second drafts?

2.   What structural problems, if any, still remain?

3.   Do any explanations still need to be expanded or reworded? If so, which?

4.   Do you notice many changes in sentence structure, word choice, or mechanics/usage?

5.   What generalizations can you make about the type of changes Charlene made in her initial draft to produce this draft?

PATI'S SECOND DRAFT

Graffiti, Liberation, and the Women's Movement

My gender was determined in 1961. Midway through 1962 I became a target of the socialization process. That is, society let me know that I, as a female, was expected to act in various situations. My purpose was clear; I was to do everything in my power to catch, marry and hang on to a man. Because bitchy women are so unattractive I was to be passive and uncomplaining, especially about sex. I was to avoid damage to the male ego at all costs.

Now the general American public may argue with those statements but a brief look at the role models we present for our children and the mass media messages we beam all over the world will show that these messages are being communicated, sometimes subtly, sometimes not. The problem is not that young people don't eventually develop enough sense to reject some ideas we are presented with, but that these particular ideas hit us so hard at such an early age that ~~we~~ they become ingrained in us before we can question them. It is my belief that a majority of women my age are trying to live up to these expectations without believing in them wholeheartedly. I have come to this conclusion from interacting with my peers for 21 years and reading the graffiti on bathroom walls.

~~Public restrooms are one of the few places where genders are completely segregated. Thus people can write messages~~   *afraid*
Women my age use graffiti to express disatisfactions they are embarassed to voice concerning their expected role in sexual relationships. To complain is to risk losing male companionship so we keep our disappointments to ourselves. But we all need to release our frustrations and graffiti is one possible method.

Women's restrooms are one of the few places men can never go. The stalls are private; the graffiti is uncensored and anonymous. What

better palce to express the feelings we don't dare communicate piblicly? *Insert I*
New ¶ Tavern graffiti is particularly revealing because alcohol tends to release
inhibitions. There the dominant topic is sex and the prevalent feeling
seems to be ~~dismay~~ anger, confusion, *or* disappointment, or even dismay.
For example:

FAMOUS LIES

    YOU WON'T GET PREGNANT.
    I'LL RESPECT YOU IN THE MORNING.

  I HUMILIATED MYSELF

      LEND YOUR LOVE TO ME TONIGHT
      DON'T ASK ME WHO OR WHAT
               IS RIGHT
      I HAVE NO STRENGTH I CANNOT FIGHT
      JUST FLOOD MY DARKNESS
             WITH YOUR LIGHT

I'M TIRED OF MEN
WHO THINK THEY OWN ME.

Insert I

We can get things off our chests w/o blowing our cover. Some women
even ~~direct~~ write their messages directly to ~~the~~ men who ~~would~~ will
never read them:

MARK— YOU DON'T
      AS WELL AS YOU
        THINK
          Kathleen

(continued)

(*more Insert I*)

OH MY LOVE, I HAVE ONE THING TO SAY TO YOU—
            "GET A GRIP"

Notice the last particularly angry outburst at men "who think they own women."   Often graffiti such as this is answered by women   who try to persuade other women that they don't really need   men.

YOU'D BE SURPRISED
    HOW MUCH BETTER YOU DO IN LIFE
    WITHOUT GUYS!

ASHES TO ASHES,
DUST TO DUST,
        THERE'S NO MAN A WOMAN CAN
                    TRUST
            SO
HAVE NO MAN AND HAVE NO SIN
    & HAVE NO SORROW
            FOR GONE TOMORROW.
                KIM AND MICHELLE

What is interesting is the responding   graffiti.

SORRY,
    BUT I NEED GUYS FOR MY SEX LIFE!

LIFE AT SCHOOL CAN BE TOLERATED
        BUT

LIFE WITHOUT MEN AND ALCOHOL
CANNOT BE A LIFE WORTH
LIVING.

In the first example the woman considers men as sex objects. The
second woman considers men in the same category with alcohol.

I do not think that either of these attitudes are typical of women
involved in healthy and fulfilling relationships with men.

Other women spoke directly of marriage.

MARRIAGE
IS
PROSTITUTION WITH ONE MAN.

DIVORCE TODAY
              PLEASURE TOMORROW

One girl wrote a long, lamenting poem about a painful relationship
in which man and woman shared a home but could not communicate.

    Continuing--
    Each one had defenses, they said
    The sheets were full of static
    Sometimes, when they went to bed
    He biting drunk, she swollen
        With silences
    They pulled the blankets to shreds
    And wrapped themselves separate as shrouds.
        In the museum, sand held skeletons
    Nothing could pry the fingers from the clench
    and the round spine reminded them
        All humans are alone.
        in time
    they must uncurl, combine, beg

And forgive one another. It is nearly
   Impossible
To live under one roof without speech
Or that slow growing into something they
   Needed
To name love, for want of another way
To say how lonely it is here on earth
And how the nights are cold.

As this writer points out, women are in a clench, but so is all of humankind. We pair ourselves off into male/female couples but neither sex fully understands the gifts and needs of the other. Women may be trapped in a lesser role, but everyone, male and female alike, suffers from this situation. ~~It-is-lonely-here-on-earth-because-we~~

   I think ~~it is clear from~~ these examples *that* make it clear that the writers are not happy in their relationships with the opposite sex. But we seldom hear these views expressed publicly anymore. We may be upset by the role society expects us to play but we are also tranquilized by the socialization process. We missed the era when liberation was popular ~~though-we-did-grow-up-to-witness-the-dismal-failure-of-the movement~~ and we are left hanging in limbo. If the graffiti of some women is any indicator of the feelings of many women (I believe it is) then we are holding in our anger and frustration, a situation which cannot continue if we are to grow into healthy, fulfilled human beings.

Exercise

1.   What is the thesis of Pati's second draft?

2.   Describe the structure of Pati's draft. What words or phrases call attention to structure?

3.   Does Pati make the concept of "role" clear enough, given the purpose of the draft? Compare Pati's use of "role" in this draft with her use of "feminist" in her predraft.

4.   Does the beginning of Pati's second draft work? Explain.

5.   What do you see as the major differences between this draft and Pati's first one?

The Final Draft

Here are the finished essays about the "function of graffiti" that Charlene and Pati wrote.

The Function of Adolescent Graffiti

Charlene Coleman

Graffiti, commonly written by adolescents, serves a useful function for people in this age group. Adolescence is a period of change and challenge. It poses many problems for young individuals because they are exposed to situations and experiences which they have never before encountered. Adolescents must develop personal codes of behavior for each kind of challenging situation in which they may find themselves. However, developing suitable and socially acceptable codes of behavior can be a trying challenge that may result in mixed-up feelings. It may be helpful for adolescents to vent their confused feelings. Therefore, writing graffiti, which is a way of communicating, can serve as an outlet for adolescents, through which they can express their feelings and thoughts. Hence, there is a possible relationship between adolescence and graffiti, but first let us look more closely at adolescence.

Adolescents, young people who are making the transition from childhood to adult life, form an entire subculture of our society. During adolescence, which occurs between the ages of 12–18 years, a young person experiences physical, emotional, and social changes that can be confusing and frustrating. But to complicate things further, in the midst of all these changes an adolescent must form a sense of identity and a personal set of values.

Since adolescence brings on confusion about values and identity, youths need outlets for self-expression. For many adolescents, writing graffiti is a useful means of expressing their frustrations, confusion, and anxieties, as well as of proving to society that they have unique identities. Therefore, particularly for youths who have no one to talk to about their feelings, writing graffiti can be the best way of getting someone to "listen."

Now that we have looked at some characteristics of adolescence, let us turn our attention to specific ways that graffiti can function in helping adolescents deal with the changes in their lives. The most common graffiti written by adolescents is that which expresses sexual desire, probably because this is a new feeling for them to experience. Also, because talking openly about sexual desire and activity is taboo, adolescents may feel free to express their sex-related thoughts only through graffiti. Graffiti on the topic of sex can serve a significant function for young people as they toy with ideas about sex and morality. Perhaps writing sex-related graffiti helps some adolescents form personal values about sex.

The second most common graffiti written by adolescents is that which expresses self-identity. The frequency of graffiti on this topic suggests each adolescent's preoccupation with his sense of self in relation to others and to the world. Much of the graffiti, therefore, deals with the "new" self and the "new" body. For example, "You do your thing, I'll do mine" and names like "Mooch" and "Kidd" refer to identity. The following graffiti also expresses identity: "Sometimes I feel like a rag doll being played with by a little girl. me . . . ." Furthermore, the following graffiti expresses concerns about the body: "Zits are gross" and "Short stuff is tuff." This self-oriented graffiti demonstrates the adolescent search for identity.

Besides graffiti that openly explores questions like "Who am I?" there is a great deal of writing on walls that is simply names. Psychologists attribute the writing of names to "crude youthful efforts to express personal identity." Name writing gives the young writer a sense of achievement and a positive self-concept; he can feel important because people will read HIS name.

In addition to helping youths express their thoughts on sex and self-identity, graffiti helps meet adolescents' growing need for independence. Since graffiti is generally not an acceptable means of expression, the writing of graffiti is an act of rebellion. Rebellion, for adolescents, is an assertion of independence. As young people mature they need to become more independent, which is part of establishing their own unique identities. Thus, for some adolescents, writing graffiti is a means of asserting independence.

Another function that graffiti serves for young people is to give them a sense of belonging. In New York City, for instance, graffitists achieve a sense of belonging because they run together in cliques and have names known by other members of the group. Adolescents have a strong need to belong and to be accepted by a peer group. Belonging and acceptance strengthen an individual's self-concept and reinforce his sense of identity. By writing a name that is known to other group members, a graffitist is able to satisfy his need to belong and be accepted.

In conclusion, we can see that an adolescent, through writing graffiti, can deal with many of the problems that he encounters during his transition from childhood to adulthood: He is able to express his feelings about his new body, new self, and new desires without fear of direct rebuttal; and he is able to express his independence and assert his self-identity. Therefore, for many adolescents who have no other or no better means of self-expression, writing graffiti helps them to deal with their changing lives.

Graffiti, Liberation, and the Women's Movement
Pati Brumfield

My gender was determined in 1961. Midway through 1962 I was targeted for socialization. That is, society let me know from day one how I, as a female, was expected to act in various situations. My purpose was clear: I was to do everything in my power to catch, marry, and hang on to a man. Because women who "bitch" are considered masculine and unattractive, I was to be passive and uncomplaining, especially about sex. I was to avoid damage to the male ego at all costs. The average American may disagree with those statements, but a brief look at the role models we present for our children and the mass media we beam all over the world will show that these messages are being communicated, sometimes subtly, sometimes not.

The problem is not that young people don't eventually develop enough sense to reject some ideas we are presented with, but that these particular ideas hit us so hard at such an early age that they become ingrained in us before we can question them. As adults we may be able to critically analyze social norms, but fear and guilt often prevent us from rebelling against them. It is my opinion that a majority of women my age are trying to live up to these expectations without believing in them wholeheartedly. I have come to this conclusion from interacting with my peers and by reading the graffiti on bathroom walls.

Women my age use graffiti to express dissatisfactions they are afraid to voice concerning their expected role in sexual relationships. To complain is to risk losing male companionship, so we keep our disappointments to ourselves. But we all need to release our frustrations, and graffiti is one method in which our risk of being found out is minimal. Women's restrooms are one of the few places men can never go. The stalls are private; the graffiti is uncensored and anonymous. What better place to express the feelings we don't dare communicate publicly? We can get things off our chests without blowing our cover—in fact, some women even write their messages to men who will never read them:

MARK —
YOU DON'T AS WELL AS YOU THINK!

KATHLEEN

OH MY LOVE —
I HAVE ONE THING TO SAY TO YOU
"GET A GRIP"

Tavern graffiti is particularly revealing because alcohol tends to release inhibitions. There the dominant topic is sex and the prevalent feelings seem to be anger, confusion, or disappointment. For example:

FAMOUS LIES — —

YOU WON'T GET PREGNANT.

I'LL RESPECT YOU IN THE MORNING.

LEND YOUR LOVE TO ME TONIGHT
DON'T ASK ME WHO OR WHAT IS RIGHT
I HAVE NO STRENGTH   I CANNOT FIGHT
JUST FLOOD MY DARKNESS WITH YOUR LIGHT.

I HUMILIATED MYSELF

I'M TIRED OF
MEN
WHO THINK THEY
OWN
WOMEN.

Notice the last particularly angry outburst at men "who think they own women." Often graffiti such as this is answered by women who argue that men aren't necessary for happiness.

ASHES TO ASHES
DUST TO DUST,

THERE'S NO MAN
A WOMAN CAN TRUST

SO HAVE NO MAN
AND HAVE NO SIN

AND HAVE NO SORROW
FOR GONE TOMORROW

        KIM & MICHELLE

YOU'D BE SURPRISED
HOW MUCH BETTER YOU
DO IN LIFE
    WITHOUT GUYS!

What is interesting is the responding graffiti:

—SORRY
    BUT I NEED GUYS FOR MY SEX LIFE

    LIFE AT SCHOOL CAN BE TOLERATED
    BUT
       LIFE WITHOUT GUYS AND ALCOHOL

    CANNOT BE A LIFE WORTH LIVING.

In the first example the woman considers men as sex objects; the second woman places men in the same category with alcohol. A possible explanation for these attitudes may be that women have long felt that men use us for various "entertainment" purposes and now we have begun to view men in the same light. In any case, it is obvious that attitudes such as these cannot exist in a healthy relationship between man and woman.

Other women speak directly of marriage:

MARRIAGE IS PROSTITUTION WITH ONE
            M A N.

DIVORCE TODAY, PLEASURE
                        TOMORROW.

One girl writes a long, lamenting poem about a painful relationship in which man and woman share a home but cannot communicate.

CONTINUING ———

EACH ONE HAD DEFENSES, THEY SAID
THE SHEETS WERE FULL OF STATIC
SOMETIMES, WHEN THEY WENT TO BED
HE BITING DRUNK, SHE SWOLLEN
   WITH SILENCES
THEY PULLED THE BLANKETS TO SHREDS
AND WRAPPED THEMSELVES SEPARATE
   AS SHROUDS.

IN THE MUSEUM SAND HELD SKELETONS
NOTHING COULD PRY THE FINGERS
   FROM THE CLENCH
AND THE ROUND SPINE REMINDED THEM
ALL HUMANS ARE ALONE
                     IN TIME
THEY MUST UNCURL, COMBINE, BEG
   AND FORGIVE ONE ANOTHER

                     IT IS NEARLY
        IMPOSSIBLE
     TO LIVE UNDER
                     ONE ROOF WITHOUT SPEECH

OR THAT SLOW

GROWING INTO SOMETHING THEY

NEEDED
TO NAME LOVE,

TO SAY HOW

FOR WANT OF ANOTHER WAY

LONELY IT IS HERE

ON EARTH

AND HOW THE NIGHTS ARE COLD.

As the poet points out, women are caught in a clench, but so is all of humankind. We may pair ourselves off into male/female couples, but until each sex fully understands the needs and the gifts of the other, all humans are alone. Women may be trapped in the lesser role, but every person, regardless of gender, suffers from the situation.

Obviously these graffiti writers are unhappy in their relationships with the opposite sex, but seldom do we hear these feelings expressed publicly. Women my age may be upset by the role society expects us to play, but as we are socialized we are also tranquilized. We were only girls when liberated women were in vogue, and rebellion out of fashion is risky business. So we continue holding everything inside. If the graffiti written by some women is any indicator of the feelings of many women (I believe it is), then we are repressing too much anger and frustration, and this situation cannot continue if we are to grow into healthy, fulfilled human beings.

Exercise

Suppose you are an editor of a local magazine. Pati or Charlene has submitted her essay to you in response to your request for a feature essay on the function of graffiti. Write a letter to Pati or Charlene in which you inform her that you are/are not going to publish the essay as it is. Explain your decision, making specific references to the essay whenever possible. You may, if you wish, decide to publish the essay with some revisions, which you, of course, must explain so that the author will be able to make the necessary changes. As you write, remember that the author is a valued staff writer.

Guidelines for Drafting

There were rather dramatic differences between the drafting behavior of Pati and Charlene. Charlene did not begin writing a draft until she had pretty must decided *what* she wanted to say and *how* she wanted to say it. Pati, on the other hand, needed to give her material textual form rather quickly, even though she had not really decided on a thesis or an intention. Neither method of drafting is superior or preferable. However, there are some guidelines that will help you draft a text successfully.

First, to draft successfully you must devote sufficient time and effort to inventing and planning. It does not matter whether you do this before you begin drafting, as Charlene did, or after, as with Pati.

Second, to draft successfully you must be able to conceptualize your thesis and your intention *in detail*. This is not to say that you must do this *before* you begin to write. But if you do not have a thesis and intention in mind before you write, you must develop a design, a global plan, *as you* write. Before you declare a text finished, you must determine whether it conforms to your design: Does its form and content express what you wish? In other words, you must be able to compare each draft you produce with a goal you have set. Each successive draft should come closer to that goal.

Third, to draft successfully you must be able to examine and evaluate each draft that you write to determine whether and/or to what extent it has met your expectations and to plan accordingly. Specifically, *each time* you produce a draft, you must be able to determine whether it is a rough draft or a predraft. If it is a predraft, you must examine it and extract what you can from it. Pati's predraft suggested a number of possible topics to her; it enabled her to engage in a second inventing and planning session that was extensive and quite successful. On the other hand, if a draft is a rough draft, you must be able to identify writer-based elements within it and devise strategies for eliminating them.

Exercise

Review Pati's drafting process and answer the following questions.

1. Explain how Pati did her inventing and planning. When did she seem to do the bulk of her inventing?
2. How did Pati benefit from writing a predraft?

3.   When do you think Pati *began* to conceptualize her thesis and her intention? How do you know that Pati had a detailed idea of her thesis and intention by the time she had completed her second draft?

4.   After comparing what she *wanted* to do, or her overall goal in writing, with what she actually *did* in her second draft, Pati was able to produce a third and final draft. Compare Pati's second and final drafts and list the major changes that she made.

Exercise

Review Charlene's drafting process and answer the following questions.

1.   Explain how Charlene devoted sufficient time to inventing and planning. When did she seem to do the bulk of her inventing and planning?

2.   Charlene's composing process seems to follow the procedure suggested by many writing textbooks. That is, she narrowed a topic, devised a thesis, created a detailed plan, wrote a draft, and then revised it. When you faithfully follow this procedure, does it seem to help you or hinder you? Explain. (You might consider the following as you answer this question: If teachers have required you to hand in an *outline* with a research paper or essay, do you habitually create the outline *after* you finish the text?)

3.   When do you think Charlene had a detailed, concrete conceptualization of her thesis and intention? When did she have a detailed plan for executing her thesis and intention?

4.   Examine the progression of Charlene's drafts toward her final draft. Did she seem to be reworking and refining her drafts in a consistent manner? Did she seem to be comparing each draft with a goal of some sort? Explain.

Writing Assignment

Reread Charlene's and Pati's final essays on graffiti (pp. 97–103). Consider both essays as you answer these discussion questions.

1.   The following statement is from the essay "Names, Graffiti, and Culture" by Herbert Kohl: "[Graffiti] may reveal more of the everyday life of times

past than do documents that are considered historically 'significant.' "[1] Do you agree? Do historians usually study "everyday, run-of-the-mill" people or famous individuals who have made a significant contribution or who have had a significant influence on events? What are the reasons for this approach? Are there any disadvantages to it? Is it interesting or important for us to understand how the "average" person lived during a particular era? Why or why not?

2. Why do people continue to write graffiti? Is graffiti writing limited to individuals of a particular social class? Is it limited to persons of a particular age or ages?

3. What are some of the ways in which graffiti functions for those who write it? What does writing graffiti accomplish for these individuals? Have you ever written graffiti? If so, why did you write it?

Here are some suggestions for writing tasks. Before you attempt any of them, we recommend that you do first what Pati and Charlene did: Gather some graffiti and read a few works about graffiti.

1. Interview several of your friends about graffiti writing. Ask them if they do it; ask them why they do it; ask them to speculate as to why other college students of your age write graffiti. Write a narrative of one of your interviews. Try to write it so that it illustrates what you believe about why your peers write graffiti. Or write a summary and critique of the findings from your interviews. First, report the findings: What did many (or most) of the interviewees say? Did they tend to say similar things, to agree with one another? Or was there a great deal of difference in what they said? Then, articulate your critical response to what you found. Address your essay to your peers; you may wish to imagine that the finished piece will be published in your school newspaper as a feature article.

2. Imagine a piece or pieces of "dangerous" graffiti, that is, graffiti that was written at great risk to the writer. Examples would be graffiti that is written on a high water tower or graffiti that is written on a highway overpass or on a high bridge. Why do you suppose the persons who wrote those pieces of dangerous graffiti were willing to take such risks? They might have been injured. Write an essay in which you speculate as to why there are graffiti risk-takers. You may want to structure your essay in a

[1]Herbert Kohl, photographs by James Hinton, "Names, Graffiti, and Culture," *Urban Review* (April 1969); reprinted in Thomas Kochman, ed., *Rappin' and Stylin' Out: Communication in Urban Black America* (Urbana: U of Illinois P, 1972) 109–133.

manner similar to the one Pati used. Or you may decide that there are several different groups of graffiti writers who are risk-takers, and that these individuals take risks for different reasons. Or you may decide to write a story about one such risk-taker, showing why he or she took these risks. Or you may be a former (or current) risk-taker, in which case you may wish to write an essay explaining why you took (or take) risks; or you may wish to vividly describe a situation in which you wrote such graffiti. You may wish to argue that such risk taking is foolish and dangerous, or you may wish to merely describe what happens and why as objectively as possible. If you choose to do the latter, reread Charlene's essay, as it may suggest a structure to you.

3.   Think about the various places in and around the campus where you frequently find graffiti, such as restrooms, desk tops, library carrels, and walls. Select one or several of these sources and gather graffiti. Be sure to copy them accurately, both in terms of wording and in terms of how the graffiti is presented—in a heart? in capital letters? with a drawing? Now begin to order and/or classify the graffiti you've gathered. For example, if you have gathered only desk-top graffiti, did you gather it from different places, such as from the English Building, the Computer Center, the History/ Sociology Building, the library, the study lounge in the Student Union? Do you notice any differences in the sorts of graffiti you found in different places? Any similarities? Write an essay, addressed to your peers, describing the graffiti you found. You have many options. You may choose to describe what you found and draw some tentative conclusions. You may choose to discuss either similarities or differences or both. You may choose to mention the similarities and/or differences you found, but to focus your efforts on speculation as to why these similarities or differences exist. Or you may have had some preconceptions about what you were going to find, and these may have been right or wrong: Write an essay comparing what you expected to find with what you actually found. Did your attitude towards graffiti change as a result of reading and/or the discussions you had in class or with friends? If so, write an essay explaining what your attitude used to be, and why, and what it is now, and why. What caused you to change it?

4   *Revising Predrafts*

Distinguishing Predrafts from Rough Drafts

As you have seen in Chapter 3, different writers have different manners of drafting. Some, like Charlene, do not begin drafting until they have done considerable inventing and planning and have formulated a concrete, well-realized thesis and intention for writing, along with a detailed design for conveying these to a reader. Other writers, like Pati, may draft in stages, producing an initial predraft in order to explore their intention and find a thesis.

   In general, creating an initial predraft can be a good strategy *unless* a writer mistakes a predraft for a rough draft. The distinction between a predraft and a rough draft is important because many inexperienced writers produce a predraft without knowing that they have done so. There are a number of possible explanations for this:

1.   Apprentice writers are taught to "think of their audience" when they write. Therefore, they perceive themselves as thinking of their audience even when they are not. Perhaps, also, they do not know exactly what "thinking of an audience" means, anyway.

2.   The way the writing process is often described precludes a "writing to oneself" stage. The process is presented in stages that involve narrowing

a topic, forming a thesis, writing a formal or informal outline, and so on.
3. "Writing to oneself" is frequently perceived as being a *type* of writing, "expressive writing," rather than a strategy a writer might use in producing a text that will, ultimately, be addressed to others.

The important point of this discussion is as follows: Creating an initial predraft is useful only if, by the time she has finished producing the predraft, the writer knows that she has written to and for herself. If a writer assumes that she has begun drafting with a clear notion of her thesis and intention, when in fact she is still searching for these, she may have considerable difficulty. Such an assumption may lead her to read her first draft with inappropriate expectations, and she may thus view it as being considerably more reader-based than it is. She may, perhaps, attempt to rewrite a predraft, a text which is largely an unstructured "dump" of ideas and impressions. We have found that it is almost always more productive and more efficient for an apprentice writer to glean ideas, possible theses, plans, and strategies from a predraft, then begin a *new* draft, rather than trying to rewrite the predraft.

But determining the nature of a first draft is not always easy. Every writing situation is unique, and different writers behave differently, both in general and with regard to the way they react to different writing tasks. There is no simple way for you to determine whether you are a writer who frequently produces predrafts or a writer who rarely does. However, being able to critically examine a draft you have produced so that you can revise predrafts and rough drafts in different ways is clearly to your advantage. This chapter, therefore, will discuss some very specific features that you can look for in a draft to help you determine whether it is a predraft. Strategies for revising a predraft will accompany the discussion of these features.

Before we formally present the features that can be indicative of a predraft, let us have an informal look at two drafts. In Chapter 3 you examined Pati's initial draft, a predraft, and Charlene's initial draft, a rough draft, so you already have a sense of how such drafts differ from one another.

Assume that each of the following drafts was written by a student reporter for the college newspaper. Draft 1 is about Walter James Burrell, who was selected by his class as Outstanding Senior. The editor felt that the paper should carry an informative article about Walter, since being chosen as Outstanding Senior was quite an honor. Draft 2 is about Evelyn Harshman, Dean of Women. In this case, the editor asked for a "human interest" profile about an administrator and suggested Dean Harshman as the subject because she was "popular with students."

As you read each draft, keep the editor's assignment in mind. How well does the draft seem to address that assignment?

Draft 1

1   Walter James Burrell, who was selected by his class as outstanding senior student, has made contributions to the welfare of other students at Bowling Green State University for nearly four years. He has never been too involved with his studies to help or to share his knowledge with others. It's important to be around persons who are sincere and who have common sense, and Walter sure has common sense and a real commitment to excellence.

2   Walter was born in Mentor, Ohio, home of many other famous Americans. His mother was also a native of Mentor, who attended the same school, Mentor High, that Walter did. Walter's mother, Martha, always has had a soft spot for Mentor and frequently has told people that she was glad her parents migrated there from Pennsylvania.

3   Walter's father, Henry, was born in Michigan, just outside of Detroit. 3 Henry's dad was an auto worker and he liked working "with his hands." His son, Walter's father, became a lawyer, but he never lost respect for the "working man" and he passed this respect to <u>his</u> son, Walter. When Henry was eight, his dad moved to Mentor, Ohio, and so Henry ended up going to school with Martha, his future wife. Martha and Henry became high school sweethearts and married after they both graduated from Bowling Green State University. Two years later Walter was born and two years after that Betty, Walter's sister, was born.

4   Walter attended elementary, junior high, and high school in Mentor. He graduated in the top 5% of his class and won a scholarship to BG, which he chose as his school because his parents went there. At BG Walter decided to be a premed student, majoring in biology. Walter, a second semester senior, has a 3.9 gpa. His professors all speak very well of him.

5   Walter just hasn't been a "book worm" while at BG. He has been a part of the Student Government Association since his sophomore year, and he has also been active in the Union Activities Organization, planning such events as ski weekends and trips to Florida over Spring Break. To quote Walter, "Studying is important, but I want to be a well-rounded individual. I'll be a better doctor that way, I'm sure."

All of Walter's friends speak well of him; they think he's fair, hard-working, sincere, and fun to be with. They particularly admire Walter's commitment to important social issues. Walter has frequently written letters to the BG News when he feels something is important. For example, he wrote several letters on the topic of student rights. He thinks students must learn responsibility and they won't be able to do that unless they are given the opportunity to make important decisions that effect them.   6

Walter plans to specialize eventually in colorectal surgery; he's particularly interested in the recently developed technique of pull through circular stapling anastomosis, which involves making the anastomosis on the perineum.   7

Walter, an all around wonderful student, will make a great physician. He will be a credit to his profession.   8

Draft 2

Evelyn Harshman wasn't always Dean of Women at Bowling Green. She had to work hard to graduate from college, much less become a Dean.   1

Born of a rural, Michigan family, Evelyn doesn't remember much of her childhood except that it was hard. "In the early days we didn't have indoor plumbing; and that meant an Outhouse. It wasn't so bad during the spring and summer, but during the winter I remember I used to dread having to go." She doesn't complain about the difficulty of her childhood, though. In fact, Evelyn has some good things to say about it: "You know, sometimes I think it was that time back in Michigan--on the farm--that has the most to do with, well, my success. Although I hate to call it 'success'; that embarrasses me." (Evelyn Harshman is modest.) "We kids had to do a lot, helping around. Fed the stock; helped weed the garden; helped Mom do around the house with the cooking and dishes and such. Mom and Dad expected us to keep up in school, too. I remember that much of the time I really resented having to do so much. But I was stubborn, so I always did everything--even if I didn't like it much."   2

When asked about how she chose philosophy as her major and why she left teaching and became an administrator, Evelyn can provide no clear answers. She speaks of the "times" during which she attended undergraduate school (World War II) and of her disillusionment with people: "I was young and I couldn't believe that what was happening was <u>really</u> happening." She also speaks of the study of philosophy as   3 something which, at the time, provided some needed answers for her. She pursued these "answers" and received her doctorate.

4   She decided to pursue an administrative career because "I'd been teaching for almost two decades and so I wondered if I couldn't somehow do more as an administrator." Evelyn won't comment as to whether she is "doing more"—she's still undecided. But she says her goal as dean is to "provide the college with leadership so that our students will receive the very best education they possibly can." Evelyn is hard at work on a plan which will increase the availability of funding for good students, and which will provide the university with additional facilities for helping all students improve their skills in such basics as writing, reading, and critical thinking.

5   Many students have personal relationships with Dean Harshman and speak of her "availability" and her "concern." One student (and this is a fairly representative "story") tells of the time she was experiencing personal problems: "I didn't even go to see the Dean; I was just there to get some forms that I needed in order to drop classes, and she noticed me. She told me to come into her office." This student goes on to relate a remarkable story, the gist of which is that the Dean not only talked her out of dropping her classes, she also on several occasions helped her so that she could make up missed work. According to this student, "I wouldn't be graduating this May if it weren't for Dean Harshman."

6   I know it seems "corny" to talk about hard work and dedication 6 and all of that. But something made Evelyn Harshman the way she is. Whatever it is, all of us here at BG have benefitted from it.

As you read and compared the drafts about Walter James Burrell and Evelyn Harshman, what did you notice about each? Did you wonder, for example, why so much of the essay about Walter was devoted to a discussion of his mother and dad, Martha and Henry, or whether Walter was chosen Outstanding Senior primarily because of his academic performance or because of his service to students? Did you ask yourself why Walter's interest in colorectal surgery, particularly the technique of "pull through circular stapling anastomosis," was important?

Recall what you know about *writer-based* prose and *reader-based* prose and answer these questions about Draft 1.

1. If you were asked to *write out* the thesis and intention of the draft, could you do it easily? Explain.

2.   Does the draft have a definite structure, or does it seem to ramble on from one thing to another? Do individual paragraphs seem to be focused, or do they seem to be catch-alls for lots of different things? Examine paragraph 4, for example.

3.   Obviously, the student reporter who wrote Draft 1 couldn't write *everything* about Walter James Burrell. Does she seem to have found a way to determine what information to present and what not to present, or does she seem to be *searching* for one?

4.   How *writer-based* is Draft 1? Are isolated portions of the draft writer-based, or does most of it seem to be written for the writer's benefit? Would you characterize the draft as a predraft or a rough draft? Explain.

5.   If a friend of yours had written Draft 1, how would you suggest she go about revising it? Should she work with the draft, adding, deleting, rearranging, and rewording, or should she read the draft, perhaps jotting down ideas, to determine what she should write about and to get ideas about how to do this?

Now reconsider Draft 2. Paragraph 2 of this draft about Evelyn Harshman contains information regarding her girlhood. As you read, did you wonder why this information was included, or did it seem relevant? The student reporter was asked to produce a "human interest" profile. Is the presentation of Dean Harshman personal or impersonal? Should the story about one student's personal problems, given in paragraph 5, have been included? Here are some additional questions to answer about Draft 2.

1.   What are the thesis and intention of the draft?

2.   How does the structure of the draft help reveal the thesis and intention? What is the purpose of paragraph 3: what is it about, and why is it included?

3.   What principle did the student reporter use in *selecting* information to be included in the draft?

4.   Is Draft 2 written for a *reader* or for the *writer*? If there are portions of the draft that are not crafted for the reader, are they isolated or do they occur throughout the text? Would you characterize Draft 2 as a predraft or a rough draft? Explain.

5.   If a friend of yours had written Draft 2, how would you suggest she go about revising it? What portions of the draft need attention?

Writing Task

Interview a person in your writing class. You should probably talk with that individual at least twice, for about 30 to 60 minutes each time. Prepare a list of questions before the first session. These questions should elicit information about your subject's background, professional academic pursuits, and special interests. Background information might include place of birth, current residence, information about immediate family, etc.; academic pursuits would include the subject's major and minor, courses currently enrolled in, career goals, etc.; while special interests would include such things as hobbies, talents, and social activities. Tape record or take notes on your subject's answers to your questions. Later, examine your notes and recordings to determine what additional information you would like to have. For example, if your subject is a swimmer, you might like to ask questions about past or current competitions, practice, skill development, and so forth. Write out a second list of questions, and bring this list with you to your second session. Again take notes or tape record the session.

Write the *first draft* of an informative essay about your subject. This will be read or duplicated and passed out to the rest of the class. *You* must decide on your thesis and your intention for writing. You will need to select a special aspect or quality about your subject so that you will know which information to include in your essay and which to leave out. Later in this chapter, you will be asked to *read, evaluate,* and *revise* your draft.

Reading for Revision

Whenever you examine a draft to determine what you should do next, you are revising. Revising a draft involves at least *two* steps: The writer (1) examines and evaluates what she has written, and (2) responds appropriately by rewriting, rethinking, replanning, or performing a combination of these activities.

Reading and evaluating your own draft is not easy. You must view your own writing as another person would. However, such reading and evaluation is essential if you are to move toward completion of a writing task. To help you become proficient in evaluating your own drafts, the following discussion illustrates characteristic features of writer-based prose. These features fall into three broad categories:

1. text structure
2. sentence form
3. word choice

Recognizing these features in your draft and assessing the *extent to which they are present* will help you determine whether you have produced a predraft or a rough draft and what revision strategies are likely to be most effective. This chapter will also suggest ways to use these features as guides for revising a predraft. Chapter 5 will cover techniques for dealing with incidences of writer-based prose in rough drafts, since even isolated episodes of writer-based prose can weaken the effect of a piece of writing.

Text Structure

You should carefully examine the structure of any draft you produce for the presence of three key features. If one or more of these features is present in your draft, this indicates that you may have written the draft—to some extent—to and for yourself.

Narrative Structure

The form of discourse that we are most familiar with is the narrative form. Think about the conversations you engage in. You say something, such as "What a lousy math exam." Then you get a response: "Really? Was it hard or didn't you study for it?" You do not usually produce long, uninterrupted pieces of spoken discourse. However, there are times when you do produce fairly long, uninterrupted, unified pieces of talk—when you tell a story: the story you told your friends last week about your weekend in Cleveland; the story you told your roommate yesterday about the trouble you had with the bursar about that bill that you had *already* paid; the story you told your mother to explain why the family car, which you borrowed, has a dent in it. Because you have had a lot of experience telling stories, you are already familiar with the narrative form, and you have some skill in ordering occurrences chronologically. All of us are quite comfortable with this form, so it is not at all unusual for us to use it to present information to others, whether or not it is the form that is best suited for the purpose.

Suppose you are enrolled in an introductory sociology class that you have been unable to attend for the last week. Your professor has asked you to "see her after class"; she wants an explanation for your absences. So you respond like this:

> Well, you see, I have this job in Lima and I work the 7 to 3 shift. And last Monday my boss told me that this guy Arnold couldn't work his 8 to 5 shift for a whole week. But my boss told me that Arnold *could* work the 7 to 3 shift and asked me to switch with Arnold because this is a real heavy production time and he needs every available person on the job. He also reminded me that he gave me the time I asked for, for vacation last summer, when I wanted to take a week off. And he told me what a valuable employee I was and how he really thought that I might soon be promoted and get a raise. And so I agreed to switch with Arnold for a week. And now I'm back to my regular schedule and so I can attend class regularly again. This job is really important because I am putting myself through school, and if I lose the job I'll have to drop out because my parents can't help me much. My dad has been laid off a lot lately. I'm sorry I didn't notify you, but the whole thing happened really suddenly.

If you examine your response to the sociology professor, you will notice that it is largely a narrative of what happened. You have responded to your professor by relating a series of incidents. But is this *narrative structure* the best and most useful structure for producing the intended effect? Remember that your intention was to convince your sociology professor that your absences were unavoidable and that you really couldn't notify her in advance. Therefore, which information was more important: that your boss gave you time off for vacation last summer, or that you need the job in order to finance your education? Did your sociology professor *really* need a fully detailed account of your conversation with your boss? Your response to all of this might be, "All right. Probably telling the prof a story wasn't the best way of handling the situation. But come on. This was sprung on me. I didn't have much time to prepare a response." Exactly. But writing is a different matter. When you write, you have time to think, to plan, to write, and to rewrite. Had your sociology professor required you to respond *in writing,* your first written draft might have been very much like the oral one, but your *final* draft should have been structured quite differently.

Narrative structure is a legitimate form that writers often use to good effect. But frequent and lengthy narrations that include lots of material that is seemingly unrelated to what you *think* your intention for writing is require attention. Examine your written drafts, therefore, for *narrative structure*. Do large portions of the draft seem to merely record events, whether or not the narrative format and the information presented are appropriate and/or useful to the reader? If they do, you may begin to suspect that your draft is *writer-based,* perhaps a *predraft*.

If you conclude that you have written a predraft, the narrative portions of your text are not just passages to be excised. Reread them carefully. They often include useful information that can help you do additional inventing and planning for your next draft. Pay particular attention to the portions of your text that come *immediately after* narrative passages. These may contain essential information, summations, or conclusions. If you reexamine the narration to your sociology professor, for example, you will see that important information is presented immediately after the story is finished: "This job is really important because I am putting myself through school. . . . If I lose the job I'll have to drop out. . . . My dad has been laid off." Narrative passages also can tell you what *you* consider crucial about a series of events. The fact that you have chosen to record *this* particular aspect at length and not *that* one can often be vital as you search to discover or clarify your intention for writing and/or to find a means of conveying that intention to your reader.

For an illustration of this, read the following short story and then the two drafts produced in response to this writing assignment:

> In a brief essay, discuss the changes in the relationship among the narrator, the audience, and the characters in "Birthday Party" by Katharine Brush.

A discussion of the drafts will follow.

Birthday Party
Katharine Brush

They were a couple in their late thirties, and they looked unmistakably married. They sat on the banquette opposite us in a little narrow restaurant, having dinner. The man had a round, self-satisfied face, with glasses on it; the woman was fadingly pretty, in a big hat. There was nothing conspicuous about them, nothing particularly noticeable, until the end of their meal, when it suddenly became obvious that this was an Occasion—in fact, the husband's birthday, and the wife had planned a little surprise for him.

It arrived, in the form of a small but glossy birthday cake, with one pink candle burning in the center. The headwaiter brought it in and placed it before the husband, and meanwhile the violin-and-piano orchestra played "Happy Birthday to You" and the wife beamed with shy pride over her little surprise, and such few people as there were in the restaurant tried to help out with a pattering of applause. It became clear at once that help was needed, because the husband was not pleased. Instead he was hotly embarrassed, and indignant at his wife for embarrassing him.

You looked at him and you saw this and you thought, "Oh, now, don't *be* like that!" But he was like that, and as soon as the little cake had been deposited on the table, and the orchestra had finished the birthday piece, and the general attention had shifted from the man and woman, I saw him say something to her under his breath—some punishing thing, quick and curt and unkind. I couldn't bear to look at the woman then, so I stared at my plate and waited for quite a long time. Not long enough, though. She was still crying when I finally glanced over there again. Crying quietly and heartbrokenly and hopelessly, all to herself, under the gay big brim of her best hat.

Draft A

1   In the story "Birthday Party," by Katharine Brush, there are a number of changes in the relationship among the narrator, the characters in the story, and the readers. These changes occur as both the reader and the narrator become involved with the wife and feel compassion towards her.

2   The story starts with a couple "in their late thirties" having dinner in a restaurant. The couple look "unmistakably married." They are ordinary looking, except that the woman is wearing a big hat. And soon it becomes evident that the couple is eating in the restaurant because it is an "Occasion," the husband's birthday. The wife has planned a surprise for him—a cake.

3   The head waiter brings a small, "glossy" cake to the table. And when the cake arrives, the violin-and-piano orchestra plays "Happy Birthday." There aren't very many people in the restaurant, but they "try to help out" by applauding. Unfortunately, the husband is embarrassed by all the fuss, and so he gets angry with his wife "for embarrassing him."

4   In fact, the husband is so angry that it is obvious to anyone who might be looking. The narrator notices this and gets upset—especially

when the husband says something to his wife, which is "punishing" and "quick and curt and unkind." The wife gets upset and begins to cry. She is still crying when the narrator, who had looked away out of embarrassment, looks back at the table: the wife is crying "heart-brokenly" under the "gay big brim of her best hat."

The relationship between the narrator, the readers, and the characters in the story changes because at first the narrator and the readers are not involved with the characters. They are only curious about them. However, as the story progresses, the narrator becomes more involved with the husband and wife and less objective about both of them. The narrator begins to dislike the husband, who is described as being needlessly unkind. After all, he gets angry with his wife for trying to do something nice for him. On the other hand, the wife becomes an object of sympathy, crying "all to herself, under the gay brim of her best hat." The readers "agree with" the narrator. They think that the hubsand is cruel and they sympathize with the wife: "You looked at him and you saw this and you thought, 'Oh, now, don't be like that.'" 5

In conclusion, the relationship among the reader, the narrator, and the characters in the story "Birthday Party" changes several times. Both the readers and the narrator become more emotionally involved with the characters in the story as the story progresses. The narrator also becomes less objective about the characters and so, therefore, does the reader. 6

Draft B

The relationship among the narrator, the characters, and the readers changes several times within the story, "Birthday Party." This change in relationship is shown by a number of elements within the story, the most obvious way of which is point of view. The point of view of the story starts out as third person, shifts to second person, and then shifts again to first person. 1

"Birthday Party" begins as an observation of a couple having dinner in a restaurant and it is portrayed in an objective manner: "They were a couple in their late thirties, and they looked unmistakably married." The use of third-person point of view plays down the narrator and focuses the reader upon the couple being observed. Initially both the reader and the narrator seem to be impartial observers, so it is easy to overlook the narrator's use of adjectives such as "self-satisfied" 2 when the husband is described. As the story goes on, the narrator continues to use third-person point of view to describe the couple and circumstances surrounding them. It is the husband's birthday and his wife has attempted to "surprise" him with a cake. But by this time, the narrator is no longer objective even though using third person. For example, when the cake is brought to the husband, the people in the restaurant try to "help out with a pattering of applause." And it is "clear" that help is needed because the husband is angry with his wife "for embarrassing him." Although the narrator is using a point of view (third person) that seems to make her objective, she has become "involved" with the characters, and wants the reader to view the scene as she does.

3   Immediately after she tells about the husband's anger, the narrator stops using the third-person "objective" point of view and switches to second person. The third, and last, paragraph begins with a bold attempt to make the reader's point of view just like the narrator's: "You looked at him and you saw this and you thought, 'Oh, now, don't be like that.'" The narrator doesn't say "People looked at him and saw this and thought. ..." The narrator also doesn't say, "I looked at him and saw this and thought. ..." Instead, she tries to bring herself and the reader together by means of the use of the second person point of view. The narrator and reader are disturbed by the husband's anger. They both don't approve. At this point in the story, the relationship between the narrator and the readers is interesting because if the readers have gone along with the narrator's attitude toward the characters in the story, and think the woman is being treated badly by her husband, who is a louse, the narrator and readers have merged into one.

4   Once she's made the obvious attempt to grab the reader in the first sentence of the last paragraph, the narrator shifts her point of view again. This time she shifts to first person: "I saw him say something to her under his breath—some punishing thing, quick and curt and unkind." This seems to show that the narrator is personally involved and distressed by events, so she expresses a very personal reaction. "I couldn't bear to look at the woman then. ..." You can tell she thinks the woman in the story is a victim and an object of pity, "crying quietly and heartbrokenly and hopelessly, all to herself, under the gay big brim of her best hat." The narrator empathizes with the woman; and the reader does too.

If you examine paragraphs 2, 3, and 4 of Draft A, you will notice that the *sole* purpose of these paragraphs is to paraphrase the paragraphs of the story, "Birthday Party." Paragraphs 2, 3, and 4 do little more than *narrate* the events of the story. Remember, the writing assignment was to comment on the relationship among the narrator, the reader, and the characters in the story. Do you think it is necessary or helpful for the *reader* to sit through a detailed account of every occurrence in the story, including the number of people in the restaurant? Also compare the amount of writing devoted to *narration* with the amount devoted to *discussion* or *analysis* of the relationship. It is clear, especially if you examine Draft B, that such a detailed narration of the plot is neither necessary nor useful for the reader.

Draft A is a predraft. It was written for the writer, who can put it to good use by gleaning information and ideas from it. This gleaning will certainly focus the writer's attention on the fifth paragraph, which seems to contain a great many potentially useful conclusions, and on paragraph 6, which contains a possible thesis: "The relationship among the reader, the narrator, and the characters in the story 'Birthday Party' changes several times. Both the readers and the narrator become more emotionally involved with the characters in the story as the story progresses. The narrator also becomes less objective about the characters and so, therefore, does the reader." The writer now has some useful ideas for a new draft: A concrete analysis of the changes in the relationship about which she is to write, and perhaps a means of structuring her text.

In contrast to Draft A, Draft B, while it contains some narrative, does not rely on narration for its structure or framework. If you reread the first paragraph of Draft B, you will see that the writer has chosen to discuss changes in relationships by examining changes in point of view. The writer claims that the point of view changes three times, from third person to second person to first person, and that these changes reflect changes in the relationships among the narrator, the reader, and the characters. Now examine paragraphs 2, 3, and 4 of Draft B. Paragraph 2 discusses the use of the third-person point of view, paragraph 3 discusses the use of the second-person point of view, and paragraph 4 discusses the use of the first-person point of view. There are, of course, many ways to discuss the changing relationships in "Birthday Party," but the writer of Draft B, although clumsy at times, has recognized that if a reader is to understand a discussion of the changing relationships within the story, the writer must choose a structure that focuses attention *on the nature of those relationships*, not on a narration of the incidents. Draft B is, therefore, a reader-based text. It is a rough draft.

Exercise

Examine the following draft, which was written in response to this writing assignment: "By now most of us have heard the argument that 'inside every overweight person is a thin person trying to get out.' Americans are definitely concerned with diet; they expend a great deal of energy, time, and money to become 'picture perfect' images of the human form. Do you think this preoccupation may, in fact, be an unhealthy one? Discuss or argue for a position favoring or rejecting this concern with diet."

Draft

It is true that Americans are overly concerned about diet. Every year they spend billions of dollars on diet products. New fitness fads come and go almost constantly. The most recent is jogging.

Last night I watched television for about two hours and what did I see? I saw three programs (two comedies; one "serious"), all of which contained men and women in various states of undress. One of the comedies was typical of most of the comedies on television (including the other comedy I saw last night). One of the characters on the comedy is a "dumb blond." The plot of the show was about how she was dating a married man—only she didn't know it. She gets up in the morning to make breakfast and while she's making breakfast she tells her friend how wonderful this man she's dating is. Of course she's wearing babydoll pajamas during the entire scene. Later she gets ready for a date with the man, and of course, she's wearing a dress that's tight and also low-cut in front, low-cut enough for some cleavage to show.

The "serious" show I watched wasn't any better. It was a detective drama, but of course one of the female "sidekicks" of the detective was prancing around in a bikini. She didn't have very many lines ("There weren't any calls while you were out"), so I can only assume she was there in order to stand around in a skimpy bikini. She certainly wasn't necessary in the plot of the show, which is about how the hero tries to locate the little boy of a former girlfriend, who had been kidnapped by the former girlfriend's ex-husband a while back. The hero of the show also must have not been chosen strictly for his acting ability (or lack of it) because *he* appeared in his underwear, when his old girlfriend first shows up. Then later when he and his old flame are having a little ''romantic interlude'' they go swimming, so he's in a tiny bathing suit, and then much of the time he's running around in shorts (with no shirt).

The shows I watched were frequently interrupted by commercials. One commercial told me to drink Diet Blah and in it was a woman in a bikini, another woman in a bikini, another woman in short shorts, and a man in a bathing suit. Even commercials that didn't have anything to do with dieting had skinny, undressed people in them. One car commercial had a young man in short, tight shorts and no shirt and a young woman in short, tight shorts and *barely* a shirt riding around in a car; they were *experiencing* the car. Then in another commercial this woman comes up out of the water in a bathing suit. She was talking about the wet look and she was wet all right. Finally, there was a commercial that showed this woman lying by a pool and a man in a teeny weeny bikini comes up out of the pool and stands by her.

After I was done watching television I went back up to my room and there was my roommate exercising to a record. She was dancing all around and huffing and puffing. And she said she'd only eaten six hundred calories so far that day. I asked her what she had for supper and she said she had a dish of ice cream and a glass of pop. I asked her why she didn't have any meat and she said that she'd ''already had too many calories.'' I got disgusted and went down to the hall lounge, but there were some people there talking about dieting.

I think it's important for people to be concerned about other things besides how they look. It may sound like a cliché, but it is true that you ''can't judge a book by its cover.'' It's what's inside that counts!''

Now that you have read the draft about ''diet,'' answer the following questions.

1. How is the draft structured? What seems to give it its shape? What seems to give each paragraph its shape or structure?

2. Which narrative elements, if any, within the draft seem justified? Which do not?

3. To what extent does the structure of the draft seem related to its purpose? To the audience to whom it is addressed?

4. Is this draft more writer-based or more reader-based? Explain your answer, making specific references to the draft. If you consider this to be a writer-based draft, is it a predraft? Why or why not? Justify your answer.

5. If you had produced this draft in response to the assignment, how would you begin to revise it? What portions seem significant to you? Explain. Does the draft contain any possible theses? What are they? What does the draft suggest might be an intention for writing?

Shifting Focus

As you have seen, one of the clues a writer might look for in order to determine how writer-based her draft is concerns its structure: a narrative structure may indicate a writer-based draft. Another indication of a writer-based draft is a structure that seems to shift focus or change topic often, especially if there is no apparent reason for such shifts. Writer-based prose is produced so that the writer can think about what she wants to say and, perhaps, how she wants to say it. Sometimes a writer's thinking process may appear quite logical. Other times it may appear totally disorganized: The writer has freely associated with regard to her topic; facts, attitudes, emotions, and assumptions have raced through her mind, in no particular order.

Few writers, even those with limited experience, would mistake a "stream of consciousness" draft such as the following for anything *but* a predraft: "Dogs. Man's best friend—woman's worst enemy?—slobbery, messy. Hair everywhere all over the furniture. Have to walk him. Loyal. Kind to children. Protection. Expensive. Eat eat eat. Noisy. Bark bark bark." But an inexperienced writer can quite easily overlook shifts in focus if a piece of writing *seems* unified.

Let us reexamine the draft that was written about Walter James Burrell.

1   Walter James Burrell, who was selected by his class as outstanding senior student, has made contributions to the welfare of other students at Bowling Green State University for nearly four years. He has never been too involved with his studies to help or to share his knowledge with others. It's important to be around persons who are sincere and who have common sense, and Walter sure has common sense and a real commitment to excellence.

Walter was born in Mentor, Ohio, home of many other famous Americans. His mother was also a native of Mentor, who attended the same school, Mentor High, that Walter did. Walter's mother, Martha, always has had a soft spot for Mentor and frequently has told people that she was glad her parents migrated there from Pennsylvania.

Walter's father, Henry, was born in Michigan, just outside of Detroit. Henry's dad was an auto worker and he liked working "with his hands." His son, Walter's father, became a lawyer, but he never lost respect for the "working man" and he passed this respect to *his* son, Walter. When Henry was eight, his dad moved to Mentor, Ohio, and so Henry ended up going to school with Martha, his future wife. Martha and Henry became high school sweethearts and married after they both graduated from Bowling Green State University. Two years later Walter was born and two years after that Betty, Walter's sister, was born.

Walter attended elementary, junior high, and high school in Mentor. He graduated in the top 5% of his class and won a scholarship to BG, which he chose as his school because his parents went there. At BG Walter decided to be a premed student, majoring in biology. Walter, a second semester senior, has a 3.9 gpa. His professors all speak very well of him.

Walter just hasn't been a "book worm" while at BG. He has been a part of the Student Government Association since his sophomore year, and he has also been active in the Union Activities Organization, planning such events as ski weekends and trips to Florida over Spring Break. To quote Walter, "Studying is important, but I want to be a well-rounded individual. I'll be a better doctor that way, I'm sure."

All of Walter's friends speak well of him; they think he's fair, hardworking, sincere, and fun to be with. They particularly admire Walter's commitment to important social issues. Walter has frequently written letters to the BG News when he feels something is important. For example, he wrote several letters on the topic of student rights. He thinks students must learn responsibility and they won't be able to do that unless they are given the opportunity to make important decisions that effect them.

Walter plans to specialize eventually in colorectal surgery; he's particularly interested in the recently developed technique of pull through circular stapling anastomosis, which involves making the anastomosis on the perineum.

8   Walter, an all around wonderful student, will make a great physician.
        He will be a credit to his profession.

This essay seems to have a purpose, to talk about how wonderful Walter James Burrell is. It also seems to be unified, since it is *only* about the good qualities of Walter James Burrell. However, a careful examination will show that the focus of this draft shifts frequently, and that it is, in fact, a predraft.

The best way to see this frequent shifting of focus is to try to determine what each paragraph is about. The purpose of many, and perhaps most, paragraphs can be paraphrased briefly, often in less than a sentence. Paraphrasing the purpose of each paragraph is a technique you might like to use until you can *easily* detect shifts in focus merely by reading a draft. Let us examine each paragraph of the Walter draft.

☐ *Paragraph 1:* The purpose of paragraph 1 is to inform the reader of the purpose of the essay: to show that Walter James Burrell, who was selected by his class as outstanding senior student, has made "contributions to the welfare of other students" at BGSU for "nearly four years."

☐ *Paragraph 2:* The purpose of paragraph 2 is not clear. It begins with the fact that Walter was born in Mentor, Ohio, but the rest of the paragraph seems to be about Walter's mother.

☐ *Paragraph 3:* The purpose of paragraph 3 seems to be to tell the reader about Walter's father.

☐ *Paragraph 4:* Paragraph 4 *seems* to be about the fact that Walter is a good student, but this paragraph also includes his college major, his career aspirations (premed), and the reason he chose to attend Bowling Green State University.

☐ *Paragraph 5:* The purpose of paragraph 5 is to show that Walter is a well-rounded person; he is involved in social activities.

☐ *Paragraph 6:* The purpose of paragraph 6 is not clear. Is the paragraph about the fact that Walter is well liked ("All of Walter's friends speak well of him"), or that he is committed to social issues, or that he believes in "student rights" (which is not necessarily the same as being committed to social issues)?

☐ *Paragraph 7:* The purpose of paragraph 7 is to explain Walter's career aspirations.

☐ *Paragraph 8:* Paragraph 8 *seems* to be a concluding paragraph, but it suggests that the essay was about why Walter "will make a great physician."

This is not in accord with what the essay was supposed to be about, as expressed in paragraph 1: that Walter was an outstanding student who has made contributions to the welfare of other students.

As these brief paragraph descriptions suggest, the structure of this essay frequently shifts its focus, obscuring both thesis and intention. The essay focuses on Walter's mother (paragraph 2), Walter's father (paragraph 3), how Walter's father met and subsequently married Walter's mother (paragraph 3), what schools Walter attended (paragraph 4), Walter's scholastic achievements (paragraph 4), Walter's social activities (paragraph 5), what Walter's friends think of him (paragraph 6), how Walter feels about student rights (paragraph 6), Walter's career aspirations (paragraph 7).

These shifts in focus should tell the writer that she has not yet decided what, exactly, she wants to say about Walter. She knows she wishes to praise Walter, who is worthy of praise, and she has a lot of information about him: biographical information, information about his scholastic achievements, information about his nonacademic involvements, information regarding students' and professors' attitudes toward him. But she has not as yet determined her intention in writing. Does she want to write an essay explaining how important Walter's contributions have been? Does she wish to explain how Walter's roots have made him a good student? Does she want to argue that students should follow Walter's example and take a more active role in self-government?

This draft is a predraft that contains lots of useful information and ideas. From it the writer can recover a number of possible narrower topics, any of which might provide sufficient focus for an essay. For example, she could write about Walter's service to his fellow students *or* about Walter's outstanding performance in his classes. The writer can also uncover several potential intentions for writing that could stimulate further inventing and plannning. For example, she could *argue* that students should follow Walter's example and take a more active role in self-government.

Exercise

Sometimes what appear to be shifts in focus are, in fact, not shifts in focus. For example, if the author of the "Walter" draft had chosen to argue that Walter became a students' rights activist because of his father's working-class background, selected information about Walter's father would not only be relevant, it would be necessary. On the other hand, it is not likely that detailed information regarding Walter's career aspirations would be relevant.

Reread the essay written about Evelyn Harshman (page 111).

1.   Paraphrase the purpose of each paragraph. Examine the paraphrases on page 126 if you are not certain how to do this.

2.   Describe what you think are the thesis and intention of the essay.

3.   The essay is about Evelyn Harshman, the Dean of Women, who is an adult. Do you think that the discussion in paragraph 2 of Evelyn's rural Michigan childhood is a shift in focus? Explain your answer.

"Copied" Structure

Suppose you bought a new stereo, and a friend who had not seen it asked you to describe it. Here is what you might say:

> Well, it's got two speakers and they're pretty small—each one is less than a foot high—even though they're powerful enough to go with a 30-watt amplifier. Uh, they're wood. The amp is a 30-watt amp and it's got an AM-FM tuner, which I didn't want but I don't think you can get an amplifier without a tuner very easily. Then there's the turntable; it's a Phillips [German company]. It's got an automatic changer, even though I know that's not so good, but I'm too lazy to get up every time and change the record. The turntable came with a $30 stylus and the guy at the store said if I want to upgrade the quality of the sound a lot, with the least expenditure, I should buy a more expensive stylus; so that's what I'm going to do next.

Notice that the structure of this description reflects, and even copies, the structure of the information about the stereo as you perceived it. In other words, in order to tell your friend about your stereo, you pictured it in your mind and simply described each part of your mental picture: speakers, receiver/amplifier, turntable. This is one of the simplest ways to structure speech or writing: to use the structure of the information *as* the structure of the speech or writing.

Here is another example. Suppose you are asked to write a *summary* of what you read earlier in this chapter concerning the way you should examine the structure of a draft to determine whether it is a predraft or a rough draft. Here is what you first write:

> This material starts out with an explanation of the fact that revision consists of at least two steps: The writer examines what she wrote and then she responds accordingly. Then it goes on to explain that the first step is really important because a person can't make any changes in a piece of writing, for example, unless she knows what to change. After explaining the two steps of revision and why the second one is important, the chapter goes on to talk about what to look for with regard to the structure of a piece of writing. The first kind of text structure that a person should look for is a narrative structure. Then another kind of text structure, a structure that shifts focus, is covered. Then ...

If you examine the structure of this summary, you will notice that it duplicates or copies the structure of the corresponding parts of the chapter. That is, the summary used, or copied, the structure of the parts of the chapter for *its* structure.

Using the structure of information as a means of structuring a text can be quite helpful for a writer. She has to do fewer things at the same time. Since she is using an already existing structure, she can focus her attention on *what* she wants to say and does not have to be bothered, as yet, about how she is going to organize her material.

The fact that the structure of a text mimics or copies the structure of the information being discussed does not always indicate that the text is writer-based, perhaps a predraft. Whether or not such a structure is appropriate *depends on the writer's intention*. But if the structure of a draft that you have written seems to copy the structure of the information being presented or to mimic the structure of what is being described, you should examine the draft carefully, putting yourself in the reader's place. Will this draft effectively communicate your thesis and intention? If, for example, a book you wish to evaluate has *two* major strengths, but your initial draft of your review has *six* parts, each of which describes one of the book's *six* chapters, you should be alerted. Will this structure help the reader *easily* determine that the book has two major strengths, or will it make it difficult for the reader to determine this?

Exercise

Examine each of the following writing situations and comment on whether
or not the structure of the piece of writing described is appropriate. Explain
your decision in each instance.

1.   *Writing Situation:* Mr. Bill, a movie critic, has written a review of *Kabosh,*
a film with a plot so complicated that it is impossible to understand what
is happening. He has addressed his review to the readers of the *Pickle
Tribune.* His purpose for writing the review was to tell his readers *not* to
see *Kabosh,* although he does wish to point out some merits, notably the
acting and the cinematography.

Mr. Bill's review starts like this: "*Kabosh* begins with a scene in the
woods. Two adults (it's impossible to tell whether they're men or women)
are herding some horses and some wolves into a clearing. Then the scene
changes to Frankfurt, Germany, where we meet Mr. Meems, who appears
to be . . ." The review continues to give a blow-by-blow description of the
plot. At the very end of the review, Mr. Bill comments that the film was
interesting—the acting was good, and the cinematography was wonderful.
But he does not recommend the film because the plot was hard to follow.

2.   *Writing Situation:* Professor Noteworthy has been assigned to write a
review of the writing text *Writing for Clarity* for *English Professionals,* a
journal to which high school and college English teachers subscribe. Professor
Noteworthy considers *Writing for Clarity* to be a brilliant text, especially
because it is organized so well: Students of writing can easily find things
in the text.

Professor Noteworthy begins his review by asserting that *Writing for
Clarity* is a textbook milestone. In his first, introductory paragraph he explains
that the text will be praised by both students and teachers because it is
organized so well. Students will find every explanation about any aspect
of writing that they seek with ease because the book is divided into parts,
which are—in turn—divided into sections. Following this first paragraph,
Professor Noteworthy's review consists of 14 additional paragraphs, each
of which discusses one of the text's 14 chapters.

3.   *Writing Situation:* Borthea Bornheld is a physical therapist who has
been working with Clyde Zeenon for several months. Dr. Expensive, Clyde's
physician, has requested a written report on Clyde's progress, including a
recommendation as to whether or not Clyde is ready for increased activity.

Borthea's report begins with a description of what she did with Clyde
four months ago, when he first was assigned to her. Her report continues

with a detailed description of everything she has done up to and including the session with Clyde immediately before Dr. Expensive requested a report. Then the report describes Clyde's progress *in detail,* again from four months ago until the most recent session. Finally, the report ends with Borthea's recommendation.

Exercise

Here again is the summary of the earlier parts of the chapter, discussed above.

> This material starts out with an explanation of the fact that revision consists of at least two steps: The writer examines what she wrote and then she responds accordingly. Then it goes on to explain that the first step is really important because a person can't make any changes in a piece of writing, for example, unless she knows what to change. After explaining the two steps of revision and why the second one is important, the chapter goes on to talk about what to look for with regard to the structure of a piece of writing. The first kind of text structure that a person should look for is a narrative structure. Then another kind of text structure, a structure that shifts focus is covered. Then . . .

Consider how this information about text structure might best be presented to and structured for a reader who is unfamiliar with it. Your intention in writing is to present the information as concisely as you can to someone who will find it useful. Then *rewrite* the summary. You might, for example, consider your roommate as a possible audience. How would she or he most easily acquire the information well enough to apply it to her or his own writing?

Sentence Form

When you examine a draft, you should first give its *structure* careful attention in order to determine whether the draft reveals its thesis and intention or whether it was written to discover these. If you detect a narrative structure or framework, shifts in focus, and/or copied structure, you may have written the draft primarily to and for yourself and need to revise accordingly.

Writer-based prose may have other characteristic features as well. Sometimes you may not be certain what the structure of your draft has told you about it, or you may need more evidence to bolster a tentative conclusion. The nature of the sentences and words in a draft can provide you with additional information regarding the draft and the ways in which it should be revised. The following discussion should familiarize you with the kinds of sentences that are indicative of writer-based prose.

The structure of sentences in writer-based prose often reflects the writer's thinking or discovery process. Quite often, upon examination, these sentences appear more useful for the writer than for the reader. Examine the underlined sentences in this first paragraph from an initial draft of an essay about England.

England

[1]England is one of the most beautiful countries in the world. [2]The castles and palaces are world-famous and filled with history. [3]Because of moderate weather, a visit would be enjoyable most any time of the year. [4]Meeting all sorts of people young and old, it would be exciting and instructive. [5]Especially getting to know someone who was born there and lived there all his life, this would be a rare treat.

Sentences 4 and 5 appear to have been constructed to give the writer more space to figure out what she wanted to say.

SENTENCE 4:

What do I want this sentence to be about?
Meeting different kinds of people, young and old

What do I want to say about this?
It would be exciting and instructive

SENTENCE 5:

What do I want this sentence to be about?
Getting to know someone who was born in England and lived there all his life

What do I want to say about this?
It would be a rare treat

Such sentences may be useful to the writer, who is, after all, trying to shape a text *and* put her thoughts into language simultaneously. But they tax the reader unnecessarily, often making it difficult for him to determine who or what the sentence is about.

Another sort of sentence that seems to be written for the writer rather than the reader is one in which the "real" subject of the sentence is in the writer's *mind,* not in the sentence. Sometimes such sentences are extremely awkward, even ungrammatical; their structure obscures their meaning. For example, what is this sentence about?

> Vacationing as far off as California and Florida have some wonderful water skiing resorts.

Is it about "vacationing [in] . . . far-off California and Florida"? Or is it about California and Florida and the fact that they have superior water skiing facilities? It is difficult for a reader to determine what is most important about this sentence.

Sentences with hidden subjects are not always awkward or ungrammatical, however. Reexamine sentence 3 from the paragraph about England (page 132):

> Because of moderate weather, a visit would be enjoyable most any time of the year.

The grammatical subject of this sentence is, of course, "visit." However, is this sentence about a *visit,* or is it about England's *moderate weather,* or is it about the *writer,* who would like to visit England?

In spite of what you may think, it is not unusual for a writer not to know what she wants a sentence to be about as she writes it. Perhaps she is in the process of evolving a highly complex concept and is not yet fully able to articulate the details. Perhaps she is writing to *discover* what she wishes to write about. In such instances, many sentences are likely to be affected.

To illustrate this, let us again examine the paragraph about England:

[1]England is one of the most beautiful countries in the world. [2]The castles and palaces are world-famous and filled with history. [3]Because of moderate weather, a visit would be enjoyable most any time of the year. [4]Meeting all sorts of people young and old, it would be exciting and instructive. [5]Especially getting to know someone who was born there and lived there all his life, this would be a rare treat.

Sentences 4 and 5 are confusing because the first parts of both sentences seem to modify the writer, who is not mentioned in either sentence. It is the writer who would be *"meeting all sorts of people"* and *"getting to know someone who was born there."* In the context of the paragraph, sentence 3 is also troublesome; it begins with a reference to *weather,* but its grammatical subject is *visit.* It is likely that these sentences are structured the way they are because the writer was not certain about what she wanted to say as she wrote them. Nevertheless, they may prove useful to her. Assuming that she knows that she has begun a *predraft,* these sentences indicate some of the choices she will have to make in the course of revising. For example, she must decide whether she wishes to focus her essay on *England* and its sights and tourist attractions or on *what she would do during a visit to England*—e.g., meet people. This implies that the writer may choose to write in first person ("If I ever get a chance to visit England, I most certainly . . .") or in third person ("England can provide the traveler with extraordinary attractions. Its castles and estates are . . .").

Since sentence structure often provides useful information about the nature of a draft and how to revise it, it is important that you be able to recognize some of the most common structures that may indicate writer-based, self-addressed sentences. Here is a list of these structures.

1. Sentences that have "it" or "there" as their grammatical subjects, with the "real" subject moved into a modifier of the sentence.

    EXAMPLES:

        REAL SUBJECT   GRAMMATICAL SUBJECT
    Talking about *good citizenship, it* should be of concern to all Americans.

        REAL SUBJECT   GRAMMATICAL SUBJECT
    With respect to *writing, there* is a need in the business sector for persons who can do it well.

2. Sentences that are preceded by modifiers that do not modify anything in the sentence.

    EXAMPLES:

    Lying on the beach, the sun felt hot. (What does "lying on the beach" modify?)

Examining the data, errors were found in numerous places. (What does "examining the data" modify?)

Monitoring the output, there are usually a lot of unexplained signals. (What does "monitoring the output" modify?)

In reading *The Philosophy of Symbolic Forms,* it can be asserted that Cassirer was greatly influenced by Kant. (What does "in reading *The Philosophy of Symbolic Forms*" modify?)

3.   Sentences that seem to have two grammatical subjects vying for the same role.

   EXAMPLES:
   Swimming in *Lake Erie* is ecologically improved since efforts have been made to control pollution.

   Traveling by train to *Scotland* can be reached in just a few hours.

4.   Sentences that have no grammatical subject.

   EXAMPLES:
   By adjusting to compensate for our different backgrounds has made working together much more pleasant.

   If the schedules aren't adjusted so that single parents are able to attend orientation will render the whole process useless.

   Also, if people have to pay for recreation facilities, it would encourage them to use them. *Thus enabling them to exercise and improve their health.*

5.   Sentences that seem to shift focus.

   EXAMPLES:
   The work that Marcia did, I feel she must have a college education or the equivalent.

But there are alternatives to provide a child with alternate role models, such as aunts, uncles, grandparents, and one really successful organization is the YMCA (or the YWCA).

In addition to these kinds of sentence problems, try to watch for sentences in which the grammatical subject does not tell what the sentence is about. You should probably examine your sentences to determine whether it would be difficult for a reader to figure out what they are about. Here are some examples:

In addition to all the other factors that show how school can have an effect on a person, by meeting new and different kinds of individuals, and by appreciating what you have already, is the priceless worth of the education that was gotten during the time of experience.

Although others who are older or younger than high school age can understand and perhaps appreciate it through the situations the characters get in and out of as the kids find out about themselves and if they're popular or square pegs, most of all young, high school viewers is who the show *Square Pegs* is for.

Exercise

Read the following draft. Then:

1. Examine the structure of the draft. On the basis of your examination, do you consider this a rough draft or a predraft? If it is a rough draft, how much revision is still required? Explain and justify your answer.
2. Examine the sentences within the draft. Underline any that you consider to be written in a form that is more helpful to the *writer* than the *reader.* Explain why you have selected each underlined sentence.
3. Explain what you would do to begin to revise this draft. What do the sentences you underlined suggest?

Recruiting, International Style

To help counteract, possibly even reverse, the long-predicted drop in enrollments which has already begun to affect us and which will continue to affect us until the mid-1990s, a two-year plan has been developed to increase the enrollment of international students at Sutpen State University. International students provide a university with much needed diversity and are often among the most academically talented. Recruitment is a key ingredient in attracting numbers and quality, however.

Examining recent enrollment trends, it is expected that as much as a 20% decrease in enrollment can be expected over the next decade. University administrators have been expressing concern over the decline for some time and have requested members of the university community to devise "creative" solutions to the problem. "Regarding the traditional student, we just can't expect to see as many in the near future. And this, of course, will cause our state subsidies to drop," says Dr. Marvin Frye, Vice President for Budget and Planning.

All members of the university community, students, faculty, staff, and administrators agree that quality students are "good" for everybody. Good students provide inspiration for one another and for faculty. Good students have a long-range effect on the quality of an institution. Dr. Arlin Wade, Director of Sutpen State University's International Program, asserts that efforts are made to look for international students who are—at the very least—as well qualified as their American counterparts. Both undergraduate and graduate students are screened, both in terms of their knowledge of their subject matter and in terms of their facility with the English language. Facility with and fluency in English are very important and so international students must take the TOEFL test as well as writing a proficiency test administered by the English Department. The English Department provides remedial instruction in language for those who need it.

By making a carefully planned, well-executed effort toward recruiting international students has paid off in recent years. The current "two-year" plan is in response to the recent success in recruiting, which is expected to provide Sutpen State University with an even wider field of applicants from which to choose. Future efforts at recruitment will be formulated on the basis of the success of the current program, which is to begin this fall.

Word Choice

Examining which words you selected and how you used them may also help you to determine the nature of what you have written and how to revise it. Two types of word use are often indicative of writer-based prose:

(1) pronouns without clear, specific referents, and (2) loaded expressions or "code words."[1]

Pronouns Without Clear Referents

The main principle that governs pronoun use is a crucial one: Pronouns are *substitute* words; they *stand for* something. It is essential, therefore, that the meaning of the word or words for which a pronoun stands be recoverable. If it is not, a person may not receive the message that the speaker or writer intended him to receive. For an illustration of this principle, read the following passage.

> Live musical performances are quite exciting. In addition to the music itself, members of the audience can savor visual aspects of the performance: What do the performers look like; how do they behave as they play their instruments? The most exciting part of a live performance, however, is the *excitement* generated by both the audience and the musicians as they experience the performance together. No matter how technically perfect a recording of a concert might be, no matter how faithfully the quality of the sound has been reproduced, the experience of listening to a recording is a limited one. If you have ever experienced *this* you know that *it* is true.

Notice the italicized pronouns, *this* and *it,* in the passage. The person who wrote the passage may have known to what they referred. But what about the reader? Does *this* refer to "a live performance," to "a recorded performance," to "both live and recorded performances," or what? The problem of *it* is even more complex. Does *it* refer to the same thing as *this*? Or does *it* refer to something different? For example, does *this* refer to "both live and recorded performances," whereas *it* refers to "my point about the difference between live and recorded performances, and that live performances are superior"?

Of course, the reader may not be aware of these problems at all. He may simply interpret *this* and *it* as he sees fit. In doing so, he has assumed that the writer meant something, and this may be something that the writer did not mean. It could be argued that in this passage the problems

---

[1] "Code word" is a term used by Linda Flower, to whom we are greatly indebted in this chapter.

caused by the unclear pronouns are not too serious, since many readers could probably guess at interpretations that are similar to what the writer had in mind. Regardless of the validity of that argument, it is dangerous to assume that readers will be able to guess a writer's intentions accurately *always* or *most of the time*. Examine this passage:

> The role of a cooperating teacher is an exacting one. A cooperating teacher must be certain to provide a teaching intern with ample opportunity to complete assignments. More vital, however, is the responsibility of the cooperating teacher to monitor the intern so that weaknesses can be located and thus remediated. To that end, we request that each cooperating teacher carefully complete a DAILY assessment sheet, to be forwarded to the Curriculum Coordinator. In addition, any recommendations should be written out on the appropriate form and also forwarded to the Curriculum Coordinator. All of *these* should be submitted at the end of each week (on Fridays).

Notice the italicized pronoun, *these:* To what does it refer? Does it refer to both the recommendations and the daily assessment sheets, which must be completed daily but are to be submitted weekly, or does it refer to the recommendations only? If the individual who wrote this memorandum has told the Curriculum Coordinator to expect all forms to be submitted once a week, each Friday, it will cause considerable confusion if some individuals submit assessment sheets daily and others do not. In addition, if the author of the memorandum requested weekly submissions, because it is unreasonable to expect everyone to submit assessment sheets every day, some individuals who read the memorandum incorrectly and assume that they must turn in assessment sheets every day may become angry. On the other hand, if the writer of the memorandum *does* wish to receive the assessment forms every day, he is likely to become angry with those cooperating teachers who read the memorandum as requesting weekly submissions of these forms! In either instance, whatever the writer intended, the use of *these* is bound to cause confusion, and ultimately problems. Pronouns must always have *clear referents*.

   Although vague, unclear pronouns can be troublesome for a reader, they often serve a useful function for the *writer*. Think of a writer who is writing a text to explore a topic and/or ideas. Since many of the sentences in the draft are likely to be exploratory, because the topic and/or concepts are not yet clear in her mind, pronouns that do not refer to a *specific* antecedent or referent may abound. Notice the pronouns in this first paragraph of an exploratory draft about genetic engineering:

> Human beings are a curious race: we have always been interested in finding out about <u>things;</u> we've always been interested in making new discoveries. Right now, scientists are in their laboratories performing experiments which are changing the structures of bacteria. Recently, a researcher has developed a "new" oil-eating bacteria. <u>These individuals</u> have been modifying the structures of life. As <u>this</u> is discovered it causes dilemmas: one discovery leads to another; <u>this</u> result leads to <u>that</u> one; <u>they're</u> all connected with <u>one another</u>. New techniques and discoveries create good <u>things,</u> but also potentially bad <u>ones.</u> Because of <u>this,</u> the whole human race may be affected. Therefore, it's not too soon to start thinking about the implications of <u>this</u> research. We need to be prepared to make decisions regarding <u>this</u> change and <u>that</u> one. We need to determine how many persons should be involved in making <u>these</u> decisions (everyone? a few individuals?) and whether <u>they</u> should be "experts" or common people or elected officials or what.

The writer of this passage is developing a number of issues and topics, as well as several approaches to these issues and topics. Requiring the writer to clarify all her pronouns at this time would be counterproductive and premature for several reasons:

1.   The writer is exploring her topic and her approach to it. Her exploration would be severely restricted, and perhaps even halted, if she were preoccupied with clarifying what each pronoun stands for at this stage.
2.   Much of what the writer is thinking about is vague and unfocused. She probably *can't* clearly articulate what all her pronouns mean because she is writing *in order* to clarify her ideas and, thus, be able to clearly articulate them.
3.   Once the writer has determined her thesis and intention, many of these problems will disappear in a later draft.

To summarize, writers frequently use pronouns without clear referents when they are drafting for themselves. An easy way to assess the nature of a draft, therefore, is to examine pronouns. Circle each pronoun and draw an arrow from it to the word or group of words for which it stands.

If many arrows point to nothing, you may well have produced a predraft. See if you can list the words or ideas to which these pronouns *might* refer. Such a list may help you clarify your thesis and intention as you prepare to write your next draft.

Exercise

1. Select four pronouns with unclear referents from the genetic engineering paragraph. Write out two possible referents for each pronoun. For example, "*This* can stand for all scientific inquiry in general, or it can stand for the type of experimentation that has to do with genetic manipulation."
2. Explain what the excessive number of unclear pronouns tells you about the genetic engineering paragraph. Try to isolate some of the different issues and approaches to these issues being explored in the paragraph.
3. Assuming that this paragraph is representative of the rest of the draft, what *specific* revision strategies would you suggest to the writer?

Code Words

Code words are another common feature of writer-based prose. Using them allows writers considerable latitude in expressing their thoughts. A code word or expression is a word or word group that holds, for the writer, a great deal of information, facts, experience, or ideas that are not necessarily evident to the reader. A writer may or may not be consciously aware of the information, facts, experiences, or ideas a code word expresses.

Suppose that the following excerpt is from a piece of writing Fred produced in response to a writing assignment requiring him to describe one or two of the major effects college has had on his life:

> Before I came to college I hadn't been outside of my home town of Bryan much. Bryan is a small farming community with about one thousand residents. So I was pretty <u>naive</u>. When I got to college. . . .

The word "naive" is rather vague. Does it refer to Fred's experience with members of the opposite sex? Does it refer to his inability to handle his own finances? Does it refer to his attitudes toward members of ethnic or

cultural groups with whom he has had no experience? Or what? If Fred
hands in the draft containing this excerpt, his teacher will probably respond
with something like, "What do you mean by 'naive'?" Assuming that *Fred*
knows what he meant by "naive," it will probably be relatively simple for
him to revise his draft, supplying his meaning.

Now examine the use of the word "style" in these excerpts from Chris's
draft of an essay about writing behavior:

1   Whenever I write a paper for class, I usually am quite nervous
and anxious to finish. However, when I write a more 'personal'
piece of writing, a narrative in which I express my feelings about
something, I enjoy writing a lot more. My <u>style</u> is a lot more
relaxed. . . .

2   . . . I most often do three different kinds of writing: papers for
classes, letters applying for jobs, and excerpts in my private
journal. Usually, when I write papers for classes, my sentences
can get quite long and complicated; also my word choice tends
to be formal. On the other hand, when I write job application
letters, my sentences tend to be short, and uncomplicated; the
words I use are "everyday" words that a business person would
use. When I write in my journal, though, anything goes! Sometimes sentences go on for a page; sometimes they consist of one
word. And my words? Well, I make a lot of them up. So my <u>style</u>
varies. . . .

3   . . . My <u>style</u> as a writer also depends on what I am writing.
Sometimes I need to do a lot of planning before I begin writing;
sometimes I don't do any at all. When I write a letter of application,
it is usually best for me to begin writing almost immediately,
but then I usually discard what I write, initially, and start all
over again. Most papers for class, however, require a lot of planning. . . .

Undoubtedly, most readers would have difficulty determining what Chris
means by *style*. Does it have to do with Chris's behavior as a writer, and,
if so, with what aspects of that behavior? Or does it have to do with
distinctive features, such as the structure of sentences, that are characteristic
of her writing?

Indeed, when she wrote this, Chris did not have a clear idea of what she meant by "style." She was using the word to mean just about *anything* that had to do with any *unique* aspect of her writing behavior or of her writing. This generalized use of the word "style" allowed her to think about her behavior as a writer, in order to determine the particular aspect of her behavior that she wished to write about. Excerpt 2 seems to focus on the types of writing tasks Chris is most often confronted with and the effect that these tasks seem to have on such features as sentence length and word choice in the writing she produces in response to these tasks. Excerpts 1 and 3, however, seem to describe her behavior as a writer: The first excerpt focuses on how she *feels* when she writes, and the third focuses on her planning process. Chris used the word "style" to mean a number of things as she was determining what to write about; "style" was laden with meaning, and Chris was not fully aware of that meaning.

When Chris read her completed draft, her *repeated* use of the word "style" to mean different things told her that she had produced a predraft, but it also suggested a means of revision. She probed the code word "style" for all the hidden meanings. This let her begin to clarify her intention: Did she want to *describe* how she felt when she was writing, for example? Or did she want *to explain* how the writing task affected the type of final draft she produced?

Exercise

Examine each of the following excerpts from essays. Underline any word or words that you consider to be code words. In general, you can recognize code words by two criteria: (1) Code words are usually conceptually complex, which enables them to mean different things in different contexts or to different people—remember how Chris used the word "style." (2) Code words are usually closely related, and sometimes essential, to the topic being explored. Recall Pati's use of the code word "feminist" in Chapter 3. Explain your choices.

1. Each of the songs from the album "Love Over Gold" is unique. In producing this album, the group Dire Straits has managed to avoid the overproduced hype that is so characteristic of music today.

2. The most important aspect about graffiti is that it is the result of an expressive act. Graffiti is a creative attempt to communicate, and the fact that it is produced anonymously allows the writer more room to be creative.

3.   Some urban youths who write graffiti do so in order to attain status within their groups. It is not important, under these circumstances, for persons outside of the particular group to recognize the identity of the graffiti writer. This acceptability function of graffiti is served as long as members of the particular group know who wrote the graffiti.

4.   Graffiti writers who take great risks to write in dangerous places gain satisfaction on a physical level. But, more importantly, they gain on a psychological level, too. The satisfaction of both of these levels is vital for graffiti writers.

5.   One of the most frequented bars on the campus is Bennie's. Many students go there because they are frustrated and fed up from studying, and Bennie's is a good place to go when you want to get radical. Bennie's is also an unusual bar because its clientele is varied. Lots of different kinds of students go to Bennie's: hippies, Greek types, and "serious" students. The one kind of student who might get in trouble at Bennie's, though, is a student who is radical because Josh, the owner, doesn't like radical students.

6.   The best thing about the book is its format. It is easy to find what you are looking for and the explanations are clear because of this format.

Exercise

Read the following short draft, which is an attempt to describe the feeling of loneliness through the writer's personal experience of it. Locate and circle any code words and/or pronouns with unclear referents that you find. Be able to justify and explain your choices.

Lonely

1   It is not easy to be lonely. But yet lots of students are just that when they first leave home and come to college. Some students try to overcome their loneliness by sitting in public places, such as the Student Union. Other students try to keep busy studying. Still others attend public events. I too do this. I don't like to be lonely.

2   I especially feel lonely on days when it is gray and rainy. The weather makes me feel down. That's when I try to cheer myself up. It's really hard though, because the gloomy sky makes me feel tired. So it takes a real effort to get myself up and out of my room. Sometimes I can't get the energy to go out at all and so I just lie around and brood. Then I am not

just lonely, I am depressed. If I can get myself up, I usually go first to the Parrot and the Peacock. The Parrot and the Peacock is small; plus a lot of my friends go there. Also, if I get there I don't feel embarrassed to be alone for a while to see if some of my friends will show up. It's really OK.

If no one shows up at the Parrot and the Peacock, then I might go back   3 to my room or I might call someone up. It depends on my perspective. If I go back to my room I might already feel better or I might be even more lonely and depressed. If I call someone up, this is risky because what if the person isn't home or what if he or she doesn't want to come out? Then I could be in trouble.

The fall and winter, they can be real problems because of the weather: 4 It is gloomy and it is hard to get out. No one wants to walk or drive anywhere. Loneliness is the most prevalent at these times. But there's nothing anyone can do about the weather—except try to adjust. Loneliness is a feeling we all have to learn to live with.

Exercise

The draft in the previous exercise is a predraft. First, explain *why* it is a predraft, in terms of its structure, the form of the sentences within it, and the presence of code words and pronouns with unclear referents. Then, glean it for ideas and strategies. Here are some guides that will help you.

1. Paragraph 1 contains at least one narrowed topic: What college students do to relieve loneliness. List as many other topics as you can find in paragraphs 2, 3, and 4.

2. Paragraph 1 contains a possible thesis for an essay: Students try to overcome loneliness by sitting in public places, studying, or attending public events. List at least *three* other possible theses contained in the draft. If you were to choose *one* to invent and plan with, which would it be? Why?

3. A possible intention for writing that this predraft suggests is to explain to new freshmen three strategies they can use to combat loneliness. Describe at least *two* other intentions for writing suggested by the predraft.

4. Paragraph 1 suggests a strategy for *organizing* the text. It suggests that an essay about tactics students employ to combat loneliness *could* be divided into three parts: (1) a "sitting in public places" part, (2) a "studying" part, and (3) an "attending public events" part. Examine paragraphs 2, 3, and 4 carefully. Do you see any other buried suggestions? List any that you find.

5.   If you had written the predraft "Lonely," you would have quite a few issues to decide. For example, do you want to write about *loneliness* or *depression?* Do you want to *narrate* an experience or *explain* some tactics? Do you want to focus on your *own* feelings or describe what you consider to be the feelings of college freshmen in general? List some other important decisions you would have to make.

Applying Revision Skills

Here are drafts of two different essays on the topic of capital punishment. Read each draft and determine, by examining text structure, sentence form, and word choice, whether it is a rough draft or a predraft. If it is a predraft, read through it and jot down possible theses and strategies for developing and structuring suggested by the draft. If it is a rough draft, explain how reader-based it is, making specific references to the text. Which portions seem to need more work? Why? What specific changes are needed?

Essay 1

1   There is nothing wrong with capital punishment. Although I have always heard people say that capital punishment is not the human thing to do, I wonder if the people who say this have ever had any experience with crime or murder. If they did, I don't think they'd be so worried about the rights of the criminal—whatever they are.

2   Throughout the history of time, murder, rape, stealing, and plunder have been frequent occurrances. It's a form of common behavior to many who feel that if they have a problem, then crime must be the answer to it. Right now, crime is so big that the government can't even control it. Organized crime is right out there, it's everywhere; lot's of persons are employed or controlled by illegal persons. And if there ever is a sentence it's so light the person gets right off without jail or a fine--even serious criminals.

3   Right now there's murders like Son of Sam or Charles Manson who are serving sentences of life in prison. These are elligible for parole after a few short years and what if the parole board decides to let them out? First of all these people have killed a lot of people. And so they get about ten years in jail (if they get paroled). Big deal! I wonder

how the families of the victims feel about that one. But not only that, what about the protection of innocent citizens? What if these people get upset again? Maybe they might kill somebody again. This does happen. I know about times when they let a murderer go free and the guy killed again. When will we ever learn.

Then there's the idea of who takes care of the support. Taxes are 4 always going up and there's not enough money for things like education and national defense, but we have to support these murderers for the rest of their lives. Supporters of anti-capital punishment say it's wrong to take a life, but do these people want to live out their whole lives in prison, anyway? Does anyone ever ask them?

To conclude, we all live together in society and so we have to support 5 a lifestyle that we believe in. Dangerous and destructive elements must be weeded out so that everyone can be in harmony. "An eye for an eye; a tooth for a tooth" is a good law to follow. I don't want to have to kill anyone, but if I have to I will.

Essay 2

Although this may sound very cruel, I must say that I am in favor 1 of capital punishment. I know that it is wrong to take a human life, and I have heard it said that capital punishment only adds one wrong to another. However, I feel that capital punishment is the right thing to do, especially in the case of mass murder.

My first argument in favor of capital punishment is that maybe it 2 might prevent some persons from committing murder. I know that people say that "capital punishment is no deterrent for crime" but I don't see how anyone can be entirely certain about this. And until we are certain, what if knowing there is a death penalty prevents someone from murder? Maybe lives could be saved. Even if just ten lives were saved because ten people stopped and thought about the consequences, that would be something. What are ten lives worth? So it is possible that capital punishment may save lives and until we are certain that it doesn't, it's worth it.

Another argument in favor of capital punishment is that it might 3 help the victim's family and loved ones who survive. How would you feel if your baby were murdered, but the person who did it goes to prison for a few years and then is let out? Your baby is dead, and the person who did it is around walking the streets. This also brings me to another point. Would the victim's family be safe, once the person were let out of prison? Do prisoners ever take revenge on the people who sent them to prison (even though they *did* something wrong)? And what about other citizens? Are they safe? Isn't it possible that someone who has murdered once may murder again? How can parole boards be certain that the persons they let out aren't dangerous? Is it fair to let a murderer out of jail if there is any chance he might do it again?

4   Finally, I think that capital punishment is the responsibility of law-abiding citizens. Sure, it's not pleasant to punish persons, but we have laws. We need to follow these laws and we need to enforce them; otherwise, what's the use of having laws. Capital punishment is very serious, but so is murder. In the Bible, one of the Ten Commandments says, "Thou shalt not murder." Also the Bible says "An eye for an eye. A tooth for a tooth." This means that God's law also calls for capital punishment. If you murder then you should pay with your life. So responsibility to our own laws and to the laws of God indicates that capital punishment is the responsibility of law-abiding citizens.

5   Capital punishment is harsh but it is also just.

Writing Assignment

Reread your initial draft of your essay about the person that you interviewed (p. 114). Examine the text structure, sentence form, and word choice, and determine whether it is a predraft or a rough draft.

If your draft is a predraft, read through it and jot down possible theses and strategies for developing and structuring the text that are suggested by the draft. After additional inventing and planning, write a second draft.

If you produced a rough draft, identify the *writer-based* portions that need to be rewritten. Jot down ideas for specific changes. For example, should more information be added? Should some information be deleted? Should the material be rearranged? Should some new portions be substituted for material that is currently in the draft? Then rewrite your initial draft.

Writing Assignment

Think about the writing process questionnaire you completed in Chapter 1 and about what you did as you drafted your interview essay. Then do some inventing about the way you write and revise, and draft an expository text that describes your writing process. Some of the questions you might address are: How many drafts must you write before you begin to write reader-based prose consistently? What kinds of changes do you make as you write? How and when do you make these changes? Use vivid, personal anecdotes to illustrate the kinds of things you do when you write.

5 *Revising Rough Drafts*

Revising as Rewriting

Chapter 4 helped you to understand the differences between a predraft and a rough draft and gave you practice in transforming a predraft into a rough draft. In this chapter we will look at how to revise a *rough draft*. As you learned in working with predrafts, there are two basic steps in revising: (1) evaluation, and (2) determining and executing a revision strategy. Once you have determined that you have produced a rough draft, you should move systematically through the revision process, eliminating writer-based elements and working toward a final draft that is fully accessible to a reader.

Revising a rough draft primarily involves *rewriting:* adding, deleting, substituting, and rearranging. This should involve not only solidifying the amount and relevance of the information you are presenting to the reader, but also refining your sentence structure and monitoring the quality of your word choice.

Contrast this with the way one revises a *predraft*. Essentially, revising a predraft means starting again, "harvesting" the useful ideas you have uncovered, but beginning again to look for thesis and intention. In addition, the text structure, sentence form, and word choice used in a predraft usually make it impossible to create a reader-based draft efficiently by just adding, deleting, substituting, or rearranging your material.

A rough draft, on the other hand, has the following features.

1. Text Level
    a. *Development*   The text is developed enough to permit the writer to recognize a clear thesis and intention emerging. In addition, it either contains ample evidence, illustration, or argument to support its thesis and intention *or* points to or suggests the kind of evidence needed for a subsequent draft.
    b. *Organization*   The text proceeds logically, moving from point to point or from section to section guided by the writer's intention and meeting the reader's expectations. The frame of reference, or interpretive context, for the information presented is clear, and the focus of individual units in the text (paragraphs and sentences) is unambiguous.
2. Sentence Level
    a. *Structure*   The text contains few ambiguously structured sentences. That is, most of the sentences have a clearly recognizable grammatical subject and predicate that are appropriate to the context and the writer's intention.
3. Word Level
    a. *Word Choice*   The text generally uses words that are appropriate given its intention, subject matter, and perceived audience. Words are appropriately concrete and specific. Pronouns with unclear referents and code words, although they may be present, are not a major problem.

Revising a rough draft is thus a progressive activity in which you rewrite elements to make your draft increasingly reader-based. As you learn to read through and rewrite a rough draft, spotting weaknesses and exploiting strengths, you will become more confident of your ability to communicate your ideas to the audience you are addressing.

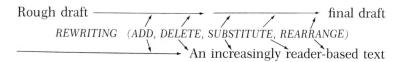

Rough draft ─────────────────────── ───────────────────→ final draft
          REWRITING   (ADD, DELETE, SUBSTITUTE, REARRANGE)
─────────────────────────────────→ An increasingly reader-based text

The fact that your draft is a rough draft does not mean that there will not be any lingering writer-based elements. However, there should be proportionally fewer such elements. In other words, there is a qualitative difference between a predraft and rough draft that distinguishes them and guides your choice of revision strategies.

Writing Task

Read the following newspaper column by Carolyn Reed that appeared in the Cleveland *Plain Dealer*. In her column Ms. Reed reflects on the way she was brought up by her father, especially his influence upon her views of patriotism. His, she says, is a "sexist patriotism," one that equates masculinity with Americanism, effectively relegating women to a subservient role. How would you characterize Ms. Reed's *intention*? Whom does she seem to consider her audience? How does she use her very personal experience to comment on what she perceives as a social evil?

What attitudes, stances, or beliefs that you may be uncomfortable with have your parents bequeathed to you? How do their views of life color your own? Which have you embraced? Which have you rejected? Explore these ideas in an inventing session in which you consider the heritage that your parents have given you, searching for a thesis and intention.

Draft a text that uses your personal experience to comment on a specific social issue on which your view has been influenced by your parents. You will be using this draft throughout this chapter for revision practice.

Contempt for Females Can Be Taught

Carolyn Reed

I was thinking about obscene phone calls. I receive about one a week. That is not unusual, because I have my full name listed in the phone book.

(Once my husband answered the phone in the middle of the night and got an earful of the obscenities meant for me. It didn't seem to matter to the caller that it wasn't a woman's voice; his fixation that it should be a woman was all that mattered.)

I am not personally offended by the language of the calls. But I am always horrified at the contempt and objectification.

I was thinking about the few women who work as artists at the theater where I'm employed. Of 47 contracts issued this year, only 13 are for women. That is less than one-third. The resident (full-time) company numbers 31 actors. Only seven are women. That is less than one-fourth.

No plays being presented this season were written by women, and no women will be directing at the Cleveland Play House. Three of the plays are two-men casts. Three other plays have largely male casts, and women are incidental. "The Tempest," which opened the new Bolton Theater has a cast of 28, and only four of them are women. Only one of those women is a member of the actor's union, earning a full salary.

I'm shocked because it has been easy for management to backslide. I'm disappointed because I am a woman. I'm embarrassed because I've made so little difference.

I was thinking about Beirut and Grenada and the Equal Rights Amendment. I was thinking about loss and feminism and misogyny when the newspaper clipping arrived in the mail.

A photographer from my home-town newspaper took my father's picture on Veterans Day, 1983. Caught him unaware. It's a close-up, and my father is saluting as the American flag goes by. The right hand at his forehead, that once-capable dentist's hand is now arthritic, swollen and crooked. The extremes of his nature are pushed and poked into a visual mediocrity under his American Legion cap. I've never seen him that way before: the old veteran.

But the expression on his face I've seen a thousand times. I've seen his mouth go into that straight line, not quite a smile, not quite a grimace. I've seen his eyes go opaque and inward like that, their light becoming a blue hardness as he takes himself away inside to the phrases and comfort and totems of his patriotism.

He's always been a super-patriot. During the 1960s he had one of those bumper stickers on the Oldsmobile which read: "America: Love It or Leave It." He wears a jeweled American flag in his lapel.

The flag from his son's coffin, the bitter memory of one more Vietnam casualty, lies in the cedar chest at the foot of my mother's bed.

He is usually Flag Day chairman at the Elks Club. For years he has helped organize the Veterans Day parade back home and bemoaned the fact that so few people line the streets to pay homage to the military, to the America of uniforms and weapons and marching drills, of patriotism, of "The Flag."

For years I measured my femaleness by my father's standards. I attempted to clarify the contradictory messages of "free and equal" on one hand and "subordinate" on the other. So much of what I was taught seemed beside the point, and anyway the point was obscure.

See, the America which has his blessing is masculine, and it is impossible for a woman to be anointed. His flag is a sexist symbol.

But that is just one part of the man. My father, raised a Catholic, has been an atheist for 60 of his 89 years. He has advocated and defended abortion as long as I can remember. He is open to new influences on many levels.

But his male-supremacy theme, his sexist patriotism, have been the sandpaper which scratched this woman. It is a connotative patriotism, not actual. He sees America not as it is, but as he was taught it was. His connotative Americanism is rigid because it substitutes received prejudices for the actuality of social change.

His idea of America is not descriptive or denotative; it does not allow for the scrutiny of atrophied ideals, nor does it heed the permutations of the social order.

The old veteran has spent a lot of his life defending the status quo. I'm pretty sure he didn't like it much: Both he and my mother have perturbable and passionate natures, quirky and emotionally excessive. Our household was a crazy one, full of shouting and hugging, conflict and sensibility, tyrannies and rebellions, and left my brothers and me with many unanswered "whys."

For years I have blamed my father for subordinating my mother (she blames him, too), for refusing to allow her to take a job when she wanted to, for fostering her dependency, for isolating her from society. I blamed my father for instilling in me the values of the old patriarchy, so that my perception of my worth and possibilities were marred because of my sex. I blamed him for his mixture of love and contempt for my femaleness.

Then, that day, that photograph and that expression on his face brought some clarity to my thoughts on misogyny. Not only my father but also my mother held being female in contempt. And the source lies in the women who raised them.

Both my parents were raised fatherless by women who spent most of their adult lives bearing the names of men who were only vague memories. They were strong women who managed to bring up three children each on the income from the sales of their family homes. When that ran out, they raised their children with the help of male relatives, or the husbands of female relatives.

They were dependent and hated it. Without husbands and homes of their own they were disenfranchised and socially anomalous. They were un-educated, unskilled and unemployable. They were not allowed to vote. Without men to mirror their value, they had no value. They held themselves in contempt, and their children learned that contempt.

It's two generations later, and almost 100 years, and the battle is still being waged. I'm asking the old veteran and my son to join me at the barricades!

Re-seeing Your Text

The biggest obstacle a writer faces in revising a rough draft is his familiarity with it. The writer *knows* what he means, or at least what he intended to mean. So when he has failed to reveal his intentions fully in a completed text, he may not recognize it. Perhaps at some time you have had a conference with a teacher in which you said, "But what I meant was . . ." All writers tend to see what they want to see in their texts, forgetting that the reader does not have access to all their thinking and planning. The writer may be asking the reader to supply support, such as illustrations or evidence and/or connections, transitions, or coherence that he has left out.

To revise effectively, the writer needs to become a *stranger* to his own text. He must "re-see" his text in light of his original goals, comparing what he has actually *done* with what he *intended* to do—not an easy task. He must, in other words, develop strategies for putting distance between himself and his text so that he can evaluate his text objectively and determine what revising strategies to use and what rewriting to do.

Before you begin to revise your rough draft, it is a good idea to wait at least twenty-four hours *between* your evaluation and the last session in which you worked on your draft. It is hard to overestimate the difference a good night's sleep will make in your ability to look at your text as a third party. Instead of one or two marathon sessions, write for shorter periods, developing your text over several days.

Many writers fail to revise their rough drafts because these drafts appear finished, and the writers have never developed a strategy for evaluating their drafts and planning appropriate revisions. The following questions can help you read a rough draft more objectively and allow you to pinpoint specific problem areas that need attention. We will first present these seven reading and planning strategies, then demonstrate how they can help you plan a revision.

Seven Reading Strategies for Revising a Rough Draft

1.   Move through *each* paragraph of your text and write a precise summary or paraphrase of its topic, or central idea.

Once you have identified the topic of the paragraph, examine each sentence. Does each bear a direct relationship to others in the paragraph, either amplifying the topic or providing a transition between other sentences?

Mark any sentences that seem off the topic or that seem ambiguous. Also, evaluate the illustrations and evidence the paragraph provides. Do they support and elaborate the topic of the paragraph adequately? Is the reader *shown* at least as much as she is *told*?

2.   Consider your audience. Are the kind and amount of support you have provided for the main topic of your text relevant and well expressed to your intended readers?

Write brief notes to yourself in the margins around the paragraph if you think you need to provide additional support: "Tell bursar story" or "put in enrollment data."

3.   Briefly describe the function of each paragraph within the text as a whole.

How does the paragraph contribute to the development of the thesis? What is the paragraph designed to do? Mark any paragraphs about which you have reservations. Jot down marginal notes suggesting future revisions: "Move this paragraph to plant discussion part of essay" or "Rewrite so this connects paragraphs 1 and 3 better."

4.   Examine the opening and closing paragraphs of your text carefully.

Does the opening paragraph accurately and consistently forecast the thesis, subject matter, tone, and direction of the text? Does it promise anything that the remainder of the text does not deliver? If it does, will you need to delete part of the introduction, or will you need to add to your text? Does the opening paragraph provide enough of a "hook" to interest the reader in continuing to read?

Does the closing paragraph adequately conclude the text without being abrupt or excessively repetitive? Does it avoid introducing new lines of inquiry that cannot be pursued? Would a reader come away with a sense of "closure," that is, a sense that the task the text was created to perform has been completed? Mark any sentences that may need to be deleted or rewritten entirely. If the text seems to end abruptly, jot down ideas for revision if they occur to you.

5.   Examine the *first* sentence in each paragraph carefully.

Does each maintain the direction of the text in a way that the reader can follow? Does each provide an adequate transition from the preceding paragraph? Put brackets around any sentences that do not seem to provide an adequate transition.

6.   Examine *each* sentence in your text carefully.

Does the sentence contain any "code words," or loaded words that may not convey to your reader what they mean to you? Is the sentence one of a group of consecutive sentences of the same length containing exactly the same subject? Circle any words or expressions that you suspect may be code words. Draw a vertical line in the margin alongside any group of consecutive sentences that seem to be of the same length or have the same subject.

7.   Examine paragraphs or sentences in your text *at random.*

Can you tell from the paragraph or sentence what its immediate function is in the text? For example, does it introduce a new idea, provide transition or connection, illustrate or support a previous idea, or reveal an organizational principle? If the paragraph or sentence were left out of the text entirely, would it make any difference to the coherence or cogency of your development? Mark any subunits of your text—paragraphs or sentences—whose functions are ambiguous.

Applying the Seven Reading Strategies

Consider the following rough draft that Frank Day drafted from his original inventing and planning notes (see Chapter 2).

Indians Fans and the Neverending Story
Frank Day

Although many Indians fans are well aware of their team's distressing   1
record in post-season play, most of them probably don't know why their team has failed so often. I do. I have made it part of my life's work to figure out the Indians' problems. It's not that when they get there that they don't do well. (Except for the 1954 World Series which I remember my dad talking about so much.) It's that they don't get there, period. Except for 1920, 1948 and 1954, the Indians have been to nary a post-season playoff. After the Cubs revival in 1984, I think Indians fans deserve the title for the longest suffering devotees to a team. This dismal record sends one looking for reasons.

There are plenty. You can start with the front office. Always strapped   2
for funds, the general manager of the team almost always had to settle for good-to-mediocre players since he couldn't entice any of the high-priced free agents to the join the Indians. And even when he did, like Wayne Garland, the Indians got damaged goods. Then there is the manager. The Indians have almost as many managers as the Yankees have had in the last decade. With so little stability, it's no wonder that the team never seems to know if it's headed up or down.

3   Of course, playing at Municipal Stadium is no treat either. When the cold winds blow off the lake, it not only makes the players cold, it chills fan interest considerably. The only park worse for the fans must be Candlestick Park.

4   With limited funds, few quality players, a disappointing stadium, it is only justice that the Indians fans also get some of the most opinionated and negative sportswriters. Whenever the Indians do something right, the press is there to say it's a fluke. When they get caught in one of their annual losing streaks, then it's the press's turn to say "I told you so." It's no wonder that few players want to play in Cleveland.

5   But I remain a diehard Indians fan anyway. Despite all the problems, something about old Chief Wahoo brings tears to my eyes and reminds me of summer nights long ago, listening to Rocky Colavito, John Romano, and Sudden Sam McDowell do battle against the forces of evil in the American League. If the Indians ever do become a winner, I'll be the first to buy season tickets. In the meantime, I'll stick by them through thick and thin. Until then rooting for the Indians is a neverending story.

Frank used these seven reading strategies to evaluate his rough draft and plan his revision strategy:

1.   Move through *each* paragraph of your text and write a precise summary or paraphrase of its topic, or central idea.
2.   Consider your audience. Are the kind and amount of support you have provided for the main topic of your text relevant and well expressed to your intended readers?
3.   Briefly describe the function of each paragraph within the text as a whole.
4.   Examine the opening and closing paragraphs of your text carefully.
5.   Examine the *first* sentence in each paragraph carefully.
6.   Examine *each* sentence in your text carefully.
7.   Examine paragraphs or sentences in your text *at random*.

Here is how his rough draft looked after he marked up his text using these seven strategies:

Although many Indians fans are well aware   1
of their team's distressing record in post-season

play, most of them probably don't know why their team has failed so often. I do. I have made it part of my life's work to figure out the Indians' problems. *unclear to reader?* [It's not that when they get there that they don't do well.] (Except for the 1954 World Series which I remember my dad talking about so much.) [It's that they don't get there, period.] Except for 1920, 1948 and 1954, the Indians have been to nary a post-season playoff. After the Cubs revival in 1984, I think Indians fans deserve the title for the longest suffering devotees to a team. This dismal record sends one looking for reasons.

weak transition

opening ¶: Attempt to place whole text in context by discussing past and present failures of Indians

Doesn't work: narrative and copied structure here — too W Based

needs a frame!

2 [There are plenty] You can start with the front office. *change in person* Always strapped for funds, the general manager of the team almost always had to settle for good-to-mediocre players since he couldn't entice any of the high-priced free agents to the join the Indians. And even when he did, like [Wayne Garland,] the Indians got damaged goods. Then there is the manager. The Indians have almost as many managers as the Yankees have had in the last decade. With so little stability, it's no wonder that the team never seems to know if it's headed up or down.

2nd ¶ - attempt to move to reasons for failure - too abrupt!

explain further

Make separate ¶ and develop

3 Of course, playing at Municipal Stadium is no treat either. When the cold winds blow off the lake, it not only makes the players cold, it chills fan interest considerably. The only park worse for the fans must be [Candlestick Park] *Explain - code word*

Expand this ¶

3rd ¶ needs development - but I want to keep it.

4 With limited funds, few quality players, a disappointing stadium, it is only justice that the Indians fans also get some of the most opinionated and negative sportwriters. Whenever the Indians do something right, the press is there to say it's a fluke. When they get caught in one of their annual losing streaks, then it's the press's turn to say "I told you so." It's no wonder that few players want to play in Cleveland.

Eliminate ¶ doesn't connect with main topic well!

4th ¶ Is too improbable - Reader will balk!

5 But I remain a diehard Indians fan anyway. Despite all the problems, something about old

5th ¶ I like the sentiment here but still too personal

Chief Wahoo brings tears to my eyes and reminds
me of summer nights long ago listening to Rocky
Colavito, John Romano, and Sudden Sam Mc-
Dowell do battle against the forces of evil in the
American League. If the Indians ever do become
a winner, I'll be the first to buy season tickets.
In the meantime, I'll stick by them through thick
and thin. Until then rooting for the Indians is a
<u>neverending</u> story.

[Marginal handwritten notes: "ambiguous", "Explain who these are", "Could be good conclusion", "cliché", "Explain ending", "losing?"]

Frank felt confident that he had produced a rough draft, not a predraft.
He could discern an intention and thesis and felt that although his development could be bolstered, it adequately outlined the territory he needed
to cover. Nevertheless, he realized that his opening paragraph did not make
his intention and thesis as clear to his readers as it should have; it used
too much narrative structure and rambled too much. He knew that this
first paragraph needed to create a *frame of reference,* or interpretive context,
for the reader. Rewriting this first paragraph was the key to other revisions,
particularly those involving paragraphs 4 and 5. Notice his notations in
the margins to mark places where development needed to be enhanced.

At the sentence level, Frank bracketed several ambiguous, writer-based
sentences and noted a few whose structure was too convoluted to be easily
understood by the reader. Similarly, at the word level he spotted several
code words and made marginal notes to himself about how to clarify his
ideas.

Having evaluated his draft and noted areas of strength and weakness,
Frank plotted a specific strategy for revising his text:

1. Create a frame of reference in the opening paragraph and sharpen
the focus in each subsequent paragraph based upon this opening
announcement of thesis and intention.

2. Develop the reasons behind the Indians' failures in three sections:
the lack of capital, the frequent change in managers, and the poor
conditions of the playing field. Make sure transitions between paragraphs are less clipped.

3. Delete information about my dad and the paragraph on the press.
Substitute a more developed paragraph on the change in managers.

4. Clarify references that are currently obscure, such as Wayne Garland,
Candlestick Park, and Sudden Sam McDowell, by adding more
information.

5. Rewrite the concluding paragraph, still using the reminiscence, but making it less a "private" memory and more a public remembrance of the Indians' heritage and possible future glory.

6. Generally eliminate code words and expressions by clarifying the focus of individual sentences or substituting a more substantial explanation of the term.

In the next two sections of this chapter we will look more closely at what Frank actually did to rewrite his draft at the text level.

Exercise

Read again the draft written about Evelyn Harshman in Chapter 4 (pp. 111–112).

1. What text-level, sentence-level, and word-level elements helped you identify it as a rough draft?

2. Using the seven reading strategies discussed in this chapter, analyze this draft and write a note to the writer explaining what you think needs to be done to make the draft more effective.

Writing Task

Carefully examine the draft you wrote in response to the writing task on page 152. If it is a rough draft, use the seven reading strategies to evaluate it and plot a revision strategy. If it is a predraft, review the revising strategies for a predraft in Chapter 4, and revise it. Once you have produced a rough draft, use the seven reading strategies to plot a revision strategy.

Revising Text Structure

Creating Frames of Reference

Since a rough draft is structured more specifically with the reader and the intention of the writer in mind, it generally does not have extensive structural problems, like inappropriate narrative or copied structure or shifting focus. But even in a rough draft there may be residual traces of these structures, and it is useful to know how to revise these kinds of writer-based elements.

One important method of revising inappropriately structured portions of a rough draft involves rewriting these portions to provide the reader with a *frame of reference* for interpreting the information being presented. To do so, the writer must explicitly attend to his intention and reveal it unambiguously to a reader. As an illustration, let us examine the following excerpt from Frank Day's rough draft. Frank was writing an explanatory text; his intention was *to explain* the reasons behind a professional baseball team's poor record to an audience of his peers. Here again is his opening paragraph:

1   Although many Indians fans are well aware of their team's distressing record in post-season play, most of them probably don't know why their team has failed so often. I do. I have made it part of my life's work to figure out the Indians' problems. It's not that when they get there that they don't do well. (Except for the 1954 World Series which I remember my dad talking about so much.) It's that they don't get there, period. Except for 1920, 1948 and 1954, the Indians have been to nary a post-season playoff. After the Cubs revival in 1984, I think Indians fans deserve the title for the longest suffering devotees to a team. This dismal record sends one looking for reasons.

As you recall from Frank's evaluation of his draft, too much of this paragraph is *about* the writer himself—a "play-by-play" of his approach to the topic and a catalogue of facts tied to no specific context. First, he generalizes about the Indians' fans and their knowledge of the game; then he moves to his own knowledge of the team, then to a reminiscence about the 1954 Indians and his dad, and finally to the real intention of his text.

Eventually, a clear thesis and intention emerges (the text is about the Indians' failures, and the author's intention is to explore the reasons for them), but the reader has to work too hard to discover this because of Frank's initial structure. His narration of his stages of discovery and his culling of certain facts about the Indians are beside the point of his *intention*: to explain and analyze the Indians' failures. In essence, the writer must get out of the way so that his readers can see the explanation he wants to give them.

The following revision is much less egocentric and distracting; it clearly establishes a frame of reference for the reader based on the writer's intention to discuss the various reasons for the Indians' lack of success.

> [1]One doesn't have to be an avid Cleveland Indians fan to be aware of their thirty-year failure to win a championship. [2]Their last post-season appearance occurred in 1954, the year of the infamous World Series in which they lost all four games to the New York Giants after a record-breaking regular season. [3]Until 1984, when the Chicago Cubs made the National League playoffs, Cubs fans were the most longsuffering of all baseball devotees. [4]Now, however, Indians fans can surpass them in patience, perseverance and pain. [5]The Indians' failure, nevertheless, is no mystery. [6]If one looks a little deeper and analyzes the factors that contribute to their lack of success, it becomes apparent that their problems are threefold.

This revised opening paragraph reveals that Frank recognized that the rambling, narrative structure of his original paragraph only confused the reader, making random facts or Frank himself the center of attention. The revision makes it clear that the writer's *intention* is to explain the Indians' failures. Having given the reader a clear frame of reference in which to interpret information, Frank can continue his revision by rewriting later paragraphs in terms of this opening. We will come back to Frank's revision of subsequent paragraphs in the next section, on focus. But let us look a little more closely at the changes Frank has made in his text by comparing the two paragraphs side by side:

ORIGINAL

Although many Indians fans are well aware of their team's distressing record in post-season play, most of them probably don't know why their team has failed so often. I do. I have made it part of my life's work to figure out the Indians' problems. It's not that when they get there that they don't do well. (Except for the

REVISED

[1]One doesn't have to be an avid Cleveland Indians fan to be aware of their thirty-year failure to win a championship. [2]Their last post-season appearance occurred in 1954, the year of the infamous World Series in which they lost all four games to the New York Giants after a record-breaking regular season. [3]Until 1984, when the Chicago

1954 World Series which I remember my dad talking about so much.) It's that they don't get there, period. Except for 1920, 1948 and 1954, the Indians have been to nary a post-season playoff. After the Cubs revival in 1984, I think Indians fans deserve the title for the longest suffering devotees to a team. This dismal record sends one looking for reasons.

Cubs made the National League playoffs, Cubs fans were the most longsuffering of all baseball devotees. [4]Now, however, Indians fans can surpass them in patience, perseverance and pain. [5]The Indians' failure, nevertheless, is no mystery. [6]If one looks a little deeper and analyzes the factors that contribute to their lack of success, it becomes apparent that their problems are threefold.

The first, or introductory, paragraph is usually crucial for providing a frame of reference, indicating the thesis and the direction and tone of the text to follow. In the revised paragraph, Frank has accomplished this admirably. In sentence 1 he has indicated that the subject matter of the text will be baseball, and in particular the failure of the Cleveland Indians. Sentence 2 elaborates on the extent of this failure and pushes the reader ahead toward a thesis, which is forthcoming. Sentences 3 and 4 place the Indians' failure in a particular context (Indians fans now surpass Cubs fans in endurance), and sentence 5 suggests that a thesis sentence is coming next. Finally, sentence 6 announces a specific intention for the text and sets the stage for an exposition of the reasons behind the Indians' failure, the main topic of the opening paragraph and the text itself.

Notice how Frank's rewriting of his opening paragraph has provided the reader with a frame of reference for understanding the rest of the text. The opening paragraph is not the only place where frame of reference is important, of course, but it usually is particularly crucial. The two examples below illustrate how *transitional paragraphs* may also provide a continuing frame of reference for the reader as she proceeds through a text:

1   Having surveyed the major sources of food poisoning in mammals, we will now turn our attention to an equally important division of veterinary pathology: the classification of diseases of the alimentary canal. In so doing, we will discuss, first, the more typical occurrences of alimentary dysfunction, and then move on to the rarer forms.

2   These, then, are the reasons I support the Equal Rights Amendment. But one must also confront opposing views honestly and fairly and I will now address the common objections to the ERA, one by one.

SUMMARY

A reader cannot just be dropped into a text. The writer must orient her; he must provide text-level signals that give the reader some sense of what the text is about and how she is to proceed in reading it. Within and between the paragraphs of a text, the writer must provide frames of reference—those bits of background information, clarifying or qualifying words, or means of transition that *restrict* the range of possible meaning and enable the reader to follow the writer's development. Such signals include text titles, headers, and introductory or transition paragraphs. For example, in this book, the title is *Roughdrafts: The Process of Writing*, and *Revising Text Structure* is an example of a header.

Consider one more example of a text that needs a frame of reference. This is the opening paragraph of a text whose purpose is to explain the popularity of suspense and horror writer Stephen King:

> [1]Stephen King is the most popular writer in America today. [2]There are many reasons for this. [3]Among them are his ability to scare people out of their wits with words and his way of squeezing the last moment of terror out of every scene in which someone is going to be killed or disfigured. [4]American readers simply cannot get enough of this kind of fiction.

One does not have to be an aficionado of Stephen King's fiction, or know anything about him at all, to see a lack of context that could be provided by a frame of reference.

Let us examine each of the sentences:

> [1]Stephen King is the most popular writer in America today.

The reader's immediate impulse may be to ask, "The most popular of what *kind* of writer, and compared to whom, and what do you mean by *popular*"? This first sentence contains no qualifying language to permit the reader to judge the validity of the generalization, or, in fact, to identify Stephen King any more particularly than as a writer.

> [2]There are many reasons for this.

The second sentence is an unsuccessful attempt to provide transition between the opening sentence and the support that follows. It speaks of "many reasons," although the rest of the paragraph mentions only two. This sentence also needs elaboration: If there are many reasons, why is the writer only going to talk about these two?

> [3]Among them are his ability to scare people out of their wits with words and his way of squeezing the last moment of terror out of every scene in which someone is going to be killed or disfigured.

Sentence 3 shows promise, since it begins to specify the unique features of King's fiction, thus giving the reader a means of locating King in the context of other fiction writers. But it suffers from the use of code expressions that may mask the writer's point. The reader asks, "What does it mean to 'scare people with words' and 'squeeze terror out of every scene'?" The reader needs further elaboration of these items—something that a preceding frame of reference might have set up, or that might be supplied later in the paragraph.

> [4]American readers simply cannot get enough of this kind of fiction.

The writer no doubt intends sentence 4 to be a capsule summary of what he has just written, but in fact it reminds the reader that the writer has not supplied enough context or elaboration to justify it. Both "topics" of the paragraph appear in this concluding sentence: (1) the popularity of Stephen King ("American readers simply cannot get enough") and (2) the features that might account for this popularity ("this kind of fiction"), but the writer has not prepared the reader for this sudden summary. The problem of context begins with the generalization in the first sentence, when King is called "the most popular writer in America," and reaches a climax in the fourth when the writer alludes to "this kind of fiction" as if he had adequately explained and illustrated the point he was making. What needs to be done?

Consider this revision:

> [1]One of the most popular horror and suspense writers in America today is Stephen King, author of such terrifying volumes as Carrie, The Shining, and Salem's Lot. [2]Though most of his early works were best-sellers in both hardback and paperback, the sales of his works have increased proportionally with the release of movie

versions of some of his more recent thrillers, <u>Christine</u> and <u>The Dead Zone</u>. [3]The reasons for his popularity are many, but two of them deserve special attention and analysis here. [4]First, King, more than almost any other contemporary horror and suspense writer, has the ability to terrify his readers with vivid description of the most grisly and horrific scenes. [5]Further, he knows how to pace his narration so that he can delay the climax of a particularly suspenseful scene long enough to make the most calloused reader breathless with anticipation. [6]It is clear that the reading public cannot get enough of this kind of gruesome and delightfully "horrible" fiction.

Let us examine this revision sentence by sentence to see what was done.

> [1]<u>One of</u> the most popular <u>horror and suspense</u> writers in America <u>today</u> is Stephen King, <u>author of such terrifying volumes</u> as Carrie, The Shining, and Salem's Lot.

Each of the underlined words or phrases helps to place the original subject in an appropriate context. Sentence 1 both qualifies King's popularity status, declaring that he is <u>one</u> of the most popular <u>horror and suspense</u> writers, and identifies King by naming a few of his better known works. This limits the writer's opening generalization, and provides a frame of reference that enables the reader to classify King as a writer.

> [2]Though most of his early works were best-sellers in both hardback and paperback, the sales of his works have increased proportionally with the release of movie versions of some of his more recent thrillers, <u>Christine</u> and <u>The Dead Zone</u>.

This sentence qualifies and specifies the nature and calibre of King's popularity even further: His books sell well, and his popularity has increased even more with the movie productions of his recent novels.

> [3]The reasons for his popularity are many, but two of them deserve special attention and analysis here.

This is a transition sentence that implies that the reason the writer's subject, Stephen King, has been introduced is in order to explain his popularity, and indicates the extent of the analysis to be offered—two of the reasons for this popularity will receive special attention. This sentence does not offer additional information about the subject. Instead, it indicates to the reader the method and scope of development that the writer will use. This sentence is an example of *metadiscourse,* which is, as you recall, language primarily devoted to helping a reader work through a text.

> [4]First, King, more than almost any other contemporary horror and suspense writer, has the ability to terrify his readers with vivid description of the most grisly and horrific scenes. [5]Further, he knows how to pace his narration so that he can delay the climax of a particularly suspenseful scene long enough to make the most calloused reader breathless with anticipation.

Both of these sentences help to document and illustrate the paragraph's main theme, establishing that King is popular—and for good reason, while offering further qualification ("more than *almost* any . . .").

> [6]It is clear that the reading public cannot get enough of this kind of gruesome and delightfully "horrible" fiction.

The final sentence summarizes the paragraph's main topics, that King is popular and that he writes horror fiction well. It also prepares the reader for further elaboration and illustration in following paragraphs.

Now let us compare the original and revised versions of the Stephen King paragraphs in their entirety.

ORIGINAL:

> [1]Stephen King is the most popular writer in America today. [2]There are many reasons for this. [3]Among them are his ability to scare people out of their wits with words and his way of squeezing the last moment of terror out of every scene in which someone is going to be killed or disfigured. [4]American readers simply cannot get enough of this kind of fiction.

REVISED:

> [1]One of the most popular horror and suspense writers in America today is Stephen King, author of such terrifying volumes as <u>Carrie,</u> <u>The Shining,</u> and <u>Salem's Lot.</u> [2]Though most of his early works

were best-sellers in both hardback and paperback, the sales of his works have increased proportionally with the release of movie versions of some of his more recent thrillers, <u>Christine</u> and <u>The Dead Zone</u>. [3]The reasons for his popularity are many, but two of them deserve special attention and analysis here. [4]First, King, more than almost any other contemporary horror and suspense writer, has the ability to terrify his readers with vivid description of the most grisly and horrific scenes. [5]Further, he knows how to pace his narration so that he can delay the climax of a particularly suspenseful scene long enough to make the most calloused reader breathless with anticipation. [6]It is clear that the reading public cannot get enough of this kind of gruesome and delightfully "horrible" fiction.

Notice that the revised version has been expanded by the *addition* of sentences 2 and 5. Sentence 2 was added to clarify and specify the nature and scope of King's popularity. Sentence 5 was added so that each of the two reasons for King's popularity, originally specified in *one* sentence, could be given its own sentence. Notice also that longer, more detailed sentences have been *substituted* for shorter ones. (Compare, for example, sentence 4 in the original text with sentence 6 in the revised version.) Additionally, code expressions in the original version, such as "scare people out of their wits," have been *deleted*. Such operations, along with *rearranging* of portions of the text, are the major rewriting operations.

Revising to provide your reader with a frame of reference thus involves, first, careful analysis to see whether you have (1) avoided exaggerations or inflated generalizations that make it difficult for your reader to interpret the scope of the information you are presenting; (2) identified important individuals, terms, and concepts that help the reader understand the context of your development; and (3) provided appropriate signals to your reader that you are presenting transitions or identifying the organization of your text.

If your analysis reveals that you have not provided your reader with an adequate frame of reference, here are some useful rewriting strategies.

1. Omit unnecessary generalizations; limit those you do use with qualifiers that adequately narrow the scope of the generalization.

EXAMPLE:
New York is the most dangerous city in America. You should take special precautions in traveling there.

REVISION:

A traveler to New York City *might* take some special safety precautions *since it has a well-known reputation for street crime and violence.*

2. Clarify key terms, individuals, and concepts by adding helpful identifying phrases, especially when terms are first used in a text.

EXAMPLE:

His only true rival is Reggie Jackson.

REVISION:

His only true rival is Reggie Jackson, *veteran slugger of the California Angels and winner of several American League home run titles.*

3. Add signals to create connections between sentences.

EXAMPLE:

One could talk all day about her beautiful hair and eyes. I want to talk about her choice of wardrobe, though.

REVISION:

One could talk about her beautiful hair and eyes indefinitely. *However, it is more to the point* to consider her choice of wardrobe.

Exercise

Read each of the following paragraphs carefully, determining whether they lack a frame of reference. Then rewrite each paragraph as needed to provide a more appropriate organizing structure.

1. *Task:* to prove that *E.T.* is a better movie than *Return of the Jedi.*

    When I went to see *E.T.* there wasn't a dry eye in the house. That cute little fellow just warmed everybody's heart in a way that no Wookie or Ewok ever could. Even though both movies came from basically the same movie producers, only *E.T.* really had what I call a true meaning. Everybody knew, I think, that Luke would eventually meet his father and win, somehow. On the other hand, the fate of *E.T.* was kept in mystery until the very end of the movie. I could not predict how it was going to end.

2. *Task:* to convince a reader to buy an American car instead of an import.

   Though the American car industry has suffered over the past decade by competition from abroad, there is no question that it has made a recovery and is making automobiles equal to or better than their foreign counterparts. All of the big three automakers are on the upswing and it is apparent from their new lines that they are ready to take on the American consumer full force. The cars are more economical to drive than ever. They are available in a wide variety of body styles and custom packages. Many of them also have an option for AM/FM cassette stereo. Now is the time to reconsider your choice of a foreign car. Try an American one, for a change.

3. *Task:* to explain the popularity of Michael Jackson.

   From the time he was five, Michael Jackson was destined to be a superstar. Looking at the early videotapes of his appearances with his four brothers, one can tell that he was talented and had that show-business "sense" that no one can teach you. His first solo effort, "Got to be There," went gold and his work with his brothers continued to bring him acclaim and income. As he entered the 80's and newer musical forms were coming into popularity, Michael Jackson did not play it safe. His album *Off the Wall* paved new ground in Black and rock-and-roll music. But his masterpiece was *Thriller*, the most innovative album since the Beatles' *Sgt. Pepper*. In it, Michael Jackson has captured the soul of the 80's, mellow, laid-back, and at peace. His videos demonstrate the same thing.

4. *Task:* to explain the main theme of the *Star Wars* saga.

   In *Star Wars*, Luke Skywalker is introduced as an innocent young boy. Although he has been raised by his uncle and aunt, he has never ceased to be curious about his father. Later in the series, when he discovers that his father is Darth Vader, one feels a sense of desperation in his heart. He becomes obsessed with confronting his father. He is not satisfied until he faces, and defeats him. And yet one is made to feel that when the battle is over, he feels remorse. When he finally redeems his father, one can see how his life was one long search for his own identity.

5.   *Task:* to explain the impact of baseball's free agent system on player salaries.

The free agent system began in 1975 when an arbitrator ruled that Andy Messersmith, then of the Los Angeles Dodgers, was a free agent because of a contract loophole. The ruling cleared the way for the overturning of baseball's old reserve system which, in effect, bound players to their teams for life, unless they were traded. This ruling set off a number of contract disputes as players began to seek greater freedom in their contracts. In order to bring some order into the chaos of litigation, the players union and the owners agreed to a free agent system in which, similar to the NFL draft, teams would select the available free agents in every calendar year and would try to sign the players that they drafted in competition with the other teams. This has been a bonanza for even the most mediocre players since this has escalated salaries nearly 200% since 1975. It is very lucrative for today's players in a position to enter the free agent market.

Writing Task

Review the rough draft you created for the assignment on page 161. Examine its frame of reference, starting with the opening paragraph. Rewrite any sections you find that lack a clear frame of reference or that contain an inappropriate structure.

Sharpening Focus

Focus is related to frame of reference in that once the writer has provided his reader with an adequate frame of reference, he can *focus* his text on the main topic more clearly. A *frame of reference* gives the reader boundaries for interpreting the information provided by qualifying generalizations; by identifying key personalities, terms, and concepts; and by supplying signals that explain how to proceed through the text. *Focus* signals the main topic in a given sentence, paragraph, or series of paragraphs. Sentences with clearly marked functions help the reader to understand a text more precisely. The effective use of demonstratives and pronouns, the repetition of key words or synonyms, and the use of signal words that identify the relationships *between* sentences, all help the writer achieve focus.

Focus is easier to illustrate than to define. Examine the first and second paragraphs of Frank Day's original draft about the Indians. Notice how ambiguous the main topic in Frank's second paragraph is.

Although many Indians fans are well aware of their team's distressing record in post-season play, most of them probably don't know why their team has failed so often. I do. I have made it part of my life's work to figure out the Indians' problems. It's not that when they get there that they don't do well. (Except for the 1954 World Series which I remember my dad talking about so much.) It's that they don't get there, period. Except for 1920, 1948, and 1954, the Indians have been to nary a post-season playoff. After the Cubs revival in 1984, I think Indians fans deserve the title for the longest suffering devotees to a team. This dismal record sends one looking for reasons.

1

[1]There are plenty. [2]You can start with the front office. [3]Always strapped for funds, the general manager of the team almost always had to settle for good-to-mediocre players since he couldn't entice any of the high-priced free agents to the join the Indians. [4]And even when he did, like Wayne Garland, the Indians got damaged goods. [5]Then there is the manager. [6]The Indians have almost as many managers as the Yankees have had in the last decade. [7]With so little stability, it's no wonder that the team never seems to know if it's headed up or down.

2

The second paragraph is confusing for several reasons. Sentence 1 is a weak transition from the preceding paragraph, which itself lacks a frame of reference. Sentence 2 slaps the reader in the face with a sudden shift in person: "You can . . . ." Sentence 3 begins a series of sentences that are filled with uninterpreted facts that are related to the thesis, but not explicitly; they are "reasons" for the Indians' failures. The final sentence attempts to summarize the paragraph, but provides an inadequate transition from this paragraph to the next.

This information needs to be refocused and rearranged to let the reader know the order of importance. Otherwise, the reader must guess how each of these factors is related to the others and which are the more important.

One can see Frank's thinking process at work in the paragraph: He is trying to document the first set of reasons for the Indians' failure. But there are two main ideas competing for the reader's attention: the Indians' front office and the frequent change in managers. The paragraph must be rewritten to clarify the focus.

Fortunately, as Frank rewrote his first paragraph, he created a frame of reference that suggested a way to rewrite the rest of the draft. Frank's plans for revising his rough draft included deleting paragraph 4 and splitting the second paragraph into two separate paragraphs, with a separate explanation of one distinct factor in the Indians' failures in each.

Here is Frank's rewriting of the first three paragraphs of his text.

1   One doesn't have to be an avid Cleveland Indians fan to be aware of their thirty-year failure to win a championship. Their last post-season appearance occurred in 1954, the year of the infamous World Series in which they lost all four games to the New York Giants after a record-breaking regular season. Until 1984, when the Chicago Cubs made the National League playoffs, Cubs fans were the most long-suffering of all baseball devotees. Now, however, Indians fans can surpass them in patience, perseverance and pain. The Indians' failure, nevertheless, is no mystery. If one looks a little deeper and analyzes the factors that contribute to their lack of success, it becomes apparent that their problems are threefold.

2   [1]The place to start in analyzing the Indians' dismal record is with the front office. [2]For more than three decades the Indians' upper management has been strapped for operating capital that might have allowed them to develop their minor league teams and dip into baseball's free agent market. [3]When a team cannot pay premium prices for rookie or veteran talent, it is destined to be uncompetitive with teams who can. [4]It is ironic that one of the few times in recent years that the Indians could afford one of the higher-priced free agents, the team landed hard-luck Wayne Garland, who found himself out of baseball within two years because of arm trouble.

3   [5]While the front office has been hard pressed to field a representative team because of funding problems, its attempt to turn its fortunes around with frequent managerial changes has been no more successful. [6]In recent years the Indians have had as many field generals as George Steinbrenner's New York Yankees, a team infamous for its "revolving door" of coaches, players and managers. [7]Such changes have only

confused players who get accustomed to one manager's style only to witness an abrupt shift in rules with a new regime. [8]Consequently, Indians' managerial replacements have only contributed to the lack of stability and consistency in team performance, one more nail in a coffin which has been shut tight on success for thirty years.

Once he had improved his opening paragraph, providing the reader with a frame of reference that would help her interpret the rest of the text, Frank could sharpen the focus of the following two paragraphs more easily. Specifically, this frame of reference helped him select the amount and kinds of information he wanted to develop in the remainder of the text. He used a threefold organizational pattern, focusing on funds, managerial changes, and the stadium.

Sentence 1 of the rewritten second paragraph provides a clear transition from the opening paragraph, orienting the reader by straightforwardly explaining where the analysis will begin. Sentence 2 clarifies the main topic of the paragraph, the Indians' lack of operating capital, and sentences 3 and 4 elaborate and exemplify this topic with specific examples and discuss the implications of the lack of operating capital.

In the third paragraph, the first sentence (5) again establishes a clear bridge to the previous discussion by repeating the key idea of the preceding paragraph. Sentence 6 explains what was a code expression, the New York Yankees, in the original. Sentences 7 and 8 round out the paragraph by interpreting the facts presented in sentences 5 and 6. Overall the reader does not have to guess what Frank's focus is in this section of his text.

Focus is thus achieved when the function of each sentence within an established frame of reference is clear to the reader. Revising for focus, then, involves a careful examination of each sentence. You must ask what the sentence is *doing* and how it relates to what comes *before* and *after*. Here are the major options one has in forming sentences. A sentence may:

1. Introduce a topic or notion
2. Limit or object to a preceding notion
3. Support or illustrate a preceding notion
4. Offer a question to be pursued in subsequent sentence(s)
5. Answer a question raised in preceding sentence(s)
6. Provide transition between sentences
7. Capsule the information in preceding sentences

Consider this base sentence and the writer's options:

EXAMPLE:
The Cleveland Indians have been consistently disappointing
as a team.

Possible follow-up sentences *to this base sentence* are:

2.   *Limit/object:* This disappointment is especially felt by their die-hard
fans.

3.   *Support/illustrate:* The Indians have only been in two World Series
in the past thirty-seven years.

4.   *Question:* How long can this torture continue?

5.   *Answer:* As long as management wastes money on inferior talent, one
presumes.

6.   *Transition:* Nevertheless, there is hope on the horizon.

7.   *Capsule of Previous Sentences:* And thus Detroit and Baltimore may
again rest easy this year as they contemplate the new season.

   If the function of each of your sentences is not clear to you at first
glance, you may use one or more of these strategies to revise them:

1.   Substitute a sentence whose function is more appropriate.

   EXAMPLE:
   [1]The Indians will need a back-up shortstop soon. [2]They
   already have a back-up third baseman.

   REVISION:
   [1]The Indians will need a back-up shortstop soon. [2]Their
   current shortstop is injury-prone.

The new second sentence provides effective elaboration of the first; the
previous second sentence bore no relationship to the first.

2.   Repeat key words or appropriate synonyms.

   EXAMPLE:
   [1]The cancer grows without abatement in the later stages.
   [2]The patient languishes in torment. [3]The end comes
   mercifully soon.

REVISION:

[1]The cancer grows without abatement in the later stages. [2]As *the disease* progresses, the patient languishes in torment. [3]The end of *this torment* comes mercifully soon.

3.   Effectively use pronouns and demonstratives (that, those, this, etc.).

EXAMPLE:

[1]Fabric softeners have come a long way in the past decade. [2]The clothes do get softer and fluffier. [3]The towels especially become less abrasive.

REVISION:

[1]Fabric softeners have come a long way in the past decade. [2]When *they* are used appropriately, one's clothes emerge from the wash softer and fluffier. [3]*These* additives are especially effective in making towels less abrasive.

4.   Supply signal words that make the relationship between sentences explicit. Possible relationships between sentences and some *signal words* that indicate them include the following:
   a.   *Contrast:* but, however, on the other hand, to the contrary
   b.   *Similarity:* likewise, similarly
   c.   *Consequence:* therefore, as a result, consequently, thus
   d.   *Emphasis:* indeed, equally important, in fact
   e.   *Restatement:* in other words, that is, to put it another way
   f.   *Elaboration:* and, again, also, in addition, further, too
   g.   *Sequence/time/location:* first, second. . . , finally, later, after this, formerly, at the same time, above, below, until now
   h.   *Summative:* in conclusion, in the final analysis, all in all

EXAMPLE:

[1]The London Symphony receives income from wealthy patrons of the arts. [2]The Philadelphia Orchestra receives income from business and industry.

REVISIONS:

[1]The London Symphony receives income from wealthy patrons of the arts. [2]*Similarly,* the Philadelphia Orchestra receives income from business and industry.

However, the Philadelphia Orchestra . . .
On the other hand, the Philadelphia Orchestra . . .
Indeed, the Philadelphia Orchestra . . .

Notice how Frank used all four of these strategies in his revision of paragraphs 2 and 3 of his text:

1. Substitution of sentence with more appropriate function; creates transition

2. Use of synonyms bridges the two sentences to help with cohesion

3. Repetition of key words

4. Effective use of pronoun

5. Repetition of key words

6. Signal word indicating consequence

[1]The place to start in analyzing the Indians' dismal record is with the front office.[1,2] [2]For more than three decades the Indians' upper management[2] has been strapped for operating capital that might have allowed them to develop their minor league teams and dip into baseball's free agent[3] market. [3]When a team cannot pay premium prices for rookie or veteran talent, it is destined to be uncompetitive with teams who can. [4]It is ironic that one of the few times in recent years that the Indians could afford one of the higher-priced free agents,[3] the team landed hard-luck Wayne Garland, who found himself out of baseball within two years because of arm trouble.

[5]While the front office[4] has been hard pressed to field a representative team because of funding problems, its[4] attempt to turn its fortunes around with frequent managerial[5] changes has been no more successful. [6]In recent years the Indians have had as many field generals as George Steinbrenner's New York Yankees, a team infamous for its "revolving door" of coaches, players and managers.[5] [7]Such changes have only confused players who get accustomed to one manager's[5] style only to witness an abrupt shift in rules with a new regime. [8]Consequently,[6] Indians' managerial[5] replacements have only contributed to the lack of stability and consistency in team performance, one more nail in a coffin which has been shut tight on success for thirty years.

Toward the end of this chapter you will find a final version of Frank's rough draft, in which you will see how he continued to revise at the text, sentence, and word levels.

Exercise

Read each of the following paragraphs carefully. Examine each sentence and determine its function in the paragraph. Which sentences provide a frame of reference or clearer focus to the paragraph? Write a brief analysis of each paragraph, identifying the features that help make the paragraph effective.

1. *Task:* commentary on the press censorship during the U.S. invasion of Grenada.

   [1]Was it a good idea to keep the press away during the first day? [2]It would appear to me that there are two reasonable positions on the question. [3]The first one would have press representatives saying: The safety of our reporters is our problem, not the Pentagon's, and if we choose to risk their lives that's our business, not theirs. [4]The second would have the Pentagon saying: Look that's all very well, but it is in the nature of things that our military would seek to provide protection for the press, and we simply do not want that kind of distraction. [5]Both points are defensible. [6]They do not draw a line between those who favor and those who oppose the First Amendment to the Constitution.*

2. *Task:* opening paragraph for an article exploring the reasons why video games have become popular without the use of sexually provocative graphics.

   [1]Anyone entering an arcade where pinball machines and video machines stand poised to swallow quarters will note an interesting contrast. [2]The pinball machine playing surfaces and backglasses are festooned with all manner of picturesque graphics while the video games are relatively modest in their decorations. [3]The contrast is especially noteworthy since the graphics on pinball machines—although a recent respectability has toned them down somewhat—frequently feature scenes which are sexually provocative. [4]Now this question may be asked: "Why are the pinball machines oversexed and the video machines celibate?" [5]If over the years sex has been successful in extracting nickels, dimes and quarters from mainly male pinball machine players, why not also for video games?**

*William F. Buckley, Jr., "On the Right," *National Review* 35 (1983): 1505.
**Sidney Kaplan and Shirley Kaplan, "Video Games, Sex, and Sex Differences," *Journal of Popular Culture* 17 (1983): 61.

3. *Task:* to explain the care-taking function of families.

[1]The care-taking function of parents begins to appear among animals somewhere around the level of spiders. [2]Few fish or reptiles, either male or female, go to any trouble over their offspring. [3]Most of the species in these groups lay large numbers of eggs and then leave them to fend for themselves. [4]However, as organisms become more complex, their offspring seem to be more dependent at birth and to need their parents' care for a longer period of time. [5]Just how this care is provided, though, varies greatly within classes of animals.*

Exercise

Read each of the following paragraphs carefully. Where necessary, revise them to provide the reader with a frame of reference and greater focus.

1. *Task:* to explain conflicting American positions on nuclear weapons.

Nuclear weaponry is not a subject easy to discuss. There are many positions on the issue. There are those who say that we should have no nuclear weapons whatsoever and call for disarmament. Then there are those who favor a freeze, but agree that we should have some nuclear weapons. Finally, there are those who say that a freeze cannot be verified and we should continue to make weapons because the Soviet Union will. The public hardly knows who to listen to since all spokespersons make their points enthusiastically and quote hard evidence. The issue will not go away.

2. *Task:* to establish that universities should let students devise their own degree programs.

After twelve years of public schooling, the university system ought to trust their students. Nevertheless, we come here and immediately we're told that we must take this course or that course, even if it is not something we are interested in. It is time for a revolution in the way college students get their degrees. We should be able to pick our own courses according to our own needs and career choices. Then we will see fewer drop-outs and less absenteeism in our classes.

*Virginia Stem Owens, *A Feast of Families* (Zondervan Publishing Co., 1983) 102.

3. *Task:* to convince a reader to choose his or her spouse carefully.

Even though many in our society think that marriage is outdated, people continue to marry—and divorce. The trouble is too many kids jump into marriage without preparation or counsel. And then again, most of them don't have a pastor or rabbi to talk to anymore since religion is on the downswing too. I think it is important that all of us be taught to choose our future spouses carefully. Too many of us have suffered the tragedy of divorce and separation in our parents' homes. If we could instruct people in how to choose a mate, the fabric of our society would be mended and we could once again look to a *united* state.

4. *Task:* to explain the popularity of the soap opera *General Hospital*.

Have you ever noticed that between 3:00 and 4:00 the campus is virtually deserted like a ghost town? Did you know that at drop/add you can usually add a class that starts at 2:30 or 3:30? Ask a girl who watches *General Hospital* why she blew off her 2:30 class and nine times out of ten she will tell you that she just "had to see *General Hospital*." Guys should know not to even bother to try to call a girl at 3:00. Either she won't be there or she'll be busy. *General Hospital* is the most popular soap opera on TV today. The reason why it is so popular is because of its many characters. The main characters may remind us of ourselves, someone we know, or they may be the type of person we wish we were like.

Writing Task

Review your rough draft from page 172, checking especially for focus problems. Rewrite any sections of your text in which the focus needs adjusting.

Voice, Stance, and Tone

Although some writer-based elements in rough drafts are the result of structural problems, others are more resistant to such cataloguing. Some of these belong in that vague catch-all category called *style*. The meaning of *style* is elusive. The style of a text includes, among other things, the writer's choice of voice, stance, and tone. In this section we want to survey some of the common features of each of these qualities.

Though we called voice, stance, and tone "choices," in some sense they are determined by the writer's intention as he drafts his text. The important thing for the apprentice writer is to find an appropriate voice, stance, and tone and to maintain them throughout the text. Sudden, inappropriate shifts in any of these qualities will confuse and annoy the reader and encourage her to dismiss the text.

VOICE

Voice is the "you" that you want to be manifested in the text. It may be the academic "you," which is detached and objective, usually but not always present in the text in the third person; or it may be the personal "you," less detached and less interested in presenting an "objective" face to the reader, present in the text as "I."

For most of your college writing tasks, the *academic* voice will be more appropriate. It is the voice you use to convey a sense of objectivity and deliberate neutrality in the presentation of information. Writing in this academic voice goes beyond avoiding the use of "I" and "me". It includes pruning attitude-laden words and drawing conclusions modestly, allowing the reader to be convinced by the facts presented.

The risk in using the academic voice is becoming too stuffy or too pompous in an attempt to maintain neutrality. The academic voice does not rule out the judicious use of "I." In particular, it is preferable to use the first person pronoun rather than trying to be coy, using such expressions as "this writer" or "we." Nor does the academic voice rule out vividness and liveliness. Its main function is to avoid casual intimacy that appeals to the reader on the basis of the writer's personal credentials or feelings.

When using the personal voice, on the other hand, the writer does not try to minimize the effect of his personality; indeed, he implies at each juncture that he is drawing on personal experience and observation for the information he is conveying. It is not that the academic voice is used for "serious, objective" purposes, and the personal voice for "frivolous, subjective" ones. Rather, the choice of voice depends on the writer's familiarity with his audience, the level of detachment he wishes to maintain, and the overall effect he wants his prose to project. Usually one will be more appropriate than the other. Here are a few examples.

1.   Complaint Letter

ACADEMIC VOICE:

The stereo arrived safely Tuesday morning. However, after it
was unpacked, it became apparent that both the speed control
and the anti-skating devices were defective. Please forward a
replacement for this model as soon as possible.

PERSONAL VOICE:

When I opened my stereo box Tuesday morning I was really
excited. But my excitement dwindled when I realized that the
speed control and anti-skating devices were broken. I would
like you to send me another one immediately.

2.   Exposition

ACADEMIC VOICE:

The Baskilic tribe of western Greenland shares with its
eastern neighbors a penchant for cooked goose. Many of the
Baskilic feasts are centered around the ceremonial
defeathering and preparation of the goose, including the
Baskilic equivalent of Thanksgiving, Qualonah. The only
major holiday among the Baskilics which is not celebrated by
the cooking of a goose is Ghetanjay, a solemn and tranquil
day in which no animal flesh is eaten.

PERSONAL VOICE:

I found the most interesting cultural fact about the Baskilics
to be their enthusiasm for cooked goose. I noticed that many
of their holy days centered around the preparation of this
feathered creature, save one: Ghetanjay. Unfortunately,
during the week I spent with the Baskilics, none of their
boisterous feast days was on the calendar. I plan to go back
someday.

3.   Argument

ACADEMIC VOICE:

It will better serve the interests of this university if the
current president resigns and the Board of Regents begins an

immediate search for a replacement. The faculty has nothing to gain by delaying this unpleasant task, and neither has the current president any grounds for seeking to remain in his position.

PERSONAL VOICE:

I believe that the best course of action, given the president's clear violation of the charter, is to call for his resignation and to seek an immediate replacement. He has consistently demonstrated to me and to others that he has his own interests, and not the faculty's, at heart. I urge him to resign within the week.

STANCE

Stance is the posture a writer takes in his text: either forthright, in which case the writer intends the text to be taken at face value, or ironic, in which case a writer intends the text to be taken in a manner opposite to or different from what its surface meaning would imply.

In most of your texts, your stance will be forthright—that is, you will ask your reader to take your text as a whole seriously and not ironically. Though ironic elements may have a place in your text, maintaining an ironic stance throughout a text is most difficult. To be effective, irony must be handled with a light touch, or it quickly grates on the reader and becomes burdensome. Irony undercuts the surface message of a text, saying one thing but meaning another. Here is an illustration of both kinds of stance:

FORTHRIGHT:

The play opened with a dreadful monologue which compared life to a rolling sea—one of the oldest clichés known to man. This beginning was unfortunately representative of the entire play, and many of the theatre-goers left at intermission.

IRONIC:

A play opened last night which is destined to go down in theatrical history. So startling was its opening monologue, so compelling was its theme and characterization that half the audience left at intermission.

TONE

Tone is the mood the writer wishes to project to the reader. One may speak of the tone of a text in such terms as matter-of-fact, neutral, clever, sensitive, shrill, relaxed, playful, somber, arrogant, mocking, facetious, and many others. Tone is a subtle quality, a function of both voice and stance, and of the writer's word choice. Here is an example of a "matter-of-fact" tone, followed by one which might be labeled "agitated."

> MATTER-OF-FACT:
>
> The President today announced that he would veto House Bill 3056, better known as the Consumer Housing Bill. He explained that he agreed with the spirit of the bill, but felt that it would be an inflationary measure which would eventually hurt, not help, the American consumer.

Here the tone is dispassionate and moderate.

> AGITATED:
>
> Our *tight-fisted* President *killed* another bill today that would have helped the American home buyer secure reasonable interest rates for the first time in a decade. This is just one in a series of *high-handed* rejections of legislation which would remove the burden from the middle-class and place it on the backs of the wealthy. When are the people of this nation going to *wise up?*

Italicized words indicate word choices that affect the *tone* of the text, expressing the writer's agitation.

REVISING VOICE, STANCE, AND TONE

To revise the voice, stance, and tone of a text, the writer must revise for *appropriateness* and *consistency*. Each of these qualities is controlled by such factors as the writer's intention in writing the text, his perception of the audience, and the mode of development being employed. Further, much of the substance of these textual qualities comes from the writer's *word choice*. Chapter 12 will discuss formal versus informal word choice and the appropriate contexts for each.

It is impossible to provide a list of rules that will direct your choices in these matters. You may have been solemnly warned never to use "I" in your text, and certainly never to address the reader as "you." But there may be a reason to do both, *if* your writing task and intention call for it. When James Beard, a famous chef, writes a cookbook, his audience expects a personal voice, even in giving mundane directions. Likewise, referring to the reader as "you" is perfectly legitimate in an argumentative text that directly calls for some sort of immediate action. Like many elements of the writing process, these choices depend on others.

Generally speaking, though, you will use the academic voice and forthright stance for most of your college writing tasks. The tone will vary, depending upon the intention of your text. You should use the personal voice for any task in which your personal involvement is itself a relevant factor, or for any personal narrative.

Apprentice writers seem to have the most difficulty in mastering the academic voice. They confuse it with mere verbosity or pretentiousness. The important thing to ask is: what voice, stance, and tone *best serve* my intention in writing and the ultimate response I wish to evoke in my reader? Does my audience merely want my opinion, or does it want something more objective and dispassionate? Is my audience interested in what I have to say because *I* am saying it, or because the issue or information is relevant to them? Will my choices unnecessarily alienate my audience, causing them to reject my text? What kind of text is my audience expecting, given my topic, thesis, and intention? If you are in doubt about the appropriateness of the personal voice, use the academic voice.

Exercise

Examine again these two versions of Frank Day's opening paragraphs of his Indians text, and answer the following questions: What kind of "voice" does Frank use in the original version? Is it consistent throughout the text? What stance and tone does he establish in the original? What changes has he made in voice, stance, and tone in the second version of paragraphs 1 to 3? How would you advise him to revise the remaining paragraphs (4 and 5) in his original?

ORIGINAL	REVISED
1 Although many Indians fans are well aware of their team's distressing record in post-season play, most of them probably don't know why their team has failed	1 One doesn't have to be an avid Cleveland Indians fan to be aware of their thirty-year failure to win a championship. Their last post-season appearance occurred in

ORIGINAL

so often. I do. I have made it part of my life's work to figure out the Indians' problems. It's not that when they get there that they don't do well. (Except for the 1954 World Series which I remember my dad talking about so much.) It's that they don't get there, period. Except for 1920, 1948 and 1954, the Indians have been to nary a post-season playoff. After the Cubs revival in 1984, I think Indians fans deserve the title for the longest suffering devotees to a team. This dismal record sends one looking for reasons.

2   There are plenty. You can start with the front office. Always strapped for funds, the general manager of the team almost always had to settle for good-to-mediocre players since he couldn't entice any of the high-priced free agents to the join the Indians. And even when he did, like Wayne Garland, the Indians got damaged goods. Then there is the manager. The Indians have almost as many managers as the Yankees have had in the last decade. With so little stability, it's no wonder that the team never seems to know if it's headed up or down.

3   Of course, playing at Municipal Stadium is no treat either. When the cold winds blow off the lake, it not only makes the players cold, it chills fan interest con-

REVISED

1954, the year of the infamous World Series in which they lost all four games to the New York Giants after a record-breaking regular season. Until 1984, when the Chicago Cubs made the National League playoffs, Cubs fans were the most longsuffering of all baseball devotees. Now, however, Indians fans can surpass them in patience, perseverance and pain. The Indians failure, nevertheless, is no mystery. If one looks a little deeper and analyzes the factors that contribute to their lack of success, it becomes apparent that their problems are threefold.

2   The place to start in analyzing the Indians' dismal record is with the front office. For more than three decades the Indians' upper management has been strapped for operating capital that might have allowed them to develop their minor league teams and dip into baseball's free agent market. When a team cannot pay premium prices for rookie or veteran talent, it is destined to be uncompetitive with teams who can. It is ironic that one of the few times in recent years that the Indians could afford one of the higher-priced free agents, it landed hard-luck Wayne Garland, who found himself out of baseball within two years because of arm trouble.

3   While the front office has been hard pressed to field a representative team because of funding problems, its attempt to turn its fortunes

ORIGINAL

siderably. The only park worse for the fans must be Candlestick Park.

4   With limited funds, few quality players, a disappointing stadium, it is only justice that the Indians fans also get some of the most opinionated and negative sportswriters. Whenever the Indians do something right, the press is there to say it's a fluke. When they get caught in one of their annual losing streaks, then it's the press's turn to say "I told you so." It's no wonder that few players want to play in Cleveland.

5   But I remain a diehard Indians fan anyway. Despite all the problems, something about old Chief Wahoo brings tears to my eyes and reminds me of summer nights long ago, listening to Rocky Colavito, John Romano, and Sudden Sam McDowell do battle against the forces of evil in the American League. If the Indians ever do become a winner, I'll be the first to buy season tickets. In the meantime, I'll stick by them through thick and thin. Until then rooting for the Indians is a neverending story.

REVISED

around with frequent managerial changes has been no more successful. In recent years the Indians have had as many field generals as George Steinbrenner's New York Yankees, a team infamous for its "revolving door" of coaches, players and managers. Such changes have only confused players who get accustomed to one manager's style only to witness an abrupt shift in rules with a new regime. Consequently, Indians' managerial replacements have only contributed to the lack of stability and consistency in team performance, one more nail in a coffin which has been shut tight on success for thirty years.

Exercise

Examine each of the following paragraphs. Given the writing task, how appropriate is the writer's voice, stance, and tone? For each paragraph, write a brief analysis that critiques these elements and, where necessary, offers suggestions for revision.

1.   *Task:* to convince an audience of 18-year-olds that revising the drinking laws to allow only 20-year-olds to buy beer is a trivial issue.

   I remember when I was 17. The only thing I thought of was how important it was to get to 18—so I could buy my first six-pack. By the time I got to 18, however, that "license" to buy alcohol paled in importance to the other responsibilities being foisted upon me. Off on my own at college, in pursuit of an engineering degree, I found that there were more pressing issues and problems in the world than whether I could purchase a few intoxicants. Now that I am 21 and I look back on those years, I realize that being able to buy beer was not a major factor in my maturity and responsibility.

2.   *Task:* to explain how to purchase license tags.

   The first step in buying auto license tags is to find the stupid county office that sells them. That's a job in itself. When you do find it, you'll discover that there are a whole bunch of papers you need to have that you probably lost or forgot to bring. These include a registration for the car, your driver's license, and the title to the car. I don't know why they need to look at these things every year, but they do. Then, there's the waiting in line for two hours. So plan to miss your lunch and a few hours at the assembly line. Once you get them, it's one more thing not to worry about for another year.

3.   *Task:* to vent one's exasperation at the etiquette of some people.

   I am convinced that some people could do themselves a favor by taking some walking lessons. Walking lessons? Certainly! How many times have you entered a hallway, eyeing the errant steps of a person somnambulating toward you, aware that you have the right-of-way, but also knowing that you're the one who'll have to yield? You've seen the kind I mean. She's oblivious to your presence; she owns the whole darn hallway; she walks with her feet, not her eyes; in short, she needs elementary instruction in the common courtesies of entering buildings, navigating hallways, and negotiating staircases. Walking lessons. If you need them, call me at 555-8765; my remedial course begins Monday.

4.   *Task:* to tell a story about one's grandfather to illustrate his tenderness with small children.

The grandfather is a wonderful piece of work, a marvelous invention. One can always depend on a grandfather to have pockets full of small treasures: a whittling stick, a candy cane, a whistle, an old key. One wonders where they get their patience. Lord knows most of us lose ours early on at the first sign of childishness in a kid. But there he is, the grandfather, hour after hour, weaving a spell that will last a lifetime in the hearts of the little ones. Whatever makes the grandfather tick at 70 ought to be patented and available at 45.

5.   *Task:* to describe the crowd at a college basketball game for a metropolitan newspaper.

The thunder began in the second half with 5:43 left in the game, as the cheerleaders whipped the crowd into a frenzy. The lightning came later—when the Blue Devils rallied from a 10-point deficit with 34 seconds to go. No one in the arena had ever seen, of course, a 10-point-rally-with-34-seconds-left before, and one could tell the place was going to explode. Explode it did. When Grayson's shot ripped the nets for a 65-64 miracle victory, all 6789 Blue Devil fans swarmed to the court. If there had been any goalposts to tear down, they would have been quickly demolished. As it was, the scorer's table, the usual barrier between boisterous fans and their beloved team, was trampled over, smashed, and its pieces distributed as the spoils of victory to the exuberant crowd.

Writing Task

Examine your rough draft again, this time focusing on voice, tone, and stance. If any of these are inappropriate, rewrite your text, using your intention as your overall guide.

Revising Sentence Form

In revising a rough draft, you must devote some attention to the sentence and word levels, as well as the text structure. In this section, we will introduce you to elements of sentence structure that will help you make your rough draft more reader-based.

Ineffective sentences, as opposed to sentences that contain *errors*, make your reader work too hard in understanding and interpreting the information they present. Such sentences may be (1) *convoluted* sentences, which are indirect or excessively passive, or which camouflage the true subject/actor and verb/action of a sentence; (2) *ambiguous* sentences, which can mean more than one thing; or (3) *verbose* sentences, which use more words than necessary, needlessly repeating what has already been said. In this section we will deal primarily with *convoluted* sentences and ways to revise them. Sections in Chapter 11 (pp. 401–447) will help you revise ambiguous and wordy sentences.

Convoluted Sentences

The writer has packed the following sentence full of information he plans to sort out later:

> In regard to the Cleveland Indians player salaries, and in addition to the poor management of the past, the fact is, no major star has yet consented to accept any of their offers.

The writer knows what he wants to say here, but he has not taken the time to clean the sentence up, preferring instead to get on with the development of his text. If he does not return to this sentence, however, the reader will get lost in the forest of unprocessed ideas it contains. A revision might sort out the problems in the sentence this way:

> Given the low salaries of Cleveland Indian players and their poor managerial record of the past thirty years, it is no wonder that no major stars have agreed to sign with them.

Convoluted sentences like this one are puzzles that writers unintentionally present to their readers. Though there are many sources of convolution in sentences, most have one structural problem in common: they force the reader to look too hard for the *subject* and *action* of the sentence, thus blunting its force and directness. Here are some sample convoluted structures.

OVERNOMINALIZED STRUCTURE

Some writers store the *action* of their sentences in *nominalizations,* that is, nouns derived from verbs or adjectives. Here are some sample nominalizations:

VERB/NOMINALIZATION	ADJECTIVE/NOMINALIZATION
investigate/investigation	equal/equality
resist/resistance	careful/carefulness
analyze/analysis	intelligent/intelligence
prepare/preparation	difficult/difficulty

There are many occasions when nominalizations are helpful in sentences, for instance, when the nominalization is the subject and refers to a previous sentence: "The faculty voted overwhelmingly to support an early retirement system. This *decision* will affect the annual budget considerably." The problem comes when a writer consistently strings such nominalizations together. The effect is to make the sentences more abstract and less direct— and, usually, more wordy:

1.   A *need* for a *reevaluation* of the organization exists.
2.   There is an *expectation* that the *submission* will meet the deadline.
3.   The *appearance* of the team before the court is a *necessity*.

Revising Overnominalized Structures   Revision of overnominalized structures involves locating (1) the true *action* of the sentence and (2) the true *subject*. That is, look at your sentence and determine *who* or *what* is actually participating in or causing the *action* of the sentence. The subject—or *agent*, the entity responsible for the action—and the action may be buried in a nominalization, as in our three previous examples. Here is how they might be revised:

1.   *We need* to *reevaluate* the organization.
2.   *The governor expects* the submission to meet the deadline.
3.   *The team must appear* before the court.

In each case, in the revision the true subject has been located or supplied, and the true action has been made the verb of the sentence.

EXCESSIVELY PASSIVE STRUCTURE

Another troublesome sentence pattern is the excessively passive structure, a structure that employs an inordinate number of "to be" verbs, such as *is/are, was/were*. Like nominalization, passive constructions tend to blunt the directness and force of sentences by hiding the agent and action. Passive structure also tends to be more wordy. Still, there are some effective uses of the passive that should be mentioned. The passive is appropriate when the *agent* of an action is irrelevant: "When a gymnasium *is adequately air-conditioned*, the crowd will be comfortable." In addition, the passive is helpful when a writer is intentionally avoiding naming an agent: "A number of items *have been stolen* lately, and a few more *were taken* this morning."

The problem with excessive use of the passive is that it consistently deemphasizes the *agent*, whoever or whatever is responsible for the action of the sentence, by placing it after the verb:

ACTIVE:

AGENT/GRAMMATICAL SUBJECT
   Jack hit the ball.
AGENT/GRAMMATICAL SUBJECT
   The committee ratified the agreement.
AGENT/GRAMMATICAL SUBJECT
   We found the evidence inadequate to convict her.

PASSIVE:

GRAMMATICAL SUBJECT   AGENT
   The ball was hit by Jack.
GRAMMATICAL SUBJECT   AGENT
   The agreement was ratified by the committee.
GRAMMATICAL SUBJECT   AGENT
   The evidence was found by us to be inadequate to convict her.

When it is used throughout a text, the passive forces the reader to work overtime to find out what is *happening*. When passive structure is combined with nominalizations, the stultifying vagueness and density of the resulting sentences prevents the reader from easily understanding your point, as in these examples:

1. The application rejection was accomplished because its acceptance would become problematic for the organization.

2. The information was presented by the national group in order to preserve the insulation of the value system.

3. The assessment of the patient's mobility was delayed by the medical board until permission could be granted by the patient's parental guardians.

Revising Excessively Passive Structures Like revision of overnominalized structures, the revision of passive structures involves determining the true *agent* and *action* of each sentence and making them the subject and verb, respectively, of the sentence, as in these revisions of the above examples:

1. The organization rejected the application, since it would cause more problems than it would solve.

2. The national group presented the information in order to insulate their values.

3. The medical board delayed their assessment of the patient's mobility until his guardians gave their permission.

COMPOUND NOUN STRUCTURES

A third source of convoluted sentences is the compound noun phrase, a structure that strings together nouns as adjectives. Such a structure usually employs nominalizations and abstract nouns, each of which blunts the writer's meaning, as in these examples:

1. Early *childhood mobility impairment* often limits a child's participation in physical activity during the early grades.

2. *Software utilization facilitation* is of concern to programmers at Wetco Industries.

Revising Compound Noun Structures As with other convoluted, indirect sentences, the revision of compound noun structures involves, primarily, determining the *agent* and the *action* of the sentence and making them the subject and verb. Then: (1) each compound noun structure must be examined to determine which nouns are being used as adjectives; (2) each compound noun phrase must be "unpacked" by converting nominalizations into other parts of speech or grammatical structures, such as verbs or prepositional phrases; and (3) these new structures should be redistributed throughout the "new" sentence:

AGENT/GRAMMATICAL SUBJECT   *ACTION/VERB*
   A child whose mobility is impaired in early childhood *may*
   participate in physical activity very little in the early grades.
AGENT/GRAMMATICAL SUBJECT   *ACTION/VERB*
   The programmers at Wetco Industries *design* software that is
   easy to use.

All three of these forms of convoluted, indirect sentence structure make the reader work too hard. If a writer can maintain an active sentence structure, one that makes the true agent of the sentence the subject and uses action verbs in the predicate, most of these problems will take care of themselves.

Exercise

Rewrite each of these sentences as needed to avoid overnominalization, excessive use of the passive voice, and compound noun phrases.

1. There was uneasiness among the team's coaches over the result of the final three games.
2. The performance of the investigation by the detectives in the crime most recently occurred with little fanfare.
3. Agreement as to the need of future revisions in the state budget was reached by the two negotiation education development teams.
4. Based on extensive training needs assessment review, there was the identification of the main topics of discussion to be offered to the board at the following meeting.
5. It is the belief of the committee that the true social ramifications of the housing depreciation ordinance bill by the city council will not be understood until the formation of a neutral evaluation structure committee has occurred.

Writing Task

Examine your rough draft carefully at the sentence level, noting any problem sentences and rewriting them using the strategies discussed in this section.

Revising Word Choice

Even a rough draft that is on the way to becoming a final draft may contain a few code words. As discussed in Chapter 4, code words often stand for a number of concepts, ideas, or attitudes that a writer wishes to express, but that are inaccessible to the reader. In this chapter we are limiting our discussion of word choice to revising code words. Other problems, such as informal/formal diction and unclear pronoun referents, are dealt with in Chapters 12 and 13.

Code Words

As we noted in Chapter 4, code words are typically vague. They reflect a writer's private meaning, which a reader unacquainted with the writer's vocabulary would never guess. The question for a writer is how to *recognize* code words in his own text. A writer who uses code words as a strategy in drafting a text will naturally return to these words, developing and defining them before the text reaches his readers. On the other hand, every writer must be careful not to overlook words that may mislead or confuse the reader if used inappropriately. Here are a few reading strategies to uncover code words in a rough draft:

1.   Look at any words in your text that seem conceptually complex. Are you certain how you are using each term? Have you made this clear to your *reader* in each case?

2.   Look at words that are essential or closely related to the topic being developed. Are you using any "carry-alls" for ideas and concepts that you have not yet defined or articulated fully, either for yourself or for the reader?

3.   Look at recurring words, especially those that express an attitude or judgment on your topic. Have you given your reader a definition or illustrated what you mean by a term with appropriate examples that would clarify its meaning in your text?

4.   Look at any technical or jargon words in your text, especially any word(s) that you suspect have a *more specific and narrow meaning* than you intended in your text. Consider the kind of text you are writing and, as always, your *intention*. How do these words fit with your goals in the text? Are they *precise* enough? Do they *hide* or *reveal* what you hope to communicate to the reader?

5.   Look at any words that are used frequently and that seem to *change*

meaning over the course of your text, meaning one thing at the beginning, something else in the body of the text, and still something else in the conclusion. Unless your intention is actually to discuss the evolution of a word or concept, and it is germane to your argument to survey the word's various meanings, a *shifting meaning* for a word may indicate that it is a code word.

Code words are useful in the early stages of drafting a text. However, if they remain in the final draft, they only alienate and perplex the reader, who must ask, "But what do you mean by _____?"

The key to revising code words is, of course, being able to recognize them. Once you are convinced that you have used a code word in your text, you may employ one or more of the following strategies:

1. *Replace the word* with another word or phrase that expresses your meaning more clearly.

> EXAMPLE:
> I was really *naive* when I got to high school.

> REVISED:
> I was really *afraid of women* when I got to high school.

2. Leave the word in place, but *define it* or *illustrate it* with examples that convey the meaning you intend.

> EXAMPLE:
> The *Star Wars* trilogy was very *eastern* in concept.

> REVISED:
> The *Star Wars* trilogy was very *eastern* in concept; that is, *it presented good and evil as opposite ends of the same pole, unlike the western view which sees good and evil as absolutely distinct and irreconcilable.*

> EXAMPLE:
> Our homecoming game was *different.*

> REVISED:
> Our homecoming game was *different, considering that the snowstorm spoiled our gala halftime show, kept the crowd down to 400 spectators, and allowed East Tech to tie us 0–0.*

3.   *Maintain consistency* in your text by using a word in *one, unequivocal fashion* in your discussion, unless you explain to your reader why you may be shifting the word's meaning.

> Example:
>
> The most *clever* athlete I have ever seen is Walter Payton of the Chicago Bears. He just seems to know what holes to pick when he heads to the line of scrimmage. Talent, not *cleverness,* is the reason for his success and no one has quite matched his success in the past five years. You can't coach *cleverness* or talent. It's just there. And Walter has it.

> Revised:
>
> The most *talented* athlete I have ever seen is Walter Payton of the Chicago Bears. He just seems to know what holes to pick when he heads to the line of scrimmage. A running back needs more than *cleverness* to be successful in the NFL, and Walter Payton has proven that his *talent* is more than mere trickery. His quickness and endurance cannot be "coached"; an athlete either has them or he doesn't. Walter does.

Exercise

Below is Frank Day's original draft. Circle any code expressions you find, and explain to Frank why you think each of these is a code word and how he might rewrite it to avoid ambiguity.

Indians Fans and the Neverending Story
Frank Day

1   Although many Indians fans are well aware of their team's distressing record in post-season play, most of them probably don't know why their team has failed so often. I do. I have made it part of my life's work to figure out the Indians' problems. It's not that when they get there that they don't do well. (Except for the 1954 World Series which I remember my dad talking about so much.) It's that they don't get there, period. Except for 1920, 1948 and 1954, the Indians have been to nary a post-season playoff. After the Cubs revival in 1984, I think Indians fans deserve the title

for the longest suffering devotees to a team. This dismal record sends one looking for reasons.

There are plenty. You can start with the front office. Always strapped for funds, the general manager of the team almost always had to settle for good-to-mediocre players since he couldn't entice any of the high-priced free agents to the join the Indians. And even when he did, like Wayne Garland, the Indians got damaged goods. Then there is the manager. The Indians have almost as many managers as the Yankees have had in the last decade. With so little stability, it's no wonder that the team never seems to know if it's headed up or down.   2

Of course, playing at Municipal Stadium is no treat either. When the cold winds blow off the lake, it not only makes the players cold, it chills fan interest considerably. The only park worse for the fans must be Candlestick Park.   3

With limited funds, few quality players, a disappointing stadium, it is only justice that the Indians fans also get some of the most opinionated and negative sportswriters. Whenever the Indians do something right, the press is there to say it's a fluke. When they get caught in one of their annual losing streaks, then it's the press's turn to say "I told you so." It's no wonder that few players want to play in Cleveland.   4

But I remain a diehard Indians fan anyway. Despite all the problems, something about old Chief Wahoo brings tears to my eyes and reminds me of summer nights long ago, listening to Rocky Colavito, John Romano, and Sudden Sam McDowell do battle against the forces of evil in the American League. If the Indians ever do become a winner, I'll be the first to buy season tickets. In the meantime, I'll stick by them through thick and thin. Until then rooting for the Indians is a neverending story.   5

Exercise

Locate any code words in the following sentences and use an appropriate strategy to revise them and make them accessible to a reader.

1. *Gone with the Wind* is really an interesting movie.

2. In my day, a guy only invited someone very special to his senior prom.

3. The problem at the recital was that none of the musicians could really play their instruments.

4. There is no question that the team has been unsuccessful because of its individualistic style of play.

5.   Unless the Soviet Union, China, and the United States negotiate, we will all be the losers.

6.   Her laugh is quite unique.

7.   My teacher always complained about my writing style. I happen to think that my style is very good and I don't intend to change it.

8.   I don't like to read fantasy novels because they aren't scientific enough to suit my tastes.

9.   Certain TV shows, like *Three's Company* and *Saturday Night Live*, should be banned because they are immoral.

10.   At first I didn't like all the robots and gadgets in science-fiction novels, but now I read them voraciously. One can learn so much in science-fiction novels that other kinds of realistic books don't usually present. Science fiction has its own kind of realism and it speaks to us just as truly about the present as it does the future.

Writing Task

Check your rough draft for code words or expressions that may mislead or confuse the reader. Use the strategies discussed in this chapter to revise it.

Revising Rough Drafts

As you have seen, to revise a rough draft, you must first *analyze* it at the text, sentence, and word levels to determine whether and to what extent it reflects your intention, then *rewrite* it until it ably communicates that intention.

The preceding pages have given both strategies for spotting writer-based elements in rough drafts and strategies for revising and rewriting them once you have discovered them. The following exercises are designed to give you practice at working with all three levels of a text. As you work through these exercises, continue to revise your own draft(s), using the strategies you have learned in this chapter.

Exercise

Here is Frank Day's final draft of his text about the Indians. As you read through this draft, compare it with the original version and his plan for revision (page 157). Carefully note places where Frank has specifically used the operations of adding, deleting, substituting, and rearranging. How successful has Frank been in making his text more reader-based? What features, specifically, has he changed at the text, sentence, and word levels? Write Frank a note telling him what you think the strengths and weaknesses of his draft are, making suggestions for any rewriting or editing you would perform before giving it to a third reader.

Indians Fans and the Neverending Story
Frank Day

One doesn't have to be an avid Cleveland Indians fan to be aware of   1
their thirty-year failure to win a championship. Their last post-season appearance occurred in 1954, the year of the infamous World Series in which they lost all four games to the New York Giants after a record-breaking regular season. Until 1984, when the Chicago Cubs made the National League playoffs, Cubs fans were the most longsuffering of all baseball devotees. Now, however, Indians fans can surpass them in patience, perseverance, and pain. The Indians' failure, nevertheless, is no mystery. If one looks a little deeper and analyzes the factors that contribute to their lack of success, it becomes apparent that their problems are threefold.

The place to start in analyzing the Indians' dismal record is with the front office. For more than three decades the Indians' upper management has been strapped for operating capital that might have allowed them to develop their minor league teams and dip into baseball's free agent market. When a team cannot pay premium prices for rookie or veteran talent, it is destined to be uncompetitive with teams who can. It is ironic that one of the few times in recent years that the Indians could afford one of the higher-priced free agents, the team landed hard-luck Wayne Garland, who found himself out of baseball within two years because of arm trouble.

While the front office has been hard pressed to field a representative   2
team because of funding problems, its attempt to turn its fortunes around with frequent managerial changes has been no more successful. In recent years the Indians have had as many field generals as George Steinbrenner's New York Yankees, a team infamous for its "revolving door" of coaches,

players, and managers. Such changes have only confused players who get accustomed to one manager's style only to witness an abrupt shift in rules with a new regime. Consequently, the Indians' managerial replacements have only contributed to the lack of stability and consistency in team performance, one more nail in a coffin which has been shut tight on success for thirty years.

3   With limited upper management and handicapped field management, the final blow to the team's chances for success comes on the playing field itself. Major league teams play a minimum of 81 games in their home parks and for the Indians that means 81 games played on generally wet ground in a giant air conditioner called Cleveland Municipal Stadium. When the air blows off Lake Erie into the summer Cleveland night, players and fans alike are chilled. There is probably no more unpleasant place to play baseball than in this stadium—unless it is San Francisco's Candlestick Park, a stadium where fans have been literally awarded medallions of achievement for making it through a night game. When baseball players, even professionals, anticipate playing half of their games on an inadequate surface in frozen conditions, it is no wonder that their enthusiasm can be dulled. The risk of injury is simply too great. The fans can hardly be expected to attend en masse and cheer vigorously in such conditions.

4   But most of us remain diehard Indians fans anyway. Despite all the problems, something about old Chief Wahoo, the Indians' mascot, brings tears to our eyes, reminding us of summer nights long ago, listening on the radio to legendary Indians Rocky Colavito, John Romano, and Sudden Sam McDowell do battle against the forces of evil in the American League. If the Indians ever do become a winner—despite all the obstacles—we'll be the first to buy playoff and season tickets. In the meantime, Indians fans can only dream. Rooting for the Indians is a neverending story. Only a Cubs fan can really understand it.

Exercise

The following rough draft purports to be an expository text designed to help parents of college freshmen help their children adjust to college life and to be more supportive of them when they run into difficulties. Examine its text structure, sentence form, and word choice for writer-based features. Write the writer a note explaining what you think needs to be done to this text at the text, sentence, and word levels to revise and rewrite it.

A Guide for Parents of College Freshmen

A college freshman must learn to change and adapt to being away from home for the first time. The student no longer has his parents around to guide him; therefore, he must make his own decisions, set his own goals, and fulfill his own responsibilities. Likewise, the parents must be able to understand and sympathize with their child and be of help when needed. 1

As a freshman at Big State University, I left my home obtaining an education for starting a career. I was excited, yet scared about the changes I knew I would encounter. One thing that scared me was leaving a school of 2000 students for a university of 50,000 people. In this group of 50,000, there are a variety of races, ages, and personalities, whereas in high school everybody was basically the same age and had similar interests. I was scared to know I was younger than so many people and that my personality and interests would clash with many other people on campus. I made several adjustments which involved being away from my parents and their supervision. For example, I had to develop new study habits on my own, which were different from my high school habits. My courses required much more studying than I was used to, which forced me to change my old habits and form new ones. I started going to the library, using highlighter pens for reading, and devoting many more hours to preparing for exams. Another adjustment I made was learning to budget my money. I have had a checking account for two years, which has given me some background on handling money. However, I am limited to a monthly allowance, which forces me to cut out many things I could buy while living at home. For example, I can no longer go shopping and buy everything I want; I must be careful in choosing how I spend my money. Another change I faced was not having my parents here to enforce a curfew, so I had to learn when I needed to come home and get enough sleep to function the next day. For example, I try to be in around eleven on weekdays, and on weekends, around two depending on what I am doing. Without my parents around, I have no one to "make" me do anything; therefore, I must motivate myself and use my best judgment. I have been forced to become a more independent and responsible person by being away from my parents. 2

The hardest change I made when coming to college was adjusting to a dorm and a roommate. At home, I've always had my own room, which gave me plenty of privacy from my sisters. I had access to a kitchen, living room, and a backyard. I chose to let the university assign my roommate at random by what they call "pot luck." I like my roommate real well, and I'm lucky that we get along better than many "pot luck" roommates. Other 3 girls in our all girls dorm are constantly coming to us complaining about stereos and phone calls while trying to study. My roommate and I are very considerate of each other and never seem to have too many problems.

4   As parents, you need to be aware of the changes your child will go through. There are adjustments you must make as your child is becoming an adult. For example, allow your child to come to you for advice when he needs it. My parents are always willing to help me and offer advice when I call them long distance. A weekly phone call is helpful in letting them know how I am because I know they are interested to hear of my experiences while growing up and becoming an adult. You must realize that your child is growing away from you seeking independence and responsibility. As parents, let your child know that you are willing to lend a helping hand and try to understand the changes he is going through.

5   I like college very much and have looked forward to coming to Big State University for two years. These are my experiences of adjustments I have made as a college freshman away from home and many freshmen will face changes similar to mine. I hope you, as parents, will sympathize with your child now that you are aware of some typical changes a freshman encounters. The best help to your child is just letting him know that you really care.

Writing Assignment

Think of a "guide to" text that would be especially helpful to a new college student on your campus, for instance, "A Guide to Cafeteria Food at Fairfax State College: Warnings and Admonitions." Such a guide might be written tongue-in-cheek, but would still provide the incoming student with valuable information. Work through an initial inventing period, brainstorming and treeing possible topics and intentions. Then, using more structured inventing strategies like the 5W+ procedure, settle upon an appropriate thesis and intention. As you write your guide, determine a voice, stance, and tone your readers will find appealing and effective.

Writing Assignment

Choose a burning issue in your community or on your campus, perhaps some social issue like co-ed dormitories or some national policy issue like arms control, that is capable of causing your blood to boil. Do some inventing that helps you articulate how you feel about the issue. After you have sorted out some of your opinions and feelings, write an editorial appropriate for publication in your campus newspaper. Be sure to marshall appropriate evidence to support your assertions, and be equally sure to choose the proper voice, stance, and tone for this editorial directed toward your fellow students.

Part Two

Writers at Work

I n this section of *Roughdrafts*, you will be reading, examining, and practicing several kinds of texts that you will be likely to read and write during college and in your career. Real writing, of course, arises from a particular context, and the final form of a piece of writing is influenced and shaped by that context: Who is the audience being addressed? What is the writer's intention? What choices must the writer make to accomplish his purposes in writing the text?

The title of our textbook, *Roughdrafts*, indicates the major premise upon which it is based: Apprentice writers can benefit tremendously from peering over the shoulders of writers while they are in the act of producing a successful text. Therefore, Part Two contains five chapters, each of which illustrates or describes the drafting process of our students and gives several examples of particular types of texts that reveal how professional writers may deal with such matters as thesis, intention, audience, voice, content, and organization.

Think of these chapters as a series of time-lapse photographs, snapshots of initial thoughts, ideas, essay "seeds," which germinate into a seedling, a young growth, and finally, a mature plant. Or, think of them as a series of snapshots of a sculpture as it emerges from the clay: first, some vague, formless ideas; next, a shapeless form coming in stages into a recognizable pattern; finally, a finished work. We hope that when you have finished Part Two, you will never regard a "finished" text in quite the same way again, since you will detect the resonances of the process that culminated in the finished piece.

Each chapter begins with a brief discussion of one of these five kinds of essays: personal experience, process, informative, persuasive, evaluative. Writers do not always begin with the intention of writing a particular kind of text, such as "comparison and contrast," and we realize that you will write many other kinds of texts in college and in your careers. However, it is valuable to examine and to practice these five ways of presenting and organizing information as building blocks for future writing tasks you will encounter. The student texts we have chosen represent a wide range of writing strategies and behavior; each writer faced different choices as he or she worked to complete the text.

Each chapter also contains example texts from professional writers. These are not presented as models for you to emulate; rather, they should serve as repositories of ideas to be harvested for options and strategies for writing. Consequently, each text is followed by a series of questions that encourage you to examine it critically. You will begin to notice structures that successful writers use to get specific effects. In addition, you will begin to recognize problems that writers face as they construct texts and the options they have in choosing strategies to solve those problems. Three of the chapters contain a writing assignment that is interspersed throughout the chapter, presented in various steps to give you practice in the conventions of the particular genre of essay under consideration. All five chapters also have writing assignments at the end.

To help you make generalizations about writing strategies, we have organized Chapters 6, 7, and 8 in the following way:

1.   Explanation of the characteristic features of the genre of essay under consideration, followed by two professional examples.

2.   Description of the writing task that our student faced.

3.   Description and illustration of the student's inventing and planning.

4.   The actual drafts that the student wrote and an analysis of how he or she evaluated each draft and made appropriate changes.

5.   The final, reworked draft and a description of the student's editing process.

6.   Additional writing assignments.

Chapters 9 and 10 contain an explanation about and professional examples of the kind of essay under consideration; a brief description of the student's written task and a summary of her or his response to it; the student's final draft; and writing assignments that will encourage you to produce polished texts on your own.

Writing About Personal Experience 6

The Personal Experience Essay

The personal experience essay invites the reader to explore an episode in the life of another person, one that may reveal interesting information about the writer but that often illuminates the life of the reader himself. Andy Rooney's tribute to his mother, which you read in Chapter 2, is the kind of text that causes a reader to reflect on his own relationships with his parents and friends at least as much as it informs him about the author. The fact is, many readers read personal experience essays to find out how similar or different someone else's life is from their own, and they frequently come away knowing as much about themselves as the people they're reading about.

Since we live in an age of inordinate interest in the private lives of public persons, perhaps we have become accustomed to the sensational biography or autobiography that reveals intimate facts about such persons. We are used to reading about what Prince has for breakfast, what Princess Di wore to the theater, or whether our senator has a happy home life. But a personal experience essay need not be spectacular or sensational to be effective, interesting, or moving. All of us share personal memories and experiences that are worth exploring in writing.

Unlike expository texts, such as the process or informative essays that will be discussed in later chapters, the personal experience essay is *about* the writer herself: her experiences, her attitudes, her outlooks, her feelings, and the impact of specific events and relationships upon her life and the lives of others she knows. More than anything else, the personal experience essay is a way for the writer to *explore,* to examine her past critically and come to some conclusions about her life's meaning and direction. In the personal experience essay a writer looks for insights into her own behavior and the behavior of others as she traces patterns in her life and surroundings and seeks to explain her present circumstances.

Some personal experience essays simply *report.* That is, they give the facts and circumstances of an experience and allow the reader to judge their meaning and implications for himself. Much biography and auto-biography is written this way. More commonly, however, the personal experience essay serves a larger purpose or intention for its writer. Rather than merely telling a story for its own sake or reporting events that the reader can interpret on his own, a writer may choose to use her personal experience as a medium for saying something more, as in the following examples of intentions:

1. *Teaching the Reader a Lesson:* "I'll never the forget the evening dad warned me not to go drinking with Ralph and Ed."
2. *Presenting a Hard-won Insight into Human Behavior:* "Teaching the handicapped that summer convinced me that no human life is so limited that it cannot maintain dignity and purpose."
3. *Explaining How the Writer Has Come to Be the Sort of Person She Is:* "When I was 16, no one could have told me that I would become a selfish, irascible person."

Though the personal experience essay is essentially "about" the writer, the reader cannot be taken for granted or ignored. Such an essay is not merely an expanded diary entry, purely expressive in intent, an overflow of emotion and nostalgia. Rather, the personal experience essay must be crafted with the reader and his needs in mind, lest its larger purpose remain obscure or inaccessible.

In writing the personal experience essay in Chapter 2, you made choices about such matters as intention, audience, and voice, and we will be looking closely at these choices in a later section of this chapter. Also, the skillful use of *narration* and *description* is integral to the development of the personal experience essay. As you recall from Chapter 2, narration involves the sequencing of events and experiences in a specific order or pattern, frequently *chronological,* depending upon the writer's intention. Description involves the vivid depiction of events and experiences, employing all five senses—visual, aural, tactile, oral, and olfactory. An effective personal experience essay thus is built upon formative experiences in the writer's life that have been carefully chosen and vividly presented to the reader. A finished, *reader-based* personal experience essay will have these characteristics:

1.   The nature and meaning of the personal experience will be clear to the reader.
2.   Each event or experience that is related will contribute to the overall intent of the essay. Readers will understand why some events are selected and others are omitted, and why some are compressed and others are given central focus and elaboration.
3.   The ordering of the essay will be logical, not disjointed or obscure, and will present no problems for the reader. If the writer has chosen not to use chronological order or has departed from chronology for a specific effect, the reader will be able to follow the organization of the essay.
4.   The voice and tone of the essay will be appropriate and consistent, governed by the writer's overriding intention.
5.   The intention of the essay, although perhaps not explicitly stated, will become apparent to the reader by the end of the essay.

Examples

Read the following two personal experience essays carefully, noting their effective use of narration and description. Answer the accompanying questions, which focus your attention on the choices of intention, organization, voice, and tone that the two writers have made.

Once Upon a Time
Frederick Buechner

On a Saturday in late fall, my brother and I woke up around sunrise. I was ten and he not quite eight, and once we were awake, there was no going back to sleep again because immediately all the excitement of the day that was about to be burst in upon us like the sun itself, and we could not conceivably have closed our eyes on it. Our mother and father were going to take us to a football game, and although we were not particularly

1

interested in the game, we were desperately interested in being taken. Grandma Buechner had come down from the city to go with us and was asleep in another room. Our parents presumably were also asleep, and so were the black couple who worked for us, downstairs in a room off the kitchen. It was much too early to get up, so just as on Christmas morning when you wake up too early to start opening the presents, we amused ourselves as best we could till the rest of the house got moving and it came time to start opening the present of this new and most promising day. We had a roulette wheel, of all things—black and glittery with a chromium spindle at the hub which it took only the slightest twirl to set spinning and the little ball skittering clickety-click around the rim until the wheel slowed down enough for it to settle into one of the niches and ride out the rest of the spin in silence.

2   We had a green felt cloth with the numbers and colors marked on it and a box of red, white, and blue poker chips; and all of this we had spread out on the foot of one of our beds, playing with it, when something happened that at the moment neither of us more than half noticed because it was such an ordinary thing in a way, set next to all the extraordinary things that we had reason to believe were going to happen as soon as the day got going. What happened was that our bedroom door opened a little, and somebody looked in on us. It was our father. Later on, we could not remember anything more about it than that, even when we finally got around to pooling our memories of it, which was not until many years later.

3   If he said anything to us, or if we said anything to him, we neither of us have ever been able to remember it. He could have been either dressed or still in his pajamas for all we noticed. There was apparently nothing about his appearance or about what he said or did that made us look twice at him. There was nothing to suggest that he opened the door for any reason other than just to check on us as he passed by on his way to the bathroom or wherever else we might have thought he was going that early on a Saturday morning, if either of us had bothered to think about it at all. I have no idea how long he stood there looking at us. A few seconds? A few minutes? Did he smile, make a face, wave his hand? I have no idea. All I know is that after a while, he disappeared, closing the door behind him, and we went on playing with our wheel as I assume we had kept on playing with it right along because there was nothing our father had said or done or seemed to want that made us stop. Clickety clickety click. Now this number, now that. On one spin we could be rich as Croesus. On the next we could lose our shirts.

How long it was from the moment he closed that door to the moment   4
we opened it, I no longer have any way of knowing, but the interlude can
stand in a way for my whole childhood up till then and for everybody else's
too, I suppose: childhood as a waiting for you do not know just what and
living, as you live in dreams, with little or no sense of sequence or consequence
or measurable time. And that moment was also the last of my childhood
because, when I opened the door again, measurable time was, among other
things, what I opened it on. The click of the latch as I turned the knob
was the first tick of the clock that measures everything into before and
after, and at that exact moment my once-below-a-time ended and my once-
upon-a-time began. From that moment to this I have ridden on time's back
as a man rides a horse, knowing fully that the day will come when my
ride will end and my time will end and all that I am and all that I have
will end with them. Up till then the house had been still. Then, muffled
by the closed door, there was a shout from downstairs. It was the husband
of the black couple. His voice was fruity and hollow with something I had
never heard in it before. I opened the door.

All over the house doors opened, upstairs and down. My grandmother   5
loomed fierce and terrified in the hallway, her nightgown billowing around
her, white and stiff as a sail, her hair down her back. There was a blue
haze in the air, faintly bitter and stifling. In what I remember still as a
kind of crazy parody of excitement, I grabbed hold of the newel post at
the top of the stairs and swung myself around it. "Something terrible has
happened!" my grandmother said. She told us to go back to our room. We
went back. We looked out the window.

Down below was the gravel drive, the garage with its doors flung wide   6
open and the same blue haze thick inside it and drifting out into the crisp
autumn day. I had the sense that my brother and I were looking down
from a height many times greater than just the height of the second story
of our house. In gray slacks and a maroon sweater, our father was lying
in the driveway on his back. By now my mother and grandmother were
with him, both in their nightgowns still, barefoot, their hair uncombed.
Each had taken one of his legs and was working it up and down like the
handle of a pump, but whatever this was supposed to accomplish, it accomplished nothing as far as we could see. A few neighbors had gathered
at the upper end of the drive, and my brother and I were there with them,
neither knowing how we got there nor daring to go any farther.

Nobody spoke. A car careened up and braked sharp with a spray of   7
gravel. A doctor got out. He was wearing a fedora and glasses. He ran
down the driveway with his bag in his hand. He knelt. I remember the

black man who had roused us sitting somewhere with his head in his hands. I remember the dachshund we had wagging his tail. After a time the doctor came back up the drive, his tread noisy on the gravel. The question the neighbors asked him they asked without words, and without a word the doctor answered them. He barely shook his head. It was not for several days that a note was found. It was written in pencil on the last page of *Gone with the Wind*, which had been published that year, 1936, and it was addressed to my mother. "I adore and love you," it said, "and am no good. . . . Give Freddy my watch. Give Jamie my pearl pin. I give you all my love."

8   God speaks to us through our lives, we often too easily say. *Something* speaks anyway, spells out some sort of godly or godforsaken meaning to us through the alphabet of our years, but often it takes many years and many further spellings out before we start to glimpse, or think we do, a little of what that meaning is. Even then we glimpse it only dimly, like the first trace of dawn on the rim of night, and even then it is a meaning that we cannot fix and be sure of once and for all because it is always incarnate meaning and thus as alive and changing as we are ourselves alive and changing.

9   A child takes life as it comes because he has no other way of taking it. The world had come to an end that Saturday morning, but each time we had moved to another place, I had seen a world come to an end, and there had always been another world to replace it. When somebody you love dies, Mark Twain said, it is like when your house burns down; it isn't for years that you realize the full extent of your loss. For me it was longer than for most, if indeed I have realized it fully even yet, and in the meanwhile the loss came to get buried so deep in me that after a time I scarcely ever took it out to look at it at all, let alone to speak of it. If ever anybody asked me how my father died, I would say heart trouble. That seemed at least a version of the truth. He had had a heart. It had been troubled. I remembered how his laughter toward the end had rung like a cracked bell. I remembered how when he opened the bedroom door, he had not said good-bye to us in any way that we understood. I remembered what he had written on the last page of the book he had been reading.

10   And then by grace or by luck or by some cool, child's skill for withdrawing from anything too sharp or puzzling to deal with, I stopped remembering so almost completely to remember at all that when, a year or so later, I came upon my brother crying one day all by himself in his room, I was stopped dead in my tracks. Why was he crying? When I prodded him into telling me that he was crying about something that he would not name

but said only had happened a long time ago, I finally knew what he meant, and I can recapture still my astonishment that, for him, a wound was still open that for me, or so I thought, had long since closed. And in addition to the astonishment, there was also a shadow of guilt. It was guilt not only that I had no tears like his to cry with but that if, no less than he, I had also lost more than I yet knew, I had also, although admittedly at an exorbitant price, made a sort of giddy, tragic, but quite measurable little gain. While my father lived, I was the heir apparent, the crown prince. Now I was not only king, but king in a place that, except for his death, I would probably never have known except in dreams. What I mean is that the place we moved to soon after he died—and it was there that my brother cried, in a house the color of smoked salmon overhanging a harbor of turquoise and ultramarine—was the Land of Oz. . . .

QUESTIONS ABOUT "ONCE UPON A TIME"

1.   In this excerpt, Buechner recounts the day of his father's suicide. What seems to be Buechner's intention in relating this poignant episode from his childhood?

2.   How does the idea of time play an essential part in Buechner's making sense of this experience? How does he convey the importance of time to his readers? Which of the memories captured here are those of the young Buechner? Which are the recollections of the adult Buechner? Is it important to determine which are which?

3.   Describe what happens in this excerpt. How does the organization help reveal the author's intention? What frame of reference does he use to prepare the reader for the details he cites?

4.   In the first part of the excerpt, Buechner narrates the details of that Saturday morning in late fall. What happened that morning? What does his selection of details tell his readers about the young Buechner and the effect of this experience on him?

5.   Buechner disrupts the narration of events that morning: "On one spin we could be rich as Croesus. On the next we could lose our shirts. . . . Up till then the house had been still. Then, muffled by the closed door, there was a shout from downstairs." What happens in the paragraph that interrupts the action of the narrative? What do the two phrases "once-below-a-time" and "once-upon-a-time" mean in the context of this narrative? What effect does this interruption have on the meaning of this experience?

6.   The narration of remembered events ends with the father's suicide note. The paragraph that begins, "God speaks to us," and the three paragraphs

that follow, seem to have a different function. What is their purpose? Are these paragraphs especially helpful to a reader? If so, how?

7.   In what way is the final phrase, "Land of Oz," related to the sense of time created in this excerpt?

8.   Look at Buechner's choice of words. How does he maintain control of the tone of his text so that it avoids mere emotion or sentiment?

Summer Beyond Wish

Russell Baker

1   A long time ago I lived in a crossroads village of northern Virginia and during its summer enjoyed innocence and never knew boredom, although nothing of consequence happened there.

2   Seven houses of varying lack of distinction constituted the community. A dirt road meandered off toward the mountain where a bootleg still supplied whiskey to the men of the countryside, and another dirt road ran down to the creek. My cousin Kenneth and I would sit on the bank and fish with earthworms. One day we killed a copperhead which was basking on a rock nearby. That was unusual.

3   The heat of summer was mellow and produced sweet scents which lay in the air so damp and rich you could almost taste them. Mornings smelled of purple wisteria, afternoons of the wild roses which tumbled over stone fences, and evenings of honeysuckle.

4   Even by standards of that time it was a primitive place. There was no electricity. Roads were unpaved. In our house there was no plumbing. The routine of summer days was shaped by these deficiencies. Lacking electric lights, one went early to bed and rose while the dew was still in the grass. Kerosene lamps were cleaned and polished in an early-morning hubbub of women, and children were sent to the spring for fresh water.

5   This afforded a chance to see whether the crayfish population had multiplied. Later, a trip to the outhouse would afford a chance to daydream in the Sears, Roebuck Catalogue, mostly about shotguns and bicycles.

6   With no electricity, radio was not available for pacifying the young. One or two people did have radios that operated on mail-order batteries about the size of a present-day car battery, but these were not for children, though occasionally you might be invited in to hear "Amos 'n' Andy."

7   All I remember about "Amos 'n' Andy" at that time is that it was strange hearing voices come out of furniture. Much later I was advised that listening to "Amos 'n' Andy" was racist and was grateful that I hadn't heard much.

In the summer no pleasures were to be had indoors. Everything of delight 8
occurred in the world outside. In the flowers there were hummingbirds to
be seen, tiny wings fluttering so fast that the birds seemed to have no
wings at all.

In the heat of mid-afternoon the women would draw the blinds, spread 9
blankets on the floor for coolness and nap, while in the fields the cattle
herded together in the shade of spreading trees to escape the sun. Afternoons
were absolutely still, yet filled with sounds.

Bees buzzed in the clover. Far away over the fields the chug of an 10
ancient steam-powered threshing machine could be faintly heard. Birds
rustled under the tin porch of the roof.

Rising dust along the road from the mountains signaled an approaching 11
event. A car was coming. "Car's coming," someone would say. People
emerged from houses. The approaching dust was studied. Guesses were
hazarded about whom it might contain.

Then—a big moment in the day—the car would cruise past. 12

"Who was it?" 13

"I didn't get a good look." 14

"It looked like Packy Painter to me." 15

"Couldn't have been Packy. Wasn't his car." 16

The stillness resettled itself as gently as the dust, and you could wander 17
past the henhouse and watch a hen settle herself to perform the mystery
of laying an egg. For livelier adventure there was the field that contained
the bull. There, one could test his courage by seeing how far he dared
venture before running back through the fence.

The men drifted back with the falling sun, steaming with heat and 18
fatigue, and washed in tin basins with water hauled in buckets from the
spring. I knew a few of their secrets, such as who kept his whisky hidden
in a mason jar behind the lime barrel, and what they were really doing
when they excused themselves from the kitchen and stepped out into the
orchard and stayed out there laughing too hard.

I also knew what the women felt about it, though not what they thought. 19
Even then I could see that matters between women and men could become
very difficult and, sometimes, so difficult that they spoiled the air of summer.

At sunset people sat on the porches. As dusk deepened, the lightning 20
bugs came out to be caught and bottled. As twilight edged into night, a
bat swooped across the road. I was not afraid of bats then, although I
feared ghosts, which made the approach of bedtime in a room where even
the kerosene lamp would quickly be doused seem terrifying.

I was even more afraid of toads and specifically of the toad which lived 21
under the porch steps and which, everyone assured me, would, if touched,

give me warts. One night I was allowed to stay up until the stars were in full command of the sky. A woman of great age was dying in the village and it was considered fit to let the children stay abroad into the night. As four of us sat there we saw a shooting star and someone said, "Make a wish."

I did not know what that meant. I didn't know anything to wish for.

Questions About "Summer Beyond Wish"

1. What seems to be Baker's intention in relating this boyhood experience? Why does he say at the beginning that "nothing of consequence happened" and then proceed to talk about it anyway?

2. The text is written retrospectively; that is, Baker, the adult, is looking back at Baker, the child. When is the "adult" Baker speaking? When is the "child" Baker speaking?

3. How does the vivid description of his Virginia village contribute to the effect of his narrative? Find specific phrases and word choices that create a sense of place for the reader.

4. Toward the middle of the text, Baker suddenly employs dialogue. What is the effect? Why do you think he chose to use it here but not elsewhere in the text?

5. The conclusion may seem abrupt. Does the text end abruptly or does it only seem so? How has Baker prepared the reader for this sudden ending?

Summary

Now that you have examined an explanation of personal experience writing and two examples, here are several important operations that a writer usually performs before she begins to draft a personal experience essay:

1. The writer must *select* and *explore* the experience or experiences that will serve her intention in the crafting of the essay.

2. The writer must *choose* those details of the experience(s) that will best serve her larger intention. For instance, if a writer wants to narrate the experience of witnessing a traffic accident in order to demonstrate how cowardly she had been in not coming forward with her testimony, she might provide a vivid, moment-by-moment account of the accident, including the thoughts that came to mind as she witnessed the horrible event. In contrast, how the writer got to the scene of the accident, what she was wearing at the time, and other such information might be superfluous

detail that would distract the reader from the main focus of the essay; thus some details or accompanying events might be compressed or omitted entirely.

3. The writer must *determine* the best way to order the experience(s) she is relating. A strict chronological order is easiest to manage, of course, and for short narratives it is probably the most useful organization. On the other hand, some events may not lend themselves to such a strict chronological narration. A writer might find that summarizing an experience first and then examining it in detail or using flashbacks—moving backward instead of forward in time—to recall pertinent events would be a suitable means of organizing the experience for the reader.

4. The writer must *consider the audience* for which she is writing. Among the things she must ask herself are: How common are my experiences to the audience? How much background information do they need to understand the kind of events or experiences I am talking about? What needs to be stated explicitly? If my experiences are commonplace, how will I get the audience to see that they are nevertheless unique to me and my development as a person? What tone should I adopt in relating my experience: sober, detached, playful, bitter, wiser-but-poorer, or something else? What point of view will best serve my intentions and my audience: first person/present tense? third person/retrospective? What effect do I want to leave? Should my readers feel "duly warned," properly "chastened," entertained and amused, "preached at"?

A Rhetorical Task: Anita and Being a Nurse

Initial Responses

Anita Critz, along with the rest of her class, was given the task of writing a personal experience text. The nature of the personal experience, the intention in writing about it, and the audience to whom the text would be directed were left to the discretion of each student. Because Anita had been keeping a journal about her nursing experiences, she decided to make one of her journal entries the basis of her text.

VISUALIZING THE AUDIENCE

Since Anita was already a registered nurse who was back in school to finish her B.A. in nursing, she decided to draw on her hospital experience for the basis of the text, relating her thoughts one evening as she contemplated the reasons she originally went into the nursing profession. She decided to write for an audience that would not necessarily be aware of the training and experiences nurses bring to their tasks, or the kind of interaction that occurs between doctors, nurses, and patients. Here are some of the questions she asked herself to help her make her audience more real to her:

-- What is the typical experience of most people who have been in the hospital?
-- How do people usually react to nurses and/or doctors in the hospital environment (as opposed to doctors' offices, etc.)?
-- Given that medical TV shows are popular, what stereotypes might my audience bring to an essay on nursing and hospitals?
-- Will my audience be cynical or sympathetic to the task of nursing?
-- How "technical" should I be in describing some hospital activities?

CREATING A CONTEXT

As Anita considered her audience and their potential needs as readers, a more complete frame of reference began to form in her mind. Perhaps this essay would encourage those who were thinking about becoming nurses to pursue their goals. On the other hand, she thought the essay might help to clarify some mistaken impressions the public might have about the commitment of the medical profession to its calling. She decided to do some more writing before settling on the exact context, which would provide the boundaries and direction of her essay.

ARTICULATING INTENTION

Anita's anticipation of her audience and the context for her essay led her to begin with the intention of relating a personal experience from childhood, her first desire to become a nurse, followed by a discussion of her present reflections on that childhood dream, exploring the "dream" and the "reality" that she has found in her nursing career. At this point she was still not clear about the exact "point" of her essay, although she suspected that it would become clearer as she wrote her thoughts down.

More Inventing and Planning

Anita's initial inventing involved thinking about the journal entry she had selected as the basis for her essay.

> The hospital was so peaceful last night that it seemed unreal. I worked in coronary care and the unit was full, but very quiet. We assessed our patients early in the shift. They were quite ill and would require careful watching during the night. After they went to sleep we settled in for a night of observation. We watched for changes in skin color, skin temperature, or breathing patterns. In addition we watched the monitors and the intravenous therapy. The pervading measure of our night was the EKG monitor. As long as the pattern of lights moving across the screen was steady and regular our night was quiet. All went well. The night was peaceful and time worked its miracle of healing under our watchful eyes.

After she mulled over her journal entry, she made a brief summary of how she planned to proceed. Anita *planned* to write a predraft; that is, she did not expect her first draft to be a final one. She would use her first draft as a discovery draft in order to determine her intentions in creating her essay.

1. Journal Entry
2. Brief Outline
3. Predraft
4. Adjective comparison
5. Elimination of concepts as distracting from theme
6. Rewriting of paragraphs opposing one another
7. Rough draft
8. Checking for continuity of thought patterns
9. Rewriting of paragraphs one at a time
10. Checking for structure
11. "   " adequate supportive ideas rather than a list of adjectives

After this brief planning episode, Anita did some brainstorming in which she generated some of the descriptive terms she associated with hospital personnel. She then created an outline to guide the rest of her drafting:

BRAINSTORMING

Hospitals

Fantasy	Reality
Quiet	Noisy
Peaceful	Bustling
Restful	Carts rolling & banging
Quiet zone	Pages
Big	Mazelike
Apart	Inadequately marked
Haven	TV's, newspapers
Sanctuary	

Nurses

Fantasy	Reality
Efficient	Well trained but in varying de-
Truthful	grees overworked
Loving	Harassed
Caring	Too busy
Well trained	Frustrated
Nonjudgmental	
Conscientious	
Safe confident	
Skillful observer	
Nurturing	

Doctors

Fantasy	Reality
Strong	Knowledgeable
Knowledgeable	Impatient
Wise	Overcautious
Thorough	Actually, see pts for 2 min/day
Omnicient	Stressed
Calm	Difficult to find
Omnipresent	Play golf
Marcus Welby	Spend time c families
Sense of humor	Talk at tangents
Authoritative	

OUTLINE

1. **My fantasy**
   A. Hospitals
   B. Doctors
   C. Nurses
   D. Patients
2. **Reality**
   A. Hospitals
   B. Doctors
   C. Nurses
   D. Patients
3. **Blending of fantasy and reality in one quiet night**

Writing Task

Here is a rhetorical task for you similar to the one with which Anita was presented.

Select a personal experience about which you would like to write. Be sure to consider the intention of your essay. It may help you to get started if you examine the process Anita used to begin to visualize her audience and articulate her intention for writing.

Do your own inventing and planning now by following these steps:

1. Jot down some past experiences you have had that seem to you to be formative and that have had an impact on your present life.
2. What is the impact of these experiences as you consider them? How do you know? Did you think them momentous when they originally occurred? What present conditions or circumstances did these experiences affect? To what degree?
3. Use 5W+ to explore one of these experiences further. How has your perception of this experience changed over time? How does this experience mesh with others you had since? Have other people you know experienced something similar? How unique to you is this experience? If it is rather common, how might you present it so that a reader will not dismiss it as trivial? Ask other questions from 5W+ that would provoke your thinking further.
4. What can an audience learn about you from this experience and your relating of it? What possible intention for your essay is emerging in your

thinking about this experience? What is the best organization sequence for presenting this experience and your discussion of its impact?

5.   Who is your audience? A group of peers? A specialized group of college students? Parents? Children? Who would benefit most by reading about your experience? What seems to be an appropriate tone for your essay? Somber? Frivolous? Intentionally satirical? Matter-of-fact?

6.   Examine the essays of Baker and Buechner. Can your experience be presented in a manner similar to theirs? If not, describe how you might organize your essay. How many parts will your essay have? What do you expect each part to *do?*

7.   Write a draft of your essay.

Drafting and Revising

What follows are successive drafts of Anita's personal experience essay. She produced a total of three drafts, with intervening inventing and planning episodes. We will analyze each draft at the text, sentence, and word level. We have placed our commentary in the margins to highlight specific features that needed attention as Anita proceeded through the drafting process. Anita's final draft will appear in the section "Proofreading and Editing," page 240. In that section we will illustrate how Anita moved from a rough draft to a final draft by revising her essay at the text level.

ANITA'S FIRST DRAFT

I worked last night and revisited a world of fantasy. When I was 1 younger[1] and much more idealistic I dreamed of working in a hospital as a nurse. In my imaginings a hospital was a place of quiet and rest, ~~the doctors were knowledgeable and wise~~ a refuge from the realities of pain and suffering, a place ~~to be healed~~ of healing.

1. Shift in focus

Although the patients came in with painful <u>diseases</u>[2] such as <u>heart</u> 2 <u>attacks</u>[2] and cancer, the doctors were more than capable of dealing with ~~the illness brought by their patients~~ them. They were knowledgeable, wise, ~~and caring~~ authoritative and skilled in the art of healing. In my dream they were readily available to nurses and patients. They were supportive in times of grief and calming in emergencies. In short ~~paragons of perfection~~ virtue.[3]

2. Word choice?

3. Sentence pattern choppy

A nurse was a loving, caring woman who not only had special skills 3 and training in caring for the sick but had infinite capacity for listening to and helping with personal problems. She had the special capacity to listen without judging or condemning. She was conscientious in maintaining confidentiality, but had the ability to persuade her patients to seek the help that they needed. Because of her skills in observation, she was able to know, without being told, when her patients needed pain medication, a back rub, or just left alone. In general, a very nurturing individual.[4]

4   The patients, of course, responded to all of this care with gratitude and, usually, by getting well. Even the act of dying was conducted <u>with dignity</u>.[5]

5   The reality of being a nurse in the active, busy world of a hospital has proven to be quite different from my idealized version. Reality shock has set in.[6]

6   A hospital is, of course, where many people go to obtain relief from pain and a cure from illness. ~~They~~ It most definitely ~~are~~ is not a place of rest, peace, and quiet. A good night's rest is disturbed by someone walking in and looking at you every hour, and perhaps turning on the light and taking your blood pressure every couple of hours. The laboratory technician is almost sure to wake you up around 6:30 a.m. ~~Then~~ Just as you are dozing off to sleep the nurse wants you to take a bath before breakfast. If you're fortunate you get to eat, but probably you'll get wheeled off to X-ray for some test only to have to sit in a cold hall waiting for your turn under the machine. By the time you get back it's lunch time. Of course, you're exhausted and hope to catch up on some sleep by taking a nap. Unfortunately, someone keeps rolling huge carts by your door, usually banging into the wall at least once. Just a few are the dinner cart, the central supply cart, the linen cart, the dressing cart, and the surgery cart. Of course, there are also the never ending pages to interrupt your rest.[7] A hospital is most definitely not inducive for rest.

7   Physicians are most certainly knowledgeable and skilled in the art of healing. However, they are frequently <u>autocratic</u>[8] rather than authoritative. They have the unfortunate habit of wanting time for themselves and their families rather than being available to nurses and/or patients. <u>They sometimes demonstrate a normal tendency to avoid being with families when a death occurs and they are unable to do anything to prevent it.</u>[9] I have also noted a deplorable tendency, on occasion, to get angry during stressful situations. My paragons of virtue have alarmingly human characteristics.

8   Caring for the physical and emotional needs of patients is the goal of every nurse, but the capability which she demonstrates when doing this varies greatly.[10] She carries her moral, religious and educational

---

4. Narrative text structure

5. Code expression

6. This paragraph contains an abrupt shift in focus

7. Text seems to become a list of events here.

8. Code word

9. Ambiguous sentence

10. Transition weak: shift of focus

11. Sentences form an uncohesive paragraph: functions unclear

background with her as she deals with the personal problems of her patients. The task of maintaining confidentiality is in continual conflict with the need to maintain accurate records and the desire to tell an interesting story over lunch. Her ability to know what a patient needs or wants is limited by her inability to read minds and lack of time for adequate communication.[11] Her goals are still intact, but can be sidelined by many things.

12. Focus

Gratitude is one of the emotions expressed by patients. Others are anger, fear, hostility, paranoia, frustration, depression, anxiety. Some patients are confused and disoriented. Most patients are frightened. Patients are people who have been removed from their normal environment and placed in an alien one over which they have little or no control.[12] Understandably, the emotions they have and express are not simple or necessarily positive.   9

13. No transition

14. Code word

15. Function ambiguous, lack of focus.

Last night,[13] the hospital, although real,[14] came close to being like my fantasy. The halls were hushed, the lights dim. The technicians, nurses and doctors went about their work quietly and efficiently. Patients' needs were met promptly. The world was shut out and the patients were protected and cared for.[15] It was an enjoyable, satisfying interlude blending fantasy and reality.   10

EVALUATION

Text Level Anita wrote a quick first draft in longhand, then waited for a few days before trying to evaluate it. When she did read through it, she discovered that, as she had anticipated, she had created a *predraft* too full of writer-based features to be revisable. Rather than being a cohesive draft whose intention was manifested early and maintained consistently throughout, Anita's essay was plagued with focus and transition problems, as well as using a narrative structure in places where it did not suit her intentions. Here are some of the specific items that convinced Anita that her text was a predraft:

In paragraph 1, there was a sudden shift of focus between the first and second sentences. Anita realized that the first sentence had established certain expectations in the reader about the function of the follow-up sentence, and that she had not met them. The connection between the two incidents was clear *to her,* but she had not signalled the connection to the reader. Still, these sentences helped her to realize more clearly what her intention was in crafting the essay: articulating the discrepancy between her childhood ideals of nursing and the reality of her personal hospital experience. She would need to find a better frame of reference for her opening paragraph in order to make the context and focus of her subsequent narration meaningful to the reader.

Paragraphs 3 to 6 employed a primarily *narrative* structure, basically relating information in the order in which it occurred to Anita. In other words, she had not really presented her reader with an ordering principle that indicated her intended *focus:* what was important to her discussion, how the reader should understand her intention given the order of information. Thus, this section of her essay—which was not intended as a narration— left her reader unsure about how these paragraphs fit into the larger intention of the essay.

The last two paragraphs, 9 and 10, also lacked focus, shifting from one specific aspect of nursing care, responding to the emotional needs of patients, to a sudden "concluding" paragraph that abruptly returned the reader to the contrast between reality and fantasy. Anita realized that she had not really prepared her reader for these abrupt shifts of focus and function. She knew that in her revision she would have to recast these paragraphs to make her intention clearer.

Sentence Level The sentence-level features that Anita recognized as writer-based included a choppy sentence structure in paragraph 2, a lack of variety in sentence length in paragraphs 6 to 8, and a number of sentences whose function was ambiguous: for example, "They sometimes demonstrate a normal tendency to avoid being with families when a death occurs and they are unable to do anything to prevent it" (paragraph 7) and "Her goals are still intact, but can be sidelined by many things" (paragraph 8).

The sentences that concluded the essay in paragraph 10 were most troublesome. Anita knew that the paragraph lacked cohesion, primarily because her sentences seemed clipped, obscure, and anticlimactic. She had intended bringing the reader full circle to her first mention of her childhood dreams in paragraph 1, but she realized that the repetition of these sentences had not accomplished this.

Word Level Anita noted several code words and expressions, such as "with dignity" in paragraph 4, "autocratic" in paragraph 7, and "real" in paragraph 10, but she was generally satisfied that she had avoided ambiguity in word choice, and had captured the "feel" of the hospital with concrete words and images. She felt confident that at the word level she had been successful in being reader-based.

Exercise

Examine Anita's first draft and answer the following questions.

1. If you had written Anita's first predraft, what portions of it would you consider significant? List them.

2. Does Anita's predraft suggest any strategies for structuring the next draft? Why or why not? Explain.

3. Should Anita begin a second draft immediately, or does she need to do some more inventing and planning? Explain.

Writing Task

Read the first draft of your essay and answer the following questions.

1. Describe the intention of your essay.
2. Describe the audience to whom your essay is addressed.
3. Describe the way in which you intended to structure your essay.
4. Describe the tone that you intended to use.

Now examine your own first draft at the *text, sentence,* and *word levels.* Then determine whether you have produced a predraft or a rough draft.

If you have written a predraft, carefully glean it for possible theses and for strategies that you might use in writing your next draft. Also, reexamine your inventing and planning process. Do you need to do more inventing and planning? If so, what does your predraft indicate that you should focus your efforts on: clarifying intention? defining your audience more carefully? creating a different or more explicit structure?

If you have written a rough draft, identify the portions of your text that need work. Overall, does your intention need clarification? Does your reader need additional frames of reference? Does the focus of your paragraphs need to be sharpened?

REVISION

Because Anita had determined that her first draft was a predraft, she did not try to rewrite it by merely adding, deleting, rearranging, and substituting. Instead, she read through her draft carefully, hoping to uncover ideas that would be useful in a revamped and replanned subsequent draft.

Anita decided that she needed a new and more authentic frame of reference with which to begin her essay—a personal experience that explained her entry into nursing more directly and that could sustain the themes she had inadequately explored and developed in her predraft. She also knew that she needed to articulate her intention more clearly to her readers.

Anita did most of this new inventing and planning in her head, but she did jot down some notes to guide her in her new draft, including a title. She decided that her initial inventing had not really prepared her for the scope and intention of the paper she wanted to write. She also realized that her initial outline encouraged her to alternate paragraphs about the topics she had identified, doctors, patients, nurses, and hospitals, but with little focus or cohesion. Her readers simply could not determine why she proceeded from sentence to sentence in her predraft.

Here is a summary of the plans Anita made to write another draft of her text.

Title: Nursing: The Dream and the Reality

1. Start with memory of grandma--contrast the ideal with the actual.
2. Use early paragraphs to build image of serenity and competency that most of us have of a hospital so that the later "reality" will be that much more startling.
3. "Fill out" skeleton of ideas sketched in the predraft; be more concrete, illustrative.
4. Build toward a climax that expresses my disappointment but acceptance of my dream's failure.

After this further planning, Anita wrote a second draft. She was still struggling with her intention and the focus of certain paragraphs, but she was determined to make this draft more reader-based.

Here is a summary of Anita's revision strategies.

1. Having determined that she had written a predraft, Anita read through her draft, trying to salvage the ideas and expressions that seemed to suit her original intention.
2. She discovered in her mental brainstorming an effective frame of reference with which to begin her essay: a memory of her grandmother, a nurse who had captured her granddaughter's heart at an early age.
3. She determined that she needed to pay special attention to making her sentences and paragraphs more clearly focused and her development more concrete. In addition, she planned to focus on *nurses* and *patients* primarily and to create a conclusion that solidified her main points.

Exercise

1.   Compare Anita's plans for revising her draft with her original inventing and planning. How do they differ? How successful do you think she will be in using these plans to create a second draft?

2.   What additional advice would you give Anita as she tries to write her second draft? If you were Anita, would you be ready to write a second draft, or would you need to do some more inventing and planning?

Writing Task

If your first draft was a predraft:

1.   Engage in an additional inventing and planning session, if you have determined that it is necessary.

2.   Write a second draft.

If your first draft was a rough draft: Write a second draft.

ANITA'S SECOND DRAFT

Nursing: The Reality and the Dream
Anita Critz

When I was a little girl, and dreaming of one   1
day being a nurse, I had rather vague ideas of
what nursing was like. Most of them centered
around the only nurse that I knew, my Grandma.
She was the chief She frequently regaled us with stories about her
caregiver for all hospital. Grandma was serene, soft spoken and
our friends and even-tempered. She would always help with
relatives. she had whatever illness anyone had.[1] and had the ability
                                                         most
1. Ambiguous   to sooth hurt feelings and answer all the difficult
                  questions. There was a sign outside of her hospital
that I could   that read Quiet--Hospital Zone. These memories
think of.   formed the basis for my expectations of hospitals
                  and hospital life. The hospital itself was a big
                  stone building surrounded by well kept lawns,
                  and people appeared willing to
                  obey that demand.

trees, bushes and a wrought-iron fence. They seemed to go together. The building provided a quiet, safe environment and my grandmother provided care, understanding and knowledge. These memories formed the basis for my expectations of hospitals and nursing.

2   In my imaginings,[2] a hospital would be a place of serenity, protection and healing. The building itself would be separated from the noise of the streets by spacious lawns, thick walls and double doors. The halls would be wide, free of clutter and uncrowded. All of the room would be conveniently arranged with a window overlooking the green lawns. *There would be* plenty of space for flowers and personal items from home *to make* the patient feel more comfortable.

The people who worked at the hospital there would talk softly and walk quietly. Visitors would come only at appropriate times and their visits would be of benefit to the patients. They would be treated with courtesy by the hospital staff.[3] The hospital would be a place of refuge from the realities of pain and suffering, a place to rest and be healed. The hospital would be equipped with all of the equipment necessary for diagnosing and treating any illness a patient might have.

3   A hospital is, of course, where many people go to obtain relief from pain and a cure for illness. Modern hospitals contain complex, expensive *radiologic* equipment designed to explore and visualize almost every portion of your body. They have laboratory tests and equipment which determine whether these parts of your body are functioning correctly. *After the testing is done,* your physician is then able to correlate the findings and prescribe the proper treatment. If medical treatment is necessary the hospital has the ability to make available to you the necessary drugs. If surgical intervention is necessary hospitals are equipped with the needed instruments and the equipment needed to prevent con-

2.   Code word

3.   Focus problems

If a particular test is ordered that your hospital does not have the capacity for performing, a sister hospital will have the necessary equipment.

4. Code word

5. Function of sentence unclear

tamination, as well as people skilled in their use.
A hospital is a highly technological[4] institution
designed for the diagnosis and treatment of
disease.[5]

A hospital is not a place of rest, peace or quiet.   4
A good night's rest is not only interrupted by
whatever illness the patient might have, but also
6. Focus shift   by someone walking in your[6] room, flipping *switching* on
the light and taking your blood pressure every
couple of hours. The laboratory technicians are
almost sure to wake you[6] up around six in the
morning to obtain some more of your[6] blood.
Just as you doze back to sleep, your nurse wakes
you up to take a bath before "breakfast." If you're
fortunate, you get to eat but you will probably
have to go to the radiology department instead.
While there, you'll spend most of your time sitting
in a cold, crowded hall waiting for your turn
under the machine. By the time you return to
your room you are exhausted. Hoping to catch
up on some sleep, you lay down for awhile. Unfortunately someone keeps rolling huge carts past
your door, usually banging them onto *into the* walls in
the process. It seems like a parade. First comes
the dinner cart, then the central supply cart,
linen cart, dressing cart, crash cart and surgery
cart. To add variety there are wheel chairs, scales
7. Technical term needing definition   and hoyer lifts.[7] As an additional sound effect
announcements and pages come over the loud
speaker every few minutes. Then, of course, its
Not realizing how time for visiting hours. A hospital is definitely
tired you are, not the place to rest. your visitors stay, and stay,
trying to make the time go by more quickly and
pleasantly. They never seem to notice how tired
you are. A hospital is definitely not a good place
to rest.   *would be*

8. Shift in focus; transition absent   A nurse was a loving, caring person, who not   5
only had special skills and training in caring for
the sick, but had a seemingly infinite capacity
for listening to and helping with personal prob-

would have

lems.[8] She had gone to school to learn the techniques of assisting with diagnostic tests, daily
physical care and how to observe changes and
to know when they are important. She would had *have*
practiced these tasks and was be able to implement
them successfully in a hospital setting. She had *would possess*
developed the capacity to listen to information
and from
about her patients and from them without judging
them
or condemning. She was, conscientous in main- *would be*
taining confidentiality, but also have the ability
to persuade her patients to seek professional help
clear
if they needed it. A nurse would maintain com-
lines
munication, as a result of her skills between
her patients and their doctors at all times.

6   Caring for the physical and emotional needs
of patients is the goal of every nurse, but the
ability which she demonstrates when doing this
varies greatly.[9] She carries her moral, religious
and educational backgrounds with her as she
deals with her patients.

7   The educational background most greatly effects
her technical skills. Of course There are The
training programs vary in length from 13 months
to 5 years.[9] Obviously this indicates a difference
in depth and variation of knowledge. In addition
there are several schools of thought on a nurses
which exert tremendous influence on nursing.
These vary from year to year and, the locality. *in different localities*
As a result Each nurse brings to her job differing
skills, points of emphasis, and philosophies as
well as differing abilities to put these into practise.

8   The task of helping a patient with his emotional
problems not only is difficult, but frequently too
time consuming to be included in a nurses daily
routine. Each nurse carries her moral and religious background with her as she interacts with
her patients and helps them deal with their problems.[9] This makes it difficult for her to be
nonjudgmental[10] and objective.[10] In addition her
daily routine does not allow for much care beyond

9. Focus and function of paragraphs
    6–8 unclear.

10. Code words

the physical, daily needs. If she does manage to find the time to help with personal problems and do so non-judgementally, what to do with the information she has obtained is a problem. Confidentiality is a right possessed by every patient. It is difficult, if not impossible, to balance that right with the need to maintain accurate records for legal purposes or the human desire to share an interesting story. Emotional needs are, perhaps, the most poorly administered to in a hospital setting.

On rare occasions the reality of hospital life   9 and the dreams I had as a child blend. Such experiences are tantalizingly sweet to those who still remember the dream and keep us striving to make our fantasies real.

EVALUATION

Text Level   When Anita read through her second draft, she was pleased to find that it was much more reader-based than her first draft. She was convinced that she had produced a *rough draft* that could be revised by adding, deleting, rearranging, and substituting information. Still, there were a number of trouble spots that needed attention. Here are some of the text-level problems she noted in her second draft:

The use of the anecdote about her grandmother had, indeed, given Anita a better frame of reference for the reader, allowing her to explain how her personal experiences as a child and as an adult have changed her perspective about nursing. But in the second paragraph, she noted, she had not provided the "bridge" she needed to make clear her intention clear. Why, the reader would ask, has the writer moved from the personal experience of her childhood to a very concrete description of her imaginings about the ideal hospital? Hadn't she already described this ideal in the later sentences of the first paragraph? She needed, then, either to continue the frame of reference introduced in the first paragraph, or to create a new one that would cue the reader to her intention.

As she examined each later paragraph, she realized that this initial ambiguity in the relationships between the opening two paragraphs plagued the essay's structure throughout. Because the beginning sentence of each subsequent paragraph did not help her to maintain a consistent focus,

Anita determined that a major part of her revision of this draft would involve providing specific links between paragraphs and clarifying the function of each paragraph by providing an explicit frame of reference.

This, she knew, would be both an *additive* and a *substitution* process. She would articulate the connections between sentences and paragraphs for the reader by adding additional information and substituting sentences that would offer a clearer focus.

Sentence Level   Most of Anita's sentence problems were related to the text-level problems. She found fewer outright ambiguous sentences, although there were still a few: "She would always help with whatever illness anyone had," in paragraph 1, and "A hospital is a highly technological institution designed for the diagnosis and treatment of disease," paragraph 3, for example. Anita also felt uncomfortable with the wordiness of some of her sentences, such as "These memories formed the basis for my expectations of hospitals and nursing," paragraph 1, or "A nurse would be a loving, caring person, who not only had special skills and training in caring for the sick, but had a seemingly infinite capacity for listening to and helping with personal problems," paragraph 5. Still, she thought she could tinker with their length and style *after* she had dealt with the text-level problems.

Word Level   A number of code words remained that Anita felt needed to be more explicitly defined or elaborated. Among these were: "imaginings," paragraph 1; "technological," paragraph 3; "hoyer lifts," paragraph 4; "variation," paragraph 7; and "nonjudgmental" and "objective," paragraph 9. Again, Anita was not disturbed by these few word-level problems. She would concentrate on the text-level problems first.

Writing Task

Examine your second draft at the text, sentence, and word levels, keeping your intention and audience in mind. Have you produced a predraft or a rough draft?

REVISION

Text Level: Rewriting to Clarify Intention   In examining her second draft, Anita knew that although her anecdote about her grandmother helped to provide the reader with a frame of reference for interpreting the rest of the essay, the relationship between her memory of her grandmother, her dreams of becoming a nurse, and the hospital in which her grandmother worked was still ambiguous. She determined that in rewriting she would concentrate on refining that frame of reference and providing greater focus for her text wherever necessary.

1. *Paragraph 1:* This paragraph was crucial for Anita's intention, an intention that was finally becoming clear to her. She needed to establish a stronger link between the dreams and fantasies of a young child growing up in the shadow of a loving and successful relative who was a nurse and her disillusionment by the reality of nursing that she found as an adult. Anita decided that this paragraph needed further development, including carefully selected concrete images that would express the youthful respect with which she held her grandmother and the institution she personified.

2. *Paragraph 2:* In this key elaboration paragraph, Anita had to make the connection between the nurse as an individual and her relationship to the hospital as an institution more explicit. Her "dream" institution needed to be portrayed as graphically as the "real" institution that had so disappointed her.

3. *Paragraph 3:* This was a key transitional paragraph. Anita's intention was to portray the technological aspects of hospital care as advanced but ineffectual in the absence of personal concern for the patient. She decided that she needed some "buffer" paragraphs that would summarize the "dream" aspects of her childhood impressions of nursing, and she inserted them between paragraphs 2 and 3.

4. *Paragraphs 4 to 9:* Anita decided that paragraph 5 was out of place organizationally, since it was part of her old plan to alternatively compare the dream and the reality. Her new plan was to deal with the dream and the reality separately, bunching those paragraphs together to make the text more coherent. Paragraph 4 would then be grouped with paragraphs 6 to 9, and the irony and ambivalence of the real nursing experience would be heightened with additional concrete images of hospital life. These would lead to a concluding paragraph that would bring the reader back to Anita's grandmother and the reasons why Anita stays in nursing.

Sentence Level   Anita read her draft aloud and heard only a few sentences whose structure seemed to be writer-based. Her main revision at the sentence level involved careful attention to the head sentences in each paragraph, making sure that each one provided a smooth transition from the previous one, always signaling to the reader what the function of the subsequent information would be.

Word Level   Anita excised some technical words, changed some words that unnecessarily misled the reader, and altered a few code words so that the reader could follow the text without ambiguity.

Summary   Here is a summary of Anita's revision strategies for draft two:

1.   Anita examined each paragraph carefully to determine whether its purpose was clear to the reader, noting any paragraphs whose content and organization did not further her overall intention. When she found paragraphs without adequate development, order, or coherence, she tried to determine whether this was a problem with certain sentences, with the use of "unpacked" code words, or with the kind of information she was presenting. She made changes accordingly.

2.   Anita made structural, text-level changes first, then proceeded to minor sentence and word choice adjustments.

3.   Anita read her paper aloud to detect wordiness or convoluted sentence patterns.

Exercise

Carefully re-read Anita's first and second drafts and answer the following questions.

1.   Compare the structure of Anita's first draft with the structure of the second. Discuss the differences.

2.   Compare the tone of the first draft with the tone of the second draft and explain how they are different.

3.   Why do you think Anita was able to produce a rough draft on her second attempt? How important was her first draft in enabling her to produce a creditable rough draft on her second try?

4.   Compare the revision strategies Anita used on her first draft with those she used on her second draft.

5.   Do you agree with Anita's assessment of her second draft? What other revision suggestions would you have made to Anita before she began a third draft?

6.   Which revisions seemed to be most crucial to Anita's progress? Which seemed to be the key to other beneficial changes? Explain.

Writing Task

Recall your evaluation of your second draft. Keeping your intention and your audience in mind, select appropriate revision strategies and carry them out.

If you produced another predraft, compare it carefully with your first predraft. Is your second predraft more reader-based than your first? Do you need to engage in more inventing and planning? What aspects of your text—for example, audience, intention, structure—need the most attention? Consider these questions, then write another draft. You may wish to consult your teacher for some specific strategies that you can use in writing your next draft.

If you produced a rough draft, determine the location and the nature of every problem with your text as precisely as you can. Choose rewriting strategies accordingly. Do you need to create frames of reference for your reader? Do you need to sharpen the focus of particular portions of your text? Do you need to refine your stance? Then rewrite your draft.

REVISING THE SECOND DRAFT

We cannot show all the text-level changes Anita made to arrive at the final version of the essay that follows, since that would surely tax the patience of even the most sympathetic reader, but we can show you a representative paragraph and the operations Anita used to produce her final version. Here are the changes that Anita made on paragraph 3.

ORIGINAL:

3   A hospital is, of course, where many people go to obtain relief from pain and a cure for illness. Modern hospitals contain complex, expensive radiologic equipment designed to explore and visualize almost every portion of your body. They have laboratory tests and equipment which determine whether these parts of your body are functioning correctly. If a particular test is ordered that your hospital does not have the capacity for performing, a sister hospital will have the necessary equipment. After the testing is done, your physician is then able to correlate the findings and prescribe the proper treatment. If medical treatment is necessary

the hospital has the ability to make available to you the necessary drugs. If surgical intervention is necessary hospitals are equipped with the needed instruments and the equipment needed to prevent contamination, as well as people skilled in their use. A hospital is a highly technological institution designed for the diagnosis and treatment of disease.

In revising this paragraph, Anita made a number of changes, not the least of which were reducing the wordiness and condensing the information provided. But the most important changes she made were in providing greater *focus* for the paragraph so that what this paragraph was *doing* in the essay became clear to the reader. In the original version, the paragraph had no shape or clear function; it was merely a *list of things* that described the hospital. In transforming this paragraph, Anita emphasized that although a hospital is a technological marvel, it is still a business, and therefore it may sometimes place such things as "efficiency" and "turning a profit" above the needs of patients. Through this emphasis, Anita was able to make this paragraph a suitable transitional paragraph—in fact, a crucial one. This revised paragraph sets up the dramatic difference, which the subsequent paragraphs will explore, between the hospital-as-ideal and the hospital-as-it-is. The key here is focusing phrases like "of course," "and to be sure," and "admittedly," which prepare the reader for the irony of the paragraph that follows. Note how Anita has improved the *focus* of the paragraph by organizing it around its true function.

REVISED:

A hospital is assumed to be, of course, a place where ailing   3
souls go to relieve their pain and seek a cure for their illnesses.
And to be sure, modern hospitals do contain complex, expensive
diagnostic equipment designed to probe and examine almost every
portion of the body. Admittedly, they are equipped with extensive
laboratories and skilled technicians who are able to determine
precisely how your body is functioning. This amazing technology
facilitates the physician's prescription for the patient's treatment.
But a hospital is also a *business*—with all that the term implies
about "efficiency" and routine. Perhaps it is here that the dream
begins to fade.

The tighter, less rambling sentence structure, the greater focus, and the final transition sentence, which prepares the reader for the surprising "inhospitality" of hospitals, all serve to make this paragraph more effective, more reader-based. The reader no longer has to guess what Anita's point is in providing this information. Anita performed these same operations on each section of the essay as she revised her second draft.

Proofreading and Editing

After Anita finished rewriting her second draft, she had a friend read through it, looking for sentence structure problems, poor word choice, and mechanical or usage errors. She found a few minor errors, primarily typographical. After she retyped her text, she was ready to submit it to her instructor.

Nursing: The Dream and the Reality
Anita Critz

1   As a child I dreamed of becoming a nurse. To me, nursing represented the highest goal a woman could reach. Actually, the only nurse that I knew intimately was one of the people that I loved and respected the most—my grandmother. I derived most of my impressions of nursing from her and her stories about the hospital in which she worked. Grandma was a quiet, soft-spoken aristocratic lady who was able not only to demonstrate love, but also to command respect from everyone around her. Helping with the physical and emotional needs of her family and neighbors was a normal way of life for her, and taking care of patients in a hospital seemed to be only an extension of what she did at home. I remember the hospital where she worked as a big stone building, surrounded by well-kept lawns, shade trees, and flowers, fortified by a tall wrought-iron fence. In my memory my grandmother personified a gentle care, while the building itself represented a quiet, safe environment for patient recovery. These loving, idealistic images formed the basis of my expectations of hospitals and nursing.

2   In my daydreams existed a perfect hospital, a place dedicated to the art of healing and committed to the recuperation of all its patients. The hospital edifice would shelter the sick and infirm from the noise and clatter of the streets. Its wide halls, free of clutter, antiseptic, and aesthetically appealing, would convey a holiness for the human body and its health. Each room would be equally spacious, filled with flowers and personal items to make the patient more comfortable. Visitors,

coming only at appropriate times, would be therapeutic for the patients. No piece of equipment needed for the diagnosis and treatment of diseases would be absent. In my child's eyes, the hospital would be a place of refuge from the realities of pain and suffering, a place of rest, diagnosis, treatment, and healing.

I staffed my dream hospital with flawless nurses, their education   3
including techniques of observation, patterns of diagnosis, and loyalty to dedicated physicians. Each nurse listened to her patients nonjudg- mentally, understanding the confidentiality such information deserved. Clear, concise communication between doctors and patients was skill- fully maintained. All in all, my nurses were unfailingly caring, nurturing, understanding, knowledgeable, authoritative, and polite.

That was the dream. ... I am now a nurse in a large metropolitan   4
hospital; the differences between my daydreams and the reality of hospital work have occasionally been startling and difficult to accept. Though my childhood fantasy was reinforced somewhat during school years by teachers who promoted the ideals my grandmother represented, my first weeks on the job in a hospital were an abrupt—and rude— awakening.

A hospital is assumed to be, of course, a place where ailing souls   5
go to relieve their pain and seek a cure for their illnesses. And to be sure, modern hospitals do contain complex, expensive diagnostic equipment designed to probe and examine almost every portion of the body. Admittedly, they are equipped with extensive laboratories and skilled technicians who are able to determine precisely how your body is functioning. This amazing technology facilitates the physician's prescription for the patient's treatment. But a hospital is also a *busi- ness*—with all that the term implies about "efficiency" and routine. Perhaps it is here that the dream begins to fade.

In fact, a modern hospital is not a place of rest, peace, or quiet.   6
Typically, the day begins about 4:00 A.M. with a bright light shining in a patient's face: a nurse putting a thermometer under his tongue, pumping up a blood pressure cuff around his arm. Then, when she has thoroughly roused him, she suggests, not facetiously, that he "go back to sleep." Two hours later the laboratory technician wakes him up to get some blood for more tests ordered by the doctor. Just as he dozes off to sleep, the nurse returns to set him up for a bath before breakfast trays arrive. Probably a transporter will claim him before he gets to eat, taking him to the chilly, bustling radiology department. When he returns to his room, tired and needing sleep, he is disturbed by a parade of equipment clattering past his door. First comes the

dinner cart, then the central supply cart, linen cart, dressing cart, emergency cart, wheel chairs, and surgery cart. Frequent pages and announcements over the loudspeaker climax the hospital sound effects. By this time it's visiting hours. Not realizing how tired he is, his friends settle in and attempt to help the time pass by more quickly. The myth of hospital tranquility is quickly dispelled by just one day spent as a patient. Hospitals aren't hospitable.

7   Perhaps I am being unfair. Whether the hospital is a dream or a reality, it must still be staffed by nurses. Caring competently for the physical and emotional needs of patients is the goal of every nurse—but the capacity for doing so differs in each nurse. The expectations of nurses and their patients clash in the reality of their interaction.

8   All licensed nurses are certainly required to meet technical standards of nursing skills and knowledge. But a more difficult component of nursing is how a nurse will react emotionally as she is faced with patients' problems. Just last week I had a patient who had been diagnosed as a stroke victim. Her physical symptoms originally included complete paralysis on one side and loss of speaking and comprehension ability. Her prognosis, however, seemed to be quite good. She had shown improvement in motor ability and could occasionally speak. Her physician ordered use of the typical therapies to bring her to her full potential. However, the patient clearly indicated both verbally and with gestures that she wanted to be left alone. As her nurse, I had to confront the conflicting priorities: my own commitment to healing patients, my belief that life should be lived to the fullest; and the knowledge that each human being has the right to decide the course of his own life. This particular patient chose to resist recovery—much to her doctor's dismay. Should I, as patient-advocate, have defended her or, as a healer, do what I considered to be in her best interests to promote healing? My own religious and moral beliefs made objectivity difficult to achieve. I had traveled far from the schoolgirl naivete that had made all nursing decisions facile—textbook-simple. Where was the warm pattern of grace and comfort which my grandma had manifested in my daydreams of long ago?

9   The reality of daily nursing care allows little time even to be aware of patients' emotional needs, let alone meet them. But even when the nurse does find the time and the objectivity necessary to understand her patient's psychology, she faces the problem of confidentiality. How can she protect her patient's personal dignity? It is difficult, if not impossible, to balance patient rights with the need to maintain accurate

records for legal purposes or the human desire to share an interesting story over lunch.

On occasion the reality of hospital life and the dream world I created   10
as a child merge. To me, and all of those who remember the dreams, such times are tantalizingly sweet, promising a glory and a presence which cannot be maintained. They do, however, keep us striving to turn our ideals into reality.

Although I now know that even my grandmother's world was not   11
as simple and straightforward as it appeared, the dreams that she fostered have helped sustain me in my career as a nurse, and continue to inspire me to greater service to those under my care.

Exercise

Answer these questions about Anita's final draft.

1. How successful was Anita in following her revision plans for this final draft?
2. Compare this final draft with Anita's first and second drafts. What are the most dramatic changes between these three versions? Which of Anita's revision strategies seemed to be most productive?
3. This personal experience essay does not depend on a narrative structure. How does Anita use description to carry the reader from point to point?
4. Can you articulate for yourself the intention of the essay?

Writing Task

Read the next draft of your essay and examine it at the text, sentence, and word levels. Revise it until it is as reader-based as you can make it. Then proofread and edit your final draft.

Writing Assignment

Read the following essay, "Champion of the World," by Maya Angelou, an excerpt from her autobiographical work, *I Know Why the Caged Bird Sings*.

Champion of the World

Maya Angelou

1   The last inch of space was filled, yet people continued to wedge themselves along the walls of the Store. Uncle Willie had turned the radio up to its last notch so that youngsters on the porch wouldn't miss a word. Women sat on kitchen chairs, dining-room chairs, stools and upturned wooden boxes. Small children and babies perched on every lap available and men leaned on the shelves or on each other.

2   The apprehensive mood was shot through with shafts of gaiety, as a black sky is streaked with lightning.

3   "I ain't worried 'bout this fight. Joe's gonna whip that cracker like it's open season."

4   "He gone whip him till that white boy call him Momma."

5   At last the talking was finished and the string-along songs about razor blades were over and the fight began.

6   "A quick jab to the head." In the Store the crowd grunted. "A left to the head and a right and another left." One of the listeners cackled like a hen and was quieted.

7   "They're in a clinch, Louis is trying to fight his way out."

8   Some bitter comedian on the porch said, "That white man don't mind hugging that niggah now, I betcha."

9   "The referee is moving in to break them up, but Louis finally pushed the contender away and it's an uppercut to the chin. The contender is hanging on, now he's backing away. Louis catches him with a short left to the jaw."

10   A tide of murmuring assent poured out the doors and into the yard.

11   "Another left and another left. Louis is saving that mighty right . . ." The mutter in the Store had grown into a baby roar and it was pierced by the clang of a bell and the announcer's "That's the bell for round three, ladies and gentlemen."

12   As I pushed my way into the Store I wondered if the announcer gave any thought to the fact that he was addressing as "ladies and gentlemen" all the Negroes around the world who sat sweating and praying, glued to their "master's voice."

13   There were only a few calls for R. C. Colas, Dr. Peppers, and Hires root beer. The real festivities would begin after the fight. Then even the old Christian ladies who taught their children and tried themselves to practice turning the other cheek would buy soft drinks, and if the Brown Bomber's victory was a particularly bloody one they would order peanut patties and Baby Ruths also.

14   Bailey and I laid the coins on top of the cash register. Uncle Willie didn't

allow us to ring up sales during a fight. It was too noisy and might shake up the atmosphere. When the gong rang for the next round we pushed through the near-sacred quiet to the herd of children outside.

"He's got Louis against the ropes and now it's a left to the body and a right to the ribs. Another right to the body, it looks like it was low. . . . Yes, ladies and gentlemen, the referee is signaling but the contender keeps raining the blows on Louis. It's another to the body, and it looks like Louis is going down." 15

My race groaned. It was our people falling. It was another lynching, yet another Black man hanging on a tree. One more woman ambushed and raped. A Black boy whipped and maimed. It was hounds on the trail of a man running through slimy swamps. It was a white woman slapping her maid for being forgetful. 16

The men in the Store stood away from the walls and at attention. Women greedily clutched the babes on their laps while on the porch the shufflings and smiles, flirtings and pinching of a few minutes before were gone. This might be the end of the world. If Joe lost we were back in slavery and beyond help. It would all be true, the accusations that we were lower types of human beings. Only a little higher than apes. True that we were stupid and ugly and lazy and dirty and, unlucky and worst of all, that God Himself hated us and ordained us to be hewers of wood and drawers of water, forever and ever, world without end. 17

We didn't breathe. We didn't hope. We waited. 18

"He's off the ropes, ladies and gentlemen. He's moving towards the center of the ring." There was no time to be relieved. The worst might still happen. 19

"And now it looks like Joe is mad. He's caught Carnera with a left hook to the head and a right to the head. It's a left jab to the body and another left to the head. There's a left cross and a right to the head. The contender's right eye is bleeding and he can't seem to keep his block up. Louis is penetrating every block. The referee is moving in, but Louis sends a left to the body and it's an uppercut to the chin and the contender is dropping. He's on the canvas, ladies and gentlemen." 20

Babies slid to the floor as women stood up and men leaned toward the radio. 21

"Here's the referee. He's counting. One, two, three, four, five, six, seven . . . Is the contender trying to get up again?" 22

All the men in the store shouted, "NO." 23

"—eight, nine, ten." There were a few sounds from the audience, but they seemed to be holding themselves in against tremendous pressure. 24

25   "The fight is all over, ladies and gentlemen. Let's get the microphone over to the referee . . . Here he is. He's got the Brown Bomber's hand, he's holding it up . . . Here he is . . ."

26   Then the voice, husky and familiar, came to wash over us—"The winnah, and still heavyweight champeen of the world . . . Joe Louis."

27   Champion of the world. A Black boy. Some Black mother's son. He was the strongest man in the world. People drank Coca-Colas like ambrosia and ate candy bars like Christmas. Some of the men went behind the Store and poured white lightning in their soft-drink bottles, and a few of the bigger boys followed them. Those who were not chased away came back blowing their breath in front of themselves like proud smokers.

28   It would take an hour or more before the people would leave the Store and head for home. Those who lived too far had made arrangements to stay in town. It wouldn't do for a Black man and his family to be caught on a lonely country road on a night when Joe Louis had proved that we were the strongest people in the world.

Answer the following questions about Angelou's essay.

1.   What is the experience that Angelou is writing about in this essay? Why does it qualify as a pivotal or poignant experience worth exploring and articulating for a reader?

2.   What seems to be Angelou's point in relating this experience? To whom would you say this essay is addressed?

3.   There is an abundance of dialogue in this essay. Why is it an effective strategy for evoking the atmosphere and immediacy of the experience she is relating?

4.   How is it that the experience of one person—Joe Louis, in this case—is related to the experience of a whole strata of society, Blacks?

5.   How much of the experience is Angelou's own and how much is filtered through the experience of others who shared this experience with her? In other words, how much of this experience is collective and how much intrinsically personal?

6.   How does Angelou handle the irony of the episode she describes?

7.   What is the overall tone of the essay?

Write an essay describing an experience that you have shared with others as a group or as a family, perhaps something that you have thought about many times since and have discussed with others. It could be a historical event you witnessed in person or on TV, such as the moon landing of 1969, a sporting event in which your team or a specific individual was particularly heroic, or a tragedy that affected the lives of a number of people. Or it could be a poignant confrontation within a family, a group of friends, a club or special interest society, etc., whose ramifications you are still grappling with.

I. Getting Started: Inventing and Planning
    A. Jot down several experiences that you feel qualify for the purposes of this assignment.
    B. What were the circumstances of these experiences? (Who? What? Why? When? How?)
    C. What makes these experiences particularly memorable and important to you and the people with whom you shared them?
    D. Choose one of these experiences. Explore it, using the inventing strategies discussed in Chapter 2.
    E. Discuss the audience to which you will direct this essay. What will they need to know about the experience for it to make sense to them, and also strike them as something significant? How common might this experience be for them?
    F. Describe the organization you intend to use.
    G. What point of view will you use? What tone?

II. Drafting and Revising
    A. Write the first draft of your essay.
    B. Read your draft and answer the following:
        What is the intention of your essay?
        To whom is the essay addressed?
        What is the actual organization of your essay?
        What point of view is evident? What tone?
    C. Evaluate your answers to these questions. Examine your draft at the text, sentence, and word levels. Is it a predraft or a rough draft?
    D. Describe your plans for revising or rewriting your draft.
    E. Repeat steps *b* to *d* if necessary.

III. Proofreading and Editing
    A. Allow some time to go by, then read your final draft out loud.
    B. Correct errors in sentence structure, word choice, and mechanics and usage.

Writing Assignment

Select a fictional character and write a personal essay *as if* you were that fictional character. You might choose a cartoon character, a movie character, a TV character, or some other fictional character. Keep your tongue "out of your cheek"; that is, write the essay without intentional satire or parody. If, for instance, you chose Hawkeye Pierce of the M*A*S*H TV series, you might select the experience you think most affected his character during the run of the series, perhaps the death of Henry Blake, and write an essay that explores this event and its implications for Hawkeye.

I.   Getting Started: Inventing and Planning
    A.   List several characters you are interested in writing "for."
    B.   Choose one of these characters and do some brainstorming about experiences in his or her fictional life and their effect on his or her development within the particular medium in which they exist (movies; tv; record album; cartoon; book). The 5W+ procedure should be particularly useful here.
    C.   Once you have familiarized yourself with various experiences in this character's life, determine how you will proceed. Where will you begin your discussion? Which experiences will you relate? How will you maintain the "voice" of the character you are pretending to be? What are some characteristic personality traits of the person that would become evident in this personal experience he or she is relating?
    D.   To whom would this character write his or her essay? In the case of Hawkeye, he might write to his father in Maine, to whom he addressed several letters in various episodes of the TV series, or, perhaps, to Father Mulcahy, several years after the Korean War has ended, as he writes about how he has changed. How would the choice of audience affect the selection and arrangement of the experiences the person would relate?
    E.   With what intention might this character write the essay? For example, you could assume that Hawkeye would write an "anti-war" essay, or you could imagine him changing his attitudes radically after several years back home in civilian medical practice, and offering a surprising defense of what he formerly opposed.
    F.   How can you ensure that the character stays in character, or, articulate and defend the change for the reader if he or she departs

from it? To what extent do you, the writer, identify with the character you have chosen? Should you keep your distance, or should you reveal your own solidarity with the views of your fictional persona?

II.   Drafting and Revising
   A.   Write the first draft of your essay.
   B.   Read your draft and answer the following:
     What is the intention of your essay?
     To whom is the essay addressed?
     How is your essay organized?
     Is the point of view consistent? Is the tone appropriate for the character you have chosen?
   C.   Evaluate your draft in terms of your answers to these questions. Examine your draft at the text, sentence, and word levels. Is it a predraft or a rough draft?
   D.   Describe your plans for revising or rewriting your draft.
   E.   Repeat steps *b* to *d* if necessary.

III. Proofreading and Editing
   A.   Allow some time to go by, then read your final draft aloud.
   B.   Correct errors in sentence structure, word choice, and mechanics and usage.

7 *Explaining a Process*

The Process Essay

In Chapter 6 you read several examples of personal experience essays and wrote one. Reading an essay about an experience that was significant enough to inspire a piece of writing can be satisfying, moving, disturbing, or perhaps inspirational. Through reading such pieces, we can understand—and even experience—events through another person's eyes. Sometimes we find that others' experiences and feelings are remarkably similar to our own; this can strengthen our ties to others, making us feel more a part of the human community. Other times, we are amazed to find that people have been shaped by events and/or feelings that are totally foreign to our experience. Writing such as this may force us to view the world from a different perspective; we may begin to examine critically attitudes and behaviors that we never before questioned.

Another kind of discourse that you have read and written is writing that *explains*. This is often referred to as *exposition*. People read exposition for a variety of reasons: they may wish to become informed about a situation, an event, or a person; they may wish to learn a body of information so that they may become certified in some profession; they may be curious about a concept, idea, or process.

One of the most common types of exposition is writing that tells readers how to do something or that explains the sequence of events that lead (or have led) to a particular outcome. This type of writing, sometimes called "process" exposition, is extremely valuable to readers. Through reading it, an individual may learn such things as how to write a professional vita, how to apply for a job, how to invest wisely, how to buy the "right" car, how to shop for clothes, how to sew a dress, how to bake a mocha-almond layer cake, and so forth. Or an individual can learn about a process that he may never personally engage in but considers important or interesting, such as how a bill becomes a law or how a professional mountain climber scales a rock face. You are already familiar with various types of process exposition: recipes, instructions that explain how to assemble an item, directions accompanying sewing patterns, descriptions of election procedures, and so forth. You also may remember why you needed to read these process expositions and your reactions to them as a *reader*. For example, you may have read a set of directions or a description of a procedure because you had a specific goal: to fill out your tax form properly or to present your "best" self during a job interview. But you probably became frustrated, or even hostile, if the writer used terms with which you were not familiar. For example, you were instructed to "sauté the shrimp in clarified butter," but you do not know the meaning of "sauté" or "clarified butter." You also might have become angry if steps in the process seemed to be left out, or if the order in which the operations were to be performed was not clear.

Writers create process essays to share information with readers. Their intention for writing, therefore, is to explain something to someone. A scientist will explain his methods and procedures so that other scientists can reproduce his steps and recreate his outcome. A professional photographer may explain a simple means of developing pictures so that other people may develop their own at home. An avid rose breeder may explain how hybrids are created so that rose lovers can understand and appreciate the complexity of the process, even though they may never create a hybrid themselves. An explanation of a process differs from a narrative of personal experience because the writer's intention in writing differs. The purpose of process exposition is to instruct or explain, not to share personal insights or experience. A good process essay will be written in such a way that the information being presented, not the writer's attitudes, beliefs, experiences, or perceptions, is the focus of the essay.

Since the focus of a process essay is the information being conveyed, the tone and point of view should reinforce this emphasis. If a writer attracts undue attention to himself or to his attitudes toward the process he is describing, his readers may become confused as to his intention in writing. For example, readers may wonder whether a writer's intention is to explain the steps to follow when purchasing a used car or to discourage a person from buying one, if the process being described is burdensome, ridiculous, or unreasonable. This is not to say that a writer must entirely mask his attitude toward the process he's explaining. A professional photographer who writes an essay directed toward amateur photographers about the process of developing film does not have to eradicate all traces of enthusiasm from his text. Rather, he should keep his intention in writing in mind: to explain how to develop film, *not* to describe how excited and wonderful developing film makes him feel.

In structure, process exposition often relies on a chronological ordering of events; it thus resembles narration. However, since the writer's intention in writing a process essay is to explain how to do something or how something happens or happened, the structure must be carefully designed to convey the particular process being described. The order of steps must be clear and logical; if there are many steps, the writer must devise some means of grouping them. The writer must also present the reader with all pertinent information, at the appropriate place or places. For example, most essays that explain how to prepare a particular dish, such as spinach lasagna, begin with a list or list plus discussion of the foods and cooking utensils needed.

A finished, *reader-based* process essay will exhibit these characteristics:

1.   The nature and scope of the information presented will match the requirements of the particular audience being addressed. For example, if the audience consists largely of readers who know little about the process being described, sufficient background information will have been provided. No aspects of the process will have been left to the readers' imagination; vivid, concrete details will have been supplied. If, in addition to being ignorant of the process, the audience of readers is largely uninterested in it, a serious attempt to capture that audience's interest—perhaps by demonstrating the relevance and/or importance of the process—will have been made.

2.   When appropriate, the process or procedure being described will be divided into clear steps, presented in a logical order. Complex or complicated steps will, if possible, be divided into substeps: Step 1; Step 2; Step 3 (which includes three substeps, a, b, c); Step 4. If a complex or complicated

step cannot be broken down into smaller steps, it will be adequately covered in terms of length, explanation, and illustration. Steps and substeps will be clearly labeled so that the reader knows "where she is" at all times. Steps that might easily be reversed, confused with one another, or deleted will be given special attention. If necessary, the reader will be warned not to omit a particular step, to be sure to perform certain steps in the prescribed sequence, etc.

3. Each step or substep will be described precisely and in detail. If the process being described is highly intricate (such as blowing bubbles with bubble gum), cannot be observed (like a nuclear chain reaction), or is global in scope (like a social process), the essay will—if possible—contain metaphorical comparisons. For example, a nuclear chain reaction can be compared to what happens if a room is filled wall to wall with mousetraps laden with golf balls; one ball is thrown into the room, which causes a trap to spring and set an additional ball free, which causes other traps to spring, which causes. . . .

4. The relationship between a step and the steps that precede and follow it will be clear and logical, whether the process being described is one the reader hopes to be able to *do,* such as developing film, or one the reader hopes to be able to *understand,* such as how a baseball player is recruited for a professional baseball team.

Examples

Here are two examples of effective process essays. Read each one carefully and answer the accompanying questions. The questions will help you glean these models for ideas and strategies you can use in writing and revising your own texts.

Freewriting
Peter Elbow

The most effective way I know to improve your writing is to do freewriting   1
exercises regularly. At least three times a week. They are sometimes called "automatic writing," "babbling," or "jabbering" exercises. The idea is simply to write for ten minutes (later on, perhaps fifteen or twenty). Don't stop for anything. Go quickly without rushing. Never stop to look back, to cross

something out, to wonder how to spell something, to wonder what word
or thought to use, or to think about what you are doing. If you can't think
of a word or a spelling, just use a squiggle or else write, "I can't think of
it." Just put down something. The easiest thing is just to put down whatever
is in your mind. If you get stuck it's fine to write "I can't think what to
say, I can't think what to say" as many times as you want; or repeat the
last word you wrote over and over again; or anything else. The only re-
quirement is that you *never* stop.

2   What happens to a freewriting exercise is important. It must be a piece
of writing which, even if someone reads it, doesn't send any ripples back
to you. It is like writing something and putting it in a bottle in the sea.
The teacherless class helps your writing by providing maximum feedback.
Freewritings help you by providing no feedback at all. When I assign one,
I invite the writer to let me read it. But also tell him to keep it if he prefers.
I read it quickly and make no comments at all and I do not speak with
him about it. The main thing is that a freewriting must never be evaluated
in any way; in fact there must be no discussion or comment at all.

3   Here is an example of a fairly coherent exercise (sometimes they are
incoherent, which is fine):

> I think I'll write what's on my mind, but the only thing on my mind
> right now is what to write for ten minutes. I've never done this before
> and I'm not prepared in any way—the sky is cloudy today, how's that?
> now I'm afraid I won't be able to think of what to write when I get
> to the end of the sentence—well, here I am at the end of the sentence—
> here I am again, again, again, again, at least I'm still writing—Now
> I ask is there some reason to be happy that I'm still writing—ah yes!
> Here comes the question again—What am I getting out of this? What
> point is there in it? It's almost obscene to always ask it but I seem
> to question everything that way and I was gonna say something else
> pertaining to that but I got so busy writing down the first part that
> I forgot what I was leading into. This is kind of fun oh don't stop
> writing—cars and trucks speeding by somewhere out the window,
> pens clittering across peoples' papers. The sky is still cloudy—is it
> symbolic that I should be mentioning it? Huh? I dunno. Maybe I
> should try colors, blue, red, dirty words—wait a minute—no can't do
> that, orange, yellow, arm tired, green pink, violet magenta lavender
> red brown black green—now that I can't think of any more colors—
> just about done—relief? maybe.

QUESTIONS ABOUT "FREEWRITING"

1.   In this excerpt, Elbow discusses freewriting exercises. What seems to be his intention in writing?

2.   What point(s) of view did Elbow select: first person ("I"), second person ("you"), third person ("writers," "individuals," "a person," etc.), or a combination? How does this help the reader focus his or her attention on the process being described? Does this excerpt make you feel that you could try freewriting? To what extent does Elbow refer to himself? Do these references increase the effectiveness of the text? How do they affect the tone?

3.   Elbow presents a fairly extensive example of freewriting. Why is the example helpful? The writer of the example claims never to have done freewriting before and is "not prepared in any way." Does this make a difference to the reader? Explain.

4.   Describe the structure of the essay: what happens first, next, and so on. What seem to be the major parts? How does the structure help reveal the author's intention to his readers?

5.   Describe the characteristics of the audience you think is being addressed. Does the amount of information being presented seem to be adequate for that audience? Explain. Does the choice of words seem appropriate? Explain. How often does Elbow provide specific illustrations and details of the process he is describing? List some of the details and illustrations. How do they strengthen the text?

When You Camp Out, Do It Right

Ernest Hemingway

Thousands of people will go into the bush this summer to cut the high cost of living. A man who gets his two weeks' salary while he is on vacation should be able to put those two weeks in fishing and camping and be able to save one week's salary clear. He ought to be able to sleep comfortably every night, to eat well every day and to return to the city rested and in good condition.

But if he goes into the woods with a frying pan, an ignorance of black flies and mosquitoes, and a great and abiding lack of knowledge about cookery the chances are that his return will be very different. He will come back with enough mosquito bites to make the back of his neck look like a relief map of the Caucasus. His digestion will be wrecked after a valiant battle to assimilate half-cooked or charred grub. And he won't have had a decent night's sleep while he has been gone.

3   He will solemnly raise his right hand and inform you that he has joined the grand army of never-agains. The call of the wild may be all right, but it's a dog's life. He's heard the call of the tame with both ears. Waiter, bring him an order of milk toast.

4   In the first place he overlooked the insects. Black flies, no-see-ums, deer flies, gnats and mosquitoes were instituted by the devil to force people to live in cities where he could get at them better. If it weren't for them everybody would live in the bush and he would be out of work. It was a rather successful invention.

5   But there are lots of dopes that will counteract the pests. The simplest perhaps is oil of citronella. Two bits' worth of this purchased at any pharmacist's will be enough to last for two weeks in the worst fly and mosquito-ridden country.

6   Rub a little on the back of your neck, your forehead and your wrists before you start fishing, and the blacks and skeeters will shun you. The odor of citronella is not offensive to people. It smells like gun oil. But the bugs do hate it.

7   Oil of pennyroyal and eucalyptol are also much hated by mosquitoes, and with citronella they form the basis for many proprietary preparations. But it is cheaper and better to buy the straight citronella. Put a little on the mosquito netting that covers the front of your pup tent or canoe tent at night, and you won't be bothered.

8   To be really rested and get any benefit out of a vacation a man must get a good night's sleep every night. The first requisite for this is to have plenty of cover. It is twice as cold as you expect it will be in the bush four nights out of five, and a good plan is to take just double the bedding that you think you will need. An old quilt that you can wrap up in is as warm as two blankets.

9   Nearly all outdoor writers rhapsodize over the browse bed. It is all right for the man who knows how to make one and has plenty of time. But in a succession of one-night camps on a canoe trip all you need is level ground for your tent floor and you will sleep all right if you have plenty of covers under you. Take twice as much cover as you think that you will need, and then put two-thirds of it under you. You will sleep warm and get your rest.

10   When it is clear weather you don't need to pitch your tent if you are only stopping for the night. Drive four stakes at the head of your made-up bed and drape your mosquito bar over that, then you can sleep like a log and laugh at the mosquitoes.

Outside of insects and bum sleeping the rock that wrecks most camping 11
trips is cooking. The average tyro's idea of cooking is to fry everything and
fry it good and plenty. Now, a frying pan is a most necessary thing to any
trip, but you also need the old stew kettle and the folding reflector baker.

A pan of fried trout can't be bettered and they don't cost any more than 12
ever. But there is a good and bad way of frying them.

The beginner puts his trout and his bacon in and over a brightly burning 13
fire the bacon curls up and dries into a dry tasteless cinder and the trout
is burned outside while it is still raw inside. He eats them and it is all
right if he is only out for the day and going home to a good meal at night.
But if he is going to face more trout and bacon the next morning and
other equally well-cooked dishes for the remainder of two weeks he is on
the pathway to nervous dyspepsia.

The proper way is to cook over coals. Have several cans of Crisco or 14
Cotosuet or one of the vegetable shortenings along that are as good as lard
and excellent for all kinds of shortening. Put the bacon in and when it is
about half cooked lay the trout in the hot grease, dipping them in corn
meal first. Then put the bacon on top of the trout and it will baste them
as it slowly cooks.

The coffee can be boiling at the same time and in a smaller skillet 15
pancakes being made that are satisfying the other campers while they are
waiting for the trout.

With the prepared pancake flours you take a cupful of pancake flour 16
and add a cup of water. Mix the water and flour and as soon as the lumps
are out it is ready for cooking. Have the skillet hot and keep it well greased.
Drop the batter in and as soon as it is done on one side loosen it in the
skillet and flip it over. Apple butter, syrup or cinnamon and sugar go well
with the cakes.

While the crowd have taken the edge from their appetites with flapjacks 17
the trout have been cooked and they and the bacon are ready to serve.
The trout are crisp outside and firm and pink inside and the bacon is well
done—but not too done. If there is anything better than that combination
the writer has yet to taste it in a lifetime devoted largely and studiously
to eating.

The stew kettle will cook your dried apricots when they have resumed 18
their predried plumpness after a night of soaking, it will serve to concoct
a mulligan in, and it will cook macaroni. When you are not using it, it
should be boiling water for the dishes.

In the baker, mere man comes into his own, for he can make a pie that 19
to his bush appetite will have it all over the product that mother used to

make, like a tent. Men have always believed that there was something mysterious and difficult about making a pie. Here is a great secret. There is nothing to it. We've been kidded for years. Any man of average office intelligence can make at least as good a pie as his wife.

20   All there is to a pie is a cup and a half of flour, one-half teaspoonful of salt, one-half cup of lard and cold water. That will make pie crust that will bring tears of joy into your camping partner's eyes.

21   Mix the salt with the flour, work the lard into the flour, make it up into a good workmanlike dough with cold water. Spread some flour on the back of a box or something flat, and pat the dough around a while. Then roll it out with whatever kind of round bottle you prefer. Put a little more lard on the surface of the sheet of dough and then slosh a little flour on and roll it up and then roll it out again with the bottle.

22   Cut out a piece of the rolled out dough big enough to line a pie tin. I like the kind with holes in the bottom. Then put in your dried apples that have soaked all night and been sweetened, or your apricots, or your blue-berries, and then take another sheet of the dough and drape it gracefully over the top, soldering it down at the edges with your fingers. Cut a couple of slits in the top dough sheet and prick it a few times with a fork in an artistic manner.

23   Put it in the baker with a good slow fire for forty-five minutes and then take it out and if your pals are Frenchmen they will kiss you. The penalty for knowing how to cook is that the others will make you do all the cooking.

24   It is all right to talk about roughing it in the woods. But the real woodsman is the man who can be really comfortable in the bush.

QUESTIONS ABOUT "WHEN YOU CAMP OUT, DO IT RIGHT"

1.   What seems to be Hemingway's intention in writing?

2.   Describe what happens in this essay. What are the major sections? Are any sections subdivided into smaller parts? Choose *one* section that is subdivided and list the subdivisions. How do these help the reader digest the information?

3.   On pages 257 to 258, Hemingway describes how to bake a pie. Comment on the steps into which he divided this process. Which did he choose to combine? Why? Did he delete any? Why?

4.   What does Hemingway present as *the* most significant determinants of whether or not a person will enjoy a camping trip? Might he have chosen others? How does he convince a reader that his choices are significant? How do his choices contribute to the effectiveness of his essay?

5. To whom is the essay addressed? Describe the characteristics of the intended audience. Then comment on the point of view of the essay. Notice that the camper Hemingway talks about is referred to as "he" or addressed as "you." For what readers might such a point of view be appropriate? For what readers might such a point of view be inappropriate? How has the audience being addressed affected the information presented? The choice of language? Look again at Hemingway's discussion of pie baking.

6. How does Hemingway focus his reader's attention on the information he is presenting? To what extent is Hemingway a "presence" in this essay? Does he portray himself as an "expert" camper? What are the advantages of doing so? What are the disadvantages?

7. Describe the tone of the essay. What major factors seem to have shaped the tone? How does the tone help reveal the writer's intention to his readers?

Summary

Now that you have examined an explanation and two examples of process exposition, here is a list of several important operations that a writer usually performs before he begins to draft a process essay.

1. The writer must thoroughly *familiarize* himself with the process he is going to describe.

2. The writer must *analyze* the process in order to make at least preliminary decisions about each of the following:

    a. The best order (chronology) in which to present the information.

    b. The number of steps in which to present the information. Specifically, which "small" steps can and should be combined into single steps, which steps, if any, can be deleted, and so forth.

    c. What aspects or steps of the process are difficult to grasp and, therefore, should be given special treatment. What steps might readers overlook or reverse.

    d. How may connections between steps best be established.

    e. What tools, implements, or aids, if any, are required for the process, and in what way and when should these requirements be presented to the reader.

3. The writer must *analyze* his audience in order to determine strategies for adapting the information to that audience: the nature and amount of

background information to be included; where readers might experience difficulty in comprehension; how to best present the sequence of steps and their relationship to one another.

A Rhetorical Task:
Joe and Writing a Complaint Letter

Initial Responses

Joe Norris, along with the rest of his class, was asked to write a process essay. The nature of the process to be explained, the reason for explaining that process, and the audience to whom the essay would be directed was left to the student. Since Joe was preparing to be an English teacher and had an interest in writing, he decided to explain the process of writing a letter of complaint.

VISUALIZING THE AUDIENCE

Joe began thinking about and forming the rhetorical context for his essay by selecting and then visualizing his audience. Since he planned to be a high school teacher, he decided to address his essay to high school students, specifically juniors and/or seniors. Here are some of the questions he asked himself to help him visualize his audience:

--What are high school juniors and seniors interested in?

--Do they have personal experience with faulty goods or services?

--How much do they already know about writing complaint letters?

--How interested are they likely to be in the subject?

--How much background information do I need to present: what can I assume they already know; and what *can't* I assume they already know?

CREATING A CONTEXT

As Joe thought about his audience, a complete context started to form in his mind. He thought about the circumstances under which he might present such an essay to his readers. Perhaps he would distribute his essay to his students as a reading assignment, then give them study questions that would be used in a subsequent class discussion of writing complaint letters. Finally, he would give his students a writing assignment: They would each be required to write a letter of complaint in response to a real-life situation.

ARTICULATING INTENTION

Joe thought more about his readers and the context for his essay. This enabled him to articulate his goal in writing: to show his students, through information and example, how to write an effective letter of complaint. Joe felt that his students would appreciate learning how to write such letters. He also thought that in learning to write an effective letter of complaint, his students would be exposed to some important rhetorical principles and strategies, such as the importance of considering an audience, the importance of focus and organization, and how to choose a convincing tone.

More Inventing and Planning

Much of Joe's initial inventing and planning involved visualizing the audience and creating the context for writing. Joe did most of this mentally; his efforts, therefore, cannot be observed. However, at some point, he was ready to think about the text itself, and this led him to do some thinking about letters of complaint, since his essay would be devoted to describing how such letters are written. Now Joe began to invent and plan in writing. He used lines, numbers, letters, headings, and spacing to organize his inventing and planning and labeled the larger portion of his written inventing and planning "Format of Paper." Some parts of his design are quite detailed; others are quite sketchy. Finally, Joe used a variety of inventing and planning strategies: for example, he asked himself questions, such as "why write a complaint letter?"; he categorized and subcategorized data; he talked to himself. Here is a reproduction of his written inventing and planning:

JOE'S INVENTING AND PLANNING

1. Audience--High School Jrs/Srs.
2. Purpose--to ~~give~~ show info/through examples ~~to audience~~ how to write letters of complaint.

3. Why write a complaint letter?
--dissatisfaction w/service
--   ″   w/product
--to correct problem w/product or service after local in person &
telephone conversations have proved fruitless

4. to whom is the letter
written--President of firm   Send it to pres.--he/she might see
Complaint department   it & expedite claim--at least,
Service rep.   proper   dept.   will   get   it
                                              immediately.

5. Tone that should be used for letter
--Businesslike--i.e. formal to semi-formal w/touch of humor, perhaps.

6. Information to be included
--Specific data re: source of complaint
   Purchase date/price of product/service
   name of product/service
   Serial #/Invoice #
   Cost
   Name of (Salesperson/servieeperson)
   where purchased
   Reason for dissatisfaction
   Copies of receipts/other correspondence
   Request satisfaction by certain date
   (Sincere threat--one that is practical/effective)

7. Format of Letter--business format
--typewritten correctly & neatly
--Proper Salutation
-- #1--Give info. re: Purchase date of prod./serv., identification (i.e.,
        serial) # of purchased item; location of purchase
-- #2--Tell Ask Co. what is necessary to resolve problem Nature
        & history of problem including copies of receipts, warranties,
        etc.
-- #3--Request (again) satisfactory assistance; length of time you
        will wait before taking further action.
--After signature, include address & phone #
--Keep copies of letters.

Things to avoid
   informal/silly stationery
   Angry, vitriolic tone--nastiness/sarcasm

Idle/unrealistic threats
Wordiness--letter should be brief--only include info. necessary for
person to handle complaint.

Format of Paper

I pretty much know at this point what the body of the paper will
be--the basics of writing a letter of complaint w/maybe an example
of some sort. My major concern at this point is coming up w/the
proper intro. or "hook." I've been toying w/3 different ways of opening.
(1.) Use a generic opening--i.e., relate how important it is to be able
to write a good letter of complaint, which seems a rather lame intro.
(2.) Describe a fictional, rather humorous situation & use it to as a
paradigm of complaint writing. (3.) Show how not to write complaint
letters by giving as an example one of Mark Twain's famous complaint
letters, such as the one to his local gas company.

I tend to lean toward #2 for several reasons:

1)   I feel most comfortable w/a humorous tone.
2)   Most high school students would rather read something funny
     than serious--even if it's educational.
3)   It seems the best format to describe the specific process involved
     from start to finish.
4)   The other two ideas don't seem to have the desired focus.

So, #2 it is.

Situation--One winter's day you buy a brand new, top of the line widget
(Model 47-CXY, Serial #9) & take it home & put it on the shelf. The
first nice day of spring comes along (ideal for using your widget), so
you take it outside. You start it up only to realize that not only is the
hemulator warped, but it is also ready to fall off (or whatever). What
do you do?

1.   Put it back in box & take it back to store for replacement.
2.   Salesman says "No can do"--90 day warranty.
3.   Store Manager--"No can do"- "   "   "

4. Initial reactions--
    a. turn widget on dept store & hemulate them
    b. beat up the sales clerk & store manager
    c. write a nasty letter to the manufacturer (Empire Widgets of
        California, EWOC)

All three responses, though understandable, are wrong.

12. They don't fail to solve the basic problem--the faulty hemulator
     on your long-awaited widget.
21. They set up nasty vibrations that are especially dangerous around
     a non-hemulated widget.

What to do?
What do you do to get satisfaction if the store doesn't help you?

1. Write a letter of complaint.
    Preferably to President--he might read it himself or at least someone
    on his staff will--and forward it to the proper dept.
2. Things to avoid
    2. Purple lace stationary--use standard white
    1. Anger, nastiness, sarcasm--be objective neutral in tone though
        firm
    2. Unrealistic threats--don't threaten to blow their headquarters
        up--but do tell them you will take your complaint to a 3rd
        party
    3. Wordiness--just give them the info. needed to resolve problem.
        1. Use business tone--semiformal/to formal
3. Things to include
    1. Proper salutation, etc.
    2. ¶ 1--purchase (complete w/Model & Serial #s), date & location
        & other significant details
    3. ¶ 2--tell what the problem is & history (include copies of re-
        ceipts, etc.) Ask for satisfaction
    4. ¶ 3--politely, but firmly ask for satisfaction w/in certain time
        or you will contact 3rd party. Include address & phone #.

Write example letter.

Conclusion--list advantages of letter over force, etc.

Happy Hemulating!

Change from 2nd Person to 3rd.

Writing Task

Here is a rhetorical task for you similar to the one with which Joe was presented:

Choose a relatively *simple* process with which you are thoroughly familiar and write an essay explaining that process to an audience of your choice. Be sure to pick a process that you perform often and know well. You may choose a process that you can explain in a manner similar to the one used in one of the example essays. Be sure to consider the intention of your essay: what is your overall goal in explaining this process? Examining the process Joe used to visualize his audience and articulate his intention for writing may help you get started.

Do your inventing and planning by following these steps:

1.   Write down some processes that you know how to do well.

2.   What sorts of people would be interested in knowing how to do these things? Write down some of the characteristics of these persons, such as age, level of education, interests, etc.

3.   Start rearranging and grouping your information. For example, can you begin to group some of the characteristics of the people who would be interested in knowing how to do a particular process next to or underneath some of the processes you listed?

4.   Tentatively pick a process that you know well from those you have been considering. List some of the steps in performing the process.

5.   List the characteristics of the people who would be interested in learning how to do this process.

6.   Try to articulate the intention of your essay.

7.   Examine the structures of the Elbow and Hemingway essays. Can the process that you are going to describe be presented in a similar manner? If not, describe how you will modify a particular structure. How many parts will your essay contain? What do you expect to present in each part?

8.   Write a draft of your essay.

Drafting and Revising

What follows are successive drafts of Joe's essay. He produced a total of three drafts, with intervening planning and inventing sessions. Again, we have provided marginal commentary to make it easier for you to relate portions of the draft to the discussions that follow. The third, and final, draft will appear in the section on proofreading and editing.

JOE'S FIRST DRAFT

Little Johnny shoveled walks, mowed lawns, and performed sundry other tasks for his neighbors in order to earn enough money to purchase the one thing he most desired in life--a Model 47-CXY Widget. Little Johnny toiled away until, joy of joys, he had enough money in his savings to buy his long-awaited widget. Unfortuneately, even though Little Johnny had his Widget, he couldn't use it immediately because it was Winter when he bought it and everyone knows that you can't widget in the Winter. [1]

1. Narration of events: What is the intention of the text?

So, Little Johnny put his Widget away until the green grass and blue skies of Spring (the very best time for Widgeting) returned. At long last, that hoped-for day appeared as if by magic. The air was warm, the sun bright, and the grass as dry and refreshing as a grandmother's carress. [2]

Johnny ran to his closet, grabbed his brand-new, top-of-the-line Widget, and ran outside to share this wonder with his friends. Anxiously, he opened the box. Carefully, he removed his beloved Widget. Ecstatically, he pushed the "On" button. Mournfully, he watched his brand-new, never-been-used Widget smoke and heard it grind and smelled it burn.[1] [3]

Little Johnny pushed the "Off" button and peered closely inside the Widget. No wonder it didn't work! Not only was the hemulator warped, it had been faultily attached to the wocketa. So, little Johnny and his friends trooped to the store where Johnny had purchased his Widget and asked for a new one because the one Johnny had wasn't made right. [4]

2. Narrative structure continues

"No can do," said the salesclerk, because the 90-day limited-warranty had expired. (Which it had.) [5]

"No can do," said the manager, for the same reason. [6]

Little Johnny's first reaction was to overload put the Widget on overload and hemulate the department store and everyone in it. When he cooled down a little, he just wanted to beat up the clerk and the store manager. Then he just thought he'd write a nasty letter to the manufacturer [7]

(Empire Widgets of California--EWOC).[2] At last, Johnny, being the rational little bugger that he was, decided that the best thing he could do would be to write a letter of complaint to EWOC; after all, it seemed about the only practical way to get his problem resolved satisfactorily.

3. Intention only now apparent

8   Little Johnny didn't know exactly who he should write his letter to, so he went to the library and the nice lady behind the desk helped him find the address of the company and the name of its president (one D. Vedar).[3] Little Johnny figured that even if the president didn't read the letter himself, one of his staff would and, therefore, Little Johnny's letter wouldn't be lost in the shuffle, which is usually ~~happens~~ *what* when you are just a little Johnny.[4]

4. Code expression

9   Little Johnny, being the thorough bugger that he was, also asked his father about writing a letter of complaint. His father told him to avoid anger, nastiness, and sarcasm in his letter. Instead, he should be neutral[5] in tone.[5] Johnny's father also said that unrealistic threats should not be used. In other words, said Johnny's father, don't threaten to blow up EWOC's headquarters--simply tell them that if they fail to resolve Johnny's complaint, that he would take his problem to a third party, such as the Better Business Bureau.[6]

5. Code words

6. Focus unclear

7. Code word

10   Little Johnny's father also said to avoid wordiness.[7] Johnny should give just the ~~mistake~~ information that is necessary for the company to resolve his complaint. He also ~~told~~ gave Johnny some plain white ~~business~~ stationary to write his letter on. He said it was more business-like[9] than his mother's purple and yellow stationary.[8]

8. Focus unclear

9. Code word

11   Little Johnny's father was a very smart man. *his letter should*

12   Little Johnny's father also told Little Johnny ~~to~~ *should* include: all the information regarding the purchase (including model and serial number, the date and location of purchase, and any other significant facts); the nature and history of the problem and copies (not the originals) of all pertinent receipts, warranties, correspondence, and any other documents; ~~and, finally,~~ a polite, but firm, request for action to be taken[10] within a specific time period (usually, 3-4 weeks); a warning that a third-party will be notified if necessary; and, finally, Little Johnny's address and phone number.

10. Code expression

13   Here's what the letter Little Johnny wrote:

Little Johnny
143 Main Street
Greentown, Ill. 43897
~~Feb. 26,~~ 1984
April 1

Mr. D. Vedar, President
Empire Widgets of California, Inc.
2001 Leia Boulevard
Cucamonga, California 35678

Dear Mr. President:

   On November 27, 1983, I purchased a Model 47-CXY Widget (Serial Number 123454321). I purchased this product at Solo's Appliance and Hardware, located in Greentown.

   Due to the nature of the Winter in Illinois, I was unable to use my new Widget until March 28, 1984. The first time I attempted to use my new Widget, it severly malfunctioned. Upon investigation, <u>it was determined that</u>[11] not only was the hemulator warped, but it had been faultily attached to the wocketa. However, when I returned the faulty Widget to Solo's Appliance and Hardware, I was informed that they could not help me because the 90-day warranty had expired.

11. Passive:
    actor/
    agent
    deleted

misunderstanding
   Therefore, due to the nature of the ~~problem~~, I would appreciate your help in resolving this problem. Would you be so kind as to inform Mr. C. W. Backamm, the manager of Solo's, that my claim is justified and that my Widget should be replaced by a new one? Enclosed are copies of my receipt, warranty, model and serial numbers to help prove the validity of my claim.

   I am looking forward to your reply and the resolution of my problem, and will wait three weeks before seeking third-party assistance. Contact me at the above address or at my home number: 487-555-3490.

                                              Sincerely,

                                              Little Johnny

   Needless to say, Little Johnny's letter was extremely effective and   14
he received a new Widget even before the very last snowfall of the
Spring had melted.

EVALUATION

Text Level   Joe's first effort at drafting produced approximately four type-written pages. He knew that he would need to revise whatever he produced; therefore, although he *typed* his first draft, he used 8 × 11 1/4 yellow lined legal paper. And he set his typewriter at triple space, leaving himself plenty of room between lines to add things—if necessary.

Joe let some time pass after he finished his four pages. Then he began to examine and evaluate his draft. The first thing he noticed was that his draft contained a great deal of narration. In fact, the first seven paragraphs (almost the first two pages) told a story about Little Johnny and his "widget." Joe thought about the purpose of his essay, to show, through information and examples, how to write a letter of complaint, and began to wonder why he spent almost half of his draft talking about Little Johnny and his widget. Joe realized that he didn't even mention letter writing until paragraph 8—and that paragraph merely explained to whom a complaint letter should be sent and where information about a company can be obtained.

In fact, specific information about how to write a letter of complaint was not given until paragraph 9. Joe flipped to his last page and realized that it didn't explain much about how to write a letter of complaint, either—it contained the letter that Little Johnny sent. There was *only* one page in Joe's draft that gave any information about writing complaint letters.

Joe examined the major paragraphs on that page, thinking that he might be able to use them in his next draft, but he was skeptical. He suspected that since he had crammed his whole essay into one page without realizing it, the information about complaint letter writing that he presented would be squeezed together and disorganized. He was right.

Paragraph 9 was not focused. Joe could see that it did not have a specific purpose. The paragraph mentioned tone, but didn't really explain much about it. It also contained two sentences about the use of threats.

Paragraph 10 was not focused either. Joe began the paragraph by telling his readers to avoid "wordiness," but he didn't explain what he meant by wordiness. The next sentence advised the reader to include "information that is necessary for the company to resolve" complaints, but didn't describe the nature of this information. The paragraph ended with two sentences about proper stationery (white is better than purple and yellow).

Finally, paragraph 12 seemed to be a "catch-all" paragraph; it listed *everything* that a letter of complaint should contain. Joe also noticed that paragraph 12 consisted of one sentence! Paragraph 12 was more a collection of data than a unit of writing.

Joe found that a major portion of his first draft *narrated* events about Little Johnny's problems with his widget, even though the purpose of the essay was to explain how to write a letter of complaint. Joe also discovered that the paragraphs that described the process of letter writing frequently *shifted focus;* they covered many topics, and these topics were not presented in a logical order. On the basis of these discoveries about the *structure* of his text, Joe concluded that he had probably written a predraft.

Sentence Level Most of the sentences in Joe's draft were well formed. They did not provide much additional information about the state of his essay. Joe did notice a few awkward sentences, but since he had tentatively concluded that his first draft was a predraft, he knew that he would need to write an entirely new draft, possibly after an additional inventing and planning session. Consequently, he did not need to revise individual sentences.

One sentence did catch his attention, however, and he made a note of it. When Joe reread his first draft aloud, he noticed this sentence in Little Johnny's letter of complaint: "Upon investigation, it was determined that not only was the hemulator warped, but it had been faultily attached to the wocketa." It struck Joe that this sentence "didn't sound like" Little Johnny; in fact, the sentence, especially the portion "it was determined that," did not sound very natural for *anybody*. Joe remembered his purpose *and* his audience: high school students. He wondered whether his example letter was a good one. Perhaps it had other problems. He made a note to himself: After he revised his essay so that it was structurally sound, he would pay special attention to the sample letter, making certain that it was a good letter that illustrated everything he had instructed his readers to do.

Word Level While examining his essay at the text level, Joe noted that he had neglected to explain and illustrate a great many things about complaint letter writing. Therefore, he looked carefully for both pronouns with unclear referents and code words and expressions because he suspected that he had used words that contained a great deal of information for him, but did not express it to the reader. Joe did not find problems with pronoun use, but he did find a number of code words and expressions.

Joe found the first code expression in paragraph 8, which recommended that letters of complaint be addressed to the president of a company. The paragraph concluded with this sentence: "Little Johnny figured that even if the president didn't read the letter himself, one of his staff would and, therefore, Little Johnny's letter wouldn't be lost in the shuffle, which is what usually happens when you are *just a little Johnny*." What was meant by "just a little Johnny"? Did it mean "when you are just a little kid"? If so the *high school students* reading the essay would not need to address complaint letters to the president of a company, since they were not "little kids." Or did "just a little Johnny" mean "just an average, everyday consumer—not a state senator or a prominent surgeon." Joe realized that he had to be specific about this.

Joe located the next code words in paragraph 9. He had already discovered a problem with this paragraph when he examined the structure of his draft. Paragraph 9 advised the reader to be "neutral in tone." Joe realized that the use of a proper tone was important in complaint letter writing. Yet he never told his readers what he meant by "tone" or by "neutral." Again, when Joe thought of his audience, he realized how much information was contained in the expression "neutral in tone." He was expecting his readers to read his mind.

Paragraph 10 contained two code words: "wordiness" and "businesslike." The use of the code word "wordiness" was quite serious. Proper use of words was important in complaint letter writing, and yet the meaning of "wordiness" was not at all clear. Did it mean the use of several words when one would do? The next sentence, sentence 2, seemed to suggest that "wordiness" had to do instead with the presentation of unnecessary information: "Johnny should give just the information . . . necessary for the company to resolve his complaint." Or was sentence 2 not referring to wordiness at all, but rather presenting a new topic that had nothing to do with wordiness? Joe was not sure. He realized that *he* did not know what he meant by wordiness.

The use of the code word "business-like" was not disastrous, but Joe did wonder what, exactly, he was trying to advise his readers to do. Was "business-like" meant to be synonymous with "plain white"? Was he suggesting that his readers always use plain white paper when they write complaint letters? Perhaps he didn't want to use the word "business-like" at all, since it implied too much. Would "conservative" be better? Joe also began to wonder whether information about stationery was particularly important, especially since he would need to discuss such matters as tone thoroughly in his next draft.

Joe also located a code expression in paragraph 12. He advised that a letter of complaint should include a "polite, but firm, request for *action to be taken.*" Joe realized that he should not assume that his readers would know what sorts of "actions" they should request. He resolved to clarify this in a subsequent draft of his essay.

The use of these code words and expressions supported Joe's conclusion that he had produced a predraft.

Exercise

Examine Joe's draft and answer the following questions.

1.   If you had written Joe's predraft, what portions of it would you consider significant? List them.

2.   Does Joe's predraft suggest any strategies for structuring the next draft? Why or why not? Explain.

3.   Should Joe begin a second draft immediately, or does he need to do some more inventing and planning? Explain your answer.

Writing Task

Read the first draft of *your* essay and answer the following questions.

1.   Describe the intention of your essay.

2.   Describe the audience to whom your essay is addressed.

3.   Describe the way you intended to structure your essay.

4.   Describe the tone that you intended to use.

Now examine your own first draft at the *text, sentence,* and *word* levels. Then determine whether you have written a *pre*draft or a *rough* draft.

If you have written a predraft, carefully glean it for possible theses and for strategies that you might use in writing your next draft. Also, reexamine your inventing and planning process. Do you need to engage in an additional, significant inventing and planning session? If so, what does your predraft tell you you should focus your second session on: clarifying your *intention* for writing; defining your audience more carefully; creating a different or more explicit structure?

If you have written a rough draft, identify the portions of the text that need work. Overall, does your intention need to be clarified? Do you need to provide your reader with additional frames of reference; do you need to sharpen the focus within the paragraphs of your text?

REVISION

Because Joe's first draft was a predraft, he did not try to rewrite it by adding, deleting, rearranging, and substituting. Instead, he chose to read through it, searching for ideas and for strategies that he could use in writing his next draft. He would use these ideas and strategies to invent and plan again.

As Joe read through his draft, he decided that most of the first two pages, devoted to Little Johnny, were not particularly useful for a second draft, although they had served to get him started. He jotted a note to himself in the margin of his first page: "Too much story—not enough process. Shorten." On the bottom of the first page he also jotted a possible plan for shortening the Little Johnny story:

-- Para. 1--Johnny buys widget--it fails to work.
-- Para. 2--J. takes widget back to store--store won't do anything
-- Para. 3--decides to write letter of complaint--goes to library

Next, Joe wrote out a brief list of questions, strategies, and tasks for himself:

1. Shorten intro (Little Johnny & how he bought a widget)
2. Expand body to include more info. on how to go about writing letter of complaint
3. Make a general outline for a letter of complaint
4. Rewrite body first—then do intro—intro should be subordinate to body
5. Use second person to make Johnny's story more universal and get audience involved??

Unfortunately, at this point, Joe stopped inventing and planning. He started to write a second draft. Here is what he wrote:

Little Johnny was very proud of himself. He had shoveled walks, mowed lawns, and performed sundry other tasks for his neighbors in order to earn enough money to purchase the one thing he most desired in life--a Model 47-CXY Widget. ~~He was also~~ Being a wise lad, he purchased his Widget during the Thanksgiving Day Sales (when the price is the lowest), and he carefully stored it in his closet until Spring because, as we all know, you can't Widget in Winter.

However, When Little Johnny Spring arrived and Little Johnny took his Widget outside for the first time, he was the happiest kid on the block. That is, until he pushed the "On" button. Mournfully, he watched his brand-new, never-been-used Widget smoke and heard it grind. Quickly, he pushed the "Off" button and peered inside. When the smoke had cleared, he saw that not only was the hemulator warped, it had been faultily attached to the wocketa.

Tearfully, Little Johnny put the broken Widget back in its box and returned to the store where he had purchased his long-awaited toy months before. However, he was devastated when the salesclerk said that, because the 90-day warranty had expired, there was nothing that the store could do. When the store manager said the same thing, Johnny was beside himself with anger and frustration. His first reaction was to blow the store and everyone in it to smithereens!

If nothing else, Johnny was a rational little bugger and he knew that blowing up the store would not get him a new Widget.

After three paragraphs and the first sentence of the fourth, Joe gave up. He scrawled, "THIS IS KA KA!!!DO IT STRAIGHT!!!" on the bottom of the page. He then engaged in some additional, serious inventing and planning and produced a more detailed plan, which he revised as he developed. Here is the plan that resulted from Joe's second extensive inventing and planning session:

Revision 2

Tone--Fairly informal   It's easier to call than write
PV--2nd   We forget to write
Audience--H.S. Jr's or Sr's
Intro--Not a letter-writing age. It's the age of the telephone. It's the
       next best thing
       Calls--no records, tend to be informal, ill-prepared
       Letters--permanent records; clear, concise statements of what
       writer wants to say

    I. When to write letter of complaint
        A. When you're dissatisfied w/product/service

B. <u>After</u> local in-person & telephone discussions have proved futile

II. Things to avoid in letter
   A. Informal trivial stationary
   B. Angry tone, i.e., nastiness, sarcasm
   C. Idle or unrealistic threats
   D. Wordiness--"just the facts, man"

Separate and move these into other categories?

II. Who write letter to
   A. Complaint Dept. Sales Rep - OK
   B. Pres is better
   C. Address of Co., name of pres can be found in almost any public library--ask librarian

III. A letter of complaint is a business letter--so be businesslike
   A. Don't use an angry tone--the appropriate tone should be formal to semi-formal (maybe humor)--expand
   B. Don't write Appear professional
       don't wr type the letter on white stationary--not purple, etc.
   C. Be considerate--the people who will read your letter are *expand?* busy--don't be wordy--"Just the facts, ma'am."
   D. Don't make unrealistic threats--sincere ones are OK (e.g., contacting B.B.B.)

IV. The Format
move?
   A. typed neatly & correctly on plain, white stationary
   B. Use proper salutation, etc.
   C. (Para.) I --Purchase date
       Part?   --identification (Model and/or serial #)
                     --where purchased
       (Para.) II --nature & history of problem including <u>copies</u> of
       part?   all receipts, warranties, etc.
                     --tell what is necessary to satisfactorily resolve problem
       (Para.) III--Reiterate request for assistance
       Part?   --state length of time you will wait before contacting 3rd party
                     --give info where you can be reached

V. Follow up
omit
   A. Keep copies of *all* correspondence
   B. Keep records of who you talked to re: problem, where & when

      C. If problem isn't resolved satisfactorily or you simply don't
          hear from co., contact 3rd party

VI. Sample letter

VII. Summary
      A. Be businesslike
      B. Be firm--don't settle for unsatisfactory settlement
      C. As long as you act cool & rationally, the co. will be forced
          to deal w/you the same way

After this more lengthy inventing and planning session, Joe began his second draft. He decided not to take his own advice and "start with the body"; he felt that getting the first paragraph right was important. Joe wrote several beginnings before he finally got going with his second draft. Once he had a satisfactory beginning, Joe was able to follow his plan quite closely and produce a second draft.

Here is a summary of Joe's revision strategies for draft one:

1. After determining that he had produced a predraft, Joe read through his draft, searching for ideas and strategies. He jotted down some of these.

2. He made a brief list of tasks and strategies.

3. After a premature start on a second draft, Joe used his list of strategies to generate ideas for a more detailed plan, which he revised *as he wrote it*. He jotted down directions and ideas regarding his plan, such as "expand" or "separate?," next to various portions of it; he would heed these directions to himself when he wrote his second draft.

4. Joe rewrote his introduction several times. The successful completion of his introduction provided the impetus Joe needed to produce a second full draft.

Writing Task

If your first draft was a predraft:

1. Engage in an additional planning and inventing session, if you have determined that it is necessary.

2. Write a second draft.

If your first draft was a rough draft, write a second draft.

JOE'S SECOND DRAFT

1   At least once in your life you have probably wanted to write a letter of complaint about a product or a service that you felt was unsatisfactory. If you did actually write a letter, you may have written something during the heat of the moment without giving much thought to resolving the problem. In other words, your reader was probably aware that you were angry, but was unclear as to the exact nature of the problem and what you expected him or her to do about it. As a result, you were further frustrated by what appeared to be a lack of concern on the company's part, when, in actuality, the company wasn't exactly sure what the problem was or what you expected them to do about it.

1. Shifting focus; function unclear

2   However, a clear, well-written letter of complaint can often be a very effective means of resolving a problem.[1] The letter should be clear and courteous. A letter of complaint is not a forum for releasing your pent-up hostilities. Here are a few suggestions for writing an effective complaint letter.

If you are going to spend time and effort on a letter, why

3   While you can address your letter to the Complaint Department or to a sales rep, it is usually more effective to send your complaint directly to the president of the company. Even if he does not handle your case personally, you can be sure someone on his staff will expedite your problem efficiently. You can find the name of the president and the address of the company in Standard and Poor's Register of Corporations, Directors and Executives, which is available in most libraries.

4   It is important to keep in mind that a letter of complaint is a business letter--so be businesslike. Choose your words carefully so that you don't come across hostile and angry. Try to describe your problem in an objective, low-key manner. "Flying off the handle" will not help you solve your problem.

5   As in all business situations, appearance means an awful lot. It's worth your while to go to the extra effort to type your letter on regular white stationary. Write in longhand, if you must, but at all costs refrain from using that purple stationary that your little sister uses.

6   Be brief. The people who will read your letter are busy people. Don't waste their time by writing a long, windy letter. Try to be concise: give all the information/necessary without including superfluous detail. As Sgt. Friday always used to say, "We just want the facts, ma'am. Just the facts."

Also, don't make idle or unrealistic threats.

2. Function and focus need to be clearer

Be-sure-you-tell-the-company-exactly-what-it-is-that-you-want-them-to-do-in-order-to-correct-the-problem.--After-all,-you-can't-really-expect-a-corporation-to-do-any-more Remember to include what exactly what it is that you expect the company to do to resolve your problem. While it may be obvious to you that the company should replace or repair the faulty product or even reimburse you the cost, it may not be so apparent to the company.[2]

The letter itself should be short. Once again, it should be typewritten   7
neatly and correctly on plain white stationary, unless you have some
3. Focus not   stationary that identifies you with some group or organization, such
   clear   as a club or a business. Remember to use the proper format for a
                standard business letter.[3]

4. Context   The first part of a complaint letter (usually one paragraph) should   8
   for para-   contain the date of purchase, some kind of product identification (such
   graphs 8,   as model and/or serial number), and where the product was purchased.
   9, 10   Keep it short and simple. Keep-in-mind-that-the-easier-it-is Remember,
   needs to   the easier you make it for the reader to understand you, the easier it
   be made   will be to resolve your problem.
   clearer
                The second part (again, most often one paragraph) should explain   9
                the nature and history of the problem. You need to describe what
                happened when you used the product and why you are dissatisfied.
                Indicate, where appropriate, that you have enclosed copies (Never-
                enclose-the-original of all pertinent receipts, warranties, etc. (Never
                enclose the originals--they should be retained for your own records.)

                The third, and last, part of a letter of complaint should reiterate   10
                your request for assistance and explain what is necessary to satis-
                factorily resolve the problem as far as you are concerned. It should
                also give a-deadline the length of time you will wait before contacting
                a third party (such as the Better Business Bureau or a government
                agency that deals with consumer affairs). Be certain to include an
                address and a telephone number where you can be reached during
                working hours. This last part of a complaint letter may consist of
                one or two paragraphs.

                An effective letter of complaint should look something like this: 11

                                            M. V. Smith
                                            143 Main Street
                                            Greentown, Ill. 43897
                                            April 1, 1984

Mr. D. Vedar, President
Empire Widgets of California, Inc.
2001 Leia Boulevard
Cucamonga, Cal. 35678

Dear Sir:

On Nov. 27, 1983, I purchased a Model 47 Widget (serial number 3657). I purchased this product at Solo's Hardware Store, located in Greentown, Illinois.

The first time that I used my Widget was on March 28, 1984, at which time it severely malfunctioned. Upon close examination, it was determined that not only was the hemulator warped, but it had not been properly attached to the wocketa. When I returned the faulty Widget to Solo's Hardware, I was informed that they could not help me because the 90-day warranty (see enclosed copy) had expired.

Therefore, due to the nature of the misunderstanding, I would appreciate your help in resolving this problem. Would you be so kind as to inform Mr. C. W. Bakka, the manager of Solo's, that my claim is justified and that my Widget should be replaced with a new one? Enclosed are copies of my receipt and warranty to help prove the validity of my claim. I am looking forward to your reply and the resolution of our problem. I will wait three weeks before seeking third-party assistance. Feel free to contact me either at the above address or at my home number: 487/364-8567.

Sincerely,

M. V. Smith

12   As you can see, this sample letter contained all the information necessary to resolve the problem. The writer was courteous and objective from the very start. Even though he was probably very angry at both the manufacturer and the retailer, his letter was cool and rational. Such an objective, businesslike tone manner gives the writer a great deal of credibility and makes his demands seem reasonable. Remember, as long as you the writer are straightforward and polite, the company

will normally treat you in the same way. A dissatisfied customer doesn't make any money for a company. Remember, they need and want your business.

EVALUATION

Text Level   In his second inventing and planning session, Joe had devised a plan, and he assumed he had followed it when he wrote his second draft. His plan called for a general text structure something like this:

--Intro

--I-When to write a letter of complaint

--II-Who to write to

--III-A letter of complaint is a bus. letter; be businesslike
  use appropriate tone
  appear professional
  be brief

--IV-Format

--V-Sample Letter

--VI-Summary

Joe was generally pleased with his plan: It presented enough information, and the information was logically arranged. He decided, therefore, that a good strategy for evaluating his second draft would be to examine his paragraphs and see whether they did what his outline suggested they should do. This would also enable him to detect such problems as shifting focus or excessive narration, which are features of writer-based prose. Joe did not *think* he had produced a predraft this time, but he needed to be certain.

An analysis of each of the paragraphs in his second draft produced the following:

Para. 1-intro

Para. 2-tells that a letter can be effective, that it should be clear and
  courteous, that it is not a forum for releasing hostilities

Para. 3-tells who letter should be addressed to and related info.

Para. 4-talks about being businesslike--don't sound angry; be objective

Para. 5-more about being businesslike--appearance

Para. 6-talks about being brief, but supplying necessary info, including what company should do to resolve problem

Para. 7-talks about length of letter and format/appearance

Para. 8, 9, 10-talk about format; one para per part of letter

Para. 11-sample letter

Para. 12-conclusion/summary

After he compared what he had done with what he had intended to do, it was clear to Joe that he had followed his plan quite closely. His draft contained the major parts that he intended it to contain, and they were presented in the correct order. In most instances, his paragraphs were focused, containing only the information and examples that he intended them to. Joe concluded that he had produced a rough draft, a text that was finished enough to revise.

Sentence Level   Again, the sentences in Joe's second draft were well formed. They did not provide any contradictory evidence; they affirmed his conclusion that he had, indeed, written a rough draft.

Word Level   Joe had eradicated the code words and expressions that he had discovered in his first draft. He did not discover any new ones, nor did he find an excessive number of pronouns with unclear referents. He concluded, again, that he had written a rough draft.

Writing Task

Examine your second draft at the text, sentence, and word level, keeping your intention and audience in mind. Have you produced a predraft or a rough draft?

REVISION

Text Level: Rewriting to Clarify Intention   While examining the structure of his draft, Joe noticed certain problems that he would need to address when he rewrote his draft. Here are the problems he noticed and the rewriting strategies he chose for addressing these problems. Joe's main concern in rewriting at the text level was to give his readers adequate frames of reference and to sharpen the focus of his text wherever necessary.

Paragraph 2 had several topics; it exhibited shifting focus. In addition, according to Joe's plan, paragraph 2 was supposed to be an important part of the essay. It was supposed to explain when to write a letter of complaint. As it was, paragraph 2 was an "empty" paragraph. It served no purpose except to move the reader on to the next paragraph, the beginning of the body of the essay. Joe knew that he needed to do some thinking about this. Did he want to modify his plan and *not* talk about when to write a letter of complaint? If so, he could turn paragraph 2 into a short transitional paragraph; its sole function would be to move the reader gracefully into the essay. Or did he want to do some additional inventing and planning and write a *real* paragraph explaining the circumstances under which a person should write a letter of complaint instead of, say, making a phone call. Ultimately, Joe decided that his plan needed to be modified: There was not much to say about when to write a letter of complaint—it was pretty obvious. He decided to turn paragraph 2 into a transitional paragraph.

Joe expected to have trouble with paragraph 4. He assumed that the notion of "tone" might be the culprit. Joe had avoided using the code word "tone," but he still did not feel he had totally solved the problem of determining exactly what he wanted to say. He knew he wanted his readers to avoid sounding angry, but now he had thrown in the word "businesslike," and he was not sure he had defined it sufficiently. Also, he had advised his readers to "choose your words carefully." Was *that* what he meant by tone? After carefully considering the purpose of paragraph 4, as a paragraph and as part of his essay, Joe decided that since this paragraph and paragraphs 5 and 6 talked about aspects of being "businesslike," he had defined "businesslike" sufficiently. He also determined that since he had not mentioned the word "tone," he did not need to deal with the concept; mostly, he wanted to advise his readers not to sound angry, but to sound objective and low-key. Therefore, the only change he would make in the paragraph would be to reorder the sentences. He thought that the sentence about "flying off the handle" should come after the sentence that advised the reader not to sound hostile and angry rather than after the sentence advising the reader to sound objective.

Again, Joe knew he would have to work with paragraph 6 some more. As he produced his draft, he had done a great deal of crossing out and rewriting in this paragraph, but he never got it the way he wanted it, although he went on anyway. According to his plan, paragraph 6 was supposed to talk about the third subtopic related to being businesslike: being brief. Unfortunately, the relationship between being brief and being businesslike was not clearly established. Also the pieces of the paragraph did not fit together well. Joe knew that all the information fit together somehow, and that he wanted it all in one paragraph. But he needed to integrate the information so that the reader could see the relationship. Joe ultimately solved his first problem by rewording the second sentence and including the word "business"; he felt that this would link the information in the paragraph to being businesslike; "*Business* people are very busy people. Don't waste. . . ." Joe also decided to add a sentence to help integrate the information in the paragraph: "Don't waste their time by writing a long, windy letter. *This can be done through a careful selection of words and information.*" He would then go on to talk about concise word choice and the inclusion of appropriate information and exclusion of inappropriate information.

Paragraph 7 did little but repeat, in a helter-skelter, unfocused manner, what had already been said. And, in doing so, it distracted the reader, making it more difficult for her to follow the sequence of Joe's instructions. Joe decided to delete it, moving any new information elsewhere.

Joe had decided earlier that he would need to revise his sample letter in paragraph 11. He did not think that structure was a problem; the letter was structured well and followed the advice he had given his readers. However, he was concerned about its tone. He had advised his readers to produce letters that were "objective" and "low key." He was concerned that his letter sounded pompous because of such phrases and sentences as "severely malfunctioned" or "it was determined that."

Finally, Joe noticed a few minor organizational problems. For example, he needed to rework the beginning of paragraph 8 to let the reader know that the next paragraphs—8, 9, and 10—would provide the general format for a letter of complaint. He would also watch for places where he might add some additional detail, or perhaps an example.

Sentence Level   Joe read his draft aloud and was satisfied with its structure and with the sound of his sentences. He did not find many writer-based sentences. However, a number of sentences in his sample letter were causing problems with the *tone* of the essay. Here are Joe's revisions and his reasons for them:

M. V. Smith
143 Main Street
Greentown, Ill. 43897
April 1, 1984

Mr. D. Vedar, President
Empire Widgets of California, Inc.
2001 Leia Boulevard
Cucamonga, Calif. 35678

Dear Sir:

[1]On Nov. 27, 1983, I purchased a Model 47 Widget (serial number 3657). [2]I purchased this product at Solo's Hardware Store, located in Greentown, Illinois.

[3]The first time that I used my Widget was on March 28, 1984, at which time it severely malfunctioned. [4]Upon close examination, it was determined that not only was the hemulator warped, but it had not been properly attached to the wocketa. [5]When I returned the faulty Widget to Solo's Hardware, I was informed that they could not help me because the 90-day warranty (see enclosed copy) had expired.

[6]Therefore, due to the nature of the misunderstanding, I would appreciate your help in resolving this problem. [7]Would you be so kind as to inform Mr. C. W. Bakka, the manager of Solo's, that my claim is justified and that my Widget should be replaced with a new one? [8]Enclosed are copies of my receipt and warranty to help prove the validity of my claim.

[9]I am looking forward to your reply and the resolution of our problem. [10]I will wait three weeks before seeking third-party assistance. [11]Feel free to contact me either at the above address or at my home number: 487/364-8567.

                                                        Sincerely,

                                                        M. V. Smith

1. Sentence 1--OK.
2. Sentence 2--OK.
3. Sentence 3--Sentence is OK, but will have to do something about "severely malfunctioned" and "at which time."

4. Sentence 4--Poor sentence; "it was determined that" sounds awkward and takes the <u>person</u> ("<u>I</u> determined that ...") out of the sentence. If I put myself back into the sentence as a subject, I can simplify it: "Upon close examination, I determined that the hemulator was warped and that it had not been properly attached to the wocketa." I can further revise this sentence by restructuring "Upon close examination," which also sounds pretty stilted: "I examined the Widget closely and determined that the hemulator was warped and that it had not been properly attached to the wocketa." Much better.

5. Sentence 5--OK; I think I'll avoid mentioning Mr. Bakka's name at this time. Why call attention to the fact that he couldn't or wouldn't help me? I may want to shop at Solo's again.

6. Sentence 6--The sentence is OK, but "Therefore" bothers me and I don't like "due to the nature of the misunderstanding" either.

7. Sentence 7--OK, but "would you <u>be so kind as to</u>" sounds awfully wordy to me.

8. Sentence 8--OK.

9. Sentence 9--OK, but do I need to add the word "to" in order to balance the sentence: "I am looking forward to your reply and <u>to</u> the resolution of our problem."?

10. Sentence 10--OK.

11. Sentence 11--OK.

Word Level Excluding his sample complaint letter, Joe was, for the most part, satisfied with his choice of words. He made a few changes at the word level.

Here is a summary of Joe's revision strategies for draft two.

1. Joe examined each of his paragraphs to see whether it was focused and to see whether it followed his plan. He noted any paragraph that seemed to either lack focus or fail to follow his plan. When he found paragraphs that did not follow his plan, he thought about whether he should modify his plan or his paragraph. When he found unfocused paragraphs, he tried to determine *why* the paragraph was not focused and to make changes accordingly.

2. Joe made major, structural changes first; then he went on to make minor changes in structure, development, sentence structure, etc.

3. Joe read his essay aloud to detect problems in tone.

Exercise

Read Joe's first and second drafts carefully and answer the following questions.

1. Compare the structure of Joe's first draft with that of his second. Discuss the differences.

2. Compare the tone of Joe's first draft with that of his second draft, and explain how they are different.

3. Why do you suppose Joe was able to produce a rough draft the second time he wrote? Was his first draft, a predraft, important in enabling him to produce a second draft? Was his second session of inventing and planning, which produced the plan that he used, important? Explain.

4. Compare the revision strategies Joe used with his first draft to those he used with his second draft.

5. Do you agree with Joe's assessment of his second draft? Do you agree with the decisions he made regarding the revision of the draft? What suggestions would you have made to Joe?

6. Do you think Joe evaluated and made decisions about revising the sample letter within his essay *as* or *after* he made structural changes in his essay? Explain your answer.

Writing Task

Recall your evaluation of your second draft (see page 281). Keeping your intention and your audience in mind, select and execute appropriate revision strategies.

If you produced another predraft, compare it carefully to your first predraft. Is your second predraft more reader-based than your first? Do you need to do more inventing and planning? What aspects of your text—for example, audience, intention, structure—need the most attention? Consider these questions, then write another draft. You may wish to consult your teacher for some specific strategies that you can use in writing your next draft.

If you produced a rough draft, determine the location and nature of every problem with your text as precisely as you can. Choose rewriting strategies accordingly. Do you need to create frames of reference for your reader?

Do you need to sharpen the focus of particular portions of your text? Do you need to refine your stance? Then rewrite your draft.

Proofreading and Editing

After Joe finished rewriting his second draft, he typed it. Later, after several hours, he proofread it for problems in sentence structure, word choice, spelling, mechanics, usage, etc. He located and corrected a number of errors. Most of his changes were in the sample letter.

Here are the changes that Joe made in his sample letter:

1. Sentence 1—Change "purchased" to "bought" so that "purchased" is not repeated in sentences 1 and 2.

2. Sentence 3—"severely malfunctioned" and "at which time" sound stilted and overly formal. Joe discovered that he could not merely replace the words; he needed to restructure the sentence: "The first time that I used my Widget was on March 28, 1984; as soon as I switched it on, it broke down."

3. Sentence 6—Change "Therefore, due to the nature of the misunderstanding" to something more specific and more natural-sounding. In order to be more specific, Joe had to change the structure of his sentence: "Since the product was clearly defective due to factory workmanship, I believe it should be covered by the warranty, and I would appreciate your help in resolving the problem."

4. Sentence 7—Change "be so kind as to" to "please." Why use five words when one will do?

Here are the changes that Joe made in the other portions of his text:

1. He corrected the spelling of "stationary" to "stationery" in several places.

2. He corrected the spelling of "adress" to "address."

3. He changed "during" to "in" in paragraph 1.

4. He changed "*regular* white stationery" to "*plain* white stationery" in paragraph 5.

5. Since it was not entirely clear what "it" in "keep *it* short" in paragraph 8 was referring to, he provided a clearer referent.

6.   He changed "the company" to "a company" in the third-last sentence of the last paragraph, since he was referring to companies in general. And he deleted "Remember" from the beginning of the sentence, since he had begun the last sentence with "remember": "As long as you the writer are straightforward and polite, *a* company will. . . ."

7.   He replaced "they" in the last sentence of the last paragraph with its referent, since "they" could not logically refer to a nearby noun: "Remember *companies* need and want your business."

8.   He changed the tense of four verbs in the final paragraph to present tense to provide consistency.

Here is Joe's final draft.

How to Write an Effective Complaint Letter
Joe Norris

1   At least once in your life you have probably wanted to write a letter of complaint about a product or a service that you felt was unsatisfactory. If you did actually write such a letter, you may have written something in the heat of the moment without giving much thought to resolving the problem. In other words, your reader was probably aware that you were angry, but was unclear as to the exact nature of the problem and what you expected him or her to do about it. As a result, you were further frustrated by what appeared to be a lack of concern on the company's part, when, in actuality, the company wasn't exactly sure what the problem was or what you expected them to do about it.

2   If you compose it carefully, however, a well-written letter of complaint can often be a very effective means of resolving a problem. Here are a few suggestions for writing an effective complaint letter.

While you can address your letter to the Complaint Department or to a sales rep, it is usually more effective to send your complaint directly to the president of the company. Even if he does not handle your case personally, you can be sure someone on his staff will expedite your problem efficiently. You can find the name of the president and the address of the company in Standard and Poor's Register of Corporations, Directors and Executives, which is available in most libraries.

3   It is important to keep in mind that a letter of complaint is a business letter—so be businesslike. Choose your words carefully so that you don't come across hostile and angry. "Flying off the handle"

will not help you solve your problem. Also, try to describe your problem in an objective, low-key manner.

As in all business situations, appearance means an awful lot. It's 4 worth your while to go to the extra effort to type your letter on plain white stationery, unless you have some stationery that identifies you with some group or organization, such as a club or business. Write in longhand, if you must, but at all costs refrain from using that purple stationery that your little sister uses. Use the proper format for a standard business letter.

Be brief. Business people are busy people. Don't waste their time by 5 writing a long, windy letter. This can be done through a careful selection of words and information. When selecting words, try to be concise: don't use three words when one will do. When giving information, provide what is necessary without including superfluous detail. As Sgt. Friday always used to say, "We want the facts, ma'am. Just the facts." Be sure to include exactly what it is that you expect the company to do to resolve your problem. While it may be obvious to you that the company should replace or repair the faulty product or even reimburse the cost, it may not be so apparent to the company.

In order to help your reader assimilate the information that you 6 present, you need to organize that information skillfully. Here is a standard plan of organization for a letter of complaint:

The first part of a complaint letter (usually one paragraph) should 7 contain the date of purchase, some kind of product identification (such as model and/or serial number), and where the product was purchased. Keep this part of the letter short and simple. Remember, the easier you make it for the reader to understand you, the easier it will be to resolve your problem.

The second part (again, most often one paragraph) should explain 8 the nature and history of the problem. You need to describe what happened when you used the product and why you are dissatisfied. Indicate, where appropriate, that you have enclosed *copies* of all pertinent receipts, warranties, etc. (Never enclose the originals--they should be retained for your own records.)

The third, and last, part of a letter of complaint should reiterate 9 your request for assistance and explain what is necessary to satisfactorily resolve the problem as far as you are concerned. It should also give the length of time you will wait before contacting a third party (such as the Better Business Bureau or a government agency that deals with consumer affairs). Be certain to include an address and a telephone number where you can be reached during working hours. This last part of a complaint letter may consist of one or two paragraphs.

10   An effective letter of complaint might look something like this:

M. V. Smith
143 Main Street
Greentown, Ill. 43897
April 1, 1984

Mr. D. Vedar, President
Empire Widgets of California, Inc.
2001 Leia Boulevard
Cucamonga, Cal. 35678

Dear Sir:

On Nov. 27, 1983, I bought a Model 47 Widget (serial number 3657). I purchased this product at Solo's Hardware Store, located in Greentown, Illinois.

The first time that I used my Widget was on March 28, 1984; as soon as I switched it on, it broke down. I examined the Widget closely and determined that the hemulator was warped and that it had not been properly attached to the wocketa. When I returned the faulty Widget to Solo's Hardware, I was informed that they could not help me because the 90-day warranty (see enclosed copy) had expired.

Since the product was clearly defective due to factory workmanship, I believe it should be covered by the warranty, and I would appreciate your help in resolving the problem. Would you please inform Mr. C. W. Bakka, the manager of Solo's, that my claim is justified and that my Widget should be replaced with a new one? Enclosed are copies of my receipt and warranty to help prove the validity of my claim.

I am looking forward to your reply and to the resolution of our problem. I will wait three weeks before seeking third-party assistance. Feel free to contact me either at the above address or at my home number: 487/364-8567.

Sincerely,

M. V. Smith

As you can see, this sample letter contains all the information 11 necessary to resolve the problem. The writer is courteous and objective from the very start. Even though he is probably very angry at both the manufacturer and the retailer, his letter is cool and rational. Such an objective, businesslike manner gives the writer a great deal of credibility and makes his demands seem reasonable. As long as you the writer are straightforward and polite, a company will normally treat you in the same way. A dissatisfied customer doesn't make any money for a company. Remember, companies need and want your business.

Exercise

Read the final draft of Joe's essay and answer the following questions.

1. How successful was Joe at making the revisions he intended to make? Be specific.
2. Do you think that Joe's essay holds his readers' interest? Explain.
3. Summarize the structure of Joe's essay. What steps or parts seem prominent? Is the structure logical? Explain.
4. Assuming that they possessed average writing skills, do you think that high school juniors or seniors could write an effective complaint letter after reading Joe's essay? Why or Why not?
5. If Joe were given an opportunity to "publish" his essay, what revisions would you suggest that he make? Assume that the length and scope of the essay remain the same.

Writing Task

Continue to revise your essay at the text, sentence, and word levels until it is as reader-based as you can make it. Then proofread and edit your final draft.

Writing Assignment

Choose a somewhat complex process with which you are not familiar and describe it to an audience of your choice.

I.   Getting Started: Inventing and Planning
     A.   List several processes about which you are curious.
     B.   Choose one of these processes and find out more about it. You may wish to read about it, or interview persons who are familiar with it, or both.
     C.   Once you have thoroughly familiarized yourself with the process you are going to describe, begin to analyze it. What steps do you think it consists of? In what order do these steps occur? Can some steps be combined? Can some be omitted? With what steps do you anticipate people having difficulty?
     D.   Jot down the steps in the process that you have chosen. Try to list as many as you can.
     E.   Can you consolidate some of these steps? Can you break others down into substeps? Try grouping and arranging your steps.
     F.   What is the best way to order these steps? Try several possibilities if you have more than one idea.
     G.   As you were forming and arranging your steps, did you begin to think of an audience for your essay? If yes, describe that audience. If no, begin to think about the kinds of people who would be interested in learning how to do the process that you are going to describe. Jot down the qualities of these people.
     H.   Describe your audience. (If you already described your audience in G, can you add any characteristics or features?)
     I.   Go back and examine the steps in your process. Do any of them need to be modified because of the audience you have chosen? Make any necessary modifications.

    J.   What is your *intention* in the essay? If you are successful in writing your text, what do you want it to "do"? What point of view will you select? How will this help to reveal your intention?

    K.   Describe, tentatively, how you intend to structure your essay. How many parts will it have? What will you try to do in each part? Will the parts be chronological or will you follow some other plan?

    L.   What tone would you like your essay to project? Explain.

II.   Drafting and Revising

    A.   Write the first draft of your essay.

    B.   Read your draft and answer the following:
Describe the intention of your essay.
Describe the audience to whom your essay is addressed.
Describe the way in which you intended to structure your essay.
Describe the point of view (first, second, third person) and the tone that you used.

    C.   Evaluate your draft in terms of your answers to these questions. Examine your draft at the text, sentence, and word levels. Is it a rough draft or a predraft?

    D.   Describe your plans for revising or rewriting your draft.

    E.   Repeat steps B to D if necessary.

III.   Proofreading and Editing

    A.   Allow some time to go by, then read your final draft out loud.

    B.   Correct errors in sentence structure, word choice, and mechanics and usage.

Writing Assignment

Read the following text, "Family Reunion," by Jean Fields.

Family Reunion
Jean Fields

Our family Bible contains a note which reads: "June 10 1872 Fields and Barefoot reunion, 77 came." We still have reunions every other year on the "home" farm at the confluence of Kelly's Creek and the Kanawha River. We are Appalachians who have lived in the mountains of West Virginia since the 18th century. History books state that bands of Scotch and Irish landed in Virginia to find the Piedmont occupied and so settled at the foot of the Appalachian Mountains. But by a treaty with the Indians, the British agreed to pull all settlers back to the Piedmont by 1728. Instead the farmers fled to the nearly inaccessible mountains. When immigration began again, it flowed south to the rich lands of Kentucky and Tennessee and north to Ohio and Pennsylvania, leaving the mountain people isolated and forgotten. The differences of the mountain people result from this historical fact. We are clannish; we have a sense of belonging to a particular place. Because of our isolation, many of the frontier values and practices survive to this day. My family is no exception.

2   Our reunion is ritualized around preparing, serving and eating "vittles" with blood kin. Food is still a sign of hospitality and affection in the mountains. To offer food means: "Welcome, you are my friend; we will sit down together and share whatever we have with you." The variety and abundance of traditional food, traditionally prepared and eaten by the family is the equivalent of a kinship rite filled with affection and uncritical acceptance. In addition, it initiates the younger members into the history of the family.

3   The preparation of the food is very important. For example, the oldest men and the youngest children always prepare the smoked meat together. After World War I my great-grandfather cleaned out six steel drums, cut hinged doors near the bottom and bored holes in the lids. These are now rolled out. The children bring arm loads of hickory branches while the old men show them how to cut them into shavings and start smoldering fires in the bottom of the drums. Next, wires are suspended from the lids and the children are shown how to attach hams and turkeys to them. Now the lids are replaced and soon the field is redolent with hickory smoke and the smell of meat. At night around a camp fire, the old men tell the children stories of the coal mines, hunting and fishing trips, and of course ghost stories. I stood in the dark and listened to the familiar story of the headless dog who haunted his cruel master. My small niece, shivering, crawled into my lap, just as I had crawled, delightfully frightened, into my mother's lap as a child. That made me very happy. Suddenly, we were not so different after all, despite the differences in our ages. We both loved feeding the fires with hickory shavings, smelling the meat, anticipating how good it would taste, and we both loved the same ghost story.

4   Catfish are an important food at the reunion and they are caught fresh from the river. Since all the children want to help with the fishing, we make them draw straws. This year two seven year old inexperienced fishermen and two nine year old experienced fishermen won. Three adults accompanied them. We started at dusk, a Coleman lantern tied to the stern and the end of the trotline secured to a stout maple. A trotline is a heavy fishing line

approximately one hundred feet long, with hooks suspended on three inch lines every foot. The end of the line is tied to a heavy rock which acts as an anchor. Slowly the boat is rowed directly across the river, while the nine year olds put a piece of salt pork on each hook and drop it into the river. At the end of the line, the rock is tossed overboard, and everyone returns to shore and the campfire of the meat-smokers. The children were excited (no one bothers to sleep much at the reunion), and couldn't wait to run the line for the first time. They listened bugeyed as we told them the same tales we had been told about gigantic catfish that wouldn't fit in a bathtub, the number and length of those caught in past years. They listened just as I had listened as a child, as my parents and their parents before them had listened. At 3 A.M. we ran the line the first time. They were white faced, incoherent with excitement. As the bluecats began to break the surface, shouts of "Look how big he is," and "Don't let him hook you with his whiskers," rang across the water. In the dark it could have been 1872 or 1912 or . . .

The high point of the reunion for me comes at the beginning of the   5
dinner. Long tables have already been covered with sheets and spread with food. Then the oldest man in the clan moves to the front. In one hand he holds a Bible and in the other arm he holds the youngest baby. Great uncle John Fields was ninety-four years old and he held his great-great-grandchild Joseph as he gave the blessing. He spoke simply and eloquently, with a strong hill accent asking no favors, simply thanking the Lord. I am not a religious person nor have I much interest in ancestors; when a West Virginian speaks of ancestors he is usually referring to the land. Yet year after year I am moved to tears at this moment. It always reaffirms my sense of where I belong. From beginning to end the reunion allows me to re-create what was best in my heritage, to emphasize my strengths, my kinships with others. For a short while our differences are unimportant. It is a bit of order out of chaos, a circle of love.

Answer the following questions about Fields' text.

1. What process does the text describe?
2. Is the writer's intention to explain a process? Examine the tone, point of view, and structure of the text as well as the nature of the information presented.
3. Review the reasons why a person might read or write an essay or text about personal experience. Also think about the reasons why a person

might read or write an essay or text that explains or tells about a process. Why do you think Jean Fields wrote "Family Reunion"? What was Fields' intention for writing?

4.   Would you describe Fields' essay as an example of process exposition? Why or why not? Explain.

5.   Describe the audience to whom you think the essay is addressed. Where do you suppose such an essay would be published? Explain.

6.   Examine the structure of the essay. Why does the text begin with the sentence: "Our family Bible contains a note which reads: 'June 10 1872 Fields and Barefoot reunion, 77 came.' " What are the major sections of the essay? How does the structure help to reveal the writer's intention?

7.   Describe the type of information included in the text. Comment on the amount of space devoted to describing the behavior of children at the reunion. How specific is the information about what the children do and their reactions to doing it? Examine, for example, the paragraph about fishing for catfish. How does the nature of the information and examples help to reveal the writer's intention?

8.   Describe the essay's point of view. How evident is the writer within the text? Why does she share her memories about her reactions to family reunions when she was a child? How does this affect the tone? How do tone and point of view help to reveal the writer's intention?

Write an essay describing a ritual in which *your* family engages regularly. You might describe what your family does on Christmas Eve each year, for example. Or perhaps your family has a special July 4 picnic annually. Some families develop yearly rituals that have nothing to do with holidays or occasions that others celebrate. For example, members of your family might gather once a year to put in a large garden, the yield from which will be shared by all.

It is your responsibility to choose an intention for writing and an audience to address. For example, your intention might be *to explain* a ritual in detail to others, who might like to duplicate it; or *to express* your feelings about a family ritual that is deeply meaningful to you, and your audience could be your classmates, members of your church group, or readers of your school newspaper.

I.   Getting Started: Inventing and Planning
     A.   Jot down some possible rituals about which you might enjoy writing.
     B.   What are some steps associated with each of these rituals?

C.   Choose one of these rituals. Are there any special features that are not directly related to any of the steps but that are important? For example, is the setting important? Or is a certain element essential (Aunt Tillie's tomato pudding)?

D.   List and integrate the steps and features associated with your ritual.

E.   Describe the audience to whom your essay will be addressed.

F.   Describe the structure that you will use. How will this structure reveal your intention for writing?

G.   What point of view will you use: "Every year *I* feel particularly excited when . . ." or "Each year the *Brown family* celebrates Easter by . . ."? How will your point of view help to reveal your intention for writing?

H.   What tone would you like your essay to project? Explain.

II.   Drafting and Revising

A.   Write the first draft of your essay.

B.   Read your draft and answer the following:
Describe the intention of your essay.
Describe the audience to whom the essay is addressed.
Describe the way in which you intended to structure your essay.
Describe the point of view (first, second, third person) and the tone that you intended to use.

C.   Evaluate your draft in terms of your answers to these questions. Examine your draft at the text, sentence, and word levels. Is it a predraft or a rough draft?

D.   Describe your plans for revising or rewriting your draft.

E.   Repeat steps B to D if necessary.

III.   Proofreading and Editing

A.   Allow some time to go by, then read your final draft out loud.

B.   Correct errors in sentence structure, word choice, and mechanics and usage.

8 *Writing Informative Essays*

The Informative Essay

Chapter 7 introduced process exposition, writing that explains how to do something or the sequence of events that lead or have led to a particular outcome. Informative writing is another kind of writing that employs exposition—in this case to report information. As its label implies, informative writing is intended by its author to *inform* a particular audience about a particular subject. This is accomplished through clear, objective, and accurate presentation of facts and contexts in an appropriate and appealing format.

We can distinguish informative writing from the other kinds of writing we are considering in Part Two in this way: In an informative essay, the focus is on the topic under consideration and the factual presentation of information. The writer is not concerned with sharing personal experience, unless it is compellingly relevant to the topic, or advocating certain positions or platforms (see Chapter 10, "Writing Persuasive Essays"). Instead, she tries to "get out of the way" as much as possible, avoiding an explicit and overbearing *presence* in the text that would draw attention away from the information being presented. When this is done effectively, the informative essay does not depend at all on the identity, qualifications, or credibility of the writer herself.

In the following example we can see the distinction between some different intentions and the texts they produce. A writer who wishes to write about alternatives to abortion might have any of the following intentions, each of which would yield a different kind of text:

1. *Personal Experience Essay:* "My experience working at an abortion alternatives clinic." The focus in this text would be on the day-to-day events in the life of someone who worked in such a clinic and would be built on the details of the writer's own experiences.

2. *Process Essay:* "How to prepare an abortion alternatives pamphlet." The focus in this text would be on the sequence of steps to follow in producing such a pamphlet.

3. *Persuasive Essay:* "Serve the community as an abortion alternatives counselor." The focus in this text would be on exhorting and advocating its readers to seek a position as an abortion alternatives volunteer in a community agency.

4. *Informative Essay:* "What to expect when you visit an abortion alternatives clinic." The focus in this text would be on the objective presentation of facts about the activities in such a clinic.

The writer of the informative essay would avoid sharing merely personal narratives or advocating that a person visit an abortion alternatives clinic. And, although the origin of the clinic or the explanation of a process within it might be relevant to the writer's informative task in a general sense, the writer's primary intention is to answer the question that her topic raises. Put simply, process texts explain *how* or *why*; informative texts explain *what*.

Readers read informative essays with certain expectations. First, they expect to be informed; that is, they expect fresh, relevant, and current information. A text that is obviously outdated or outmoded, or that clearly ignores aspects of its topic that a reader might reasonably expect it to cover, will be dismissed. For instance, someone who picked up an essay purporting to be an up-to-date discussion of trends in computer games would be disappointed to find out that the writer had ignored the newly evolving interactive games created for sophisticated microcomputers and had concentrated instead on bang-bang-shoot'em-up video games.

Second, readers expect informative texts to be comprehensive; that is, they expect such texts to provide all the necessary and sufficient information they seek and to present this information within a clearly specified interpretive context. A reader who picks up *Time* or *Newsweek* the week following a national election rightly expects to be informed about all the senate races, whether they took place in Idaho, California, New York, or South Carolina. Anything less than a national perspective would be too provincial to be informative to a reader.

Third, readers expect informative texts to be organized and formatted to give prominence to the information they are seeking, and they expect this information to be presented in as clear, economical, and direct a fashion as possible. For example, if one wanted to know which new U.S. cars had the best gas mileage and picked up an essay that ostensibly covered all the new models and their features, he would expect to find a table or list that presented this information accessibly. A primarily narrative description of such mileage figures would unnecessarily frustrate a reader who was seeking such information, and thus would defeat the intention of the writer. Not all information, of course, can be put in tables or listed as statistics, but the organization and format of an informative text are crucial considerations for the writer beginning the drafting process.

Writers create informative texts, therefore, to provide their readers with useful, interesting, and important information. In writing an informative text, authors use all the forms of exposition mentioned in Chapter 2: definition; division; illustration; comparison/contrast; and analysis. Newspapers and newsweeklies contain informative discourse. Likewise, publications like *Scientific American*, *Psychology Today*, and *Sports Illustrated* seek to give their readers factual treatments of various topics: events, personalities, human behavior, medicine, science, social conditions, and political movements.

Of course, one can write informatively about the past and future as well as the present. In such cases, informative texts may include the interpretation of facts, that is, the creation of a context for understanding the facts the text presents. Thus, historical texts like Bruce Catton's series on the Civil War and Milton Friedman's books on economic trends are intended as informative texts as well.

The key consideration for the writer intending to be informative is quite simple: she must remember that the reader is not asking for her personal experience or her opinion or her advice; he is looking for accurately reported information presented within a clearly defined interpretive context. Anything more or less than that will thwart the writer's intention to inform. Consequently, a "finished," *reader-based* informative essay will exhibit these characteristics:

1.   The writer will create an appropriate context for the presentation of her information that will draw her audience into the text early and effectively, conveying the relevance, usefulness, and/or entertaining elements of the information to be provided.

2.   The subject matter of the text will be clearly and accurately conveyed to the reader in an objective manner that focuses on the information, not the writer herself.

3.   The relationships between all the facts and explanations provided and the subject matter under consideration will be clear to the reader. The reader will never have to ask, "Why is the writer telling me this?" or "What does this have to do with anything?"

4.   The writer will present the information in an accessible and attractive format that leaves the reader with a sense of completeness and comprehensiveness (appropriate to the subject matter) by the end of the text.

Examples

Following are two examples of effective informative essays. Read them carefully and answer the accompanying questions. The questions will help you glean these models for ideas and for strategies you might use in writing and revising your own texts.

Germs

Lewis Thomas

Watching television, you'd think we lived at bay, in total jeopardy, surrounded on all sides by human-seeking germs, shielded against infection and death only by a chemical technology that enables us to keep killing them off. We are instructed to spray disinfectants everywhere, into the air of our bedrooms and kitchens and with special energy into bathrooms, since it is our very own germs that seem the worst kind. We explode clouds of aerosol, mixed for good luck with deodorants, into our noses, mouths, underarms, privileged crannies—even into the intimate insides of our telephones. We apply potent antibiotics to minor scratches and seal them with plastic. Plastic is the new protector; we wrap the already plastic tumblers of hotels in more plastic, and seal the toilet seats like state secrets after irradiating them with ultraviolet light. We live in a world where the microbes

are always trying to get at us, to tear us cell from cell, and we only stay
alive and whole through diligence and fear.

2   We still think of human disease as the work of an organized, modernized
kind of demonology, in which the bacteria are the most visible and centrally
placed of our adversaries. We assume that they must somehow relish what
they do. They come after us for profit, and there are so many of them that
disease seems inevitable, a natural part of the human condition; if we
succeed in eliminating one kind of disease there will always be a new one
at hand, waiting to take its place.

3   These are paranoid delusions on a societal scale, explainable in part by
our need for enemies, and in part by our memory of what things used to
be like. Until a few decades ago, bacteria were a genuine household threat,
and although most of us survived them, we were always aware of the
nearness of death. We moved, with our families, in and out of death. We
had lobar pneumonia, meningococcal meningitis, streptococcal infections,
diphtheria, endocarditis, enteric fevers, various septicemias, syphilis, and,
always, everywhere, tuberculosis. Most of these have now left most of us,
thanks to antibiotics, plumbing, civilization, and money, but we remember.

4   In real life, however, even in our worst circumstances we have always
been a relatively minor interest of the vast microbial world. Pathogenicity
is not the rule. Indeed, it occurs so infrequently and involves such a
relatively small number of species, considering the huge population of
bacteria on the earth, that it has a freakish aspect. Disease usually results
from inconclusive negotiations for symbiosis, an overstepping of the line
by one side or the other, a biologic misinterpretation of borders.

5   Some bacteria are only harmful to us when they make exotoxins, and
they only do this when they are, in a sense, diseased themselves. The
toxins of diphtheria bacilli and streptococci are produced when the organisms
have been infected by bacteriophage; it is the virus that provides the code
for toxin. Uninfected bacteria are uninformed. When we catch diphtheria
it is a virus infection, but not of us. Our involvement is not that of an
adversary in a straightforward game, but more like blundering into someone
else's accident.

6   I can think of a few microorganisms, possibly the tubercle bacillus, the
syphilis spirochete, the malarial parasite, and a few others, that have a
selective advantage in their ability to infect human beings, but there is
nothing to be gained, in an evolutionary sense, by the capacity to cause
illness or death. Pathogenicity may be something of a disadvantage for
most microbes, carrying lethal risks more frightening to them than to us.
The man who catches a meningococcus is in considerably less danger for

his life, even without chemotherapy, than meningococci with the bad luck to catch a man. Most meningococci have the sense to stay out on the surface, in the rhinopharynx. During epidemics this is where they are to be found in the majority of the host population, and it generally goes well. It is only in the unaccountable minority, the "cases," that the line is crossed, and then there is the devil to pay on both sides, but most of all for the meningococci.

Staphylococci live all over us, and seem to have adapted to conditions   7
in our skin that are uncongenial to most other bacteria. When you count them up, and us, it is remarkable how little trouble we have with the relation. Only a few of us are plagued by boils, and we can blame a large part of the destruction of tissues on the zeal of our own leukocytes. Hemolytic streptococci are among our closest intimates, even to the extent of sharing antigens with the membranes of our muscle cells; it is our reaction to their presence, in the form of rheumatic fever, that gets us into trouble. We can carry brucella for long periods in the cells of our reticuloendothelial system without any awareness of their existence; then cyclically, for reasons not understood but probably related to immunologic reactions on our part, we sense them, and the reaction of sensing is the clinical disease.

Most bacteria are totally preoccupied with browsing, altering the con-   8
figurations of organic molecules so that they become usable for the energy needs of other forms of life. They are, by and large, indispensable to each other, living in interdependent communities in the soil or sea. Some have become symbionts in more specialized, local relations, living as working parts in the tissues of higher organisms. The root nodules of legumes would have neither form nor function without the masses of rhizobial bacteria swarming into root hairs, incorporating themselves with such intimacy that only an electron microscope can detect which membranes are bacterial and which plant. Insects have colonies of bacteria, the mycetocytes, living in them like little glands, doing heaven knows what but being essential. The microfloras of animal intestinal tracts are part of the nutritional system. And then, of course, there are the mitochondria and chloroplasts, permanent residents in everything.

The microorganisms that seem to have it in for us in the worst way—   9
the ones that really appear to wish us ill—turn out on close examination to be rather more like bystanders, strays, strangers in from the cold. They will invade and replicate if given the chance, and some of them will get into our deepest tissues and set forth in the blood, but it is our response to their presence that makes the disease. Our arsenals for fighting off bacteria are so powerful, and involve so many different defense mechanisms,

that we are in more danger from them than from the invaders. We live in the midst of explosive devices; we are mined.

10   It is the information carried by the bacteria that we cannot abide.

11   The gram-negative bacteria are the best examples of this. They display lipopolysaccharide endotoxin in their walls, and these macromolecules are read by our tissues as the very worst of bad news. When we sense lipo-polysaccharide, we are likely to turn on every defense at our disposal; we will bomb, defoliate, blockade, seal off, and destroy all the tissues in the area. Leukocytes become more actively phagocytic, release lysosomal enzymes, turn sticky, and aggregate together in dense masses, occluding capillaries and shutting off the blood supply. Complement is switched on at the right point in its sequence to release chemotactic signals, calling in leukocytes from everywhere. Vessels become hyperreactive to epinephrine so that physiologic concentrations suddenly possess necrotizing properties. Pyrogen is released from leukocytes, adding fever to hemorrhage, necrosis, and shock. It is a shambles.

12   All of this seems unnecessary, panic-driven. There is nothing intrinsically poisonous about endotoxin, but it must look awful, or feel awful when sensed by cells. Cells believe that it signifies the presence of gram-negative bacteria, and they will stop at nothing to avoid this threat.

13   I used to think that only the most highly developed, civilized animals could be fooled in this way, but it is not so. The horseshoe crab is a primitive fossil of a beast, ancient and uncitified, but he is just as vulnerable to disorganization by endotoxin as a rabbit or a man. Bang has shown that an injection of a very small dose into the body cavity will cause the aggregation of hemocytes in ponderous, immovable masses that block the vascular channels, and a gelatinous clot brings the circulation to a standstill. It is now known that a limulus clotting system, perhaps ancestral to ours, is centrally involved in the reaction. Extracts of the hemocytes can be made to jell by adding extremely small amounts of endotoxin. The self-disintegration of the whole animal that follows a systemic injection can be interpreted as a well-intentioned but lethal error. The mechanism is itself quite a good one, when used with precision and restraint, admirably designed for coping with intrusion by a single bacterium: the hemocyte would be attracted to the site, extrude the coagulable protein, the microorganism would be entrapped and immobilized, and the thing would be finished. It is when confronted by the overwhelming signal of free molecules of endotoxin, evoking memories of vibrios in great numbers, that the limulus flies into panic, launches all his defenses at once, and destroys himself.

It is, basically, a response to propaganda, something like the panic-   14
producing pheremones that slave-taking ants release to disorganize the
colonies of their prey.

I think it likely that many of our diseases work in this way. Sometimes,   15
the mechanisms used for overkill are immunologic, but often, as in the
limulus model, they are more primitive kinds of memory. We tear ourselves
to pieces because of symbols, and we are more vulnerable to this than to
any host of predators. We are, in effect, at the mercy of our own Pentagons,
most of the time.

Questions About "Germs"

1. Describe the intention of the essay: Is Thomas defending germs? Is
he criticizing humans for being paranoid about microorganisms?

2. The reader is addressed as "you" and "we." Describe the point of
view of the essay. What effect does this point of view have on the reader?

3. Describe the way Thomas presents microorganisms in his essay: What
sorts of characteristics do they seem to have? Do they seem animate or
inanimate? Friendly, hostile, or indifferent?

4. Thomas says that we "live in the midst of explosive devices; we are
mined." What sort of image of the human immunological system does this
present? Why does Thomas end the essay with this line: "We are, in effect,
at the mercy of our own Pentagons, most of the time."

5. In spite of the fact that the essay contains quite a lot of technical
terms and names, such as endocarditis, spirochete, rhinopharynx, and
lipopolysaccharide, it seems to be addressed to a "popular" audience. Why
are such terms necessary? How does Thomas get away with using such
terms without intimidating his readers?

6. How does Thomas present himself in his essay? What strategy does
he use to convince the reader that he knows what he's talking about without
seeming pompous or impersonal?

7. Comment on the effectiveness of the opening sentence: "Watching
television, you'd think we lived at bay, in total jeopardy, surrounded on all
sides by human-seeking germs, shielded against infection and death only
by a chemical technology that enables us to keep killing them off." Why
do you think Thomas chose this way of beginning his essay?

8. To what extent does Thomas's essay stress the interrelatedness of
life on earth? Think again about Thomas's intention for writing: Do you
wish to modify your answer to question 1?

9. Examine the length and complexity of the sentences within Thomas's essay. Do you think he controlled this aspect of the text carefully?

10. What assumptions do you think Thomas made about his readers? Be as specific as you can. In what ways do you think he adapted his text for them? It may help you to answer this question if you compare this text with one Thomas might have addressed to other biologists.

The Black and White Truth About Basketball
Jeff Greenfield

1   The dominance of black athletes over professional basketball is beyond dispute. Two thirds of the players are black, and the number would be greater were it not for the continuing practice of picking white bench warmers for the sake of balance. The Most Valuable Player award of the National Basketball Association has gone to blacks for eighteen of the last twenty-one years. In the 1979–80 season, eight of the top ten All-Stars were black. The NBA was the first pro sports league of any stature to hire a black coach (Bill Russell of the Celtics) and the first black general manager (Wayne Embry of the Bucks). What discrimination remains— lack of opportunity for lucrative benefits such as speaking engagements and product endorsements—has more to do with society than with basketball.

2   This dominance reflects a natural inheritance; basketball is a pastime of the urban poor. The current generation of black athletes are heirs to a tradition half a century old: in a neighborhood without the money for bats, gloves, hockey sticks, tennis rackets, or shoulder pads, basketball is accessible. "Once it was the game of the Irish and Italian Catholics in Rockaway and the Jews on Fordham Road in the Bronx," writes David Wolf in his brilliant book, *Foul!* "It was recreation, status, and a way out." But now the ethnic names are changed; instead of Red Holzmans, Red Auerbachs, and McGuire brothers, there are Julius Ervings and Darryl Dawkins and Kareem Abdul-Jabbars. And professional basketball is a sport with a national television contract and million-dollar salaries.

3   But the mark on basketball of today's players can be measured by more than money or visibility. It is a question of style. For there is a clear difference between "black" and "white" styles of play that is as clear as the difference between 155th Street at Eighth Avenue and Crystal City, Missouri. Most simply (remembering we are talking about culture, not chromosomes), "black" basketball is the use of superb athletic skill to adapt to the limits of space imposed by the game. "White" ball is the pulverization of that space by sheer intensity.

It takes a conscious effort to realize how constricted the space is on a   4
basketball court. Place a regulation court (ninety-four by fifty feet) on a
football field, and it will reach from the back of the end zone to the twenty-
one-yard line; its width will cover less than a third of the field. On a baseball
diamond, a basketball court will reach from home plate to just beyond first
base. Compared to its principal indoor rival, ice hockey, basketball covers
about one-fourth the playing area. And during the normal flow of the game,
most of the action takes place on about the third of the court nearest the
basket. It is in this dollhouse space that ten men, each of them half a foot
taller than the average man, come together to battle each other.

There is, thus, no room; basketball is a struggle for the edge: the half   5
step with which to cut around the defender for a lay-up, the half second
of freedom with which to release a jump shot, the instant a head turns
allowing a pass to a teammate breaking for the basket. It is an arena for
the subtlest of skills: the head fake, the shoulder fake, the shift of body
weight to the right and the sudden cut to the left. Deception is crucial to
success; and to young men who have learned early and painfully that life
is a battle for survival, basketball is one of the few games in which the
weapon of deception is a legitimate rule and not the source of trouble.

If there is, then, the need to compete in a crowd, to battle for the edge,   6
then the surest strategy is to develop the *unexpected;* to develop a shot
that is simply and fundamentally different from the usual methods of
putting the ball in the basket. Drive to the hoop, but go under it and come
up the other side; hold the ball at waist level and shoot from there instead
of bringing the ball up to eye level; leap into the air and fall away from
the basket instead of toward it. All these tactics take maximum advantage
of the crowding on a court; they also stamp uniqueness on young men
who may feel it nowhere else.

"For many young men in the slums," David Wolf writes, "the school   7
yard is the only place they can feel true pride in what they do, where they
can move free of inhibitions and where they can, by being spectacular,
rise for the moment against the drabness and anonymity of their lives.
Thus, when a player develops extraordinary 'school yard' moves and shots
. . . [they] become his measure as a man."

So the moves that begin as tactics for scoring soon become calling cards.   8
You don't just lay the ball in for an uncontested basket; you take the ball
in both hands, leap as high as you can, and slam the ball through the
hoop. When you jump in the air, fake a shot, bring the ball back to your
body, and throw up a shot, all without coming back down, you have proven
your worth in uncontestable fashion.

9   This liquid grace is an integral part of "black" ball, almost exclusively
the province of the playground player. Some white stars like Bob Cousy,
Billy Cunningham, Doug Collins, and Paul Westphal had it: the body
control, the moves to the basket, the free-ranging mobility. They also had
the surface ease that is integral to the "black" style; an incorporation of
the ethic of mean streets—to "make it" is not just to have wealth, but to
have it without strain. Whatever the muscles and organs are doing, the
face of the "black" star almost never shows it. George Gervin of the San
Antonio Spurs can drive to the basket with two men on him, pull up, turn
around, and hit a basket without the least flicker of emotion. The Knicks'
former great Walt Frazier, flamboyant in dress, cars, and companions,
displayed nothing but a quickly raised fist after scoring a particularly important
basket. (Interestingly, the black coaches in the NBA exhibit far less emotion
on the bench than their white counterparts; Al Attles and K. C. Jones are
statuelike compared with Jack Ramsey or Dick Motta.)

10   If there is a single trait that characterizes "black" ball it is leaping agility.
Bob Cousy, ex-Celtic great and former pro coach, says that "when coaches
get together, one is sure to say, 'I've got the one black kid in the country
who can't jump.' When coaches see a white boy who can jump or who
moves with extraordinary quickness, they say, 'He should have been born
black, he's that good.' "

11   Don Nelson, former Celtic and coach of the Milwaukee Bucks, recalls
that in 1970, Dave Cowens, then a relatively unknown Florida State graduate,
prepared for his rookie season by playing in the Rucker League, an outdoor
Harlem competition that pits pros against playground stars and college
kids. So ferocious was Cowens' leaping power, Nelson says, that "when
the summer was over, everyone wanted to know who the white son of a
bitch was who could jump so high." That's another way to overcome a
crowd around the basket—just go over it.

12   Speed, mobility, quickness, acceleration, "the moves"—all of these are
catch-phrases that surround the "black" playground style of play. So does
the most racially tinged of attributes, "rhythm." Yet rhythm is what the
black stars themselves talk about; feeling the flow of the game, finding
the tempo of the dribble, the step, the shot. It is an instinctive quality,
one that has led to difficulty between systematic coaches and free-form
players. "Cats from the street have their own rhythm when they play,"
said college dropout Bill Spivey, onetime New York high-school star. "It's
not a matter of somebody setting you up and you shooting. You *feel* the
shot. When a coach holds you back, you lose the feel and it isn't fun
anymore."

Connie Hawkins, the legendary Brooklyn playground star, said of Laker   13
coach Bill Sharman's methodical style of teaching, "He's systematic to the
point where it begins to be a little too much. It's such an action-reaction
type of game that when you have to do everything the same way, I think
you lose something."

There is another kind of basketball that has grown up in America. It is   14
not played on asphalt playgrounds with a crowd of kids competing for the
court; it is played on macadam driveways by one boy with a ball and a
backboard nailed over the garage; it is played in Midwestern gyms and on
Southern dirt courts. It is a mechanical, precise development of skills (when
Don Nelson was an Iowa farm boy his incentive to make his shots was
that an errant rebound would land in the middle of chicken droppings),
without frills, without flow, but with effectiveness. It is "white" basketball:
jagged, sweaty, stumbling, intense. A "black" player overcomes an obstacle
with finesse and body control; a "white" player reacts by outrunning or
outpowering the obstacle.

By this definition, the Boston Celtics are a classically "white" team. The   15
Celtics almost never use a player with dazzling moves; that would probably
make Red Auerbach swallow his cigar. Instead, the Celtics wear you down
with execution, with constant running, with the same play run again and
again. The rebound triggers the fast break, with everyone racing downcourt;
the ball goes to Larry Bird, who pulls up and takes the jump shot, or who
fakes the shot and passes off to the man following, the "trailer," who has
the momentum to go inside for a relatively easy shot.

Perhaps the most classically "white" position is that of the quick forward,   16
one without great moves to the basket, without highly developed shots,
without the height and mobility for rebounding effectiveness. What does
he do? He runs. He runs from the opening jump to the last horn. He runs
up and down the court, from base line to base line, back and forth under
the basket, looking for the opening, for the pass, for the chance to take a
quick step and the high-percentage shot. To watch San Antonio's Mark
Olberding, a player without speed or moves, is to wonder what he is doing
in the NBA—until you see him swing free and throw up a shot that, without
demanding any apparent skill, somehow goes in the basket more frequently
than the shots of any of his teammates. And to have watched Boston Celtic
immortal John Havlicek is to have seen "white" ball at its best.

Havlicek stands in dramatic contrast to Julius Erving of the Philadelphia   17
76 ers. Erving has the capacity to make legends come true; leaping from
the foul line and slam-dunking the ball on his way down; going up for a
lay-up, pulling the ball to his body and throwing under and up the other

side of the rim, defying gravity and probability with moves and jumps. Havlicek looked like the living embodiment of his small-town Ohio background. He would bring the ball downcourt, weaving left, then right, looking for the path. He would swing the ball to a teammate, cut behind a pick, take the pass and release the shot in a flicker of time. It looked plain, unvarnished. But there are not half a dozen players in the league who can see such possibilities for a free shot, then get that shot off as quickly and efficiently as Havlicek.

18   To former pro Jim McMillian, a black with "white" attributes, himself a quick forward, "it's a matter of environment. Julius Erving grew up in a different environment from Havlicek—John came from a very small town in Ohio. There everything was done the easy way, the shortest distance between two points. It's nothing fancy, very few times will he go one-on-one; he hits the lay-up, hits the jump shot, makes the free throw, and after the game you look up and you say, 'How did he hurt us that much?' "

19   "White" ball, then, is the basketball of patience and method. "Black" ball is the basketball of electric self-expression. One player has all the time in the world to perfect his skills, the other a need to prove himself. These are slippery categories, because a poor boy who is black can play "white" and a white boy of middle-class parents can play "black." Jamaal Wilkes and Paul Westphal are athletes who seem to defy these categories. And what makes basketball the most intriguing of sports is how these styles do not necessarily clash; how the punishing intensity of "white" players and the dazzling moves of the "blacks" can fit together, a fusion of cultures that seems more and more difficult in the world beyond the out-of-bounds line.

QUESTIONS ABOUT "THE BLACK AND WHITE TRUTH ABOUT BASKETBALL"

1.   What is the intention of the essay? To what extent, if any, does it seem to have been written to describe and to express appreciation of cultural differences?

2.   Examine the structure of the essay, especially those portions that compare "black" and "white" ball. How, exactly, does Greenfield structure his comparison? What criteria does he use to make it? How important is the comparison within the overall structure of the text? Explain.

3.   Do you suppose Greenfield's essay would be interesting to readers who are not basketball fans? Explain. In answering, consider the nature and amount of background information provided within the essay, the use of "technical" terminology, the sort of examples provided within the text.

4.   Describe the tone of the essay. How formal is the writing? Quite formal? Rather informal?

5.   Examine the description of Havlicek's playing style (pages 309–310). How effective is the language? Does the description enable the reader to visualize what Havlicek does on the court? How important are this and other similar descriptive passages within the text? How do these descriptive passages function?

6.   Why did Greenfield select the title "The Black and White Truth about Basketball" for his essay? What expectations might such a title create in the reader?

7.   Comment on the effectiveness of the opening two lines of the essay. Why does Greenfield begin by asserting that the "dominance of black athletes over professional basketball is beyond dispute"? Compare these opening lines with the last sentence in the essay: "And what makes basketball the most intriguing of sports is how these styles do not necessarily clash." When does Greenfield's intention become clear to the reader?

8.   Greenfield mentions a great many basketball players by name in a relatively short essay. Why do you suppose he did so? How do these specific references function within the text?

Summary

Now that you have examined an explanation about and two examples of informative writing, here is a list of important operations that a writer usually performs before she begins to draft an informative essay.

1.   The writer should thoroughly *familiarize* herself with the subject matter her informative essay will consider.

2.   The writer must *decide* which aspects of the subject matter she is going to discuss, in what detail, in what order, and in what context.

3.   The writer must *determine* how to present the information so that her audience perceives it as fresh, interesting, and relevant. This means the writer must *analyze* her audience to discover:
   a.   how much the audience already knows about the subject, and what and how much they may want to know.
   b.   how to relate unfamiliar to familiar information in the essay so that the audience can follow the presentation of the information. This is especially important in highly technical texts written for the non-expert.

A Rhetorical Task: Brenda and the Study of Historical Jesus

Initial Responses

Brenda Green, along with the other members of her history class, was asked to write an informative essay about a historical or contemporary figure about whom she wanted to know more. The choice of a subject and the audience to which the text would be directed were left to the writer. Since Brenda was interested in religious figures and had read some challenging articles about the "quest for the historical Jesus," she decided that she would write an informative essay about Jesus and the way historians have approached him and his times. She decided to direct her essay to an audience unfamiliar with the controversy surrounding Jesus and the processes of historical inquiry.

VISUALIZING THE AUDIENCE

Brenda began to brainstorm about the audience to whom she would be writing by thinking about the kinds of questions people might have about the "historical Jesus":

-- Did he really live, or was he "made up" by zealous believers?

-- How much of his deeds have come down to the twentieth century accurately and faithfully presented?

-- What do modern historians and Biblical critics think of the records and stories that arose in the first century?

-- How are twentieth century interpretations of the "historical" Jesus affected by the motives, beliefs, and education of the interpreters?

-- Does historical accuracy make any difference in a person's belief, i.e., if the "historical" Jesus was different from the "Christ of faith," should it matter to believers or skeptics?

CREATING A CONTEXT

As Brenda further considered her audience and the material with which she was working, she began to see the kinds of materials she needed to gather and how she might need to order her presentation. She knew that she would have to begin with a brief introduction to the "historical question" of Jesus or any other historical figure, explaining to her audience the nature of historical investigation and how a historian might have to distinguish between the "real person" and the legend if the facts established a discrepancy. Next, she would survey the opinions of respected scholars and Biblical critics. Lastly, she would have to draw all the information into a concluding section that suggested possibilities and alternatives for understanding the "historical Jesus." She knew that it would be hard to separate her own beliefs and feelings from the information, but she was determined to "get out of the way" of the material as much as possible and let the audience make up its own mind.

ARTICULATING INTENTION

Brenda was ready to enter into her inventing and planning with a fairly clear idea of her audience and her writing task, but she still was unsure about how her intention would mesh with the material she was surveying. She would have to control the tone of her essay very carefully so as not to offend the readers to whom she was writing. Her goal was to provide a helpful overview of the historical process of understanding someone as "notorious" as the first century Jesus while maintaining objectivity and distance.

More Inventing and Planning

Brenda's next inventing and planning involved several things. First, she did some more reading about the "historical Jesus" in various journals and books, making an outline of this information for later use in her essay. Second, she *intentionally* wrote a brief predraft to help her understand what she herself thought about the "historical Jesus." She did this so that she would be able to write her actual text—an *informative* essay—more objectively; by spending some time exploring her own feelings about the subject, she could distance herself more effectively from the information she wanted to present to her audience. After she wrote this draft for herself, she would know more specifically what facts to include and which to leave out: her intention to *inform*, rather than to *persuade* or *express*, would guide her selection and arrangement of details. Third, Brenda "blocked out" the structure of her essay by imagining how she would proceed in her discussion, starting with an overview of the controversy about the "historical Jesus." Here are Brenda's inventing and planning materials:

NOTES--"Who Was Jesus?"

1. Scholars' views
   A. each gospel presents a different picture of Jesus for different communities
   B. gospels limited in reconstructing the ministry and message of Jesus
   C. focus on meaning of texts to 1st century Christians
   D. do not seek to undercut the message of Christian faith; quote; do not dispute spiritual truth

2. The Gospels
   A. contains sayings & stories based on memories of Jesus' ministry
   B. believed that story of Jesus developed backwards; Messiah to earthly ministry
   C. the author of each gospel gives a different picture of Jesus
      --Mark
      Jesus as miracle worker; not understood by those closest to him; disciples do not know of the resurrection
      --Matthew
      Jesus as royal Messiah, King of Israel; antagonist towards Jewish establishment; fulfillment of prophecy; mercy and compassion in miracles
      --Luke
      Jesus as innocent savior; forgiveness & love; biography of Jesus; Christians have to live ordinary lives; ready forgiveness of sinners
      --John
      Jesus immediately identified as Son of God; under full control; not shown suffering in Gethsemane

3. My reading
   A. Mark--power, apostles lack of understanding of Jesus' teachings

  B. Luke--John the Baptist, genealogy of Jesus, compassion, detail, patient, forgiving even at death

4. Conclusions(?)
  A. outline of article
  B. reader should look at article and gospels critically
  C. will audience know the gospel accounts?
  D. is there a divorce between faith & history?

5. Tone
  A. keep out of the way: <u>inform</u>, <u>inform</u>
  B. let readers decide

BRENDA'S INTENTIONAL PREDRAFT

If one faith is thought to be predominant throughout the United States and Europe, it is Christianity. Yet without any regard to faith, Jesus Christ himself presents a <u>unique</u> <u>historical</u> <u>figure</u>. His story is one of an individual in conflict against the society in which he lives and also the religious leaders of that time. Here I want to deal with the reasons, methods, and outcome of the conflict in which Christ was involved in.

One of the main factors that brought opposition to Christ was his willingness to speak out against the religious leaders of that day. The Pharisees and Saducees were an elite sects of the Jews that were respected for their knowledge of the Law of Moses, the Scriptures, and for their apparent righteousness. However, Christ openly confronted these people and accused them of being hypocrites. This act alone caused many of the Jewish leaders to try and find fault with Christ's actions and teachings. When he healed on the Sabbath, Christ was accused of violating the Law. Christ also proved to be an outstanding teacher and in time gathered many followers, which only served to turn the priests and other religious leaders against him more. As a final reason for the conflict that resulted because of Christ, there is the fact that by saying that God was his Father, Christ placed himself on the same level as God. To the Jews, this was considered blasphemy and caused even further separation between the two groups.

In several ways, it appears that Christ went out of his way to bring about conflict. He often taught to great crowds of people, and even went to the Jewish temple to teach. By exposing himself to large numbers of people, he automatically exposed himself to the dangers of opposition. When the scribes and Pharisees would attempt to trick him with their questions, Christ would answer in a way that they could not find fault. Then he would confront them directly and convict these religious leaders of wrongdoing. Also, Christ on at least one occasion, walked into the temple in Jerusalem, turned over the tables of the moneychangers, and drove out the buyers and sellers. All of these actions, including his many good works, brought attention to Christ and acted to separate him from many of the Jews.

The outcome of the conflict caused by Christ began with a plot by the chief priests and scribes to kill him. One of Christ's personal followers worked with these men by betraying Christ for the price of thirty pieces of silver. Once he had been arrested, and though the governor could find no fault in him, Christ was sentenced to death even though the people had respected him as a teacher, and had thought of him as a prophet. The Jews chose to have a criminal released instead of Christ, resulting in Christ's crucifixion. According to Roman custom, he was beaten, scourged, and forced to carry his own cross. After suffering physically, Christ had to endure verbal mocking, and humiliation by having a robe and a crown of thorns placed on him. When he finally died the slow, painful death of crucifixion, Christ was alone as an individual punished and sentenced to death.

Although Christ had a great number of faithful followers, at the time of his death he was truly an individual against society. Betrayed by one of his apostles and abandoned by the rest, Christ the conflict between Christ and Jews ended in his death.

BRENDA'S PLANS FOR ORGANIZING HER ESSAY

I.   Views of Jesus
    A.   People who believe
    B.   People who doubt he existed
    C.   Views of scholars and authorities

II. Jesus of faith vs. Jesus of history
    A.   Views
    B.   New Testament picture
    C.   How they were written

III. Conclusion
    A.   How biases affect the way one sees things
    B.   The case of the historical Jesus
    C.   Balance and perspective

Writing Task

Here is a rhetorical task similar to the one with which Brenda was presented.

Choose an historical event or person about which you would like to know more and about which there may be a controversy as to whether it actually happened the way many people believe or as to whether the person actually lived. For instance, many people dispute the number of people involved in the assassination of President Kennedy, believing that more were responsible for his shooting than Lee Harvey Oswald. Or, you might investigate a recent controversial issue with the purpose of presenting the facts about the issue—instead of taking a position or advocating a stance, as you would in a persuasive essay (see Chapter 10). For instance, you might examine the debate between the tobacco industry and the American Cancer Society, articulating the scientific evidence against smoking or the counterclaims of the tobacco producers. You may select any audience you wish for this task, but you should do some careful inventing to analyze the audience and the sorts of information they would need to follow your presentation.

You may find it helpful to examine the process Brenda used when she began to visualize her audience and articulate her intention.

Do your own inventing and planning now:

1. Jot down some persons, events, or issues that you would like to explore and craft an informative essay about.

2. Which ones do you know the most about? Which ones would you have to do some research about? Are any of these items controversial, i.e., do any of them reflect public doubt about their "reality" or "historicity"? Why?

3. Use 5W + (see Chapter 2) to explore one of these items. What kinds of information do you generate? Which of these bits of information need further exploration and examination? Which would contribute the most to your emerging ideas for the essay?

4. Consider your audience. Who are you writing to? Would they be interested in finding out more about this person, event, or issue? What do they already know about it? What do they *think* they know about it? What do you imagine they would like to know about it?

5. Will you have any difficulty keeping yourself out of the way of the information you wish to present? How do you feel about the person, event, or issue? Will you be tempted to turn your essay into a persuasive essay that tries to move the audience to a position, instead of merely presenting them with facts in an orderly, accessible manner?

6. Examine the "example" essays in this chapter. Can you use a similar organization in your essay? If not, describe how you might organize your essay differently. How many "parts" will your essay have? What do you expect each part to *do?*

7. When you finish your essay, what do you hope your readers will know about the subject matter you have presented? Can you summarize that knowledge in a paragraph?

8. Write the first draft of your essay.

Drafting and Revising

What follows are the successive drafts of Brenda's essay, two of which are accompanied by marginal commentary. She produced a total of four drafts, with intervening planning and inventing sessions. The fourth, and final, draft will appear in the section on proofreading and editing.

BRENDA'S FIRST DRAFT

1. Code expression
2. Opening frame of reference problem
3. Code expression
4. First sentence convoluted
5. Code expressions
6. Convoluted sentence

There are some doubts in the world today[1] in relation to the man   1
Jesus. In some instances, it is questioned as to whether he was actually
the Son of God, and in others, there are doubts as to whether he
actually existed at all.[2] This paper will point out some of the *viewpoints*
findings in relation to the of Biblical scholars about the gospels of
Jesus,[3] as suggested by the important question, "Who Was Jesus?" Also,
the gospels of Mark and Luke will be looked at in relation discussed
as to how they compare agree or disagree with the views held by the
Biblical scholars. Finally, a conclusion will be drawn concerning the
usefulness of the scholarship's findings will be drawn.

One of the first points *which should be* mentioned states that most of the scholars   2
today do not make a separation between "the historical Jesus"[5] and
"the Christ of faith."[5, 4] This is an important point in understanding
the basis point of view that the Biblical scholars are speaking from.
Their emphasis is on the creative role differences of the gospels according to the needs of the community it was written communities
they were written for.[6] Also, they tend to focus on the meaning of
the that the Bible New Testament texts had to the first-century Christians to which they were written. As a final statement of the viewpoint
taken by Biblical scholarship, there is the idea that nearly all of the
scholars are keeping the message of Christianity Finally, nearly all of

the Biblical scholars conduct their studies from the viewpoint ~~that~~ which is the core of Christianity--"that God was incarnate in human form and that He died and rose again from the dead to redeem mankind from sin." What ~~aff~~ effect these basic viewpoints have ~~when those who~~ on those who are not scholars will be examined later in this paper.[7]

3   As far as the scholarship's findings in relation to the gospels, the consensus believes that ~~in the early~~ Christians worked backwards ~~to develop~~ in developing their ^accounts^ ~~writings~~ about Jesus. That is, the early Christians first ~~told of Christ~~ focused on the death and resurrection of Jesus and then took into account his ministry on earth. ~~As~~ When looking[9] at the gospels individually, ~~there appears~~ their authors give four different views of the man Jesus. The scholars see the gospel ^(sp)^ according to Mark as presenting Jesus as a miracle worker who's mission is not understood by anyone close to him, and even his followers fail to see him as the Messiah.[8] In this account, Jesus dies alone and is never reconciled with his disciples after his resurrection.[10] The Jesus presented in Matthew is looked at as the Son of God and the last King of Israel. The Biblical scholars ~~see~~ find here that Jesus is the fulfillment of ~~the Old~~ Jewish prophecy, and that Christianity is the development of Judaism. In Luke, the consensus finds that Jesus is an innocent savior, filled with peace, love, and forgiveness for all men. Here, the emphasis is on the ~~ordinary~~ everyday lives of people and how ~~their~~ those lives should be lived. ~~is emphasized.~~ The gospel according to John presents a Jesus who is immediately recognized by his disciples, and focus on his conflict with the Jews.[11] The scholarship sees the emphasis in each gospel focusing on a different aspect of Jesus' personality, and his listeners' reactions to him. In Mark, the emphasis is on power, ~~in Luke; faith;~~ in Matthew--faith, in Luke--joy, and in John--self-control.

4   In looking at the gospels according to Mark and Luke more in-depth and apart from the views of the Biblical scholarship, a greater insight[12] is gained in regards to Jesus. Mark shows Jesus as having a great amount of power which is displayed through healing, miracles, and authoritative teaching. In addition to this, the apostles consistently display a lack of understanding; they see Jesus as a teacher, not as the Son of God or the Messiah.[13] Jesus is constantly having to explain his parables to his apostles, and even then, they do not show true understanding. Luke approaches the story of Jesus in a different ~~matter~~ manner, taking into account the birth and ministry of John the Baptist, and also the birth and genealogy of Jesus. ~~When Jesus begins his ministry~~ During his ministry, Jesus is constantly showing compas-

7. Copied structure; focus unclear

8. Focus again

9. Agent missing in sentence: *who* is looking?

10. Ambiguous sentence

11. More copied structure: Intention is obscured

12. Agentless sentence

13. Focus again unclear

14. More copied structure

sion,[14] and ~~has-an-attitude-of~~ relates himself as a physician ministering to the sick. ~~Luke's-account-is-much-more-in-depth-than-Mark's~~ Luke's account goes into much more detail than Mark's, even though some of the events and teachings are paralelled. (sp) There is no emphasis on the apostles' lack of understanding; instead the emphasis ~~on-the-Christian~~ is on ~~prin~~ matters that concerned the lives of ~~Christ's~~ Jesus' followers, such as prayer, service, faithfulness, and gratitude. Jesus himself is shown as a prayerful and patient, and forgiving teacher, even to the point of asking forgiveness ~~that~~ for those who had him crucified.[15]

15. Focus problem

16. Code expression

In conclusion, it can be seen where religious biases[16] ~~tend-to-creep-in~~ can easily affect how the gospels are viewed. ~~Although-the-statements-made-in-this-article-in-general-seemed-to~~ In this article, the general statements made by the scholars gave an idea of the content of each gospel.[17] Yet the reader of the New Testament would be more rounded by studying the gospels as they are presented, and also taking into consideration the viewpoints of the Biblical scholars.[18] It seems that the greatest danger would be for the reader to hold one view, whether his own, or someone else's, as absolute and not taking into ~~account~~ consideration the possible weaknesses in human character.[19] 5

17. Ambiguous sentence

18. Focus

19. Code phrasing

EVALUATION

Text Level When Brenda wrote her intentional predraft (pp. 315–316) to discover how she felt about the historical identity of Jesus, she knew that in drafts addressed to an audience she would have to take care to keep her private views out of what was to be an *objective, informative* essay. When she read through her first draft (pp. 318–320), in which she *had* attempted to be objective, she was dismayed to discover that she had not succeeded. Her first draft contained some obvious marks of a *predraft*. Despite her outline, her notes from readings, and her strong sense of intention, her first draft tended to ignore the needs of the reader. She simply had not provided an adequate frame of reference to make the information she was presenting easy to grasp. Consequently, her thesis and intention remained unclear throughout the first draft. Here are her notes to herself as she examined each paragraph.

1. Para. 1: I guess it doesn't set up the context for my material very well. "Doubts in the world today in relation to the man Jesus," is too ambiguous, and my follow-up sentences are awkwardly placed. I don't

like it when I make the organization so explicit in the text: "I will do this, then this, then, finally ..." It's "objective" but very dull.

2. <u>Para. 2:</u> The first sentence is terrible--"points" don't "state" things. Need to define "historical" Jesus and "Christ of faith." Need to set up the context for these Biblical scholars better. Structure just seems to copy the order in which I researched my subject.

3. <u>Para. 3:</u> Transition weak. What do I want the reader to make of this information--needs focus, more explicit connection to the point of the essay. I seem to have two or three theses--which one should emerge?

4. <u>Para. 4:</u> This is too much me; I need to get out of the way--this is too much like my inventing to myself. More copied structure.

5. <u>Para. 5:</u> Conclusion is out of whack! I see I've announced my "findings" without letting the reader follow me through the evidence. I can see it--but the reader can't. Too writer-based. That last sentence is a killer.

Sentence Level   Brenda saw a number of sentence problems. Many of the sentences simply had no energy—they were too passive, or lacked a clear agent. Several, however, were classic writer-based sentences, clearly indicating that she had probably written a predraft. Here are some of the sentences she found troubling when she read her text carefully:

-- <u>Para. 1:</u> "Finally, a conclusion concerning the usefulness of the scholarship's findings will be drawn." (convoluted; passive)

-- <u>Para. 2:</u> "One of the first points which should be mentioned states that most of the scholars today do not make a separation between 'the historical Jesus' and the 'Christ of faith.'" (First half of sentence could be deleted for clarity and economy)

-- <u>Para. 3:</u> "When looking at the gospel individually, their authors give four different views of the man Jesus." (agent problem, causes dangling modifier) "In this account, Jesus dies alone and is never reconciled with his disciples after his resurrection." (ambiguous sentence; unclear function)

-- <u>Para. 4:</u> "In looking at the gospels according to Mark and Luke more in-depth and apart from the views of the Biblical scholarship, a greater insight is gained in regards to Jesus." (agentless sentence)

-- <u>Para. 5:</u> "It seems that the greatest danger would be for the reader to hold one view, whether his own or someone else's, as absolute and

not taking into consideration the possible weaknesses in human character." (ambiguous function; poor focus)

Word Level   Brenda found a number of code words and expressions that
indicated a writer-based diction. She was less worried about these problems,
since she considered her word choice the easiest part to revise. Specifically,
she knew that key terms like "Jesus of history" and "Christ of faith" needed
to be unpacked, and that other expressions, like "doubts in the world today,"
"the gospels of Jesus," "religious biases," and "weaknesses in human character," would require careful rethinking and definition to be accessible to
the reader.

Exercise

Examine Brenda's first draft and answer the following questions.

1.   If you had written Brenda's first draft, a *predraft,* what portions would
you consider significant and worth reformulation for a second draft? List
them.

2.   Does Brenda's predraft suggest any structuring and development strategies for the next draft? Explain.

3.   Should Brenda begin her second draft right away, or does she need
to do some more inventing and planning? Explain.

4.   Why do you think Brenda's intentional predraft (pp. 315–316) was of
so little help in allowing her to write a more reader-based first draft of her
informative essay?

Writing Task

Read the first draft of your essay and answer the following questions.

1.   Describe the intention of your essay.
2.   Describe the audience to whom your essay is addressed.
3.   Describe the way in which you intended to structure your essay.
4.   Describe the tone you intended to use.

Now examine your draft at the text, sentence, and word levels. Then determine whether you have produced a predraft or a rough draft.

If you have written a predraft, carefully glean it for possible theses and for strategies that you might use in writing your next draft. Also, reexamine your inventing and planning process. Do you need to engage in additional, significant inventing and planning sessions? If so, what does your predraft indicate that you should focus your subsequent sessions upon: clarifying your intention; defining your audience more carefully; creating a different or more explicit structure?

If you have written a rough draft, identify the portions of the text that need work. Overall, does your intention need to be clarified? Do you need to provide your reader with additional frames of reference? Do you need to sharpen the focus within the paragraphs of your text?

REVISION

Because she had produced another predraft rather than a rough draft, Brenda knew that she could not simply tinker with the text, adding, subtracting, rearranging, and substituting. Instead she read through her draft carefully, looking for the elements worth preserving and for the sources of ambiguity and lack of focus so that she could compensate for them in subsequent drafts.

Brenda moved through the paragraphs of her predraft, noting what she wanted the new version of each paragraph to do and writing a fairly detailed plan for revising each one to make it more reader-based. Here are her revision plans.

-- Para. 1: Use this paragraph to establish the intention of the essay more explicitly, supplying a frame of reference for the whole essay: what do we think of when we hear the name "Jesus"? What range of opinions are there? How can historical analysis help us decide?

-- Para. 2: Transition paragraph introducing the findings and activities of Biblical scholars, putting the contemporary research in the context of what had preceded it. Jesus/history vs. Christ/faith: explain more fully.

-- Para. 3, 4: Discuss what use the contemporary scholar makes of the Biblical records. Relate this to other kinds of historical figures. Why did anybody write about Jesus in the first place? Why are there four different "gospels"?

-- <u>Para. 5:</u> What is the importance of any of this for understanding history and remarkable people like Jesus, Alexander, Moses, etc.? Explain the part the Biblical narratives played in the growth of the church.

-- <u>Para. 6:</u> Big conclusion! Tie everything together--history, analysis, judgment, bias, Jesus, decision. Watch your tone--don't push, don't overract--just present the facts.

After thinking further about such matters as eliminating some of the passive sentences, which she realized were the cause of her agentless structures, and clarifying key terms, Brenda felt confident about attempting a second draft. She checked over her intentional predraft, her reading notes, and her revision plans and forged ahead in revising her first draft. Here is a summary of the steps Brenda took in planning her revision.

1.   Having determined that she had written a predraft, Brenda read through her draft, looking for the trouble spots and noting their causes.

2.   She worked through each paragraph very meticulously, asking herself the purpose of each one and then crafting an analysis for each in which she planned a new version of the paragraph for the second draft.

3.   She planned to be even more careful in getting out of the way of the information she was presenting. Her intention would be to tell her audience about recent views of Jesus and how historical figures come to be known and understood by later historians.

Exercise

1.   Compare Brenda's plans for revising her draft with her original inventing and planning. How do they differ? How successful was she in anticipating her readers' needs?

2.   On the basis of her revision plans, how successful do you think she will be in drafting a second version of her essay? Explain.

3.   What additional revision advice would you give Brenda as she begins to write her second draft? Would you be ready to write a second draft if you were Brenda, or would you need to do some more inventing and planning?

Writing Task

If your first draft was a predraft:

1. Engage in an additional inventing and planning session, if you have determined that this is necessary.
2. Write a second draft.

If you produced a rough draft, write a second draft of your essay.

BRENDA'S SECOND DRAFT

Who Was Jesus Really? A Critical View

Brenda Green

1   Though few of us fail to recognize the name "Jesus" when it surfaces in print or conversation, our attitudes about ~~of~~ his place in history and his actual identity would not be unform. At the two extremes are those who doubt his historicity[1] altogether--that is, who maintain skepticism even of his actual 1st century existence--and those who are confirmed believers not only in his existence but in his divinity.as well.[2] Somewhere in between are those who believe he lived but are not quite sure about what to make of him. Clearly, it is one thing to believe that someone once walked the earth, and another entirely to believe he walked on water.

   1. Code word
   2. Sentence convolu- ted

2   One may get some help in assessing[3] the historical identity and meaning of Jesus by consulting the work of Biblical scholars who have been grappling with the question of "Who was Jesus" for several centuries.[4] At the turn of the century, many scholars distinguished the "Christ of faith" from the "Jesus of history," arguing that the "real" Jesus--the "nonmiraculous, painfully human" Jessus--must be understood as separate from the "Christ of faith" whose exploits were embellished and exaggerated by well-meaning believers. Chief of the exponents of this view was Albert Schweitzer, whose investigations into the psychology[5] of Jesus led him to make this rigid distinction. However, more recent scholarship has rejected this dichotomy, countering that it is very difficult if not impossible to keep the two portraits separate.[6] Whereas earlier scholarship seemed intent upon disproving

   3. Code word
   4. Focus: link with previous sentence?
   5. Code word
   6. Intention unclear: Who is Schweit- zer?

the divintity of Jesus, contemporary critics and researchers are more interested in discovering what it was about the man which compelled so many first century people to consider him the unique Son of God.

The main focus, then, of today's inquiry into the historicity and   3
identity of Jesus are the Biblical narratives themselves--the Gospels of Matthew, Mark, Luke and John, each evidently written for a differing audience and with a specific purpose. Rather than beginning with the premise that the Jesus of history was different than the popularly conceived miracle worker of later centuryes, these scholars are ex-

7.   Code   amining the Biblical gospels as <u>literary and historical documents</u>[7]
     expression   which deserve the same care and consideration that other documents of historical investigation.

                       The present consensus about the source and motivation for these   4
8.   Focus   Biblical texts is the early church's belief in the resurrection and con-
                       tinued life of Christ.[8] The composition of the four gospels followed the already-established belief structure about Jesus. That is to say, after the story of Jesus's resurrection spread and was accepted by enough people, there arose a need for someone to write down, to document what was being believed--a kind of explanation of the faith to the people who had already accepted it.

9.   Frame of   When the Biblical scholar looks at each individual gospel, he finds   5
     reference   a text specially suited to a certain audience. Mark's gospel, for instance,
     somewhat   presents Jesus as a miracle worker whose mission is not understood
     obscure   by anyone close to him: even his followrts fail to recognize him as
     here   the Messiah.[9] Matthew's Jesus is pictured as the Son of God, the last King of Israel and seemed to have been directed to a Jewish audience. The Greek-oriented Gospel of Luke, focuses on jesus as an innocent
10. Intention   saviour, one filled with peave, love and forgiveness for all men. The
     of these   most "theological" gospel, that is, the one most concerned with <u>in-</u>
     bits of   <u>terpreting</u> Jesus's exploits as well as chronicling them, is John's
     evidence   gospel, in which Jesus is the eternal "Logos," or word, who preexisted
     unclear   with God before Genesis and everything else.[10] *new*

                       These findings by contemporary scholars shed light on the historical   6
                       process by which persons are understood. The effect of Jesus and his
11. Frame?   life on the first century world was staggering.[11] His appeal to both Jewish and non-Jewish audiences was unprecendented in the ancient
12. Function   world as charismatic figures go. Part of this process was the written
     of   documents which subsequently emerged after the apparent death of
     sentence   Jesus.[12] Each gospel and each New Testament letter helped to further
     unclear   the notoriety and the interest which Jesus and his message had orig-

inally engendered. As faith spread, so did the need for "authoritative" guides or documents to help explain, interpret and preserve the structure and maintenance of this new movement.

7   It is easy to see how religious and personal biases can thus color the way an observer responds to a historical event ir personage.[13] Not only must an observer strive for objectivity in approaching the identity and historical circumstances of the event or person under review, he must also respect the written documents which provide the source materials for the individual he is investigating. The scholars at the turn of the century too easily divorced the Jesus of history from the Christ of faith, guaranteeing that they would find discrepancies or contradictions between "normal" history and the life of some spectacular individual. Contemporary scholarship is thus more tempered, more responsible in it seeks to understand what is there--seeks to explain the existence of a faith and not to explain it away. What to think of the "real" Jesus becomes a matter of personal decision rather than an inevitable conclusion drawn from conclusive evidence. His claims to divinity, the reports of his miraculous exploits, are part of the record and must be confronted head on.[14] Historians may not be able to answer questions about what has happened to whom and for what reasons; they may even be able to invalidate erroneous views with careful analysis; what they cannot do, finally, is tell us unequivocally what to believe when the historical record speaks ambivalently[15] and *unclearly about a historical figure.*

13.	Focus: transition weak
14.	Writer "in the way" structurally
15.	Quite convoluted

EVALUATION AND REVISION

Text Level   When Brenda read through her second draft, she knew that she had written a more reader-based text—in fact, she had produced a rough draft, and she felt it was very close to being finished. She seemed to have solved most of her frame of reference problems and had made progress toward eliminating the unclear focus of many sections of her first draft. However, some text-level items still needed revision. Here are some that she noted:

-- Para. 1: The frame is better--but I still need to clarify what I mean by "historicity," and the question of understanding the problems of historical analysis is not clearly raised. I like the way the paragraph ends; keep it.

-- <u>Para. 2</u>: First sentence doesn't really make the bridge I need from the opening paragraph. This paragraph is crucial, since it sets up my whole thesis. I should highlight the dichotomy between the "Jesus of history" and the "Christ of faith" more and explain a bit more carefully what the debate was. I should identify Schweitzer more explicitly, too.

-- <u>Para. 3</u>: I should explain better why modern scholars start from different premises than turn of the century scholars; and will my reader understand why I am mentioning "literary and historical" documents?

-- <u>Para. 4</u>: Key paragraph--I want it to say, "Here's why examining the original source materials is important and why they are the object of attention." It is unclear, I guess, why I mention the resurrection--I need better focus.

-- <u>Para. 5</u>: This paragraph is supposed to explain why there are four different pictures of Jesus--and why that makes it difficult for a historian to get a single view of Jesus. The material is there, but it needs better organization.

-- <u>Para. 6</u>: I'm winding the turn into the home stretch: I've got to make the historical problem more explicit--distinguishing fact from legend, truth from mere wishing. Maybe I need two separate paragraphs here.

-- <u>Para. 7</u>: My climax. Comes off too persuasive--too argumentative at the end. Basically I want it to say, "history has limitations," part of it is in the eye of the beholder. Tone down the private views!

Sentence Level   Brenda had eliminated all her agentless sentences by carefully examining the structure of each sentence and making sure that the subject was the real "doer" of the action. She also minimized her use of the passive voice, and this helped to reduce some of the wordiness. Several sentences, however, seemed to her to be convoluted, too packed with information, like "At the two extremes are those who doubt his historicity altogether—that is, who maintain skepticism even of his actual 1st century existence—and those who are confirmed believers not only in his existence but in his divinity as well" (paragraph 1) and the concluding sentence of the essay: "Historians may be able to answer questions about what has happened to whom and for what reasons; they may even be able to invalidate erroneous views with careful analysis; what they cannot do, finally, is tell us unequivocally what to believe when the historical record speaks ambivalently and unclearly about a historical figure." In the latter sentence, the thrust and clarity of the conclusion were obscured by the complex structure and the ambiguous tailing off of the writer's point. Overall, however, Brenda's second draft had avoided most of the writer-based structures that had made her first draft hard to follow.

Word Level   Brenda felt that in this second draft she had dealt with most of the ambiguities and private meanings. Nevertheless, she noted several remaining code expressions that needed replacement or clarification. Two key code expressions occurred early in the second draft: (1) "historicity," a needlessly technical term used by historians that could be replaced by a more accessible expression; and (2) "Christ of faith"/"Jesus of history," two terms that were better explained in the second draft, but that were still somewhat ambiguous. Brenda also noted that some terms, such as "assessed" in paragraph 2 and "psychology" in paragraph 2, could have more than one meaning as she used them, and she determined to find more helpful replacement words.

Writing Task

Examine your second draft at the text, sentence, and word levels, keeping in mind your intention and audience. Have you produced a predraft or a rough draft?

Exercise

Carefully read the first and second drafts of Brenda's essay, and answer the following questions.

1.   Compare the structure of Brenda's two drafts. Discuss the differences.
2.   Compare the use of information in each draft. How is the second draft more effective in its presentation of what is basically the same material? How effective is Brenda in getting out of the way of her information in the second draft?
3.   Why do you think Brenda was able to produce a more reader-based draft on her second try? How important was her first draft in enabling her to produce a creditable rough draft?
4.   Compare Brenda's revision strategies for the first draft with what she actually did in her second draft. How successful was she in following her own plan? Did she depart from it in any way?

5. Do you agree with Brenda that her second draft is close to being "finished" and that she can now concentrate on proofreading and editing?

6. Which revisions seemed to be most crucial to Brenda as she progressed through the drafting of her text—frames of reference? controlling point of view? organizing information? eliminating agentless sentences?

Writing Task

Recall your evaluation of your second draft. Keeping your intention and audience in mind, select and execute appropriate revision strategies.

If you produced another predraft, compare it carefully to your first predraft. Is your second predraft more reader-based? Do you need to engage in more inventing and planning? What aspects of your text need the most attention: audience, intention, structure? Consider these questions; then write another draft. You may wish to consult your teacher for some specific strategies that you can use in writing your next draft.

If you produced a rough draft, determine the location and nature of every problem with your text as precisely as you can. Choose your revising strategies accordingly: Do you need to create frames of reference for your reader? Do you need to sharpen the focus of particular portions of your text? Do you need to refine your stance? Then revise your draft.

BRENDA'S THIRD DRAFT

Who Was Jesus Really? A Contemporary Perspective
Brenda Green

Few of us would fail to recognize the name "Jesus" when it surfaces in print or in conversation, but our attitudes about his place in history and his actual identity would not be uniform. At one end of the spectrum are the skeptics who doubt that Jesus actually ever lived; at the other end are those who believe not only in his existence, but in his divinity as well. Somewhere in between are those who concede his historical existence but who are unsure about what to do with the claims that are made for his identity. Clearly, it is one thing to believe that someone once walked the earth, and another entirely to believe that someone walked on water.

One may get some help in assessing the meaning of Jesus in history by consulting the work of Biblical scholars, all of whom have been grappling with the question of "Who was Jesus really?" for many centuries. As recently as the turn of the century, many scholars distinguished the "Jesus of history" from the "Christ of faith," arguing that the miracle-working Christ of popular faith must be understood as a creation of those who believed in him and not a fair representation of the "real," all-too-human Jesus who lived in first century Palestine. The chief exponent of this view was none other than Albert Schweitzer, whose investigations into the psychology of Jesus led him to make this rigid distinction. More recent scholarship, however, has rejected this dichotomy, countering that it is difficult to keep the two identities separate, and that, even if historians could, the records clearly point to an extraordinary individual figure whose exploits captured the imagination of thousands in the first century. Whereas earlier scholarship seemed intent upon disproving the divinity of Jesus, contemporary critics and researchers are more interested in understanding the first century documents as they are, determining the source of interest in this remarkable man.

The main focus, then, of contemporary inquiry into the historicity and identity of Jesus are the Biblical narratives themselves--the "Gospels" of Matthew, Mark, Luke, and John, each evidently written for a differing audience and with consequent differing purposes. Rather than beginning with the premise that the Jesus of history can and should be distinguished from popular conceptions of him, these scholars are examining the Biblical texts as literary and historical documents which can be analyzed using the same tools of scholarship which are applied to other similar texts.

The present consensus about the origins of faith in this charismatic figure and the motivation for the documents written about him, is that both stem from the early church's belief in Jesus' resurrection. The composition of the gospels seemed to have been precipitated by the need for an "authoritative" account of the life of Jesus for those who already believed--a kind of explanation of the faith for the initiated which followed the common belief structure of the early church.

When the present day Biblical scholar examines each individual gospel, he finds a text specially suited to a certain kind of audience. Mark's gospel, for instance, presents Jesus as a miracle worker whose mission is not understood by anyone close to him: not even his closest followers are able to recognize him as the awaited Messiah. Matthew's Jesus is pictured as the last King of Israel, the Messiah prophesied of old, and is clearly directed to a Jewish audience. The Greek-oriented gospel of Luke focuses on Jesus as an innocent savior, one filled with peace, love, and forgiveness for all men. The most "theological" gospel, that is, the one most concerned with interpreting Jesus's exploits as well as recording them, is John's gospel, which depicts Jesus as the eternal "Logos," or word, who preexisted with God before Genesis and everything else.

6   These analyses by contemporary scholars thus shed new light on the way historical figures come to be understood and interpreted by later observers. The appeal of the "Jesus story" in the first century-- to Jewish and Gentile audiences alike--was staggering, unprecedented in the ancient world as charismatic leaders and their careers usually go. Part of this understanding and interpreting process involves the written documents which survive the historical period of the figure under review. Each gospel and New Testament letter helped establish and further the notoriety and interest which the original message and presence of Jesus had engendered. As the faith spread in the ancient world, there emerged a need for written documents to help explain, interpret, and preserve the structure of this new movement.

7   It is thus easy to understand the difficulty of distinguishing the factuality of a historical personage or event from the interpretations which quickly arise to support the prevailing view. In the particular case of Jesus of Nazareth, it is clear that religious and personal biases can color the way one responds to his life as it is depicted in the Biblical narratives. The scholars of the turn of the century too facilely divorced the Jesus of history from the Christ of faith, distorting both his "actual" historical presence and his effect on first century audiences. Their stance guaranteed that they would discover "discrepancies" and "contradictions" between Jesus and his followers' perceptions of him. Contemporary scholarship is thus more tempered, more responsible in its attempt to balance the concerns of "normal" history with investigation into the sometimes spectacular or fantastic, seeking only to explain, and not to explain away.

8   What to think about the "real" Jesus becomes not so much a function of inevitable conclusions drawn from irrefutable evidence as of personal decision and commitment. While historians can help answer many of the what and why questions of historical periods, and can often invalidate erroneous views which grow up around dubious events and personages, they cannot, finally, tell us unequivocally whether we should believe this or that. The final court of historical analysis is always the human reason and the human heart.

EVALUATION AND REVISION

After Brenda had completed this draft, she had no reservations about the text being ready for proofreading and editing. All the previous problems at the text, sentence, and word levels had been dealt with. What remained to be done was careful retyping, minor editing, and a reading by a friend to spot any ambiguities that Brenda could not locate because of her closeness to the text.

Writing Task

Keep revising your essay until it is as reader-based as you can make it and you are ready to proofread and edit your final draft.

Proofreading and Editing

After Brenda finished rewriting her third draft, she had a friend read through it carefully, looking for awkward sentences, ambiguous word choice, and text-level organizational problems. She was happy to find that there were very few, although she did make some changes before typing a fourth, *final* draft. Here are some of the changes she made.

1. Rephrased the sentence in paragraph 2 to better identify Albert Schweitzer: "The chief exponent of this view was none other than humanitarian and missionary Albert Schweitzer, whose investigations into the psychology of Jesus led him to make this rigid distinction."
2. Rephrased a clause in paragraph 2 to make it less awkward: "the records clearly point to Jesus as an extraordinary figure who captured the imagination of thousands in the first century."
3. Added "Biblical" to the last sentence in paragraph 2: "first century Biblical documents," for clarity.
4. Added "ly" to "consequent" in the first sentence of paragraph 3.
5. Reworked paragraph 4 to clarify focus (see final draft).
6. Added information to the second sentence in paragraph 5 to balance it with the content of other sentences in the paragraph: "Mark's gospel, for instance, presents Jesus as a miracle worker whose derring-do and rhetorical skills appealed to a Roman audience."
7. Added a sentence to paragraph 5 to complete the unity of the paragraph: "John's gospel seems to be addressed to all audiences."

8.   Added words to sentences in paragraph 6 and deleted others for greater clarity.

9.   Added words to sentences in paragraph 7 to achieve parallelism and to clarify its topic: "distorting his 'actual' historical presence and dismissing his effect on first century audiences" and "between Jesus's life and his followers' perceptions of him."

BRENDA'S FINAL DRAFT

Who Was Jesus Really? A Contemporary Perspective
Brenda Green

1   Few of us would fail to recognize the name "Jesus" when it surfaces in print or in conversation, but our attitudes about his place in history and his actual identity would not be uniform. At one end of the spectrum are the skeptics who doubt that Jesus actually ever lived; at the other end are those who believe not only in his existence, but in his divinity as well. Somewhere in between are those who concede his historical existence but who are unsure about what to do with the spectacular claims that are made for his identity. Clearly, it is one thing to believe that someone once walked the earth, and another thing entirely to believe that someone walked on water.

2   One may get some help in determining the meaning of Jesus in history by consulting the work of Biblical scholars, all of whom have been grappling with the question of "Who was Jesus really?" for many centuries. As recently as the turn of the century, many scholars distinguished the "Jesus of history" from the "Christ of faith," arguing that the miracle-working Christ of popular faith must be understood as a creation of those who believed in him and not a fair representation of the "real," all-too-human Jesus who lived in first-century Palestine. The chief exponent of this view was none other than humanitarian and missionary Albert Schweitzer, whose investigations into the psychology of Jesus led him to make this rigid distinction. More recent scholarship, however, has rejected this dichotomy, countering that it is difficult to keep the two identities separate, and that, even if historians could, the records clearly point to Jesus as an extraordinary individual figure who captured the imagination of thousands in the first century. Whereas earlier scholarship seemed intent upon disproving the divinity of Jesus, contemporary critics and researchers are more interested

in understanding the first-century Biblical documents as they are, determining the source of interest in this remarkable man.

The main focus, then, of contemporary inquiry into the historicity   3 and identity of Jesus are the Biblical narratives themselves--the "Gospels" of Matthew, Mark, Luke, and John, each evidently written for a differing audience and with consequently differing purposes. Rather than beginning with the premise that the Jesus of history can and should be distinguished from popular conceptions of him, these scholars are examining the Biblical texts as literary documents which can be analyzed using the same tools of scholarship which are applied to other similar texts.

Their present consensus about the origins of faith in this charismatic   4 figure and, thus, the motivation for writing the documents which depict him is that both stem from the early church's belief in Jesus' resurrection. The composition of the gospels seemed to have been precipitated by the need for an "authoritative" account of the life of Jesus for those who had come to believe--a kind of "primer" of the faith for the newly initiated which reflected the commonly held beliefs of the early church.

When the present day Biblical scholar examines each individual   5 gospel, he finds a text specially suited to a certain kind of audience. Mark's gospel, for instance, presents Jesus as a miracle worker whose derring-do and rhetorical skills appealed to a Roman audience. Matthew's Jesus is pictured as the last King of Israel, the Messiah prophesied of old, and is clearly directed to a Jewish audience. The Greek-oriented gospel of Luke focuses on Jesus as an innocent savior, one filled with peace, love, and forgiveness for all men. The most "theological" gospel, that is, the one most concerned with interpreting Jesus' exploits as well as recording them, is John's gospel, which depicts Jesus as the eternal "Logos," or word, who preexisted with God before Genesis and everything else. John's gospel seems to be addressed to all audiences.

These analyses by contemporary scholars thus shed light on the   6 way historical figures come to be understood and interpreted by later observers. The appeal of the "Jesus story" in the first century--to Jewish and Gentile audiences alike--was unprecedented in the ancient world among such charismatic leaders. Crucial to this understanding and interpreting process are the written documents which survive the historical period of the figure under review. Each gospel and New Testament letter helped establish and further the notoriety and interest which the original message and presence of Jesus had engendered.

As the faith spread in the ancient world, there emerged a need for written documents to help explain, interpret, and preserve the structure of this new movement.

7   It is thus easy to understand the difficulty of distinguishing the factuality of a historical personage or event from the interpretations which quickly arise to support the prevailing view. In the particular case of Jesus of Nazareth, it is clear that religious and personal biases can color the way one responds to his life as it is depicted in the Biblical narratives. The scholars of the turn of the century too facilely divorced the Jesus of history from the Christ of faith, distorting both his "actual" historical presence and dismissing his effect on first-century audiences. Their stance guaranteed that they would discover "discrepancies" and "contradictions" between Jesus' life and his followers' perceptions of him. Contemporary scholarship is thus more tempered, more responsible in its attempt to balance the concerns of "normal" history with investigation into the sometimes spectacular or fantastic, seeking only to explain, and not to explain away.

8   What to think about the "real" Jesus becomes not so much a function of inevitable conclusions drawn from irrefutable evidence as of personal decision and commitment. While historians can help answer many of the what and why questions of historical periods, and can often invalidate erroneous views which grow up around dubious events and personages, they cannot, finally, tell us unequivocally whether we should believe this or that. The final court of historical analysis is always human reason and the human heart.

Exercise

Read Brenda's final draft carefully and answer these questions.

1. How successful was Brenda in following the revision plans she had prepared for her final draft? Do you think there are other strategies she should have used?

2. How reader-based is her "final" draft? Are there any other changes you would make or suggest to her?

3. Read the first draft of Brenda's essay again and compare it with her final version. What major differences do you find? How much change in organization, information, tone, and point of view do you find as her essay evolved?

4. Which revision strategies seemed to be most helpful to her? What

inventing and planning strategies did she seem to rely most on after she began to draft her text?

Writing Task

Examine your latest draft at the text, sentence, and word levels. Continue revising it until it is as reader-based as you can make it. Then proofread and edit your final draft.

Writing Assignment

Choose a person—an historical figure, a living person whom you know personally, or a living person you know of because he or she is a celebrity or public figure—about whom you wish to know more than you do now. Write an informative essay about that individual, addressed to an audience of your choice.

I.   Getting Started: Inventing and Planning
      A. List several persons whom you find interesting or intriguing.
      B. Choose one of these persons and find out more about him or her. If you know this individual, an interview is a good way to find out more. But you should prepare your questions in *advance*. You may wish to set up some additional, follow-up interviews, because as your intention in writing becomes clear to you, you may need to ask more questions—concerning matters you had not anticipated you would want to know about. If this individual is a well-known figure, you will probably find information about him or her in a variety of sources at the library. Be sure to examine periodicals if the person is alive or recently deceased.
      C. Once you have thoroughly familiarized yourself with the person you are going to write about, examine your information and begin to decide which aspects of this person you want to discuss, how much detail you want to include, and how you wish to order the information.
      D. Jot down the information and the particular details you want to use. Can you think of any way of ordering the information?
      E. As you were jotting down information and thinking about ways of ordering it, did you begin to think about the audience for the essay?

If not, think about your readers: Who would be interested in finding out about this person? Jot down some of the characteristics of your audience: their age, interests, level of education, occupation, etc.

F. Keeping your audience in mind, answer these questions: What are some strategies that you might use to get your readers interested in your subject? How much does your audience already know about this person? How much background information about the person or about the person's significance or importance does your audience need?

G. Describe your intention in writing. Describe the context in which you will present the information. For example, are you a staff writer for *Rolling Stone* who is doing a piece about the lead singer of Van Halen because many of your readers think he's sexy and want to know about him?

H. Tentatively describe the structure of your essay. How will you present your information so that it is accessible and interesting?

II. Drafting and Revising
A. Write the first draft of your essay.
B. Read your draft and answer the following:
Describe the intention of your essay.
Describe the audience to whom your essay is addressed.
Describe the way in which you intended to structure your essay.
Describe the point of view (first, second, third person) and the tone that you used.
C. Evaluate your draft in terms of your answers to these questions. Examine your draft at the text, sentence, and word levels. Is it a rough draft or a predraft?
D. Describe your plans for revising or rewriting your draft.
E. Repeat steps B to D if necessary.

III. Proofreading and Editing
A. Allow some time to go by, then read your final draft out loud.
B. Correct errors in sentence structure, word choice, and mechanics and usage.

Writing Assignment

Read the following essay, "The Effects of a Nuclear Explosion," by Jonathan Schell.

The Effects of a Nuclear Explosion

Jonathan Schell

One way to begin to grasp the destructive power of present-day nuclear   1
weapons is to describe the consequences of the detonation of a one-
megaton bomb, which possesses eighty times the explosive power of the
Hiroshima bomb, on a large city, such as New York. Burst some eight-five
hundred feet above the Empire State Building, a one-megaton bomb would
gut or flatten almost every building between Battery Park and 125th Street,
or within a radius of four and four-tenths miles, or in an area of sixty-one
square miles, and would heavily damage buildings between the northern
tip of Staten Island and the George Washington Bridge, or within a radius
of about eight miles, or in an area of about two hundred square miles. A
conventional explosive delivers a swift shock, like a slap, to whatever it
hits, but the blast wave of a sizable nuclear weapon endures for several
seconds and "can surround and destroy whole buildings" (Glasstone). People,
of course, would be picked up and hurled away from the blast along with
the rest of the debris. Within the sixty-one square miles, the walls, roofs,
and floors of any buildings that had not been flattened would be collapsed,
and the people and furniture inside would be swept down onto the street.
(Technically, this zone would be hit by various overpressures of at least
five pounds per square inch. Overpressure is defined as the pressure in
excess of normal atmospheric pressure.) As far away as ten miles from
ground zero, pieces of glass and other sharp objects would be hurled about
by the blast wave at lethal velocities. In Hiroshima, where buildings were
low and, outside the center of the city, were often constructed of light
materials, injuries from falling buildings were often minor. But in New York,
where the buildings are tall and are constructed of heavy materials, the
physical collapse of the city would certainly kill millions of people. The
streets of New York are narrow ravines running between the high walls of
the city's buildings. In a nuclear attack, the walls would fall and the ravines
would fill up. The people in the buildings would fall to the street with the
debris of the buildings, and the people in the street would be crushed by
this avalanche of people and buildings. At a distance of two miles or so
from ground zero, winds would reach four hundred miles an hour, and
another two miles away they would reach a hundred and eighty miles an
hour. Meanwhile, the fireball would be growing, until it was more than a
mile wide, and rocketing upward, to a height of over six miles. For ten
seconds, it would broil the city below. Anyone caught in the open within
nine miles of ground zero would receive third-degree burns and would
probably be killed; closer to the explosion, people would be charred and

killed instantly. From Greenwich Village up to Central Park, the heat would be great enough to melt metal and glass. Readily inflammable materials, such as newspapers and dry leaves, would ignite in all five boroughs (though in only a small part of Staten Island) and west to the Passaic River, in New Jersey, within a radius of about nine and a half miles from ground zero, thereby creating an area of more than two hundred and eighty square miles in which mass fires were likely to break out.

2   If it were possible (as it would not be) for someone to stand at Fifth Avenue and Seventy-second Street (about two miles from ground zero) without being instantly killed, he would see the following sequence of events. A dazzling white light from the fireball would illumine the scene, continuing for perhaps thirty seconds. Simultaneously, searing heat would ignite everything flammable and start to melt windows, cars, buses, lampposts, and everything else made of metal or glass. People in the street would immediately catch fire, and would shortly be reduced to heavily charred corpses. About five seconds after the light appeared, the blast wave would strike, laden with the debris of a now nonexistent midtown. Some buildings might be crushed, as though a giant fist had squeezed them on all sides, and others might be picked up off their foundations and whirled uptown with the other debris. On the far side of Central Park, the West Side skyline would fall from south to north. The four-hundred-mile-an-hour wind would blow south to north, die down after a few seconds, and then blow in the reverse direction with diminished intensity. While these things were happening, the fireball would be burning in the sky for the ten seconds of the thermal pulse. Soon huge, thick clouds of dust and smoke would envelop the scene, and as the mushroom cloud rushed overhead (it would have a diameter of about twelve miles) the light from the sun would be blotted out, and day would turn to night. Within minutes, fires, ignited both by the thermal pulse and by broken gas mains, tanks of gas and oil, and the like, would begin to spread in the darkness, and a strong, steady wind would begin to blow in the direction of the blast. As at Hiroshima, a whirlwind might be produced, which would sweep through the ruins, and radioactive rain, generated under the meteorological conditions created by the blast, might fall. Before long, the individual fires would coalesce into a mass fire, which, depending largely on the winds, would become either a conflagration or a firestorm. In a conflagration, prevailing winds spread a wall of fire as far as there is any combustible material to sustain it; in a firestorm, a vertical updraft caused by the fire itself sucks the surrounding air in toward a central point, and the fires therefore converge in a single fire of extreme heat. A mass fire of either kind renders shelters useless by burning up all

the oxygen in the air and creating toxic gases, so that anyone inside the shelters is asphyxiated, and also by heating the ground to such high temperatures that the shelters turn, in effect, into ovens, cremating the people inside them. In Dresden, several days after the firestorm raised there by Allied conventional bombing, the interiors of some bomb shelters were still so hot that when they were opened the inrushing air caused the contents to burst into flame. Only those who had fled their shelters when the bombing started had any chance of surviving. (It is difficult to predict in a particular situation which form the fires will take. In actual experience, Hiroshima suffered a firestorm and Nagasaki suffered a conflagration.)

In this vast theatre of physical effects, all the scenes of agony and death   3
that took place at Hiroshima would again take place, but now involving millions of people rather than hundreds of thousands. Like the people of Hiroshima, the people of New York would be burned, battered, crushed, and irradiated in every conceivable way. The city and its people would be mingled in a smoldering heap. And then, as the fires started, the survivors (most of whom would be on the periphery of the explosion) would be driven to abandon to the flames those family members and other people who were unable to flee, or else to die with them. Before long, while the ruins burned, the processions of injured, mute people would begin their slow progress out of the outskirts of the devastated zone. However, this time a much smaller proportion of the population than at Hiroshima would have a chance of escaping. In general, as the size of the area of devastation increases, the possibilities for escape decrease. When the devastated area is relatively small, as it was at Hiroshima, people who are not incapacitated will have a good chance of escaping to safety before the fires coalesce into a mass fire. But when the devastated area is great, as it would be after the detonation of a megaton bomb, and fires are springing up at a distance of nine and a half miles from ground zero, and when what used to be the streets are piled high with burning rubble, and the day (if the attack occurs in the daytime) has grown impenetrably dark, there is little chance that anyone who is not on the very edge of the devastated area will be able to make his way to safety. In New York, most people would die wherever the blast found them, or not very far from there.

If instead of being burst in the air the bomb were burst on or near the   4
ground in the vicinity of the Empire State Building, the overpressure would be very much greater near the center of the blast area but the range hit by a minimum of five pounds per square inch of overpressure would be less. The range of the thermal pulse would be about the same as that of the air burst. The fireball would be almost two miles across, and would

engulf midtown Manhattan from Greenwich Village nearly to Central Park. Very little is known about what would happen to a city that was inside a fireball, but one would expect a good deal of what was there to be first pulverized and then melted or vaporized. Any human beings in the area would be reduced to smoke and ashes; they would simply disappear. A crater roughly three blocks in diameter and two hundred feet deep would open up. In addition, heavy radioactive fallout would be created as dust and debris from the city rose with the mushroom cloud and then fell back to the ground. Fallout would begin to drop almost immediately, contaminating the ground beneath the cloud with levels of radiation many times lethal doses, and quickly killing anyone who might have survived the blast wave and the thermal pulse and might now be attempting an escape; it is difficult to believe that there would be appreciable survival of the people of the city after a megaton ground burst. And for the next twenty-four hours or so more fallout would descend downwind from the blast, in a plume whose direction and length would depend on the speed and the direction of the wind that happened to be blowing at the time of the attack. If the wind was blowing at fifteen miles an hour, fallout of lethal intensity would descend in a plume about a hundred and fifty miles long and as much as fifteen miles wide. Fallout that was sublethal but could still cause serious illness would extend another hundred and fifty miles downwind. Exposure to radioactivity in human beings is measured in units called rems—an acronym for "roentgen equivalent in man." The roentgen is a standard measurement of gamma- and X-ray radiation, and the expression "equivalent in man" indicates that an adjustment has been made to take into account the differences in the degree of biological damage that is caused by radiation of different types. Many of the kinds of harm done to human beings by radiation—for example, the incidence of cancer and of genetic damage—depend on the dose accumulated over many years; but radiation sickness, capable of causing death, results from an "acute" dose, received in a period of anything from a few seconds to several days. Because almost ninety per cent of the so-called "infinite-time dose" of radiation from fallout—that is, the dose from a given quantity of fallout that one would receive if one lived for many thousands of years—is emitted in the first week, the one-week accumulated dose is often used as a convenient measure for calculating the immediate harm from fallout. Doses in the thousands of rems, which could be expected throughout the city, would attack the central nervous system and would bring about death within a few hours. Doses of around a thousand rems, which would be delivered some tens of miles downwind from the blast, would kill within two weeks everyone who was exposed to them. Doses of around five hundred rems, which would be delivered as far as a hundred and fifty miles downwind (given a wind speed of fifteen miles per hour), would kill half of all exposed able-bodied young adults. At this level of exposure, radiation sickness proceeds in the three stages observed at Hiroshima. The plume of lethal fallout could descend, depending on the direction of the wind, on other parts of New York State and parts of New Jersey, Pennsylvania, Delaware, Maryland, Connecticut, Massachusetts, Rhode Island, Vermont, and New Hampshire, killing additional millions of people. The circumstances in heavily contaminated areas, in which millions of people were all declining together, over a period of weeks, toward painful deaths, are ones that, like so many of the consequences of nuclear explosions, have never been experienced.

A description of the effects of a one-megaton bomb on New York City   5
gives some notion of the meaning in human terms of a megaton of nuclear explosive power, but a weapon that is more likely to be used against New York is the twenty-megaton bomb, which has one thousand six hundred times the yield of the Hiroshima bomb. The Soviet Union is estimated to have at least a hundred and thirteen twenty-megaton bombs in its nuclear arsenal, carried by Bear intercontinental bombers. In addition, some of the Soviet SS-18 missiles are capable of carrying bombs of this size, although the actual yields are not known. Since the explosive power of the twenty-megaton bombs greatly exceeds the amount necessary to destroy most military targets, it is reasonable to suppose that they are meant for use against large cities. If a twenty-megaton bomb were air-burst over the Empire State Building at an altitude of thirty thousand feet, the zone gutted or flattened by the blast wave would have a radius of twelve miles and an area of more than four hundred and fifty square miles, reaching from the middle of Staten Island to the northern edge of the Bronx, the eastern edge of Queens, and well into New Jersey, and the zone of heavy damage from the blast wave (the zone hit by a minimum of two pounds of overpressure per square inch) would have a radius of twenty-one and a half miles, or an area of one thousand four hundred and fifty square miles, reaching to the southernmost tip of Staten Island, north as far as southern Rockland County, east into Nassau County, and west to Morris County, New Jersey. The fireball would be about four and a half miles in diameter and would radiate the thermal pulse for some twenty seconds. People caught in the open twenty-three miles away from ground zero, in Long Island, New Jersey, and southern New York State, would be burned to death. People hundreds of miles away who looked at the burst would be temporarily blinded and would risk permanent eye injury. (After the test of a fifteen-megaton bomb

on Bikini Atoll, in the South Pacific, in March 1954, small animals were found to have suffered retinal burns at a distance of three hundred and forty-five miles.) The mushroom cloud would be seventy miles in diameter. New York City and its suburbs would be transformed into a lifeless, flat, scorched desert in a few seconds.

6   If a twenty-megaton bomb were ground-burst on the Empire State Building, the range of severe blast damage would, as with the one-megaton ground blast, be reduced, but the fireball, which would be almost six miles in diameter, would cover Manhattan from Wall Street to northern Central Park and also parts of New Jersey, Brooklyn, and Queens, and everyone within it would be instantly killed, with most of them physically disappearing. Fallout would again be generated, this time covering thousands of square miles with lethal intensities of radiation. A fair portion of New York City and its incinerated population, now radioactive dust, would have risen into the mushroom cloud and would now be descending on the surrounding territory. On one of the few occasions when local fallout was generated by a test explosion in the multimegaton range, the fifteen-megaton bomb tested on Bikini Atoll, which was exploded seven feet above the surface of a coral reef, "caused substantial contamination over an area of more than seven thousand square miles," according to Glasstone. If, as seems likely, a twenty-megaton bomb ground-burst on New York would produce at least a comparable amount of fallout, and if the wind carried the fallout onto populated areas, then this one bomb would probably doom upward of twenty million people, or almost ten per cent of the population of the United States.

Answer the following questions about Schell's essay.

1.   Describe the intention of the essay. What, overall, did Schell wish to accomplish in writing the text?

2.   How, exactly, does Schell get out of the way of the information he is presenting?

3.   Obviously, no one has ever experienced a nuclear explosion of the kind Schell describes. Discuss the ways Schell makes the explosion real to the reader. For example, to what extent does the text appeal to the reader's senses?

4.   Examine the beginning of the essay. Is it effective? Does it make the reader want to read more? Explain.

5.   The essay ends with a sentence that claims "a bomb would probably doom upward of twenty million people, or almost ten per cent of the

population of the United States." Why did Schell choose to provide the reader with this piece of information last?

6. To whom is the essay addressed? Describe some of the characteristics of the audience. How much background information or explanation is provided for the readers?

7. How is the essay structured? What information does Schell present first, next, and so on? What kind of details does he include?

Select a topic of a rather technical nature and write an informative essay for an audience of your choice. For example, if you are majoring in fashion design, you may wish to write an essay about the nature of a particular type of fabric that is frequently used to make sportswear. Or, if you are majoring in business with a specialization in insurance, you may wish to inform an audience about whole life insurance—what it is, what it is used for, and so on. Or, if you have recently taken a computer science course, you might want to write an informative text about home or personal computers: what they are good for, what they cost, what software and peripherals are best for the first-time buyer.

I.   Getting Started: Inventing and Planning

A.   Choose a subject with which you are familiar, either because you have studied about it or because you have experience with it, or both. Jot down various aspects of this subject. For example, if you know a lot about dogs, you might jot down such things as pedigrees, showing dogs, raising dogs in a kennel, and boarding dogs. Select *one* aspect that you would like to inform an audience about, and use the 5W+ procedure (see Chapter 2) to explore this topic.

B.   Arrange the information you have generated, "treeing" the items in related branches. Do you see any gaps in your information? Do you need to do some research to fill those gaps, or do you need to do some more inventing?

C.   Which aspects of your material do you want to discuss? How much detail do you need to provide?

D.   Describe the characteristics of the audience to whom you will address your essay. Also consider these questions: Will your readers already be interested in what you have to say, or do you need to *show* them that it is relevant, entertaining, intriguing, or whatever? How much do you think your audience already knows about the subject? How will you relate unfamiliar information so that your readers will understand it? How much background information do they need?

E.   Describe the context in which you will present this information to your audience. What is your intention in writing? If your essay is successful, what do you want it to have *done?*

F.   Will you need to make a special effort to keep yourself out of the way so that you will not overshadow the information or intrude between it and your reader?

G.   Tentatively describe how you intend to structure your essay. How many parts will it have? What will you try to do in each?

II.   Drafting and Revising

A.   Write the first draft of your essay.

B.   Read your draft and answer the following:
Describe the intention of your essay.
Describe the audience to whom your essay is addressed.
Describe the way in which you intended to structure your essay.
Describe the point of view (first, second, third person) and the tone you used.

C.   Evaluate your draft in terms of your answers to these questions. Examine your draft at the text, sentence, and word levels. Is it a rough draft or a predraft?

D.   Describe your plans for revising or rewriting your draft.

E.   Repeat steps B to D if necessary.

III.   Proofreading and Editing

A.   Allow some time to go by, then read your final draft aloud.

B.   Correct errors in sentence structure, word choice, and mechanics and usage.

Writing Evaluations 9

The Evaluative Essay

In the next two chapters you will read essays that achieve their writers' intentions by using argumentative discourse, writing that marshals evidence and employs logical reasoning explicitly to lead the reader to certain conclusions that the writer wants her to adopt. You will also gain experience in writing these kinds of texts. Chapter 10 will deal more specifically with strategies for drafting persuasive essays. This chapter introduces the evaluative essay, another kind of text you will often find yourself writing.

Writing that is meant to ascertain or fix the value of something or someone is *evaluative* writing. Reviews of movies, records, or books that try to assess whether these works are "good," "bad," or "just fair" are examples of evaluative writing. Evaluative texts may also assess the performance of machines or of individuals: "The Fordrolet Wildcat is the best of the new subcompacts: It handles well under a variety of road conditions; it . . ."; "Ivan Borschtikoff's performance of Chopin's nocturnes was outstanding, characterized by technical virtuosity as well as . . ." Writing that tries to establish the importance or significance of a person or phenomenon is also evaluative: "President Denton was the best administrator Technical State University has ever had. His commitment to academic excellence was. . . ."

Why do readers read evaluative texts? Obviously, they read them to help guide their own choices, viewpoints, or courses of action. After reading a review, you may decide to see or not see a movie. An assessment of a particular product may discourage you from buying it. In addition, writers' evaluations of persons, events, and phenomena are often entertaining in themselves, providing food for thought and increasing your curiosity about the matter being discussed.

Evaluative writing differs significantly from both personal experience writing and expository writing in that it employs primarily argumentative discourse, a mode of writing that is explicitly concerned with *the reader's* sensibilities—her feelings and perspectives. The writer of an evaluative text is attempting to *persuade* the reader that his viewpoint is valid or correct. Of course, all writing is intended to be "persuasive" in the sense that every writer wants to convince the reader that his text presents a valid viewpoint. The writer of a process essay or an informative essay intends to alter the reader's viewpoint by providing her with new and relevant information. Likewise, the writer of a personal experience essay must persuade the reader that his experience was authentic and worth reading about.

However, there are important differences in the strategies for producing these kinds of texts. In expository writing, like process or informative writing, the writer's main intention is to *instruct* or *inform,* not to *advocate* specific conclusions that he wants the reader to adopt. Likewise, the intention of the writer of a personal experience essay is to *express himself,* to explore his own attitudes, outlooks, and feelings. Thus, the writer's primary *intention* distinguishes evaluative writing from these kinds of texts.

In order for an evaluative text to be successful, the reader must be convinced of the validity of the writer's assessment or judgment. A person may be motivated to read evaluative discourse for help in making a decision— "Should I read *The Purple Turtle Murders*?" "Which car should I buy?" "What graduate school should I attend?" Or a person may read evaluative texts out of curiosity or vague interest. In any case, the reader will expect to be presented with information in a clear and *persuasive* manner. She will expect to be provided with examples supporting any assertions that are made, and she will expect objectivity; in fact, overt bias on the part of the author may well cause the reader to reject his evaluation or judgment.

Since evaluative discourse presents an assessment, the clear presentation of the means by which he reached his judgment is a vital concern of the writer. Thus, an important part of all evaluative writing is the set of criteria used to make judgments. Suppose we wanted to perform a comparative evaluation of two cars, a Lincoln Continental and a Toyota Corolla, arguing that one is better than the other. Our judgment would vary dramatically depending on the set of criteria we used in making the assessment. If we choose the following criteria, which car will be "better"?

☐ Prestige value
☐ Head and leg room
☐ Smooth, quiet ride

But what if we use these criteria to make the assessment:

☐ Good gas mileage
☐ Economical purchase price
☐ Handling ease as related to size

As we have just illustrated, well-chosen, clearly described, and persuasively justified criteria are an important part of all evaluative texts. Additionally, evaluative discourse must be structured so that such criteria and the reasons behind them are clear.

The stance a writer adopts in evaluative discourse is also important. The tone of such a text should, under normal circumstances, convey objectivity. If the writer *does* intrude in the text and/or reveal his biases, he must convince the reader that his reasons for doing so are valid. Otherwise, he may only succeed in expressing his personal response, failing to convince his readers that he has performed an evaluation or that his evaluation is worth considering.

Here are some of the characteristics that a finished, *reader-based* evaluative essay should exhibit.

1.   The nature and results of the evaluation—even if it is complex—are clear to the readers.

2.   The criteria that were used in making the evaluation are clearly presented, appropriate to the evaluation being made, and, where needed, justified as being either valid or appropriate, or both.

3.   The writer's qualifications for making the judgment are established as being suitable and sufficient, if necessary.

4.   The results of the evaluation are convincing. For example, if the evaluative essay was a movie review that judged the movie "good" or "one of the best," readers should want to *see* that movie.

Examples

Following are two examples of effective evaluative essays. Read each carefully
and answer the accompanying questions.

John O'Hara: The Best Conversation in America
Frank MacShane

1   The ability of a writer to capture the speech of his characters is often
underestimated or even dismissed in favor of other qualities, but it is far
more important than subject matter or theme if his stories are to have life.
Comte de Buffon said "Style is the man" and it follows that a writer who
has the power to reproduce his character's voice has taken hold of the
character himself, and the story starts from there.

2   Because of their intimacy and lack of sociological detail, short stories
are especially dependent on the voice. Reading the dialogue of a short
story is like eavesdropping on a good conversation. The enduring popularity
of Dickens, Poe and Maupassant is based to a considerable degree on our
ability to hear the voices of Ebenezer Scrooge, Roderick Usher and the
habitués of the Maison Tellier.

3   The American writer of recent years who best represents this tradition
is John O'Hara, whose short stories seem as fresh as they were when they
were first written. This achievement is due mainly to O'Hara's ear for the
way people talk. From his beginnings as a reporter in Pottsville, Pa., he
developed his powers of observation and imitation. He began at a time
when newspaper columnists were far more influential than they are today.
The most famous column, "The Conning Tower," was edited by Franklin
P. Adams for the New York World. But newspapers everywhere ran regular
features by such writers as H. L. Mencken, Ring Lardner, Robert Benchley
and Alexander Woollcott. They were topical, and generally relied on the
rich resources of the American language for their flavor.

4   O'Hara imitated his elders by writing satirical monologues and conversations, and he made his first national appearance in "The Conning Tower"
in 1927 at the age of 22. Within the year, he moved to New York, where
nearly 20 daily newspapers were still being published. He got a job at the
Herald Tribune and was soon part of the easy democracy of Bleeck's,
Tony's, Jack and Charlie's "21" Club and other speakeasies. There he met
all sorts of people—journalists, sports figures, politicians, actors, stock brokers,
and playwrights—and he began to write sketches of them, usually imitating
their patterns of speech in the manner of Sinclair Lewis.

The New Yorker was then a young magazine, and O'Hara soon began   5
writing for it. He extended his narrative range, and he took his apprenticeship
so seriously that he published 43 stories in The New Yorker before considering
one of them worthy of inclusion in a book. O'Hara was not a satirist by
nature. Rather, he had a fiction writer's interest in human character. For
him, dialogue was a way of revealing human traits without spending much
time on description or setting. He found that when he had a precinct cop
pick up the telephone and say, "Wukkan I do fya?" the whole police station
stood revealed in those few words. When a teen-age girl from a private
school like Brearley or Chapin said, "Robert didn't come with she or I,"
her grammatical error suggested her breathless concern to appear grown
up.

"If people did not talk right, they were not real people," O'Hara observed   6
when he was a small boy, and it was as true of life as of art. "I do not
believe," he later wrote, "that a writer who neglects or has not learned to
write good dialog can be depended on for accuracy in his understanding
of character and his creation of characters."

Talk was, for O'Hara, the beginning of many of his stories. Often he   7
would sit at his typewriter and start by thinking of a couple of faces he
had seen. He would put them together in a restaurant or on an airplane,
and they would begin to talk. "I let them do small talk for a page or two,"
said O'Hara, "and pretty soon they begin to come to life. They do so entirely
through dialog. I start by knowing nothing about them except what I
remember of their faces. But as they chatter away, one of them, and then
the other, will say something that is so revealing that I recognize the signs
of created characters. From then on it is a question of how deeply I want
to interest myself in the characters."

Dialogue was not the only device O'Hara used to get into his stories,   8
but in general he relied on actual things that were as revealing as speech.
He was interested in the telling detail, the phrase or name that had some
resonance. A Brooks Brothers suit or a Swaine and Adeney's umbrella, the
Racquet Club or Palmer Stadium, Romanoff's or the Twentieth Century
Limited all carry much more than their surface identities. When O'Hara
writes about a woman pounding "her Delman heels on the Penn Station
floor," he creates a whole person in the phrase, just as he does with another
who, getting into her car in the parking lot of a suburban railway station,
"kicked off her shoes and put on a pair of loafers that lay on the floor."

If Napoleon was right in calling the Piazza San Marco "the best drawing   9
room in Europe," O'Hara's stories as a whole provide the best conversation
in America. Although he was for years associated with the upper-class

world of New York, Philadelphia and Long Island, he had a remarkable range of subjects, more so than Faulkner or Fitzgerald or even Hemingway, whose work influenced him in many ways. The central characters of his stories are not only club men and business executives, they are country doctors, movie stars, beauticians, bartenders, schoolgirls, nightclub singers, gas-station attendants, telephone operators and bus drivers. America in the 20th century is what he knew, and in 1960 he said, "It is my business to write about it to the best of my ability, with sometimes the special knowledge that I have. I want to record the way people talked and thought and felt, and to do it with complete honesty and variety."

10   Behind the modesty of this statement lies O'Hara's vision of America and, by extension, of humanity everywhere. He saw society as a structure that rarely succeeded in covering up the disorders that lay beneath the surface of human intercourse. He saw decency and hope routinely destroyed by selfishness and cruelty, leaving individuals with little solace to face the essential solitude of life and death. Yet O'Hara's vision is not a cheerless one, for he also celebrated individual acts of kindness and imagination, and he does not pass judgment or apportion blame. His stories are peopled with such varied individuals, pretentious, gentle, deranged or simply pensive, that for all his doubts about humanity, O'Hara was evidently in love with life itself, and his esthetic purposes were a direct extension of this attitude.

11   It is at their endings that O'Hara's stories give their greatest pleasure. Just when the story ends, or perhaps a few moments afterwards, when all the pieces fall into place, the reader grasps what it is really all about. A sort of epiphany occurs. It can produce chill or warmth, depending on the story, but it is an organic part of the story itself. It is not a surprise ending like one in Saki or Ambrose Bierce which loses its force once it is expressed. Rather, it deepens the feelings that come from beneath the surface of the story. Emerging from O'Hara's skillful mixture of fact and feeling, it lingers on, like a phrase of music, in the memory.

12   At the end of "We're Friends Again," one of the novellas in "Sermons and Soda-Water," the narrator asks: "What really can any of us know about any of us, and why must we make such a thing of loneliness when it is the final condition of us all?" Then he adds, "And where would love be without it?"

13   The idea that arises in this last question, suggesting that even love needs loneliness so as to express itself, casts the story in a new light. But this is not merely a device to hold the reader. It, too, is part of O'Hara's vision. "Life goes on," he wrote as a young man, "and for the sake of verisimilitude and realism, you cannot positively give the impression of an ending: you

must let something hang. A cheap interpretation of that would be to say that you must always leave a chance for a sequel. People die, love dies, but life does not die, and so long as people live, stories must have life at the end."

QUESTIONS ABOUT "JOHN O'HARA: THE BEST CONVERSATION IN AMERICA"

1.   In this essay, Frank MacShane talks about John O'Hara's writing. What seems to be MacShane's intention in writing?

2.   What does MacShane mean by a writer's ability to "capture the speech of his characters"? How does MacShane convince the reader that this ability is important for a writer? Does he provide the reader with adequate justification for his assertion that this is an appropriate criterion for judging the quality of an author's writing? Explain. Does MacShane present the reader with any other criteria for judging the quality of an author's writing? If so, what are they?

3.   Describe the structure of the essay. When does MacShane present evaluation criteria? Initially? At several places within the text? How does he relate these criteria to his assessment of O'Hara's skill as a writer? At which places in the essay does MacShane provide the reader with specific examples or information? What effect does the narration of O'Hara's early experiences as a writer in paragraphs 3, 4, and 5 have on the reader? How do they help reveal the writer's intention to the reader?

4.   How do the information and details MacShane has selected influence the reader? Does his inclusion of specifics regarding O'Hara's reliance "on actual things that were as revealing as speech. . . . A Brooks Brothers suit or a Swaine and Adeney's umbrella, the Racquet Club" in paragraph 8 lead the reader to draw the conclusions that MacShane wants her to adopt? Explain. In what way has MacShane marshaled evidence?

5.   How does MacShane establish his qualifications for making a judgment about O'Hara? Does he appear well informed about O'Hara's work? About his career? How does MacShane's reference to other writers reinforce the validity of his evaluation of O'Hara's work?

6.   Does MacShane appear evident in his essay about O'Hara? To what extent does he reveal his feelings or appear emotional? Do you think that the tone changes at the end of the essay, especially in the last paragraph? How does the strategy of ending the essay with a quote from O'Hara "as a young man" affect the reader? Does it help MacShane achieve his intention? Explain.

7. Do you consider the results of MacShane's evaluation to be convincing? Do you consider the nature of the evaluation and the means by which he supports it appropriate for the audience he was addressing?

Sisters Under the Skin

Richard Schickel

1   The movie begins with anxious, ferocious Aurora Greenway (Shirley MacLaine) clambering up over the side of her baby's crib and hurling herself on the tot, hysterically convinced that she has only seconds to administer the kiss of life to her darling Emma and save her from crib death. Naturally, all she does is disturb a healthy infant's sleep. From this scene it is obvious that *Terms of Endearment* is a comedy.

2   The story ends, some three decades later, with the same mother and daughter (played from adolescence onward by Debra Winger) confronting the same issue, the possibility of the younger woman's premature death, this time a very realistic one, in a cancer ward. From this sequence it is clear that *Terms of Endearment* is a serious film that is trying to say something important about how people can triumph over the worst kinds of adversity.

3   Between that first intimation of mortality and the final acknowledgment of its certainty, Emma grows up to endure marriage with feckless, womanizing Flap Horton (Jeff Daniels) and have more children than they can afford on his itinerant teacher's pay. She manages to ignore the many opportunities life now offers to raise her feminist consciousness to that minimum daily level of awareness required for the modern woman's mental health (having an affair with the nice man down at the bank doesn't really count). This clearly means *Terms of Endearment* is a cautionary tract for the times, something Phil Donahue can really get behind.

4   But wait. What about uptight Aurora and that raffish former astronaut, Garrett Breedlove (Jack Nicholson, giving a joyously comic display of just the kind of wrong stuff that appalls and attracts her)? Merely thinking over the possibilities he presents takes some comical time. He has been living next door to Aurora for ten years before she hints that she might entertain a luncheon invitation from him. Five years later she actually accepts it. Thereupon a woman who once told an admirer not to worship her unless she deserved it plunges giddily into a relationship with a man she knows suffers that common cold of the male psyche, fear of commitment. This is, without question, the stuff of romantic comedy. Is that, finally, the way to describe this picture?

Well, no. And that, perhaps, spells trouble. According to Hollywood's   5
favorite adage, it is impossible these days to sell a film successfully if it
cannot be summarized in a single catchy line of ad copy. If this is true,
then what are the guys over in marketing going to do with a movie that
its own maker defines largely by negatives. "It was rarely 'Wouldn't it be
great to do that?', but more often 'Better not do this,' " says Director James
L. Brooks, who shared creative credit for both *The Mary Tyler Moore Show*
and *Taxi* on television and who spent four years adapting Larry McMurtry's
novel to the screen. How, indeed, are they going to handle the writer-
director's entirely accurate description of the way his film works: "There
is never a moment in the picture that takes you to the next moment or
the next place. You just arrive and it seems inevitable—I hope."

But not to worry. What may, at first, be a commercial inconvenience   6
will surely, in the end, turn into an artistic coup. *Terms of Endearment*
does work off the conventions that rule more ordinary movies, but only to
enrich its own singular voice. Its quirky rhythms and veering emotional
tones are very much its own, and they owe less to movie tradition than
they do to a sense of how the law of unintended consequences pushes us
ceaselessly through the years, permitting no pause for perspective. *Terms*
comes to at least glancing terms with almost every problem a person is
likely to encounter in life, but it really has only one important piece of
business in hand: an examination and resolution, in comic terms, of the
relationship between a mother and a daughter. Everything else is in effect
a diversionary tactic, a way of placing this brilliantly devised and disguised
core of concern within the context of lifelike randomness.

As Brooks sees them, his movie's mother and daughter are actually sisters   7
under the skin, connected not just by kinship but by subtle parallels of
emotions and experience. Aurora appears initially to be no more than that
familiar figure of satire, the American Mom as American Nightmare, all
coy snarls and fierce demureness, while Emma, protected only by a thin
skin of perkiness, seems to be her victim. "You aren't special enough to
overcome a bad marriage," Aurora snaps on the eve of Emma's wedding,
voicing her own fears about what might happen if she ventured outside
her perfectly tended Texas house and garden. "I am totally convinced that
if you marry Flap Horton tomorrow you will ruin your life and make
wretched your destiny," she adds. As always with Brooks, locution is character.

But when Emma moves out, Aurora discovers that her child has no   8
corner on inappropriate males. After Flap takes a job in Des Moines ("You
can't even fail locally," cries Aurora, whose contempt for her son-in-law is
her one immutable, hilarious quality), a plaintive note creeps into her

obsessive phone calls to her daughter. Parent is now becoming a dependent, in need of a confidante, especially with that astronaut orbiting around her.

9   This is a new role for Emma, but one that she is entirely up for. Her ability to cope with each new child and all of Flap's croupy vagaries suggests that somehow even a so-so family life actually makes happy her destiny. If this were an ordinary comedy, that medium-sized irony would have been enough to satisfy its creator and send the audience home happy. But Brooks has one more question in mind. Could these two find it in themselves to reverse this role reversal one more time and arrive at a balanced acceptance of each other? Emma's illness provides the occasion for that final adjustment. Inevitably her growing weakness draws the young woman back toward childish dependency, and the need to defend her daughter against suffering summons forth Aurora's old ferocity. Whether she is questioning empty medical pieties or keeping poor Flap shaped up ("One of the nicest qualities about you is that you always recognized your weaknesses; don't lose that quality when you need it most") or bullying the nurse into administering a delayed sedative, MacLaine achieves a kind of cracked greatness, climax to a brave, bravura performance. Winger has an uncanny instinct for inhabiting a role, for implying that she knows even more about the character than words permit.

10   But then there are no bad performances, no slack scenes, no inattention of any kind in *Terms of Endearment*. The impulse in praising a film for which there are almost no analogies is to define it by what it is not, but that is really not good enough. It deserves some blunt declaration of respect and unguarded affection. Therefore, these three: no film since Preston Sturges was a pup has so shrewdly appreciated the way the eccentric plays hide-and-seek with the respectable in the ordinary American landscape; no comedy since *Annie Hall* or *Manhattan* has so intelligently observed not just the way people live now but what's going on in the back of their minds; and finally, and in full knowledge that one may be doing the marketing department's job for them, it is the best movie of the year.

QUESTIONS ABOUT "SISTERS UNDER THE SKIN"

1.   What seems to be Richard Schickel's intention in writing?

2.   Describe the structure of the essay. What effect does the beginning of the essay, "The movie begins with anxious, ferocious Aurora Greenway," have on the reader? What effect does the ending of the essay have on the reader? Is Schickel taking a risk by ending the text as he does? Explain. Examine also the use of expressions like "But wait," "Well no," "But not

to worry" at the beginnings of paragraphs. What *organizational* function do they serve?

3.   List the criteria that Schickel uses in his evaluation of the film. Are these criteria primarily subjective or objective? Explain. Choose *one* of the criteria and explain how Schickel demonstrates that it is appropriate and/ or valid.

4.   How much of the essay is devoted to plot synopsis? Does this synopsis occur in one or in several places? Is this strategy effective? Explain. The film *Terms of Endearment* was based on a novel of the same name, but Schickel chose not to devote much time to a discussion of the similarities or differences between the two. Instead, he discusses Brooks's (the director) conception of the relationship between the mother and daughter. How does this information help persuade the reader that Schickel's evaluation of the movie is valid? Would a comparison of the book and movie have been as effective? Explain.

5.   How does Schickel establish his credibility? What sort of credentials does he present to the reader? Is Schickel a "presence" in his review? What relationship between Schickel and his readers does the use of such expressions as "But wait," "Well, no," and "But not to worry" create? How would you describe the tone of the essay? How does this relationship encourage readers to adopt the conclusions Schickel wishes them to adopt?

6.   Describe the characteristics of the audience you think Schickel was addressing. Do you think the nature of the evidence that Schickel chose and his means of presenting it were convincing to that audience?

Summary

Now that you have examined an explanation about and two examples of evaluative writing, here are several important operations that a writer usually performs before he begins to draft an evaluative essay.

1.   The writer must thoroughly *familiarize* himself with the item that he is evaluating in order to determine the criteria he will use to make a judgment about that item.

2.   The writer must *examine* this set of criteria in order to make at least preliminary decisions about each of the following:

a. Are the criteria more *objective* or more *subjective?* Objective criteria are usually observable, such as size, and/or "provable," such as repair incidence; they are frequently used and therefore more likely to be accepted as valid. Whether or not something is *economical* is an example of an objective criterion. Subjective criteria are often based upon or derived from the writer's experience, values, and knowledge. In general, subjective criteria require more explanation as to their nature; they also must be supported with a rationale for their suitability and validity, since the reader is less likely to accept them. Whether or not a film is suitable viewing for "the entire family" is an example of a subjective criterion.

b. Are the criteria appropriate to the particular evaluation being made? For example, if a distributor is evaluating a film to determine whether it is a good film for drive-in audiences, the length of the film may be an appropriate evaluation criterion. On the other hand, if the same film is being evaluated for an Academy Award, its length may not be an appropriate evaluation criterion.

c. Are any of the criteria particularly complex or difficult to understand? The presentation of such criteria will require extra care.

3. The writer must consider how he will establish his credibility, considering at least these possibilities:

a. What personal qualifications should he present to the reader: fairness? objectivity? trustworthiness? "I'm just like you"?

b. What formal training, if any, has he had that he should mention?

c. What is the nature and amount of his experience with the entity being evaluated? Was it direct, or indirect but closely related? How much of it should he present to the reader, and in what manner?

4. The writer must consider the nature and amount of evidence to be presented.

5. Most important, the writer must *analyze* his audience and keep them in mind as he performs operations 2, 3, and 4. He must consider his audience as he determines which criteria need to be provided with support for their appropriateness and/or validity, the nature and amount of background information to be included, how *best* to establish his credibility, and how much and what kind of evidence will best convince the audience to accept his judgment about the quality and/or worth of the item or person being evaluated.

A Rhetorical Task:
Jeff and Reviewing a Movie

Initial Responses

Jeff Mauch was presented with the task of writing an evaluative essay. He and his classmates could choose the person or object to be evaluated, the intent for evaluating that person or object, and the audience to whom the essay would be addressed. At first, Jeff felt overwhelmed by the various options. He could not decide whether he wanted to write a review of a film or a television series or a record album or whether he wanted to write an evaluative comparison of two or more products, perhaps videocassette recorders, or what. A few days after the task was assigned, however, Jeff saw a film that he really liked. He decided that the film was worth seeing because it was well made and because it presented what he considered to be an important "message." Jeff decided, therefore, to write an evaluative essay about the film *King of Hearts*.

VISUALIZING THE AUDIENCE

As soon as Jeff had made this decision, he began to think about his audience. He decided that he would write for the readers of a movie review section of a periodical of "high literary value." Such readers, he assumed, would view films often, although their taste might be different from that of the "average" movie consumer. That is, his readers would appreciate and therefore attend foreign films, experimental films, and film festivals. Jeff also assumed that members of his audience were well educated and well read; thus he could make literary allusions, as long as they weren't *too* obscure, and use terms such as "absurd" in a more specialized sense. Here are some of the questions that Jeff asked himself about his audience so that he could visualize them more fully.

--What sorts of intellectual problems are my readers interested in? Specifically, how interested are they in the question of how one determines what is and is not abnormal?
--What leisure activities do they enjoy? With what other activities is seeing this film competing?

--How interested are they in the subject matter of the film? The film is rather intricate; how tolerant are they likely to be about this?

--What problems about "the world" concern my readers most?

--How interested and/or knowledgeable are they regarding the technical aspects of films?

--To what extent do they demand that a film *entertain* them, as opposed to instructing or enlightening them?

CREATING A CONTEXT

As Jeff thought about his audience, he began to solidify his initial ideas regarding the context for his essay. He decided to go to the library to examine the sort of periodical—magazine or newspaper—that would have a film review section in which his essay might be included. Then he would select one such periodical and read a number of reviews from several issues. Jeff assumed that he could get a good sense of the audience to whom he was writing by doing this. He also decided to pretend that his review was actually going to be published in this periodical, a strategy that would enable him to visualize his context quite vividly.

ARTICULATING INTENTION

As he was thinking about his audience and about the periodical for which he was writing his essay, Jeff began to make his intention for writing more concrete. He realized that he could not really *know* whether most of his readers would be reading the film review section primarily to find out "what the good films were" or to "get advice regarding what films to see." But he decided that *he* was not much interested in evaluating a film if his intention in doing so was not to convince people that they ought or ought not to see it. He decided, therefore, that his overall goal in writing would be to convince his readers that *King of Hearts* was a significant film, a film worth viewing. Jeff felt that he could persuade his readers that his evaluation was sound by establishing the importance and universality of the message the film presented and by discussing its effectiveness in presenting this message. Jeff concluded that a truly successful review would encourage readers to go and see the film.

Inventing and Planning

Jeff did most of his inventing and planning mentally. He spent a great deal of time thinking about the theme of *King of Hearts* and about how he would argue that the theme was both important and universal, i.e., valid for all people, regardless of their time or culture. He also reviewed the elements of the film. He knew that he had a limited amount of space—500 to 1000 words—in which to make his point, and so he had to be selective about which aspects of the film to discuss: the cinematography, the script, the acting?

To help him focus his ideas, Jeff began to write down some of his thoughts. He selected four major aspects of the film: themes, characterization, conflict, and plot. Under each of these headings he listed topics, such as "injustice" or "cultural norms." Following this brief brainstorming session, Jeff produced about a page of freewriting.

Drafting and Revising

From his past writing experience, Jeff knew that he often began drafting early in his writing process. He did not necessarily expect, therefore, to produce a rough draft. However, his brief freewriting and brainstorming session had helped him unearth the main strands of the argument he wished to pursue. He decided to argue that *King of Hearts* is an excellent and important film because it deals with a vital issue: Our world seems "lost to reason," and this compels all of us to search individually for the "moral and ethical fiber" that we need if we are to survive.

As he was drafting, Jeff found that he was still freewriting. As a result, the text he produced was long and somewhat rambling, somewhere between a rough draft and a predraft. He was satisfied that his draft included all the information and argumentation that he wished to use, but he did not see that it had much structure, nor did he think his presentation of material seemed focused. He decided, therefore, to glean his draft for information, marking portions that he *might* be able to reuse.

Keeping his readers in mind, Jeff jotted down a rather detailed plan before he began writing his second draft. It included a written statement of his intention for writing, a description of the organizing principle and frame of reference for the opening paragraph, and a list of the major parts of the essay. He also thought about the tone of the essay and the extent to which he would need to provide his readers with a summary of the movie's plot. He then wrote a new, second draft. After examining it at the text, sentence, and word levels, he was pleased to conclude it was a rough draft.

Jeff waited several hours before he examined his rough draft again for the purpose of revising it. He was largely satisfied and made only two changes at the text level. He added a few sentences to his opening paragraph to strengthen his frame of reference and to eliminate any doubts in the reader's mind about his intention. He also rewrote his concluding paragraph to give readers a better sense of closure. Finally, he clarified several expressions that bordered on being code words and adjusted the tone of the essay in places where he felt he had become too preachy or shrill.

Proofreading and Editing

After a good night's sleep, Jeff reexamined his draft. He eliminated or changed some of the words in his opening paragraph, since a few of these words still seemed to interfere with the tone he wished to convey. He also discovered and rewrote a few sentences that seemed to him overlong and convoluted. Then Jeff typed his essay and read it twice, looking for typographical errors and for errors in spelling and mechanics or usage that might have escaped his attention.

The Finished Essay

The Trouble with Normalcy: A Review of <u>King of Hearts</u>
Jeff Mauch

1   In an age characterized by alienation and technological obsession, the "real" value and meaning of human existence seems to have become a pondersome question for all of us. Who are we? Why are we? What are we here for? What and who is normal? These are basic questions of existence, and philosophers have been seeking answers to them through time. In every culture, as time and society changes, these questions and the factors affecting the way we respond to them convey a great deal about how mankind is faring in the world at the time. In ancient Greece, man stood beneath the heavens, relatively naked

in his ignorance and vulnerability, and brashly sought the truths which governed his existence. Men such as Socrates searched for natural laws which they hoped would provide people with fair and just limits—boundaries within which to organize their understanding of reality and human potential. Socrates wound up scorned and mistrusted. He probably asked too many troubling queries for his society. He probably questioned the unjust elements of his society and the individuals responsible so vigorously that he had to be silenced.

Now, twenty-five hundred years later, man is still subject to social injustice, is still asking questions, and is still persecuted by social planners who control his everyday existence. These "truths" are poignantly demonstrated in the movie <u>The King of Hearts</u>, a cinemagraphic inquiry into the definition of normalcy in a world overwhelmed by technological absurdities. This movie, set in the now dim era of World War II, sheds light on elements of human existence which haven't changed since the time of Socrates.

The movie revolves around a comical plot involving a British protagonist (the "king of hearts"), a squad of bumbling German soldiers, a townful of some European partisans and, most importantly, a contingent force of escaped "lunatics." The word "lunatics" is set off here by quotation marks because, by the end of the movie, the audience wonders just who should be labelled insane and who shouldn't. This is accomplished through a deliberately planned manipulation of the most ludicrous act of man against man: war--which serves as the milieu for this picture. In the movie, the idiotic approach to war assumed by all parties concerned betrays the fact that man is often a pathetic social animal, finding himself caught in the middle of battles that make no sense to him or anyone else. In <u>The King of Hearts</u>, a German patrol force occupies a partisan town somewhere in Europe during World War II and leaves as a token of appreciation for hospitable services, a bomb. A British patrol force learns of the diabolical scheme of the Germans to blow up the innocent town and decides to take retaliatory action. They seek to occupy the town and decide to dismantle the bomb, since, as the patrol brigadier general-or-whatever boisterously proclaims, it is only to their advantage to secure this town now as a symbol of freedom and liberation ... and then blow it up later if need be. They send a scout (our hero) into the town to find the bomb. Instead of encountering the hidden bomb, though, our protagonist is accosted and virtually kidnapped by a group of escaped lunatics. They crown him their "king of hearts" and this is where the philosophical parody really begins.

4   As our hero becomes enchanted by this subculture, oblivious to the dictates of "normal" everyday order and assumption, he--and we--begin to question the necessity and justice of traditional social norms. In the midst of meaningless destruction of property and life, our hero encounters a representative humanity which serves as symbols of resistance to all that is wrong with being human. As the group of lunatics dances and sways through the town, parodying every element of "normal" social custom from prostitution (the female lunatic protagonist is a virgin prostitute) to the crowning of a king (our reluctant hero), the value of all human mores and social rituals fall prey to doubt and trivialization.

5   The audience laughs at the absurdities portrayed by the lunatics, then realizes that the basis for satire, the patterns of existence which we all call normal, are even more absurd. We wonder, along with our protagonist, whether normal behavior is or should be accepted as the only means of existence for the individual. After all, life should be an individual matter, shouldn't it, and how to live it should be a matter of individual choice, right?

6   Ultimately, the movie becomes a parable for individualism--at least it does for me. It begins by asking the questions "What is normal?" and "Who should decide what is 'right' and 'correct' in life?" and ends up delegating the responsibility for answering these questions to the only element of society vested with the "true" right to make that decision--the individual. At the end of <u>The King of Hearts</u>, our hero makes an individual decision <u>not</u> to accept certain elements and dictates of his social order, and this decision serves as a triumph for individualism throughout time. In a world dominated by rigid, unyielding pressure on the individual to conform to standards, customs, and boundaries he often should not have to accept, it is truly heartwarming to witness an individual making a conscience-based choice <u>not</u> to conform. We are all, and have always been subject, to the dictates of society; and societies are imperfect institutions. But Socrates probably said that too.

Writing Assignment

This is a rhetorical task for you that is similar to the one with which Jeff was presented.

Choose a movie, book, or record album with which you are thoroughly familiar and write an evaluative essay about it. Select and carefully consider the audience to whom you are addressing your text; think about your intention for writing. Visualize the context in which you are writing. For example, you may wish to write a review of a new record album for readers of *Rolling Stone*, the intention of which is to convince the readers to buy or not to buy the album. Or you may imagine that you are a member of the panel of judges who decide which record album receives the Grammy Award for "best album of the year." In this case, you might write an evaluative essay about a particular record album, claiming that it is the "best" of the year.

I.   Getting Started: Inventing and Planning
    A.   List the names of several films, record albums, or TV series with which you are *very* familiar. Divide them into three columns: "good," "bad," and "not sure."
    B.   Decide whether you would enjoy writing an evaluative essay arguing that a film, book, or TV series is good or bad. Be honest! If you decide that you would like to write an essay that makes a negative evaluation, select a film from your "bad" column. If you decide that you would like to write an essay that makes a positive evaluation, select a film from your "good" column. If you cannot decide whether you would like to write a positive or negative essay, choose a film, book, or TV series that you find interesting from either column. Do *not* select anything from your "not sure" column unless you are willing to devote the time and effort needed to sort out and clarify your response to it. Even so, your evaluation may turn out to be "mixed." This is certainly a legitimate evaluation, but the selection, presentation, and justification of criteria will require considerable care. It will also challenge you as you articulate your intention for writing. Again, be certain that you are thoroughly familiar with the film, book, or TV series that you select; you cannot convincingly evaluate something with which you are not familiar.
    C.   What sorts of persons would be interested in reading your evaluation of one of the items you listed? Why would they be interested? Jot down the characteristics of these individuals: their age, interests, familiarity with music or TV or film, etc. Also jot down possible reasons why they would be interested in your evaluation: It will help them decide whether to purchase the album; it will help them

decide whether or not they should encourage their children (aged 6 to 12) to watch the show, etc.

D.   Tentatively list the criteria that you will use to form your judgment. You may find that one of the inventing activities discussed in Chapter 2 will help you with this.

E.   Examine your criteria. Are they more objective or subjective? Keeping your audience in mind, do you need to justify either the validity or the appropriateness of any of them? Do any need special care in presentation because they are complex, not easily understood, or unusual? Again, one of the inventing activities described in Chapter 2 may be useful; it may help you to generate arguments, illustrations, and examples that you can use to establish the validity and/or appropriateness of your criteria.

F.   Begin to think about how you would like to appear to your audience. What personal qualities do you want to project? Confidence? Modesty? Honesty? Objectivity? Also begin to think about how else you want to establish your credibility: By virtue of your experience? Your formal training?

G.   Keeping your audience in mind, consider the kinds of evidence, examples, facts, and illustrations you will need to include in your essay. Will you need to provide any background information? If so, how much and with regard to what? For example, if you are going to write an essay about the Pretenders' latest album, do you need to provide any background information about the performers—as individuals and/or as a group? Do you need to provide information about earlier record albums produced by the Pretenders? Do you need to provide any information about recent albums produced by other rock groups?

H.   Try to articulate the intention of your essay.

I.   Examine the structures of the essays presented earlier in the chapter. Try to describe the structure you want your essay to take. What do you think you want to do first, next, last?

J.   Examine your answers to the questions in F. Given the intention of your essay, what tone do you wish to use: serious or humorous? What point of view do you think you would like to use? In part, your decision will be influenced by the extent to which you want to be "present" in your essay.

II.   Drafting and Revising

A.   Write a first draft of your essay, making careful use of your inventing and planning.

B. Read your draft and answer the following:
Describe the intention of your essay.
Describe the audience to whom your essay is addressed.
Describe the way in which you intended to structure your essay.
Describe the point of view (first, second, or third person) and the tone that you used.

C. Evaluate your draft in terms of your answers to the above questions. Examine your draft at the text, sentence, and word levels. Is it a rough draft or a predraft?

D. Describe your plans for revising or rewriting your draft.

E. Repeat steps B to D if necessary.

III. Proofreading and Editing
A. Allow some time to go by, then read your final draft out loud.
B. Correct errors in sentence structure, word choice, and mechanics and usage.

Writing Assignment

Read the following essay, "Las Vegas (What?) Las Vegas (Can't Hear You! Too Noisy) Las Vegas!!" by Tom Wolfe.

Las Vegas (What?) Las Vegas
(Can't Hear You! Too Noisy)
Las Vegas!!

Tom Wolfe

Hernia, hernia, hernia, hernia, hernia, hernia, hernia, hernia, hernia, hernia, hernia, hernia, hernia, HERNia; hernia, HERNia, hernia, hernia, hernia, hernia, HERNia, HERNia, HERNia; hernia, hernia, hernia, hernia, hernia, hernia, hernia, eight is the point, the point is eight; hernia, hernia, HERNia; hernia, hernia, hernia, hernia, all hernia, hernia, HERNia, hernia, hernia, hernia, HERNia, hernia, hernia, hernia, HERNia, hernia, hernia, hernia, hernia   1

"What is all this *hernia hernia* stuff?"   2

This was Raymond talking to the wavy-haired fellow with the stick, the   3
dealer, at the craps table about 3:45 Sunday morning. The stickman had no idea what this big wiseacre was talking about, but he resented the tone. He gave Raymond that patient arch of the eyebrows known as a Red Hook

brushoff, which is supposed to convey some such thought as, I am a very tough but cool guy, as you can tell by the way I carry my eyeballs low in the pouches, and if this wasn't such a high-class joint we would take wiseacres like you out back and beat you into jellied madrilene.

4   At this point, however, Raymond was immune to subtle looks.

5   The stickman tried to get the game going again, but every time he would start up his singsong, by easing the words out through the nose, which seems to be the style among craps dealers in Las Vegas—"All right, a new shooter . . . eight is the point, the point is eight" and so on—Raymond would start droning along with him in exactly the same tone of voice, "Hernia, hernia, hernia; hernia, HERNia, HERNia, hernia; hernia, hernia, hernia."

6   Everybody at the craps table was staring in consternation to think that anybody would try to needle a tough, hip, elite *soldat* like a Las Vegas craps dealer. The gold-lamé odalisques of Los Angeles were staring. The Western sports, fifty-eight-year-old men who wear Texas string ties, were staring. The old babes at the slot machines, holding Dixie Cups full of nickels, were staring at the craps tables, but cranking away the whole time.

7   Raymond, who is thirty-four years old and works as an engineer in Phoenix, is big but not terrifying. He has the sort of thatchwork hair that grows so low all along the forehead there is no logical place to part it, but he tries anyway. He has a huge, prognathous jaw, but it is as smooth, soft and round as a melon, so that Raymond's total effect is that of an Episcopal divinity student.

8   The guards were wonderful. They were dressed in cowboy uniforms like Bruce Cabot in *Sundown* and they wore sheriff's stars.

9   "Mister, is there something we can do for you?"

10 "The expression is 'Sir,' " said Raymond. "You said 'Mister.' The expression is 'Sir.' How's your old Cosa Nostra?"

11 Amazingly, the casino guards were easing Raymond out peaceably, without putting a hand on him. I had never seen the fellow before, but possibly because I had been following his progress for the last five minutes, he turned to me and said, "Hey, do you have a car? This wild stuff is starting again."

12 The gist of it was that he had left his car somewhere and he wanted to ride up the Strip to the Stardust, one of the big hotel-casinos. I am describing this big goof Raymond not because he is a typical Las Vegas tourist, although he has some typical symptoms, but because he is a good example of the marvelous impact Las Vegas has on the senses. Raymond's senses were at a high pitch of excitation, the only trouble being that he was going off his nut. He had been up since Thursday afternoon, and it was now about

3:45 A.M. Sunday. He had an envelope full of pep pills—amphetamine—in his left coat pocket and an envelope full of Equanils—meprobamate—in his right pocket, or were the Equanils in the left and the pep pills in the right? He could tell by looking, but he wasn't going to look anymore. He didn't care to see how many were left.

He had been rolling up and down the incredible electric-sign gauntlet of   13
Las Vegas' Strip, U.S. Route 91, where the neon and the par lamps—
bubbling, spiraling, rocketing, and exploding in sunbursts ten stories high
out in the middle of the desert—celebrate one-story casinos. He had been
gambling and drinking and eating now and again at the buffet tables the
casinos keep heaped with food day and night, but mostly hopping himself
up with good old amphetamine, cooling himself down with meprobamate,
then hooking down more alcohol, until now, after sixty hours, he was
slipping into the symptoms of toxic schizophrenia.

He was also enjoying what the prophets of hallucinogen call "consciousness   14
expansion." The man was psychedelic. He was beginning to isolate the
components of Las Vegas' unique bombardment of the senses. He was
quite right about this *hernia hernia* stuff. Every casino in Las Vegas is,
among the other things, a room full of craps tables with dealers who keep
up a running singsong that sounds as though they are saying "hernia, hernia,
hernia, hernia, hernia" and so on. There they are day and night, easing a
running commentary through their nostrils. What they have to say contains
next to no useful instruction. Its underlying message is, We are the initiates,
riding the crest of chance. That the accumulated sound comes out "hernia"
is merely an unfortunate phonetic coincidence. Actually, it is part of something
rare and rather grand: a combination of baroque stimuli that brings to mind
the bronze gongs, no larger than a blue plate, that Louis XIV, his ruff collars
larded with the lint of the foul Old City of Byzantium, personally hunted
out in the bazaars of Asia Minor to provide exotic acoustics for his new
palace outside Paris.

The sounds of the craps dealer will be in, let's say, the middle register.   15
In the lower register will be the sound of the old babes at the slot machines.
Men play the slots too, of course, but one of the indelible images of Las
Vegas is that of the old babes at the row upon row of slot machines. There
they are at six o'clock Sunday morning no less than at three o'clock Tuesday
afternoon. Some of them pack their old hummocky shanks into Capri pants,
but many of them just put on the old print dress, the same one day after
day, and the old hob-heeled shoes, looking like they might be going out to
buy eggs in Tupelo, Mississippi. They have a Dixie Cup full of nickels or
dimes in the left hand and an Iron Boy work glove on the right hand to

keep the callouses from getting sore. Every time they pull the handle, the machine makes a sound much like the sound a cash register makes before the bell rings, then the slot pictures start clattering up from left to right, the oranges, lemons, plums, cherries, bells, bars, buckaroos—the figure of a cowboy riding a bucking bronco. The whole sound keeps churning up over and over again in eccentric series all over the place, like one of those random-sound radio symphonies by John Cage. You can hear it at any hour of the day or night all over Las Vegas. You can walk down Fremont Street at dawn and hear it without even walking in a door, that and the spins of the wheels of fortune, a boring and not very popular sort of simplified roulette, as the tabs flap to a stop. As an overtone, or at times simply as a loud sound, comes the babble of the casino crowds, with an occasional shriek from the craps tables, or, anywhere from 4 P.M. to 6 A.M., the sound of brass instruments or electrified string instruments from the cocktail-lounge shows.

16   The crowd and band sounds are not very extraordinary, of course. But Las Vegas' Muzak is. Muzak pervades Las Vegas from the time you walk into the airport upon landing to the last time you leave the casinos. It is piped out to the swimming pool. It is in the drugstores. It is as if there were a communal fear that someone, somewhere in Las Vegas, was going to be left with a totally vacant minute on his hands.

17   Las Vegas has succeeded in wiring an entire city with this electronic stimulation, day and night, out in the middle of the desert. In the automobile I rented, the radio could not be turned off, no matter which dial you went after. I drove for days in a happy burble of Action Checkpoint News, "Monkey No. 9," "Donna, Donna, the Prima Donna," and picking-and-singing jingles for the Frontier Bank and the Fremont Hotel.

18   One can see the magnitude of the achievement. Las Vegas takes what in other American towns is but a quixotic inflammation of the senses for some poor salary mule in the brief interval between the flagstone rambler and the automatic elevator downtown and magnifies it, foliates it, embellishes it into an institution.

19   For example, Las Vegas is the only town in the world whose skyline is made up neither of buildings, like New York, nor of trees, like Wilbraham, Massachusetts, but signs. One can look at Las Vegas from a mile away on Route 91 and see no buildings, no trees, only signs. But such signs! They tower. They revolve, they oscillate, they soar in shapes before which the existing vocabulary of art history is helpless. I can only attempt to supply names—Boomerang Modern, Palette Curvilinear, Flash Gordon Ming-Alert Spiral, McDonald's Hamburger Parabola, Mint Casino Elliptical, Miami Beach

Kidney. Las Vegas' sign makers work so far out beyond the frontiers of conventional studio art that they have no names themselves for the forms they create. Vaughan Cannon, one of those tall, blond Westerners, the builders of places like Las Vegas and Los Angeles, whose eyes seem to have been bleached by the sun, is in the back shop of the Young Electric Sign Company out on East Charleston Boulevard with Herman Boernge, one of his designers, looking at the model they have prepared for the Lucky Strike Casino sign, and Cannon points to where the sign's two great curving faces meet to form a narrow vertical face and says:

"Well, here we are again—what do we call that?"   20

"I don't know," says Boernge. "It's sort of a nose effect. Call it a nose." 21

Okay, a nose, but it rises sixteen stories high above a two-story building. 22
In Las Vegas no farseeing entrepreneur buys a sign to fit a building he owns. He rebuilds the building to support the biggest sign he can get up the money for and, if necessary, changes the name. The Lucky Strike Casino today is the Lucky Casino, which fits better when recorded in sixteen stories of flaming peach and incandescent yellow in the middle of the Mojave Desert. In the Young Electric Sign Co. era signs have become the architecture of Las Vegas, and the most whimsical, Yale-seminar-frenzied devices of the two late geniuses of Baroque Modern, Frank Lloyd Wright and Eero Saarinen, seem rather stuffy business, like a jest at a faculty meeting, compared to it. Men like Boernge, Kermit Wayne, Ben Mitchem and Jack Larsen, formerly an artist for Walt Disney, are the designer-sculptor geniuses of Las Vegas, but their motifs have been carried faithfully throughout the town by lesser men, for gasoline stations, motels, funeral parlors, churches, public buildings, flophouses and sauna baths.

Then there is a stimulus that is both visual and sexual—the Las Vegas   23
buttocks décolletage. This is a form of sexually provocative dress seen more and more in the United States, but avoided like Broadway message-embroidered ("Kiss Me, I'm Cold") underwear in the fashion pages, so that the euphemisms have not been established and I have no choice but clinical terms. To achieve buttocks décolletage a woman wears bikini-style shorts that cut across the round fatty masses of the buttocks rather than cupping them from below, so that the outer-lower edges of these fatty masses, or "cheeks," are exposed. I am in the cocktail lounge of the Hacienda Hotel, talking to managing director Dick Taylor about the great success his place has had in attracting family and tour groups, and all around me the waitresses are bobbing on their high heels, bare legs and décolletage-bare backsides, set off by pelvis length lingerie of an uncertain denomination. I stare, but I am new here. At the White Cross Rexall drugstore on the Strip a pregnant

brunette walks in off the street wearing black shorts with buttocks décolletage aft and illusion-of-cloth nylon lingerie hanging fore, and not even the old mom's-pie pensioners up near the door are staring. They just crank away at the slot machines. On the streets of Las Vegas, not only the show girls, of which the town has about two hundred fifty, bona fide, in residence, but girls of every sort, including, especially, Las Vegas' little high-school buds, who adorn what locals seeking roots in the sand call "our city of churches and schools," have taken up the chic of wearing buttocks décolletage step-ins under flesh-tight slacks, with the outline of the undergarment showing through fashionably. Others go them one better. They achieve the effect of having been dipped once, briefly, in Helenca stretch nylon. More and more they look like those wonderful old girls out of Flash Gordon who were wrapped just once over in Baghdad pantaloons of clear polyethylene with only Flash Gordon between them and the insane red-eyed assaults of the minions of Ming. It is as if all the hip young suburban gals of America named Lana, Deborah and Sandra, who gather wherever the arc lights shine and the studs steady their coiffures in the plate-glass reflection, have convened in Las Vegas with their bouffant hair above and anatomically stretch-pant-swathed little bottoms below, here on the new American frontier. But exactly!

Answer the following questions about Wolfe's essay.

1. What, exactly, is Wolfe evaluating: Las Vegas? an aspect of American culture (if so, what)? the typical Las Vegas tourist? gambling?

2. What is the intention of the essay?

3. To whom is the essay addressed? Describe some of the characteristics of the audience.

4. Where do you suppose an essay such as Wolfe's would be published? Why?

5. What is the function of "Raymond" in the essay? Is the reader supposed to identify with him? Explain.

6. Describe the structure of the essay. What does Wolfe do first, next, last?

7. What criteria does Wolfe use to make his evaluation? Are they objective or subjective? Are they presented directly or indirectly? What is his attitude toward the phenomenon he is evaluating?

8. How evident is Wolfe within the essay? Does he "emerge" at some point in the essay? Where? How does he present himself to the reader, and why?

9. Describe the tone of the essay. Do you think that Wolfe's selection of this tone was a good strategy? Explain why or why not.

10. What sort of evidence, facts, and illustrations does Wolfe present to the reader? How extensive are they?

Write an evaluative essay about a *place* of your choice: a city, a restaurant, a theater, a dentist's office, etc. You may select the audience to whom you address the essay as well as your intention for writing. For example, you may write about a place such as The Great Smokey Mountain National Park and its environs, evaluating it as a vacation spot. Or you may write about a place such as The Great Smokey Mountain National Park and its environs, evaluating it as a good or bad place in which to invest in property.

I. Getting Started: Inventing and Planning
    A. Jot down some possible places that you would enjoy evaluating.
    B. List as many concrete, specific features about each place as you can. *Eliminate* those places about which you have difficulty listing concrete data.
    C. Select a place from your list and examine the features about it that you identified. Add as many additional features as you can. Then group these features according to similarities.
    D. Begin to think about your intention for writing. Tentatively describe it.
    E. Describe the audience to whom your essay will be addressed.
    F. Thinking of your audience and your intention for writing, make a tentative list of the criteria you plan to use in your evaluation. Are your criteria more objective or subjective? Do any of them need to be justified as to their validity or appropriateness? Do any of them seem particularly complex and/or difficult to convey?
    G. What sorts of evidence or illustrations will you use in your essay? Be sure to consult your list of features.
    H. Tentatively describe the way you intend to structure your piece. What do you intend to do first, next, last?
    I. List the personal qualities that you want your readers to ascribe to you, such as modesty, humor, objectivity, or knowledgeability. Also list any other information you want your reader to have about you, such as amount of experience or formal training. Keeping these lists in mind, what point of view do you think you want to use? Describe the tone you think you would like to use.
II. Drafting and Revising
    A. Write the first draft of your essay.

    B.   Read your draft and answer the following:
1. Describe the intention of your essay.
2. Describe the audience to whom the essay is addressed.
3. Describe the way you intended to structure your essay.
4. List the criteria that you used.
5. Describe the tone and point of view that you intended to use.

    C.   Evaluate your draft in terms of your answers to the above questions. Examine your draft at the text, sentence, and word levels. Is it a rough draft or a predraft?

    D.   Describe your plans for revising or rewriting your draft.

    E.   Repeat steps B to D if necessary.

III. Proofreading and Editing

    A.   Allow some time to go by, then read your draft out loud.

    B.   Correct errors in sentence structure, word choice, and mechanics and usage.

Writing 10
Persuasive Essays

The Persuasive Essay

In Chapter 9 you examined evaluative writing, a kind of writing in which the writer's intention is to convince her readers that her judgment of a particular phenomenon, event, or person is valid. Such reviews and critiques guide readers who are looking for advice or specific information before they make a decision. This chapter will introduce you to *persuasive* writing.

Readers take note of persuasive texts when they are interested in wrestling with an issue or idea. The "op-ed" page of the daily newspaper attracts many readers who wish to sample viewpoints on a variety of issues, offered by concerned individuals who are seeking to change the readers' views. In addition, readers read persuasive texts simply for intellectual stimulation. Out of natural curiosity, such readers seek the perspectives of others on issues that are interesting or important to them.

Writers typically write persuasive texts when they feel personally involved in an issue and feel that their viewpoint is not getting a sufficient hearing. Sometimes writers share a viewpoint in order to contribute to a joint effort to resolve a problem or reach a decision. However, there is a difference between an "opinion paper" and a persuasive essay. Opinion writing involves the writer only in expressing a view; it states, "This is what *I believe* and why." In contrast, the persuasive essay *argues* the merits of the proposition being championed to the reader on the basis of reason and evidence: "This is what *you should believe* and why."

375

Persuasive writing thus employs argumentation to alter the viewpoints of an audience and to move it to a specific action. Sermons, editorials, and political speeches are all types of texts that are intended to be persuasive to their audience: "I urge each of you to repent and save your soul!" "It is unconscionable for the city council to allow the mayor to remain in office. We therefore plead with the council to act swiftly." "We need a new energy policy in this country, and if you send me to Washington, I pledge to introduce a bill to protect the consumer."

What separates persuasive writing from the other types we have looked at is the writer's *intention*. In a persuasive essay, the writer engages the reader directly, calling upon him for a response: Believe this, do not believe this; change this, do not change this; do this, do not do this. Knowledge of one's audience, important for any writing task, is especially crucial to persuasive writing. In the persuasive essay the writer demands from her readers greater attention and commitment to the arguments and information provided than in any other kind of text.

There is much that could be said about persuasive writing, and argumentation in particular, that we cannot present here. We can, nevertheless, provide some useful criteria for planning a persuasive text.

1. *The Rhetorical Context*: The writer whose intention is to persuade faces three kinds of audiences: (1) hostile, (2) indifferent, and (3) convinced. Each audience or mix of audiences requires a different strategy, and the writer must determine on which audience she is really focusing her text. The hostile audience, one the writer knows will disagree with her proposition, will demand from the writer careful citation of evidence and detail if the readers are to accept the writer's credibility. Appeals to emotion or dubious authority will carry little weight with such an audience. The indifferent audience, on the other hand, needs to be won to the issue itself; it needs to be convinced not only about the worthiness of the writer's proposition, but also about the relevance of the issue to its own interests. Typically, a persuasive text is directed at one of these two audiences. But a writer can sometimes find herself addressing the third kind of audience, the already convinced. Such an audience may need to be challenged with new evidence, more compelling argumentation, or a more vital demonstration of the importance of the issue in order to ensure their continued support and enthusiasm. The key ingredient in writing for any audience, however, is to minimize the *threat* to the targeted audience, assuring them that you understand their present stance, respect it, and seek only to bring the issue to a mutually agreeable resolution.

2.   *The Logic of Argument*: Writing with the intention to persuade presumes that there is something to disagree *about*. In using argumentation, then, the writer's task is to identify the central claim or proposition on which she is seeking the reader's agreement and to locate a more general proposition behind it on which the two parties can agree. That is to say, in order to move from disagreement to agreement, the writer must find some common ground on which she can start and from which she can proceed logically. It is important, then, that the writer sort out the key propositions involved in resolving the issue at hand, carefully eliminating false or irrelevant issues and concentrating on those that will help bring her and her readers closer to agreement.

A writer who wants to persuade a car dealer to donate a car to the school's driver education program might proceed on the principle that if she can get the dealer to agree on a general proposition—for instance, that such a donation would be to the dealer's advantage—her central argument would be more compelling. Thus, a letter advocating the proposition that a car should be donated would contain information documenting the advantage of such a donation for the car dealer. The writer thus proceeds deductively, examining her proposition carefully, looking for elements on which she and her audience can agree.

3.   *The Structure of Argument*: The writer must be careful not to begin a persuasive text too abruptly. The reader needs to be informed about the context of the debated topic, how the writer is situated within that context, and why it is worth the reader's while to consider the writer's claims. After stating the issue's context, the writer may then proceed to discuss her proposition and introduce evidence to support it. Along the way, where appropriate, the writer may choose to note alternative viewpoints, addressing them and refuting them, or at least explaining why they do not militate against the proposition advocated by the writer. And finally, the writer should be careful to leave readers with a sense of closure as well as a challenge to action or further consideration of the writer's claims.

A successful, reader-based persuasive text will have these characteristics:

1.   The *issues and problems* that the writer addresses will be clear to the readers and placed in a context that they will find relevant to their own interests as well as compelling; likewise, the writer's own stance will be unambiguous to her audience.

2.   The *evidence and forms of argumentation* the writer uses will be appropriate to the position she is advocating and effective in advancing her stance.

3.   The writer will have *anticipated and addressed* the most compelling counterarguments and alternative positions, thus conveying to her audience a sense of informed perspective.

4.   The writer's credibility will be established, or at least will not be undermined by inappropriate diction or blatantly illogical reasoning.

5.   The writer will address her audience appropriately, with both the right tone and the right approach, and with a responsible sense of tolerance and fairness.

Examples

Following are two examples of effective persuasive essays. Read each one carefully and answer the accompanying questions.

Whose Country Is It Anyway?
Roger Rosenblatt

1   The Supreme Court last week reached a decision allowing cities to display Nativity scenes, after considering whether minority interests would be impaired. At the same time, the Senate began debate on a constitutional amendment to counteract the Supreme Court's 1962 decision on school prayer, which had come into being only because of a perceived infringement of minority rights. That these matters are hurled about the court would seem to suggest they are legal puzzles dealing with the First and 14th Amendments. But the issue also involves human feelings. When a member of a minority loses a sense of belonging to the country, the country deliberates, sometimes changes shape, and occasionally comes apart.

2   To anyone but an American this may seem preposterously unfair, not to say illogical. If most Americans, being Christian, want crèches in the public squares and prayers in the public schools, why should they be forced to back down for a discomfited handful? Whose country is it anyway? And then there is the time-honored (and politically useful) association of the national identity with God. In spite of radicals like Jefferson and Madison, who erected the so-called wall of separation between church and state, the fact is that from the start the Government has been bound up with religion. In the majority's name are there Army chaplains, House and Senate chaplains, prayers for Congress. Not even the Supreme Court meets without calling for God's blessing.

Why, then, does the majority not have the right to establish, through   3
its Government, a religious character for the country? In most cases no
harm is intended. Read the tepid nonsectarian prayer that led to the 1962
decision, and you wonder what all the breast beating was about: "Almighty
God, we acknowledge our dependence upon Thee, and we beg Thy blessings
upon us, our parents, our teachers and our country." Similarly, how could
plaster-of-paris figures in Pawtucket, R.I., have alarmed anybody but the
A.C.L.U., which brought the suit?

The two issues are not the same size. Many who could not care less   4
about the crèche in Pawtucket would go to the wall of separation on the
school-prayer decision, but both issues derive from minority protests. Without
malice or belligerence, a Christian could reasonably ask: Whose country
is it anyway?

Nor is that a question to which minorities reply automatically, "As much   5
mine as yours." No one really believes that, there being too much painful
evidence to the contrary. Still, many members of minorities wholeheartedly
enjoy their status because it gives them a useful relationship to the main-
stream. Imamu Amiri Baraka (Leroi Jones) remarked that a black writer
has an advantage because, being black, he has been forced to live in an
isolated room in the nation's house, thus when he emerges from that room
into the rest of the house, he knows the entire structure. So too for any
Irishman, Chinese, Puerto Rican, a member of a minority religion or of
none at all. Without a sense of unbelonging, one might never cast a critical
eye on the majority culture, which in a way minorities cherish for their
difference from it.

Then, too, minorities often take genuine pleasure in the culture of the   6
majority. Many Jews enjoy the Christmas season for its songs and geniality,
without feeling put upon to convert or run and hide. Buddhists may dye
Easter eggs. Things inevitably get tense whenever a minority seeks to hold
on to some cultural tenet that goes against the American grain (*e.g.,* Mormons
and polygamy), but in less extreme cases the tension works out to a compromise. Those who make concessions to the majority culture may be
scorned as Uncle Toms or assimilationists, yet accommodation does not
necessarily entail a loss of integrity or self-respect. If the hordes of immigrants
who contemplated coming to America had not envisioned some definable
majority culture that they admired, they might not have made the trip in
the first place.

What, then, is the fuss about? Why on issues such as the Nativity display   7
and school prayer cannot the majority simply say, "Take it or leave it"?
On the crèche issue, that is what the court decided it could say, though

not without a lot of irrelevant hand wringing about the "passive symbolism" of the Nativity display as opposed to the "active symbolism," say, of the cross. (The distinction is meaningless.) In the matter of school prayer, the court continues to hold its ground, but why? And why not have an amendment allowing everyone to pray to his or her God, or to none?

8   Four reasons. First, the voluntary nature of school prayer would be compromised by the fact that a public institution was handling it. Second, no matter how earnestly school officials would protest that the God referred to is anybody's God, it is almost inevitable that God in a public institution will appear to take on the religion of the majority. A Jewish child would know that he is being invited to pray to a Christian God, who seems to bear no resemblance to the God of his synagogue, and an atheist would have no place in the scheme whatever. Third, school prayer does not allow full freedom of choice because it deals with children, and in an educational situation; if a school says, "Pray (or do what you feel like)," a child assumes that prayer is a part of learning. Finally, school prayer violates a fundamental assumption of American life, one that has something to do with privacy, something with freedom of speech, and something less codified and explicit: that one ought to be able to retain one's humanity without being made to feel a pariah in one's own country.

9   Of these four, the last may be the most important, since it goes to the heart of the minority-majority relationship. This is a country of outsiders, majority and minority alike. Government in America, for all its clauses and amendments, is basically a moral contract in which the minorities make concessions, but so does the majority. And the main concession the majority makes is never to use its power at the expense of individual humanity. How can one conduct prayers in a public institution without interfering with the sacrosanct relationship of a person with himself? People in a democracy hold dual citizenship; they are citizens of their country and citizens of their souls. When the state starts imposing on the soul, democracy is in trouble.

10   That President Reagan happens to be the one proposing the socialist solution to the American faith problem has its ironic element, but is beside the point. Public opinion polls indicate there is a vast majority feeling that God is good for children and that the Government ought to say so. If by saying so, however, the Government begins to destroy its principles from the inside, what then? For a big place this is an awfully delicate country, the nettings so intricately drawn that everyone feels the same reverberations. Even schoolchildren. It seems hard to believe that the whole enterprise

could be endangered for one small child standing off to the side wondering if he belongs. But whose country is it anyway?

QUESTIONS ABOUT "WHOSE COUNTRY IS IT ANYWAY?"

1.   What is the significance of the essay's title? How does it indicate the writer's intention?

2.   The essay begins with a narration of events. How important is this background information for the argument that Rosenblatt will develop?

3.   Rosenblatt gives four reasons that answer the question, "Why not have an amendment allowing everyone to pray to his or her God or to none?" What are they? Why did he choose these four? Comment on the placement of these reasons within the essay. Why do you think Rosenblatt placed them in the order he did?

4.   The last line of the second to last paragraph reads, "When the state starts imposing on the soul, democracy is in trouble." Is this line typical of the essay, or is it unusual? Why did Rosenblatt choose to use it? Why did he place it where he did?

5.   How would you paraphrase the basic claim of the essay, i.e., what is Rosenblatt trying to prove? What does he want the reader to do, if anything?

6.   How would you describe the tone of the essay? How is the reader affected by the last line: "It seems hard to believe that the whole enterprise could be endangered for one small child standing off to the side wondering if he belongs"?

Pornography Through the Looking Glass
Charles Krauthammer

Television ushered in the new year by cracking what it breathlessly   1
billed as "the last taboo": incest. Liberal Minneapolis celebrated by back-tracking a couple of taboos and considering a ban on pornography. One would have thought that that particular hang-up had been overcome. But even though the ban voted by the Minneapolis city council was eventually vetoed by Mayor Donald Fraser, pornography is evidently a hang-up of considerable tenacity. And according to the proposed law it is more than that: it is a violation of civil rights.

Now that seems like a peculiar notion, but one has to read the proposed   2
ordinance to see just how peculiar it is. The city council proposed banning

"discrimination . . . based on race, color, creed, religion, ancestry, national origin, sex, including . . . pornography." What can that possibly mean? How can one discriminate based on pornography?

3   Anticipating such questions, the bill helpfully provides "special findings on pornography." If it ever passes (immediately after the mayor's veto proponents vowed to bring it up again), the findings are destined to be the most famous gifts from social science to law since footnote eleven of *Brown* vs. *Board of Education.** The *Brown* findings, however, were based on real empirical data. The Minneapolis findings are of a more metaphysical nature. They begin: "The council finds that pornography is central in creating and maintaining the civil inequality of the sexes." If that were true, then it would follow that where pornography is banned—as in the U.S. of 50 years ago or the Tehran of today—one should not expect to find civil inequality of the sexes. Next finding. "Pornography is a systematic practice of exploitation and subordination based on sex which differentially harms women." While it is true that some pornography subordinates women, some does not, and none is "systematic" or a "practice." Outside the Minneapolis city council chambers, pornography means the traffic in obscenity. Inside, as in Alice's Wonderland, words will mean what the council wants them to mean.

4   The liberal mayor of Minneapolis was sympathetic with the proposal's aims, but vetoed it nonetheless. He found it too vague and ambiguous, a classic complaint against obscenity laws, old and new. In simpler times Justice Potter Stewart answered the question what is pornography with a succinct "I know it when I see it." But would even he know "subordination based on sex which differentially harms women" when he saw it? After all, the new dispensation seems to exclude homosexual pornography. And only embarrassment, not logic, would prevent including those weddings at which the bride is old-fashioned enough to vow "to love, honor and *obey*."

5   The head of the Minneapolis Civil Liberties Union says, unkindly, that the ordinance "has no redeeming social value." That seems a bit harsh. Set aside for a moment the pseudo findings, the creative definitions, the

*The Supreme Court's 1954 ruling cited seven scholars to prove that separate-but-equal schooling harmed black children, and led one critic to complain that it thus needlessly gave ammunition to those who wished to see the *Brown* decision not as an expression of civilized truth but as a brand of sociology.

ambiguities. The intent of the bill is to do away with the blight of pornography. What can be wrong with that?

A good question, and an important one. Over the decades it has spawned a fierce debate between a certain kind of conservative (usually called cultural conservative) on the one hand and civil libertarians on the other. The argument went like this. The conservative gave the intuitive case against pornography based on an overriding concern for, it now sounds almost too quaint to say, public morality. Pornography is an affront to decency; it coarsens society. As Susan Sontag, not a conservative, writing in defense of pornography says, it serves to "drive a wedge between one's existence as a full human being and one's existence as a sexual being." The ordinary person, of course, does not need a philosopher, conservative or otherwise, to tell him why he wants to run pornography out of his neighborhood. It cheapens and demeans. Even though he may occasionally be tempted by it, that temptation is almost invariably accompanied by a feeling of shame and a desire to shield his children from the fleshy come-ons of the magazine rack.

That may be so, say the civil libertarians, but it is irrelevant. Government has no business regulating morality. The First Amendment guarantees freedom of expression, and though you may prefer not to express yourself by dancing naked on a runway in a bar, some people do, and you have no business stopping them. Nor do you have any business trying to stop those who like to sit by the runway and imbibe this form of expression. It may not be *Swan Lake*, but the First Amendment does not hinge on judgments of artistic merit or even redeeming value.

Now this traditional debate over pornography is clear and comprehensible. It involves the clash of two important values: public morality *vs.* individual liberty. The conservative is prepared to admit that his restrictions curtail liberty, though a kind of liberty he does not think is particularly worth having. The civil libertarian admits that a price of liberty is that it stands to be misused, and that pornography may be one of those misuses; public morality may suffer, but freedom is more precious. Both sides agree, however, that one cannot have everything and may sometimes have to trade one political good for another.

Not the Minneapolis bill, and that is what made it so audacious—and perverse. It manages the amazing feat of restoring censorship, which after all is a form of coercion, while at the same time claiming not to restrict rights but expand them. The logic is a bit tortuous. It finds that pornography promotes bigotry and fosters acts of aggression against women, both of

6

7

8

9

which, in turn, "harm women's opportunities for equality of rights in employment, education, property rights, . . . contribute significantly to restricting women from full exercise of citizenship . . . and undermine women's equal exercise of rights to speech and action."

10   Apart from the questionable logical leaps required at every step of the syllogism, the more immediate question is: Why take this remote and improbable route to arrive at a point—banning pornography—that one can reach directly by citing the venerable argument that pornography damages the moral fiber of society? Why go from St. Paul to Minneapolis by way of Peking?

11   The answer is simple. As a rallying cry, public morality has no sex appeal; civil rights has. Use words like moral fiber and people think of Jerry Falwell. Use words like rights and they think of Thomas Jefferson. Use civil rights and they think of Martin Luther King Jr. Because civil rights is justly considered among the most sacred of political values, appropriating it for partisan advantage can be very useful. (The fiercest battle in the fight over affirmative action, for example, is over which side has rightful claim to the mantle of civil rights.) Convince people that censorship is really a right, and you can win them over. It won over the Minneapolis city council. And if to do so, you have to pretend that fewer rights are more, so be it.

12   Civil rights will not be the first political value to have its meaning reversed. The use of the term freedom to describe unfreedom goes back at least as far as Rousseau, who wrote, without irony, of an ideal republic in which men would be "forced to be free." In our day, the word democracy is so beloved of tyrants that some have named their countries after it, as in the German Democratic Republic (a.k.a. East Germany). And from Beirut to San Salvador, every gang of political thugs makes sure to kneel at least five times a day in the direction of "peace." So why not abuse civil rights?

13   The virtue of calling a spade a spade is that when it is traded in, accountants can still make sense of the books. The virtue of calling political values by their real names is that when social policy is to be made, citizens can make sense of the choices. That used to be the case in the debate about pornography. If Minneapolis is any indication of where that debate is heading, it will not be the case for long.

14   That is a pity, because while it is easy to quarrel with the method of the Minneapolis ban, it is hard to quarrel with the motive. After a decade's experience with permissiveness, many Americans have become acutely aware that there is a worm in the apple of sexual liberation. That a community with a reputation for liberalism should decide that things have gone too

far is not really news. The call for a pause in the frantic assault on the limits of decency (beyond which lies the terra cognita of what used to be taboos) is the quite natural expression of a profound disappointment with the reality, as opposed to the promise, of unrestricted freedom. There are pushes and pulls in the life of the national superego, and now there is a pulling—back. Many are prepared to make expression a bit less free in order to make their community a bit more whole, or, as skeptics might say, wholesome.

That is nothing to be ashamed of. So why disguise it as a campaign for   15
civil rights? (True, liberals may be somewhat embarrassed to be found in bed with bluenoses, but the Minneapolis case is easily explained away as a one-issue marriage of convenience.) In an age when the most private of human activities is everywhere called by its most common name, why be so coy about giving censorship its proper name too?

QUESTIONS ABOUT "PORNOGRAPHY THROUGH THE LOOKING GLASS"

1.   What is the intention of the essay: To argue that pornography should be illegal? To argue that pornography is bad? To argue that pornography does not violate the civil rights of women? To argue that the strategy the Minneapolis city council used to ban pornography is not a good one?

2.   Krauthammer describes the Minneapolis bill as "perverse." Examine his evaluation of the bill: its content, its probable effect, its logic. How effective is the evaluation? How important is it within the essay? Describe its function within the essay.

3.   Describe the tone of the essay. To what extent does Krauthammer minimize—even ridicule—the efforts of the persons who drafted the Minneapolis bill? What effect does this have on the reader? Would it affect different readers in different ways? For example, how might a woman who has been raped or physically abused respond to the tone?

4.   The essay is written in the third person. Although Krauthammer does not refer to himself as "I," the author is evident within the text. Comment on how and why this occurs. Why did Krauthammer select this particular strategy? Why didn't he come out and say "I" or use the third person and make his presence less detectable?

5.   Krauthammer claims that the words "moral fiber" make people think of one sort of individual, whereas the words "civil rights" make people think of another sort. Do these claims suggest that he has made certain

assumptions about the values and attitudes of his readers? If so, what are these assumptions?

6.   Krauthammer has, in part, chosen the strategy of separating the *motive* of the Minneapolis ban from the *method*. Is this an effective strategy? Why do you suppose Krauthammer chose it?

Summary

Now that you have examined an explanation about and examples of persuasive writing, here are several important operations that a writer usually performs before she begins to draft a persuasive essay.

1.   The writer must thoroughly *immerse* herself in the issue or position she is addressing, making sure that she understands the full range of attitudes, stances, approaches, and contexts that surround this issue or position.

2.   The writer must *examine* the position she will be advocating to determine the kinds and amount of evidence she will need to support her viewpoint.

3.   The writer must determine how she will establish her credibility with the audience she is addressing, including these considerations:

    a.   What personal qualifications should she present to the reader: fairness? objectivity? trustworthiness? "I'm just a common person like yourself"?

    b.   What formal qualifications, such as education, social status, or acquaintances in high places, should she mention?

    c.   What experience does the writer have with the issues, problems, or viewpoints she is dealing with? How much of this background information, if any, should she present in the text?

    d.   To what "authorities" does she want to appeal in the course of her argumentation—special interest groups, sacred texts, tradition, noted scholars?

4.   Most importantly, the writer must *analyze* her audience and keep it in mind as she works through operations 1, 2, and 3. She must learn as much as possible about what her audience knows and believes about the issue; whether they will be neutral, sympathetic, or hostile to her position; and what their educational and socioeconomic status is. This information will help her determine the kinds of evidence and forms of argumentation that will impress and convince her audience and thus serve her intentions best. The would-be "persuasive" writer who ignores her audience may

succeed in expressing her viewpoints, but will usually fail to move her audience to the position she advocates.

A Rhetorical Task: Beth and the Issue of Alcohol on Campus

Initial Responses

Beth Boyer, along with the rest of her class, was presented with the task of writing a persuasive essay.[1] The kind of issue to be addressed and the audience to which the essay would be addressed were left to the discretion of the student. Since, at the time she was writing, alcohol abuse and the availability of alcohol on campus were burning campus issues, Beth decided to write an "editorial" for the campus paper addressing the issue of whether there should be stricter control of alcohol and, further, whether the Peacock, a campus eatery that served alcoholic beverages, should be closed.

VISUALIZING THE AUDIENCE

Beth knew that her audience would be other students like herself who were concerned about the alcohol problem, but who were reluctant to add any more rules to the already strict campus code of behavior. Here are some of the questions she considered as she visualized her audience:

--What are the extremes of solutions to the alcohol problem?

--How aware are campus residents of the alcohol abuse?

--Will college and community leaders be interested in the proposed solutions that the editorial will present?

[1]Beth's editorial is based upon a writing assignment derived from *Casebook Rhetoric*, David Tedlock and Paul Jarvie (Holt, Rinehart and Winston, 1981).

--What is the most effective way of convincing students to be more self-disciplined and appreciative of others' rights?

--How sensitive will my audience be to this issue, considering that they recently helped defeat a proposal to raise the state's drinking age to 21?

CREATING A CONTEXT

Beth decided to proceed by surveying a number of recent alcohol-related incidents in order to demonstrate the need for more control of alcoholic beverages on campus. This way, she reasoned, her audience would understand the urgency of her editorial and the need for an immediate response by the administration, by student leaders, and by the community at large. Once she had established the problem, her suggestions for solutions would be more credible and relevant to her audience.

ARTICULATING INTENTION

As she considered her audience and the issue she was addressing, Beth had a clear sense of her intention in writing the editorial. She wanted to convince her audience that, indeed, there was a drinking problem on campus, and that only with the concerted effort of administration, students, and community persons could there be a reasonable and balanced solution. She wanted her editorial to be a model of sensible and responsible argumentation—neither shrill nor heavy-handed. At the very least she hoped that when her readers finished the editorial, they would be provoked to consider the issue, whether they agreed with her stance or not.

Inventing and Planning

Beth engaged in an extensive inventing and planning session before she began her first draft. She first did a lengthy freewrite of the text she had in mind. This helped her generate the kinds of issues, side issues, and viewpoints that she hoped to deal with in her editorial. She followed this with a brainstorming session in which she focused on specific campus issues around which her editorial would revolve: alcoholism, vandalism, the Peacock (a campus restaurant), dormitories. She then did more brainstorming on possible solutions to the problem of campus drinking and vandalism. After these two inventing sessions, she briefly jotted down some notes about her potential audience, realizing that they would not be indifferent, but rather at the two extremes of the issue. This dictated a specific strategy for overcoming the gaps between the two points of view. She devised a plan for producing her first draft:

> The first paragraph should set up the problem and the context for the editorial. The following paragraph should narrow the discussion and set the stage for the alternative solutions to the drinking problem that the editorial is intended to present. The middle paragraphs, in turn, would present the alternative solutions and the reasons why I think they would work. The concluding paragraph would then capsule the preceding arguments and call for support by the student body and the administration.

Drafting and Revising

Beth wrote two drafts. She considered the first a rough draft and proceeded to revise accordingly. Her plan for drafting had been generally successful. Everything was in the right order, but she was not happy with the overall structure of the essay. There seemed to be too much narration in the middle paragraphs, and this structure seemed inappropriate given her intention to persuade; it was too much a mirror of her discovery process. She decided that she needed to build in more *reader cues* to indicate the focus of those paragraphs.

At the sentence level, Beth found a great deal of wordiness, an overuse of prepositions and passive verbs that strung out the meaning and blunted the urgency of her argument. On the other hand, she found few writer-based sentences, i.e., sentences that were ambiguous or convoluted. There were sentences that needed reworking, but only to sharpen the focus and tighten the structure.

At the word level, Beth found only a few vague words and no code words per se. She did decide that she needed to define her key terms, "drinking problem," and "alcohol abuse," better. All in all, she determined that she was ready to move on to a final draft.

Proofreading and Editing

After Beth finished rewriting her first draft, she read through it *backwards*, looking for sentence problems, word choice ambiguities, and mechanics and usage errors. Then she read it aloud, listening for awkward or wordy sentences. When she was satisfied, she had it typed as her final draft and submitted it to the campus newspaper.

The Finished Essay

Closing the Peacock Not a Solution
Beth Boyer

1   Recent drinking-related campus incidents have fueled the rumor that the Peacock will be closed down. Since the Peacock is one of the key campus recreational centers--many of the students go there to relax--its closing would be a severe blow to the social life here. While it is clear that something must be done to address the ongoing drinking problems on campus, closing the Peacock is not a viable option. Alternative solutions must be found.

2   Most of us know the symptoms of uncontrolled liquor consumption at Bennett: vandalism, encouragement to underage drinking, the undermining of peaceful dorm life. But the Peacock is not the ultimate source of these problems, and closing it would only be a stop-gap measure. Students would only find other means of obtaining alcohol. Any solutions must focus on the reality of the modern campus: students will consume alcohol. The question we must ask is: how can we minimize the effects of excessive drinking on campus. From my vantage point there are four possible, complementary actions the administration can take to address the issue.

3   First, the administration can control dormitory parties by enforcing existing regulations and adding a few more relevant ones. Among these are: restricting the number of people who can attend the parties; requiring all parties to be registered 24 hours in advance and with the approval of the resident advisor; and levelling fines on individuals and groups whose noise levels disturb other residents. The result would be fewer "spontaneous" parties and a decrease in the vandalism which usually attends such spur of the moment get-togethers.

4   Second, the administration can shorten the hours of the Peacock's operation. Instead of closing it down completely, its staff could open it later in the evening, thus leaving students fewer hours to drink and get drunk. In addition, the staff could also make entrance more

difficult for underage students by employing a more rigorous identification procedure. Students who know they will not be able to come
in because of their age will not risk embarrassment in front of their
friends. Further, leaving the Peacock open will reduce the number of
students who will leave campus, driving to nearby Canton or Guern,
to search for alcohol. How much better to keep our drinking students
on campus rather than on the road, where their consumption may
prove both dangerous and deadly.

Third, since the campus and the town offer few diversions, and   5
thereby encourage students to turn to partying for their entertainment,
it is important for the administration and town officials to collaborate
on a plan to provide alternative forms of recreation for the students.
Some short-term solutions might include specific activities at the local
beach; a town bike race; encouraging involvement in local charity
drives; these are only a few. In the long run, it is clear that the town
and the college need a recreation center for sports, theatre, and dancing.
The existing town and campus facilities do not encourage students
to get involved in healthy and non-alcoholic forms of recreation.

Finally, the larger underage drinking problem can be partially cur-   6
tailed by housing all under-20 students in a special section of each
dormitory, decreasing their chances of mingling with upperclassmen
and being tempted to drink. This may seem to be a small, even trivial
attempt at isolating the "problem drinkers," but it is clear that the
more time freshman and sophomore students spend with their older
counterparts, the more likely they will be to adopt their lifestyle.

To this point, the administration has seemed to be willing to take   7
extreme measures to solve the drinking problems--measures which
bring immediate publicity, but which do not address the true problem.
Closing the Peacock would be just such a measure. We must seek
rational and balanced solutions which will yield the results we all
want. Students will continue to drink. But, we can ask them to do so
responsibly--while we provide alternative forms of recreation for them
and others.

Writing Assignment

This is a rhetorical task for you that is similar to the one with which Beth
was presented.

Choose a campus issue that has recently provoked heat among your fellow students and perhaps the campus as a whole. Choose something that definitely gets under your skin and about which you could craft a meaningful editorial. Be sure to consider the intention of your essay: What is it that you want your readers to *believe* or *do* when they finish it?

I.   Getting Started: Inventing and Planning
   A.   List several campus issues that are currently topics of discussion on your campus.
   B.   Choose one of them and freewrite several paragraphs that (1) express the kinds of attitudes that exist regarding the issue, (2) survey the implications of the issue and the problems with which it is associated, (3) explain who is affected by the issue or problem and to what degree, and (4) make tentative suggestions for solutions to the issue or problem as you see it.
   C.   Consider the audience for your editorial. What campus groups are affected by the issue or problem? To which group or groups are you addressing your editorial: the administration? the student government? particular students? What will be the most effective point of view and tone to use in addressing your audience?
   D.   How will your editorial use facts and corresponding evidence and authority to establish its reasonableness and your credibility? What are the most pertinent facts that support your view of the issue? What are the opposing points of view? How strong are these other points of view? How will you counter alternative views and solutions?
   E.   Try to articulate the intention of your editorial. Is it to change campus attitudes? Move students or others to a particular action? Merely provoke adversaries to consider the other side(s) of the issue or problem?
   F.   Examine the structures of the example persuasion texts given earlier in this chapter. Do any of these structures seem suitable for the kind of editorial you are crafting? If not, why not? Try to describe the structure you want your essay to take. What do you think you want to do first, next, last?
   G.   Consider your answer to the preceding question. Given the intention of your essay and the audience you are addressing, how objective does your stance need to be? How "present" do you want or need to be in the actual text of the editorial?
II. Drafting and Revising
   A.   Write a first draft of your essay, making careful use of your inventing and planning.

    B. Read your draft and answer the following:
        1. Describe the intention of your essay.
        2. Describe the audience to whom your essay is addressed.
        3. Describe the way in which you intend to structure your essay.
        4. Describe the point of view (first, second, or third person) and the tone that you used.
    C. Evaluate your draft in terms of your answers to the preceding questions. Examine your draft at the text, sentence, and word levels. Is it a rough draft or a predraft?
    D. Describe your plans for revising or rewriting your draft.
    E. Repeat steps B to D if necessary.
III. Proofreading and Editing
    A. Allow some time to pass, then read your final draft aloud.
    B. Correct any errors in sentence structure, word choice, and mechanics and usage.

Writing Assignment

Read the following essay, "The Penalty of Death," by H. L. Mencken.

The Penalty of Death
H. L. Mencken

    Of the arguments against capital punishment that issue from uplifters, two are commonly heard most often, to wit: 1

1. That hanging a man (or frying him or gassing him) is a dreadful business, degrading to those who have to do it and revolting to those who have to witness it.
2. That it is useless, for it does not deter others from the same crime.

    The first of these arguments, it seems to me, is plainly too weak to need   2
serious refutation. All it says, in brief, is that the work of the hangman is unpleasant. Granted. But suppose it is? It may be quite necessary to society for all that. There are, indeed, many other jobs that are unpleasant, and yet no one thinks of abolishing them—that of the plumber, that of the soldier, that of the garbage-man, that of the priest hearing confessions, that of the sand-hog, and so on. Moreover, what evidence is there that any actual

hangman complains of his work? I have heard none. On the contrary, I have known many who delighted in their ancient art, and practised it proudly.

3   In the second argument of the abolitionists there is rather more force, but even here, I believe, the ground under them is shaky. Their fundamental error consists in assuming that the whole aim of punishing criminals is to deter other (potential) criminals—that we hang or electrocute A simply in order to so alarm B that he will not kill C. This, I believe, is an assumption which confuses a part with the whole. Deterrence, obviously, is *one* of the aims of punishment, but it is surely not the only one. On the contrary, there are at least half a dozen, and some are probably quite as important. At least one of them, practically considered, is *more* important. Commonly, it is described as revenge, but revenge is really not the word for it. I borrow a better term from the late Aristotle: *katharsis*. *Katharsis,* so used, means a salubrious discharge of emotions, a healthy letting off of steam. A schoolboy, disliking his teacher, deposits a tack upon the pedagogical chair; the teacher jumps and the boy laughs. This is *katharsis*. What I contend is that one of the prime objects of all judicial punishments is to afford the same grateful relief (*a*) to the immediate victims of the criminal punished, and (*b*) to the general body of moral and timorous men.

4   These persons, and particularly the first group, are concerned only indirectly with deterring other criminals. The thing they crave primarily is the satisfaction of seeing the criminal actually before them suffer as he made them suffer. What they want is the peace of mind that goes with the feeling that accounts are squared. Until they get that satisfaction they are in a state of emotional tension, and hence unhappy. The instant they get it they are comfortable. I do not argue that this yearning is noble; I simply argue that it is almost universal among human beings. In the face of injuries that are unimportant and can be borne without damage it may yield to higher impulses; that is to say, it may yield to what is called Christian charity. But when the injury is serious Christianity is adjourned, and even saints reach for their sidearms. It is plainly asking too much of human nature to expect it to conquer so natural an impulse. A keeps a store and has a bookkeeper, B. B steals $700, employs it in playing at dice or bingo, and is cleaned out. What is A to do? Let B go? If he does so he will be unable to sleep at night. The sense of injury, of injustice, of frustration will haunt him like pruritus. So he turns B over to the police, and they hustle B to prison. Thereafter A can sleep. More, he has pleasant dreams. He pictures B chained to the wall of a dungeon a hundred feet underground, devoured by rats and scorpions. It is so agreeable that it makes him forget his $700. He has got his *katharsis*.

The same thing precisely takes place on a larger scale when there is a crime which destroys a whole community's sense of security. Every law-abiding citizen feels menaced and frustrated until the criminals have been struck down—until the communal capacity to get even with them, and more than even, has been dramatically demonstrated. Here, manifestly, the business of deterring others is no more than an afterthought. The main thing is to destroy the concrete scoundrels whose act has alarmed everyone, and thus made everyone unhappy. Until they are brought to book that unhappiness continues; when the law has been executed upon them there is a sigh of relief. In other words, there is *katharsis*. 5

I know of no public demand for the death penalty for ordinary crimes, even for ordinary homicides. Its infliction would shock all men of normal decency of feeling. But for crimes involving the deliberate and inexcusable taking of human life, by men openly defiant of all civilized order—for such crimes it seems, to nine men out of ten, a just and proper punishment. Any lesser penalty leaves them feeling that the criminal has got the better of society—that he is free to add insult to injury by laughing. That feeling can be dissipated only by a recourse to *katharsis,* the invention of the aforesaid Aristotle. It is more effectively and economically achieved, as human nature now is, by wafting the criminal to realms of bliss. 6

The real objection to capital punishment doesn't lie against the actual extermination of the condemned, but against our brutal American habit of putting it off so long. After all, every one of us must die soon or late, and a murderer, it must be assumed, is one who makes that sad fact the cornerstone of his metaphysic. But it is one thing to die, and quite another thing to lie for long months and even years under the shadow of death. No sane man would choose such a finish. All of us, despite the Prayer Book, long for a swift and unexpected end. Unhappily, a murderer, under the irrational American system, is tortured for what, to him, must seem a whole series of eternities. For months on end he sits in prison while his lawyers carry on their idiotic buffoonery with writs, injunctions, mandamuses, and appeals. In order to get his money (or that of his friends) they have to feed him with hope. Now and then, by the imbecility of a judge or some trick of juridic science, they actually justify it. But let us say that, his money all gone, they finally throw up their hands. Their client is now ready for the rope or the chair. But he must still wait for months before it fetches him. 7

That wait, I believe, is horribly cruel. I have seen more than one man sitting in the death-house, and I don't want to see any more. Worse, it is wholly useless. Why should he wait at all? Why not hang him the day after the last court dissipates his last hope? Why torture him as not even cannibals 8 would torture their victims? The common answer is that he must have time to make his peace with God. But how long does that take? It may be accomplished, I believe, in two hours quite as comfortably as in two years. There are, indeed, no temporal limitations upon God. He could forgive a whole herd of murderers in a millionth of a second. More, it has been done.

Answer the following questions about Mencken's essay.

1.   What is the intention of the essay?

2.   Why does Mencken begin his essay with the two most commonly heard arguments against capital punishment? Does "most commonly heard" necessarily mean "most valid" or "most persuasive"?

3.   Why doesn't Mencken address the argument against capital punishment that asserts that it is arbitrarily applied? (Minority persons are executed more often than members of the dominant race.) In answering, remember that this essay was written during the 1920s.

4.   Why is background information about the term *katharsis* necessary to Mencken's argument?

5.   Comment upon the effect on the reader of this sentence: "All it says, in brief, is that the work of the hangman is unpleasant." Are there other, similar statements that are calculated to have the same effect?

6.   How does Mencken establish his credibility with the reader?

7.   Describe the tone and point of view of the essay. How do these contribute to the effectiveness of Mencken's argument?

8.   To whom is the essay addressed? Describe the characteristics of the audience as you perceive them.

9.   Describe the structure of the essay.

Form your own opinion on the subject of capital punishment: in favor or against. Then write a formal, detailed letter to the governor of your state in which you argue that he or she should or should not veto a bill *in favor* of capital punishment that has narrowly passed in both houses of the state congress.

I.   Getting Started: Inventing and Planning
    A.   What is your attitude toward capital punishment? Are you in favor of it? Against it? Neutral? Indifferent?
    B.   Investigate the issue by reading sources at your library. Then state your viewpoint regarding capital punishment. Are you for, against, or undecided?

C. Discuss the issue with several persons of your choosing. Try, if possible, to engage in an informal debate with someone who does *not* share your viewpoint.

D. Describe the range of attitudes, stances, and contexts that surround the issue of capital punishment. What are some of the strongest arguments in favor of it? Against it?

E. Examine your point of view, then list the kind and amount of evidence that you will need to support it.

F. Think of your audience—the governor of the state. Describe him or her. What do you know about his or her attitudes, values, level of education, etc.? What concerns must he or she address, as governor? For example, is it near an election year? Is the governor obligated to special interest groups?

G. Keeping your audience in mind, how do you intend to establish your credibility? What qualifications—personal, formal, or experiential—will you present? Will you appeal to authorities? If so, which ones?

H. How do you intend to structure your letter so that the issues and problems that you are addressing are clear? So that the most compelling counterarguments will be anticipated and addressed?

I. Describe the tone and point of view that you intend to use. How will these help establish your credibility and the reasonableness and justness of your view?

II. Drafting and Revising
   A. Write the first draft of your essay.
   B. Read your draft and answer the following.
      1. Describe the intention of your essay.
      2. Describe the audience to whom your essay is addressed.
      3. Describe the way in which you intend to structure your essay.
      4. Describe the point of view (first, second, or third person) and the tone that you used.
   C. Evaluate your draft in terms of your answers to the previous questions. Examine your draft at the text, sentence, and word levels. Is it a rough draft or a predraft?
   D. Describe your plans for revising or rewriting your draft.
   E. Repeat steps B to D if necessary.

III. Proofreading and Editing
   A. Allow some time to pass, then read your final draft aloud.
   B. Correct errors in sentence structure, word choice, and mechanics and usage.

Part Three

Editing

As he writes, a successful writer engages in a variety of activities that enable him to produce a finished text that ably conveys his thesis and intention to a reader. These activities include inventing, planning, drafting, and revising, all of which were explained and illustrated in Parts One and Two of *Rough-drafts*. A text is not ready for a reader, however, until it has been polished. Part Three therefore explains one more activity that successful writers consider essential: editing. Editing involves making changes at the sentence and word level, and so the three chapters in Part Three will explain strategies for editing for problems in sentence structure (Chapter 11), word choice (Chapter 12), and grammar and mechanics (Chapter 13).

Although all the *editing strategies* presented in Chapters 11 to 13 are likely to be useful for most apprentice writers, the discussion of each particular *problem* in sentence structure, word choice, or grammar and mechanics is addressed primarily to those writers who are struggling with that particular problem.

Some of these discussions require a review of basic concepts, such as "subject" or "predicate," whereas others involve rather sophisticated concepts and terminology. In all discussions, however, we have tried to use a minimum of terminology, and, where feasible, we have employed terms and concepts with which apprentice writers will be familiar.

Our explanations are by no means exhaustive; they cover only the most common problems and errors. A good handbook and dictionary are important tools for any writer, and the three chapters in Part Three are meant to supplement, not replace, these tools.

General Strategies for Editing

Regardless of when a writer begins to attend to sentence- and word-level errors, he must engage in a separate serious reading of his text when the final draft is completed. Here are some *general* strategies that will increase the effectiveness of such a reading. Experienced writers employ these strategies regardless of whether they are editing for errors in sentence structure, word choice, or mechanics and usage.

1. Allow sufficient time to elapse after completing the final draft before editing for sentence- and word-level errors. One day, a night included, is a minimum, reasonable amount of time.
2. Edit when alert and rested.
3. When reading aloud, read slowly.
4. Use a finger or a ruler to focus the eyes on a small portion of the text, especially when editing for errors in grammar, spelling, and mechanics (such as punctuation).

5.   Edit more than once, focusing on the detection of particular errors each time. Devote a separate editing session to each serious problem—for instance, sentence fragments.

As with rewriting, editing is a two-step process. First, an error must be located. Then it must be corrected. Some of the editing strategies in Part Three of *Roughdrafts* will help you to locate errors; others will help you to correct them.

Editing at the Sentence Level 11

As you recall from Chapter 1, editing, which is often used synonymously with proofreading, means to polish a text by making changes at the word and sentence levels. Although writers usually edit a piece of writing at the end of the writing process, after the piece is finished in all other respects, many notice and correct errors in sentence structure, word choice, and grammar and mechanics as they write. Indeed, for some writers, wrestling with the structure of individual sentences or with the choice of particular words is an essential component of their thinking/planning/writing/rewriting process. The time it takes to look up a word in a dictionary may be a necessary, productive break in a writer's thinking process. For another writer it can be a serious, damaging distraction.

There can be no rule, therefore, regarding when small-sentence or word-level decisions should first receive a writer's attention. That is, a writer may decide to alter the structure of a sentence because it appears awkward or because it does not seem appropriate for the context in which it is found. But it may not occur to him that the structure of a particular sentence is inappropriate until a text is very nearly completed—until he is working with small, relatively insignificant features within the text.

Although the distinction between *editing,* a process largely devoted to the detection and elimination of error, and *choice making,* an integral part of the writing and revising process, cannot always be finely drawn, in this chapter and the two to follow, editing represents the *final stage* in producing a completed text, a text *ready for a reader.* As such, it involves the elimination

401

of error, general awkwardness or ambiguity, and incorrect manuscript form in the writer's text.

This chapter is divided into six sections:

☐ Inappropriate Sentence Fragments
☐ Incorrectly Connected Sentences
☐ Sentences with Modification Problems
☐ Ineffective Passive Sentences
☐ Sentences with Faulty Parallelism
☐ General Strategies for Editing Sentences

Inappropriate Sentence Fragments

In order to be grammatically complete, a sentence must have—minimally—a subject and a predicate. The subject of a sentence must be a noun, or a word or word group that acts as a noun. The predicate of a sentence must have a verb and, if the verb is transitive or linking, an additional word or words to complete it. Here are some examples:

In response to expressions of concern from personnel, the
SUBJECT   *VERB*   *OBJECT (COMPLETES VERB)*
president of EMCO *has established* a special *"hot line"* so
that employees may voice constructive criticism.

         SUBJECT   *VERB*
What the subjects thought of the examination was not
COMPLEMENT (COMPLETES VERB)
clear from their response.

Since the applicant did not follow established procedures, *his*
SUBJECT *VERB*
file will be eliminated.

As they experiment with new and varied structures, inexperienced writers sometimes *inadvertently* punctuate incomplete sentences as if they were complete. Such incomplete sentences are called *inappropriate sentence fragments*. Unlike fragments that writers produce consciously, for a particular reason, these fragments may cause confusion. They also negatively bias a reader, causing her to consider the writer careless or "illiterate." Here are a few examples of both appropriate and inappropriate sentence fragments.

APPROPRIATE FRAGMENTS:
Why should an individual join a fraternity? *To develop a sense of community as well as a commitment to service.* (The appropriate fragment answers a question posed by the first sentence.)

Many students agree that grades are poor indicators of what they know. *Or of what they can do.* (The appropriate fragment emphasizes the last phrase.)

INAPPROPRIATE FRAGMENTS:
Awarding those who deserve it or even acknowledging their excellence in front of other people. Sometimes this is enough to attract others to the task. (Neither the "subject" nor the function of the fragment is evident; its relationship to the next sentence is not clear, either.)

At fertilization, the 23 chromosomes of the sperm join with the 23 chromosomes of the ovum. *A new entity created.* (To what does the fragment refer? Its function is not clear.)

Although the solution will not be easy. All of us must work together to find it. (The fragment appears to be a modifier carelessly separated from the sentence that it modifies.)

Most of the fragments that an apprentice writer inadvertently produces occur because the writer has misjudged where a sentence should end. That is, for some reason—most often, quite a logical reason—an inexperienced writer will consider a string of words to be "finished" or "complete" when it is not. The reasons for this kind of mistake in judgment often have to do with the content and/or nature of the string of words. A string of words that is long, that contains a verb or words that appear to be verbs, or that seems to be similar to a sentence because it contains a topic and some statement or information about that topic may be mistaken for a sentence. Here are examples of some of the more common types of sentence fragments.

Fragmented Modifier

Fragmented modifiers result when a modifying word group is separated from the sentence that it modifies or that contains the word(s) it modifies. The fragmented modifier is punctuated as a complete sentence in spite of the fact that a modifier cannot be a complete, grammatical sentence.

> EXAMPLES:
> *Since I have become a writer.* I am constantly seeking new experience which will give me something to write about. ("Since I have become a writer" modifies the verb "seeking"; it tells *why*.)
>
> *Thoroughly explaining what is meant by redundant pairs.* Williams strengthens his explanation by supplying numerous examples. ("Thoroughly explaining what is meant by redundant pairs" modifies the verb "strengthens"; it tells *how*.)
>
> The people on the show are all beautiful, wear glamorous clothes, and live in expensive mansions. *Which are located on acres of land including tennis courts, formal gardens, and of course swimming pools.* ("Which are located . . ." modifies "mansions"; it tells *what kind of* mansions.)

Fragmented Word or Word Group Plus Modifier

Sometimes apprentice writers punctuate a word plus its modifier(s) as a complete sentence.

> EXAMPLE:
> The work of the structuralists familiarized many with the term "linguist." *A term that had been used to designate someone who studies languages.* (The italicized structure consists entirely of a noun, "a term," plus a group of words that modifies it. A complete grammatical sentence cannot consist of merely a word and its modifiers.)

Fragment with "For Example" or "For Instance"

A group of words preceded by "for example" or "for instance" may be mistaken for a sentence.

> EXAMPLE:
> A poor mattress can cause problems. *For example, a backache or a sore neck.* ("For example a backache or a sore neck" does not have a verb. Therefore it is not a sentence.)

Exercise 1

Examine the structure of each of the following sentences. Then read each sentence *aloud*. Locate and underline any fragments.

> EXAMPLE:
> The reason for the increase in user fees is to transfer employees to the auxiliary enterprise budget. <u>A strategy which may save jobs.</u>

1. Paintings from the nineteenth-century artist Taylor, whose works include the murals on the post office building. Individuals are encouraged to attend the exhibit.
2. The following positions have been approved by the president for posting. However, the hiring freeze will remain in effect. Until the budget appropriations are determined by the Board.
3. Noting that a local government should be responsive to its citizenry, mayoral candidate Blake pledged to create a Citizens' Action Committee if elected. Although the committee would require funding, Blake thought the expense was justified.
4. Following the Tuesday night hearings, which will provide commissioners with information regarding the proposed ditching of the North River. Residents of Greenwood will be provided with an opportunity to file grievances. For example, grievances having to do with sewer maintenance or garbage pickup.
5. At midnight, the University Activities League (UAL) will sponsor a special

showing of *The Rocky Horror Picture Show.* A cult film that has been attracting audiences of all ages for some time.

6.   Students who are unable to attend advanced registration and who will not be able to register during the following week. These individuals should contact Dr. James, Director of Registration, immediately.

7.   Norman Underwood, chair of the Student Government Board and a member of Theta Omicron Pi. Yesterday decided that poor student attendance at university-sponsored activities was embarrassing.

8.   Most of the members of the textbook selection committee were in favor of adopting the entire curriculum program. Reasoning that they would never have another opportunity to purchase such a comprehensive set of materials, committee members voted to pursue the acquisition vigorously.

9.   Lamenting his impending fate at the hands of the Student Judgment Tribunal. Mark vowed never to cheat again. Even if that would cause him to flunk out of school.

Exercise 2

Read the following short text aloud. Locate and underline any inappropriate fragments.

   Thank heavens for places like Kidland, Toys R Wonderful, and Tots N Toys. Because without these venerable establishments. Parents would need to make (make: design *and* construct) Halloween costumes for each and every one of their children over the age of one and under the age of fourteen. As it is, beleaguered parents can take their kids to Kidland (or Toys R Wonderful) and purchase costumes for them. Outfits that will enable little BillyBobbySuzyVincentKatyEdwardoMaximilian to dress up as PacMan or Superman or Yoda or Indiana Jones—all of this at virtually no cost, too; these remarkable costumes cost about three dollars apiece.

   I took Josh to Toys R Wonderful this year, in early October. "Pick out a costume," I said. Disappearing immediately from the Halloween costume section. I had to look for Josh everywhere. "Josh." "Joshua." "JOSH-EW-A!" I finally found him—at the car section. Sounding a great deal like a race car at the Daytona 500, Josh rolled a model racing car in the aisle. "Can I buy this?" "With what?" "I only got a telescope for my birthday; that's not enough." "Who says it's not enough. It most certainly *is* enough."

"You're mean. *Mean.*" I began to think of what I could have been doing if I hadn't agreed to take Josh to Toys R Wonderful. That made me depressed.

Somehow, I lured Josh to the costume section. But once there, he couldn't decide who he wanted to be. Not Superman. (Too boring.) Not Mr. Spock. (That was last year.) Not Darth Vader. (Too scary.) At last Josh narrowed the field: Rubic's Cube or PacMan. Noticing his "final" choices. I can't say that I was delighted. Who wants to be the mother of a Game, after all?

After Josh made up his mind (PacMan). We stood in the cash register line for ten minutes. Then we drove the thirty-five miles back to Bowling Green. Unpleasant as my experience was. I was satisfied. I did *not* have to make Josh a costume. And Halloween only comes once a year.

Correcting Fragments

Once inappropriate fragments are located, there are several easy methods of correcting them. Here are three common ways to correct inappropriate sentence fragments.

Since an inappropriate sentence fragment is often a modifier or other structure that has been incorrectly separated from the sentence of which it is a part, one effective means of correcting it is to attach it to the sentence that precedes or follows it.

EXAMPLE:
Since Bill didn't prepare adequately. He failed his history exam.

CORRECTED:
Since Bill didn't prepare adequately, he failed his history exam.

EXAMPLE:
Most of the spectators sat in the arena. *Wondering when the performers would arrive.* The band was already an hour late.

CORRECTED:
Most of the spectators sat in the area, wondering when the performers would arrive. The band was already an hour late.

Sometimes it may be necessary to alter the sentence that precedes or follows a fragment before the fragment can be attached.

EXAMPLE:
Many consumers prefer the sportier models. *Paying as much as an additional five hundred dollars.* The cars are loaded with optional features such as sunroofs and AM-FM stereos.

CORRECTED:
Many consumers prefer the sportier models. *Paying as much as an additional five hundred dollars,* customers select cars that are loaded with optional features such as sunroofs and AM-FM stereos. (The final sentence has been altered. "Customers" is now the subject; "select" is the verb.)

If a sentence fragment cannot easily be corrected by attaching it to another sentence, it should be rewritten so that it is a *complete* sentence with a subject and a predicate.

EXAMPLE:
Edwina resolved to begin a diet on Monday. *Trying on her new suits in front of a full-length mirror and noticing that they made her look like a sausage.* In the meantime, she thought it a shame to waste a perfectly good weekend by dieting.

CORRECTED:
Edwina resolved to begin a diet on Monday. She made this drastic decision after *trying on her new suits in front of a full-length mirror and noticing that they made her look like a sausage.* In the meantime, she thought it a shame to waste a perfectly good weekend by dieting. ("Trying on . . ." has been made part of a modifier within a new sentence, one that has the subject "she" and predicate "made this drastic decision. . . .")

Exercise 3

Examine the fragments that you located in Exercises 1 and 2. Correct each one. Try to use each of the three strategies described above.

Incorrectly Connected Sentences

When writing, all writers connect and combine sentences in a variety of ways. However, although there are many correct ways of combining complete sentences, inexperienced writers sometimes do not connect such sentences properly. Three rather common sentence errors may result from the improper joining of two or more sentences.

Fused Sentences

A fused sentence, sometimes referred to as a run-on sentence, occurs when two or more complete, grammatical sentences are punctuated as if they were one.

FUSED:
I love the new color of my room it is pink.

SEPARATE:
I love the new color of my room. It is pink.

FUSED:
Should the tax bill be defeated, the trustees will raise tuition by approximately 25% this will provide additional, needed revenue.

SEPARATE:
Should the tax bill be defeated, the trustees will raise tuition by approximately 25%. This will provide additional, needed revenue.

You can locate fused sentences by carefully reading your draft out loud. If you listen to the way you read, you will notice that your pitch generally falls at the end of a complete sentence, unless the sentence is a question that can be answered by "yes" or "no"—for example, "Do you understand?" As you read, pay attention to the pitch of your voice. If you notice that your pitch falls as it does at the end of a sentence, but you have not punctuated the structure you are examining to reflect that, look at the structure more closely. Locate the subject and the predicate; locate the simple subject and the verb. Do there seem to be two complete sentences or one?

Exercise 4

Read each of the following sentences out loud, paying special attention to the pitch of your voice. Identify any fused sentences.

1. Olivia examined the growth of her proteins in order to determine when she would be able to proceed to the next stage of her experiment.
2. Should the tax bill be defeated, the trustees will raise tuition by approximately 25% this is to provide additional, needed revenue for the institution.
3. Arthur Nathan, newly appointed lawyer for the Lakota County Tenants Union, decided that his constituents should meet immediately he wanted to set priorities for the next fiscal year.
4. Frank Alexander gave a poetry reading at the public library. To attract as large an audience as possible, he posted announcements on bulletin boards all over town.
5. Members of the Soft Pretzel Consortium thought of a means to market soft pretzels more effectively and to introduce the product to new customers they decided to make March "Eat a Soft Pretzel" month.

CORRECTING FUSED SENTENCES

Once you have located a fused sentence, there are a variety of ways of correcting it. However, the method you use to correct a fused sentence will affect the meaning of the corrected sentence(s). In revising this or *any* sentence error, therefore, you must create a sentence that is not only grammatical but that also closely expresses your intended meaning.

A simple way to correct a fused sentence is to locate the two or more complete sentences within it, then connect these sentences properly, using either a semicolon (;) or a semicolon *plus* one of the following expressions:

after all	for example	next
also	incidentally	nonetheless
anyway	indeed	otherwise
as a result	instead	on the contrary

at any rate	in addition	on the other hand
at the same time	in fact	still
besides	in other words	then
consequently	likewise	therefore
even so	meanwhile	thus
finally	moreover	
	nevertheless	

Here are some examples of how to correct fused sentences.

FUSED:
[The catalogue wasn't available until the end of September]
[this caused many complaints.]

CORRECTED:
The catalogue wasn't available until the end of September;
this caused many complaints.

FUSED:
[Many students were confused about the procedure] [the
Associate Registrar remained in the room to answer
questions.]

CORRECTED:
Many students were confused about the procedure; therefore,
the Associate Registrar remained in the room to answer
questions.

A fused sentence can also be corrected by connecting the sentences within
it with "and," "but," "for," "nor," "or," "yet," or "so" plus a comma.

FUSED:
[Many students were confused about the procedure] [the
Associate Registrar remained in the room to answer
questions.]

CORRECTED:
Many students were confused about the procedure, so the
Associate Registrar remained in the room to answer
questions.

Another way to correct a fused sentence is to incorporate one of the
sentences into the other. For example, the fused sentence "Martha cheated

it bothered me" consists of two sentences: "Martha cheated" and "It bothered me." These two sentences can be combined to form one sentence: "That Martha cheated bothered me." Notice that the first sentence, "Martha cheated," has been made the subject of the new, combined sentence: *That Martha cheated* bothered me.

Here are some other examples.

FUSED:
[It is customary to use a comma with connecting words such as "and" or "but"] [this is not always necessary.]

CORRECTED:
Although it is customary to use a comma with connecting words such as "and" or "but," this is not always necessary. (The first sentence has been made into a sentence modifier.)

FUSED:
[The accountants completed their audit of our books] [they are now ready to present their findings.]

CORRECTED:
Having completed their audit of our books, the accountants are now ready to present their findings. (The first sentence has been made into a verb modifier.)

FUSED:
[The plumber is competent at a variety of tasks] [he doesn't overcharge.]

CORRECTED:
The plumber, *who is competent at a variety of tasks,* doesn't overcharge. (The first sentence has been made into a noun modifier.)

Exercise 5

Reread each of the sentences in Exercise 4 out loud. Use one of the methods described to correct any fused sentences.

Exercise 6

Read the following excerpt out loud. Locate and correct any fused sentences.

The Army Research Office, the Office of Naval Research, and the Air Force Office of Scientific Research have announced Phase Two of a five-year Defense Department program it is intended to upgrade university scientific research. Phase Two has been instituted so that universities can apply for funding to be used for the acquisition of laboratory equipment. Funding awards will be highly selective therefore institutions are advised to monitor proposal submissions closely.

The Department of Defense has published a list of what it considers to be the key research areas this list is available upon request. It is advisable for an individual to determine if his research is related to one or several of these areas *before* he creates a proposal—although some funding awards will be made to projects in other areas.

Cost sharing is encouraged though not required. Proposals for equipment which is purely for instruction will not be considered only proposals from institutions with graduate training programs are eligible.

Comma Splices

A comma splice is a sentence structure error similar to a fused sentence. It is a structure consisting of two or more sentences connected with *just* a comma or commas. Here are some examples of comma splices.

> I got tired, I took a nap.
> The weather turned cold, vegetables in the garden died.
> The test was difficult, many students didn't do well.

These sentences are incorrect because normally the only punctuation mark that can be used by itself to connect sentences is the semicolon (;).

Although this may be time consuming, you can locate comma splices by circling every comma that you find, in pencil. Then examine the structures that *precede* and *follow* each comma. Make sure that these structures are *not* complete sentences.

> sentence, sentence = comma splice

After you have finished examining all the structures that precede and follow commas, erase the circles.

Exercise 7

Circle the commas in the following sentences, then examine the structures that precede and follow each comma. Use this procedure to find all the comma splices.

1.   Although moderate exercise is beneficial, excessive exercise can be dangerous, especially to those persons who are not particularly active.

2.   Another aspect of my writing behavior which needs improvement is my attitude, I spend hours worrying about every assignment before I begin writing.

3.   In revising any sentence error, it is important to create a sentence which is grammatical, also the sentence must reflect the meaning intended by the writer.

4.   Here are four pictures, two illustrate the major features of the device, while the other two indicate how it is used.

5.   Having mounted the pictures with care, Professor Blunt did not appreciate the careless paint job, he complained to the President.

CORRECTING COMMA SPLICES

To correct comma splices, you can use the same methods you used to correct fused sentences. That is, the sentences within a comma splice may be *joined* with (1) a semicolon, (2) a semicolon plus an appropriate connecting word, or (3) a comma plus "and," "but," "for," "nor," "or," "yet," or "so." Or the sentences may be *combined* by making one part of the other.

Exercise 8

Correct the comma splices that you located in Exercise 7.

Exercise 9

Read the following text. Locate and correct any comma splices or fused sentences.

Science fiction films seem to be more prevalent and of higher quality these days. Although it is difficult to determine who, if anyone, we have to thank for this delightful state of affairs, Stanley Kubrick who brought us *2001: A Space Odyssey* ought to be a prime contender. And George Lucas, producer/director of the *Star Wars* films, is another obvious choice.

2001: A Space Odyssey was an important film because it was one of the first science fiction films to appeal to a mass audience, not to just an audience of "sci-fi" buffs. This mass audience appeal, however, could not have been predicted at the time it was a triumph for Kubrick and those other individuals responsible for the film. They took a considerable risk. *2001* was not a typical low-budget science fiction film; it cost a great deal to produce. The film makers gambled that superb, state-of-the-art special effects coupled with the exploration of a serious theme (the future evolution of the human race) would attract many viewers. It did.

George Lucas's three *Star Wars* films, all box office smashes, have made a powerful statement, science fiction films are lucrative. Because of the overwhelming audience response to Lucas's films, other directors who may wish to make innovative science fiction films won't have to contend with the notion that science fiction films are risky business, box office "poison." As to the qualities of Lucas's films that make them so appealing to audiences of all ages, it is difficult to determine exactly what they are certainly the remarkable special effects have a lot to do with it. But there are, very likely, other contributing factors: the characters are likable and easy to identify with (except Darth Vader, of course), the battle of good against evil depicted in all of the films is timeless.

There are certainly many other individuals and many other factors responsible for the many excellent, contemporary science fiction films, however, special thanks go to Kubrick and Lucas.

Excessively Coordinated (Run-On) Sentences

A run-on sentence is a sentence in which an excessive number of complete sentences have been connected with "and," "but," "for," "so," or "and so." Such sentences often sound loose and strung together. Examine these two examples of run-on sentences.

> The hearing was set for Friday, September 28, *but* all of the
> witnesses could not be available, *so* the hearing has been

rescheduled for the following Friday, *and* now the witnesses can attend.

Most of the students enrolled in four courses, *so* all of the sections of freshman writing were filled before classes began, *and* the Assistant Dean offered fifteen additional sections of Introductory Writing.

Most often, a run-on sentence can be improved by making one or more of the connected sentences a part of the rest. Examine these revisions of the two run-on sentences:

REVISED:
The hearing, which was originally scheduled for Friday, September 28, was rescheduled for the following Friday so that all witnesses would be able to attend.

REVISED:
Since most of the students enrolled in four courses, all of the sections of freshman writing were filled before classes began, causing the Assistant Dean to open fifteen additional sections of Introductory Writing.

Sometimes it is not possible to combine all the important information in a run-on sentence into one new sentence. In such instances two or more sentences may be necessary.

EXAMPLE:
The Council members examined all the possible solutions to the problem, *but* they were unable to agree upon one, *and* so they recommended that a subcommittee be established to study the two best solutions, *and* then this subcommittee would recommend one solution to the Council.

REVISED:
After examining all possible solutions to the problem, the Council members were unable to agree upon one. They therefore recommended that a subcommittee be established to

study the two best solutions and to recommend one to the Council.

Exercise 10

Read the following text. Locate and correct any fused sentences, comma splices, and run-on sentences.

The distinction between a *vacation* and a *trip* is a useful one, especially if you are over thirty, gainfully employed, and the parent of one or more children. Let me explain. For some time, I had been returning from *what I thought were* family vacations and I often felt worn-out and more exhausted than I felt before we left on vacation, but it never occurred to me that the reason I was exhausted was that I, in fact, had not been on a vacation. Now, I had always thought that I was suffering from imaginary exhaustion. Or perhaps I had tired blood. Recently, however, my friend, Barbara, informed me that I have never taken a vacation, only trips. What follows is an explanation of the difference between vacations and trips, which I found vastly useful, perhaps you will too.

Trips: A trip is a period of time during which you *do* something, for example explore all of Yellowstone Park in four days, or drive from Texas to New England and back again in one week. Trips are usually educational. ("Look. Isn't the Grand Canyon exciting. Did you know that it was formed by the action of water on sandstone, which causes erosion.") Children also invariably accompany parents on trips, so that they (the children) can have a fun, but educational, experience. Trips are commonly mistaken for vacations because you take off from work to go on a trip, but trips are not vacations, and trips are *work,* hard work, they leave you exhausted.

Vacations: A vacation is a period of time during which you *do nothing* (except lie around and eat). Vacations provide individuals with the opportunity to rest and to gain weight. Vacations are not educational, in fact they are downright useless. Persons who take vacations are persons who indulge themselves shamelessly. These individuals usually go to *great* lengths to leave their precious children with grandma and grandpa (or at Camp PowWow). You will know if you've really had a vacation, no matter what you think, if you feel rested—even invigorated—upon your return.

I am an individual who has long confused trips for vacations, so this distinction has proved enormously useful to me. I may never go on another trip again.

Sentences with Modification Problems

As you recall, a common type of sentence fragment is a fragmented modifier. Such modifiers are mistaken for sentences because they resemble sentences. Modifiers, especially if they are long, are often mishandled by apprentice writers, who may lose track of their function within a particular sentence. Two rather common types of awkward sentences that may result from a writer's confusion over how a modifier is operating within a sentence are awkward sentences that contain misplaced modifiers and awkward sentences that contain dangling modifiers.

Misplaced Modifiers

Word order is important in English; the language has rules that govern placement of structures within a sentence. In general, a modifier should be placed as near the word being modified as permissible. It is wise to avoid unnecessary separation of related structures within a sentence. For a modifier to convey the precise meaning the writer intended, it must be properly placed.

> MISPLACED:
> *When grading exams*, students are warned that Professor Zeal takes off points for misspelled words.

"When grading exams" is placed before "students" and seems, therefore, to be describing what students do. This confuses the reader, who assumes that Professor Zeal grades exams.

> REVISED:
> Professor Zeal warns his students that he takes off points for misspelled words *when grading exams*.

The modifier has been moved closer to the verb that it modifies. *When does Professor Zeal take off points? When grading exams.*

> MISPLACED:
> The new coffee machine attracted employees from every division *in the lounge*.

"In the lounge" is placed immediately after "division," and seems to be modifying it: the lounge has divisions.

> REVISED:
> The new coffee machine *in the lounge* attracted employees
> from every division.

The modifier has been moved so that it is placed directly after the words it modifies. *Where* is the coffee machine? *In the lounge.*

As with many other problem sentences, sentences with misplaced modifiers may sound strange if they are read aloud. Once you have located a suspicious-sounding sentence, examine word groups within this sentence to determine whether the word groups function as modifiers. If so, be certain that these modifiers are placed as near the words they modify as possible.

Exercise 11

Examine each of the following sentences. Locate and underline any misplaced modifiers.

1.   The children usually attract a lot of attention dressed up in their Halloween costumes going from door to door.

2.   My roommate agreed to attend my sociology lecture for me when he was half asleep.

3.   Making changes has enabled us to better understand one another to compensate for our differences.

4.   All of the senior citizens ordered seven-course dinners from the Belmont district after winning the bowling tournament.

5.   It's a great feeling when I go to my old neighborhood and people remember me who were friends long ago.

6.   Since my roommate refuses to turn down the volume of his stereo, I am going home to mom and dad which is shattering.

7.   Traveling to the Upper Peninsula last summer was a great idea which was breathtakingly beautiful.

8.   She studied her algebra sitting at a table in the library.

9.   Many of the dealers test drove the new cars arriving early.

10.   Those students must leave the premises word-processing in the Computer Room by 5 p.m.

Exercise 12

Read the following text. Locate and underline any misplaced modifiers.

Students who are already majoring in other areas of music and who have developed a strong interest in composition may apply to the chair of the composition department for acceptance as a major. In addition, those individuals must also be able to demonstrate an aptitude in composition with an interest in being accepted as majors. It is also permissible for a student to add a major in music composition to an already held major for a double major in music performance. Most often this is done by the student at the end of his or her sophomore year, at which time application must be submitted to the chair and subsequently to the Dean of the College of music for initial approval. A double major can be recognized by the State Department of Teacher Certification; however, the process is procedurally complicated. Therefore, students are advised to discuss this matter with one of the department Education Advisors who wish to exercise this option.

CORRECTING MISPLACED MODIFIERS

Several methods can be used to revise sentences with misplaced modifiers. One way to correct a sentence with a misplaced modifier is to move the modifier so that it *follows* the word it modifies.

Misplaced:
The university is certifying people by awarding them degrees *who are not educated.*

Corrected:
The university is certifying people *who are not educated* by awarding them degrees.

Misplaced:
The children volunteered to help rake the leaves *while they were eating dessert.*

Corrected:
The children volunteered *while they were eating dessert* to help rake the leaves.

Sometimes revising a sentence with a misplaced modifier is easier if the modifier is moved to the beginning of the sentence. Therefore, if the modified word is at the beginning of a sentence, move the misplaced modifier so that it precedes the sentence, and place a comma after the modifier.

> MISPLACED:
> The tourists found a lost purse *walking through the museum.*
>
> CORRECTED:
> *Walking through the museum,* the tourists found a lost purse.

Exercise 13

Revise the sentences with misplaced modifiers in Exercises 11 and 12. Use both of the suggested methods.

Dangling Modifiers

Sometimes, especially if a modifier is long, a writer can lose track of the modifier's function completely enough so that the sentence of which that modifier is a part *does not* contain the word, usually a noun, that is being modified. Here is an example of such a sentence:

> Lying on the beach, the sun felt hot.

It is apparent that "lying on the beach" is a modifier, but what word (or word group) is it modifying? Certainly, the *sun* cannot be lying on the beach. A modifier that is part of a sentence that does not contain the word being modified is called a *dangling modifier.* Dangling modifiers are usually found at the beginning or end of a sentence.

To locate dangling modifiers, examine structures that *precede* or *follow* a sentence, especially if those structures are separated from the sentence by a comma. Such structures should modify a specific word or words within the sentence.

Here are some examples of sentences with *introductory* or *final* dangling modifiers.

> *Trying to sleep,* the noise was deafening. (Introductory)
>
> *Although an A student,* the professor was disappointed with his performance. (Introductory)

The lawn was mowed, *instead of doing the laundry.* (Final)

The moon rose, *thinking romantic thoughts.* (Final)

Sentences with introductory dangling modifiers often have the word "it" or "there" as the subject. If you tend to write sentences with dangling modifiers, carefully examine sentences that contain introductory modifiers when those sentences have the subject "it" or "there."

Here are some examples of such sentences.

Lying on the beach, *it* was hot.

Approaching the end of the semester, *there* was a lot of frustration.

Examining the data, *there* were problems.

Exercise 14

Carefully examine all modifying structures in each of the following sentences, especially those that come at the beginning or end of a sentence. Then locate and underline any dangling modifiers.

1. Alienating everyone with his nasty remarks, we decided to leave.
2. Watching the parade from the balcony, the tubas sounded particularly loud.
3. There were numerous mistakes found in the text, proofreading it carefully.
4. When just a lad, it was hard to understand women.
5. Having examined the projections for the fiscal year 1984, the auditors determined that there would be a shortage of funds.
6. After considering all of the options, prudence was ultimately decided upon.
7. Upset by the lack of enthusiasm, the auditorium gradually became empty.
8. Spending a great deal of time evaluating his students' essays, the results weren't appreciated.
9. The rain was pouring down in sheets, becoming drenched to the bone.
10. Working diligently to compile the necessary information, the results were forwarded to the federal government.

Exercise 15

Read the following excerpt. Locate and underline any dangling modifiers.

It is very easy to plan a surprise party. Thinking of the most important thing, the birthday girl must be kept unaware of the party. Though this sounds difficult, it isn't really. The trick is to act nonchalantly about the special day, leaving no trace of unusual behavior. That way, when planning it, there will be no possible signal of the party. The second most important thing is to make sure no one else gives away the surprise. Doing all the inviting over the phone and not writing anything down, it will preserve the surprise. Finally, it is crucial to think of a way to get the birthday person to the party site, gradually leading her to the chosen location. Planning carefully, the party will be both a surprise and a success.

CORRECTING DANGLING MODIFIERS

Sometimes understanding the nature of a sentence structure problem helps one to select a means of correcting it. Dangling modifiers that come at the beginning of the sentence *should*, but do not, modify the subject of the sentence. Therefore, a good strategy for rewriting a sentence with an introductory dangling modifier is to rework the main sentence so that the subject of the sentence is also the word being modified.

DANGLING MODIFIER:
Lying on the beach, the sun felt hot.

CORRECTED:
Lying on the beach, *Marcia* thought the sun felt hot.

DANGLING MODIFIER:
Examining the data, there were problems.

CORRECTED:
Examining the data, *the auditors* found problems.

DANGLING MODIFIER:
Examining the data, it was found that there were errors.

CORRECTED:
Examining the data, *the auditors* found errors.

Since *not* all dangling modifiers precede sentences, another useful strategy for revising sentences with dangling modifiers is to alter the structure of the modifier itself.

> DANGLING MODIFIER:
> *Annoying everyone with his animal noises,* people left the room.

> MODIFIER CHANGED:
> *Because Ralph was annoying everyone with his animal noises,* people left the room.

> DANGLING MODIFIER:
> The essays were graded early, *trying to finish his work before the weekend.*

> MODIFIER CHANGED:
> The essays were graded early *because Professor Finick was trying to finish his work before the weekend.*

Notice that the dangling modifier in each of these sentences was changed into a *clause,* a structure that contains a subject and a verb. Notice also that these new clause modifiers now modify the verb in each sentence.

A problem closely related to, and sometimes caused by, a dangling modifier problem is the difficulty created when a modifier contains two or more verbals[1] that do not modify the same noun. Here are some examples.

> In protecting a child, a watchdog can bark, whenever *approaching* a stranger or *attacking* an intruder. ("Attacking" clearly modifies "watchdog"; "approaching" may modify either "child" or "watchdog.")

> *Having* an article written about the house and *realizing* that the back yard houses an apple orchard, you probably understand what an unusual structure it is. ("Realizing" probably modifies the subject of the sentence, "you," but "having" cannot logically modify "you.")

---

[1] A *verbal* is a verb form that can be used as a noun or as a modifier (adjective, adverb); a verbal can *never* function as a main verb in a sentence.

A sentence with this type of modification problem can usually be revised by altering the structure of a portion of the modifier.

> EXAMPLE:
> [Eating all of the left-over pie and *becoming furious when there was none left*,] Josie angered her dad.

> CORRECTED:
> Eating all of the left-over pie, Josie angered her dad, who became furious when he discovered that there was none left.

Exercise 16

Revise each of these sentences.

1. In examining data, an auditor can request records whenever committing fraud or suspecting wrongdoing.

2. Traveling to a warm locale and catering to your every whim, resorts offer a vacationer a pleasurable experience.

3. A teacher can offer students help whenever experiencing trouble in revising or sensing that some are experiencing difficulty.

Exercise 17

Revise all the sentences in Exercises 14 and 15 that contain dangling modifiers.

Ineffective Passive Sentences

Effective writers vary the structure of their sentences so that their discourse does not become monotonous. Likewise, they vary their sentences to meet the requirements of a particular context. One particular stylistic variant, the passive, is quite useful—perhaps indispensable—in some contexts.

However, as you learned in Chapter 5, "Revising Rough Drafts," unpurposeful passive sentence structure can result in ambiguity and convolution in a text. In editing, then, it is important that you be able to recognize the passive structure and to determine whether it is appropriate in a specific context.

When the subject *performs* the action in a sentence, the verb is *active*. When the subject *receives* the action in a sentence, the verb is *passive*. Consider these examples:

> ACTIVE:
> The singer dropped the lyrics.
> The animal pawed the meat.
>
> PASSIVE:
> The lyrics were dropped by the singer.
> The meat was pawed by the animal.

As you can see, whether a sentence is passive or active depends upon who or what is performing or receiving the action in the sentence. The passive may be formed by using the appropriate form of the verb *be*—am, is, are, was, were, been, being—with the past participle of the main verb; for example, "were dropped," "was pawed." Generally, sentences with active verbs are more direct, economical, and accessible to the reader than sentences with passive verbs. Therefore, except in specific instances, which we will discuss, active verbs are preferable, especially since inexperienced writers sometimes produce passive sentences that sound pretentious—or even silly:

> Reeva's personal hygiene should be watched by her if she wishes to be befriended by me.
>
> A rebuttal to Congressman Bean should be issued by Dr. Booth because Congressman Bean's ideas aren't liked by him.

In the remainder of this section, we will consider, in order, strategies that will help you determine whether an awkward-sounding sentence is passive, strategies that will help you correct ineffective passive sentences, and guidelines to help you recognize situations in which the passive voice is appropriate.

Overblown passive sentences often sound "funny" if read out loud. Still, in order to revise any particular problem sentence, a writer must first be able to identify the cause of the problem: Why, exactly, does a particular sentence sound odd?

The *simplest* way to identify the passive is to determine whether the subject and the object within a sentence are in reverse order:

NORMAL ORDER:
John hit Mary.

PASSIVE:
Mary was hit by John.

Unfortunately, examining the order of the subject and object within a sentence is not always possible because in passive sentences the "former" subject and the word "by" can be deleted:

NORMAL ORDER:
John hit Mary.

PASSIVE:
Mary was hit by John.

DELETED "FORMER SUBJECT + BY":
Mary was hit. (by John)

Therefore, the most *accurate* way to identify a passive is to examine the verb. If the verb is in its *past participle* form, preceded by a form of the helping verb *be*, such as is, am, are, was, or will be, the sentence is passive.

Here are some more simple examples of passive sentences.

NORMAL ORDER:
John *hit* Mary.

PASSIVE:
Mary *was hit* by John.

PASSIVE:
Mary *was hit*. (be + past participle)

NORMAL ORDER:
The dog *has frightened* the kids.

PASSIVE:
The kids *have been frightened* by the dog.

PASSIVE:
The kids *have been frightened.* (be + past participle)

NORMAL ORDER:
Joe *bought* the coupons.

PASSIVE:
The coupons *were bought* by Joe.

PASSIVE:
The coupons *were bought.* (be + past participle)

Any sentence may, potentially, have more than one passive structure within it, since modifiers within sentences may also contain verbs. Here are some examples of sentences that contain passive structures within modifiers. Note that some of these sentences contain more than one passive structure.

The children read the books that *were ordered* by their teacher.
The books *were read* by the third graders who *were transferred* from the other district.
The meeting *was adjourned* after the report *was read.*
No one could understand the lecture that *was given* by the visiting professor from Sweden.

Exercise 18

Some of the following sentences are passive or contain passive constructions. Locate any sentences that are *awkward* because of the passive.

1. The results of the survey were disseminated to all interested parties.
2. The members of the committee were angered by the mayor's charge that they were influenced by representatives from the business community.
3. Newspapers should be read by citizens of Toledo who are interested in the riverside development.
4. Consumers who request information about phosphate content in Lake Erie will be sent the most recent data.
5. The textbook, *Style,* was admired by Dr. Phelps, so a letter was written by her to the author.

6. Justin's eating habits need to be changed by him if weight is to be lost on his latest diet.

7. Graffiti is often written by adolescents as they attempt to express their feelings of frustration.

8. The books must be ordered by the Selection Committee by May 1 if they are to be received in time for classes.

9. Preliminary schedules were issued by the Office of Registration and Records so that student interest in course offerings could be assessed by department administrators.

10. Danstar and Associates conducted a market analysis prior to suggesting an advertising campaign for their client.

Exercise 19

Read the following excerpt and locate awkward passives:

Of course, the view being presented here is idealistic, but at the very least, teachers ought to be familiar with English sentence structure. Otherwise, students won't be able to be helped much by them. To illustrate this point, here is another example. Sentences such as this one are often written by students and, subsequently, encountered by teachers:

> I would advise my brother to join a fraternity because I feel
> that participate in a fraternity is a rewarding experience.

Of course, no teacher would have difficulty recognizing that there is something wrong with the form of the word "participate." Changing "participate" to "participation" or "participating" might also be suggested by the teacher. The question "why" arises, however, and "because it sounds better" is hardly a satisfactory answer. And yet half of the teachers shown this sentence by us were unable to explain *why* "participate" is wrong and "participating" or "to participate" are right.

CORRECTING INEFFECTIVE PASSIVE SENTENCES

Once you have located awkward and/or pretentious passives, you should eliminate them. Passive sentences and constructions should be rewritten so that the subject *precedes* the object. Observe the differences between the active and passive forms of the following pairs of sentences. Note that in some instances deleted subjects must be reinserted in order for a passive sentence or construction to be made active:

PASSIVE:
The container *was emptied* by the *janitor.*

ACTIVE:
The janitor *emptied* the container.

PASSIVE:
Interstate 22 *was avoided* regularly.

ACTIVE:
We *avoided* Interstate 22 regularly.

PASSIVE:
The data that *was compiled* last week *is* already *considered* to be inaccurate.

ACTIVE:
Dean Heber already *considers* the data that we *compiled* last week to be inaccurate.

Although a passive construction may not cause an individual sentence to sound awkward, too many passive constructions may cause a text to sound pompous or overblown. Passives, therefore, should be used selectively. Here are some of the circumstances in which the passive may be used.

1. Use the passive when the person or thing that performed a particular action is not known.

NORMAL ORDER:
Someone made my dress in Italy.

PASSIVE + DELETION:
My dress was made in Italy. (by someone)

NORMAL ORDER:
Something or someone knocked over our garbage can last week.

Passive + Deletion:
Our garbage can was knocked over last week. (by someone or something)

2. Use the passive in business or professional correspondence to be tactful. In business or professional correspondence, the passive may be indispensable when the writer wishes, tactfully, to avoid mentioning who was careless or who made an error.

Normal Order:
Here is another copy of the report that you misplaced.

Passive + Deletion:
Here is another copy of the report that was misplaced. (by you)

Normal Order:
Yesterday we received a corrected copy of the data that Mr. Jones compiled incorrectly.

Passive + Deletion:
Yesterday we received a corrected copy of the data that was compiled incorrectly. (by Mr. Jones)

3. Use the passive to avoid unnecessary repetition. Sometimes using the passive enables a writer to delete the subjects of sentences and thus avoid undue repetition of the same word or phrase.

Next, the experimenters obtained samples of water and infused these samples with asbestos. Following that, the experimenters diluted the samples until the amount of asbestos was one million fibers per gallon of water. The experimenters put salmon roe into the diluted samples and placed these samples in an incubator. The experimenters evaluated the growth rate of the roe every five hours for three days.

Revised with Passive + Deletion:
Next, the experimenters obtained samples of water and infused these samples with asbestos. Following that, the samples were diluted until the amount of asbestos was one million fibers per gallon of water. Salmon roe were put into the diluted samples, which were placed in

an incubator. The growth rate of the roe was evaluated every five hours for three days.

4. Use the passive to change the focus or emphasis within a sentence.

EMPHASIS ON THE SUBJECT:
Roman Klinski wrote the script for *Gang War* in 1965.

EMPHASIS ON THE OBJECT:
The script for *Gang War* was written by Roman Klinski in 1965.
The script for *Gang War* was written in 1965.

The passive is a powerful—and often indispensable—stylistic alternative available to the writer. But every text should be edited so that awkward and/or unnecessary passives are eliminated.

Exercise 20

Rewrite all the awkward-sounding sentences or constructions that you located in Exercise 18.

Exercise 21

Reread the excerpt presented in Exercise 19. Revise any *awkward* or unnecessary passive constructions.

Sentences with Faulty Parallelism

Varying sentence structure to meet the requirements of a particular context is one of the most exciting, pleasurable aspects of writing. One stylistic device that is commonly used for a variety of purposes—for emphasis, for clarity, for creating rhythm within a text—is parallelism. Parallelism involves the use of two or more structures of similar grammatical *form* within a sentence. These structures should also *function* in the same manner within the sentence. For example, a sentence with two or more predicates that are similar in form contains parallel structures.

SUBJECT	PREDICATES (PARALLEL STRUCTURES)
The children in second grade	watched a science film painted a picture worked on math problems

SENTENCE:
The children in second grade *watched a science film, painted a picture,* and *worked on math problems.*

Here are more examples of sentences that contain parallel structures.

SUBJECT	VERB	OBJECTS (PARALLEL STRUCTURES)
Evelyn and her sister	really hate	swimming laps hiking uphill playing tennis strenuously

SENTENCE:
Evelyn and her sister really hate *swimming laps, hiking uphill,* and *playing tennis strenuously.*

SUBJECT	SUBJECT MODIFIERS (PARALLEL STRUCTURES)	PREDICATE
The rationale	for the policy for the procedures for the outcome	was not clear

SENTENCE:
The rationale *for the policy, for the procedures,* and *for the outcome* was not clear.

Faulty parallelism is a sentence structure problem that results when the function and/or the form of repeated elements are/is not the same. At the very least, sentences with faulty parallelism sound "bumpy" and are considered awkward.

PARALLEL:
The children in second grade *watched a science film, painted a picture, and worked on a math problem.*

NOT PARALLEL:
The children in second grade *watched a science film, painted a picture, and were also working on a math problem.*

Here are some additional examples of sentences with faulty parallelism.

NOT PARALLEL:

                                                              VERB
The visitors from Brent State University could *visit* classes,
VERB   *COULD JUST + VERB*
tour the new Recreation Center, or *could just wander* around the campus.

PARALLEL:

                                                              VERB
The visitors from Brent State University could *visit* classes,
VERB   *VERB*
tour the new Recreation Center, or *wander* around the campus.

NOT PARALLEL:

                        ADJECTIVE   ADJECTIVE
The report was *readable, comprehensive,* and an
  ADJECTIVE + NOUN
interesting document.

PARALLEL:

                        ADJECTIVE   ADJECTIVE   ADJECTIVE
The report was *readable, comprehensive,* and *interesting.*

NOT PARALLEL:

                    OBJECTS OF VERBAL "READING"
After reading *government documents, newspapers,* and
  NEW VERBAL + OBJECT
scanning periodical articles, the investigator was ready to begin the next stage of her project.

PARALLEL:

OBJECTS OF VERBAL "READING"

After reading/*government documents, newspapers,* and *periodical articles,* the investigator was ready to begin the next stage of her project.

Sometimes when repeated elements within a sentence do not share the same form and function, ambiguity results. A reader may not be able to determine exactly how structures are supposed to function within a sentence because there are two or more possibilities. Examine this sentence that exhibits faulty parallelism:

Mike Enas and his mime troup make their audiences excited and enjoy themselves.

It is not clear whether "make their audiences excited" and "enjoy themselves" are two predicates:

SUBJECT	PREDICATES
Mike Enas and his mime troupe	make their audience excited
	enjoy themselves

or whether "excited" and "enjoy themselves" are both meant to modify "audiences":

SUBJECT   VERB   OBJECT   OBJECT MODIFIERS

Mike Enas and his mime troupe make their audiences excited /
                                           enjoy themselves

In this instance, the sentence is ambiguous because of faulty parallelism. *Who* enjoy themselves—Mike Enas and his troupe or their audiences?

CORRECTING FAULTY PARALLELISM

Revising a sentence that exhibits faulty parallelism requires at least two steps. First, the repeated elements within the sentence must be identified:

                                  1   *2*   *3*

The new senator was (idealistic,) (naive,) and (he wanted to change the world overnight.)

                                1   *2*

After surveying (high school seniors,) (high school

3
principals,) and (getting information from high school teachers also,) the Articulation Committee made several recommendations.

$\qquad$1$\qquad$2$\qquad\qquad\qquad$3
Without sufficient (food,) (water,) and (if it's not warm enough), pet lizards will not survive long.

Once the elements within a sentence that *should* be parallel are identified, the sentence may be rewritten. There are several strategies that may be used to revise a sentence with faulty parallelism. Sometimes the easiest way to correct a sentence with faulty parallelism is to rework one or more of the repeated structures so that they are similar in form and function. In general, when a problem involves three or more elements, it is most efficient to change the form of the nonparallel element so that it resembles the form of the other(s):

NOT PARALLEL:
The zoning commission decided to spend the next meeting
$\qquad\qquad\qquad\qquad$1
(assessing proposals for changes in zoning), (examining
$\qquad$2$\qquad\qquad\qquad\qquad\qquad\qquad\qquad\qquad$3
requests for zoning variances), and (engaged in a review of the budget).

Elements 1 and 2 have the same form; element 3 does not. Change element 3.

PARALLEL:
The zoning commission decided to spend the next meeting
$\qquad\qquad\qquad\qquad$1
(assessing proposals for changes in zoning), (examining
$\qquad$2$\qquad\qquad\qquad\qquad\qquad\qquad\qquad\qquad$3
requests for zoning variances), and (reviewing the budget).

Sometimes it is easier to change two similar structures so that they resemble a dissimilar third, however:

NOT PARALLEL:

$\qquad\qquad\qquad\qquad\qquad\qquad\qquad\qquad\qquad\qquad\qquad$1
Professor Blaze makes students in his class feel (excited),

2   3
(stimulated), and (free to ask questions about concepts that puzzle them).

In the case of the above sentence it is probably less time consuming to change "excited" and "stimulated" so that they resemble structure 3 than it is to change structure 3 to an adjective. Such an adjective would need to replace "free to ask questions about concepts that puzzle them."

PARALLEL:
Professor Blaze makes students in his class feel (excited
1   2
about mathematics), (stimulated by new ways of viewing the
3
world), and (free to ask questions about concepts that puzzle them).

If a sentence is ambiguous because the function or form of one or more of the elements is unclear, be certain to decide *what* you intend the sentence to mean and to remove any ambiguity through your revision.

NOT PARALLEL:
Mike Enas and his mime troupe make their audiences excited and enjoy themselves.

Question: "Do I mean that Mike Enas and his troupe make their audiences excited and also make their audiences enjoy themselves? Or do I mean that Mike Enas and his troupe excite their audiences, but he and his troupe really enjoy themselves, too?"

Answer: "I really meant to say that Mike Enas and his troupe do two things to audiences: make them excited; make them enjoy themselves. Therefore, the two structures I need to make similar in form and function are two modifiers of 'audiences.'"

Mike Enas and his mime troupe make their audiences
(happy) and (excited).

Note: If "happy" is not as accurate as you wish it to be as a replacement for "enjoy themselves," you will need to try another revision strategy, perhaps the strategy suggested next. Or you might wish to restructure the entire sentence: "Mike Enas and his troupe create both excitement and enjoyment for their audiences."

Finally, if adjusting the repeated elements so that they are parallel does not work, you can correct a sentence with faulty parallelism by making a *separate* sentence out of the element that is not similar to the others.

NOT PARALLEL:

Eben made his employees feel (resentfully)[1], (unappreciated)[2],

and (as if they never had any worthwhile ideas or made any valuable contributions)[3].

PARALLEL:

Eben made his employees feel (resentful)[1] and (unappreciated)[2]. Not only that, many of his employees felt that he thought they never had any worthwhile ideas or made any valuable contributions.

Notice the use of connective devices, both *within* the original sentence and *between* the original sentence and the new one.

Exercise 22

Examine the following sentences and rewrite any sentences that exhibit faulty parallelism.

1.   After the election, newly elected officials were requested to meet with members of the city council, with nonelected city officials, and to have a session with the city planner.

2.   The New York Opera Company inspire their audiences to attend opera more often and have a wonderful time.

3.   On Saturdays many of the undergraduate students at BSU go shopping or they stay in their rooms and play cards, watch TV, listen to the stereo, or whatever their hearts desire.

4.   The enforcement of the 55-mph speed limit is beneficial for several reasons: it lessens the number of traffic fatalities, it protects the nation's highways, and gasoline is also conserved as a result.

5.   Every member of Student Senate considered Ralph Wonderby to be intelligent, sensitive, and a good person.

6.   Grocery items are arranged to cause consumers to purchase particular items and make shoppers feel hungry.

7.   The other team members didn't want Joel Weejun to be on the team since they felt that Joel had consistently performed poorly and with no practice.

8.   Arthur Jones was concerned that his roommates wouldn't allow him to keep his pet rabbit, BunBun, that they wouldn't let him practice his bass guitar at night, or visit Mindy Lou Smith.

9.   By interviewing fifty registered nurses, forty interns and residents, and talking to eighty patients at Riverford Hospital, Dr. Sullivan was able to reach some startling conclusions.

10.   My major objectives as Director of the Hofsas Yarn Center will be to provide consumers with a variety of yarn colors, textures, and qualities as well as responsiveness to their many other yarn needs.

Exercise 23

Read the following excerpt and revise any sentences that exhibit faulty parallelism.

Super Bowl XI had everything one could want: a close game, a battle of talented quarterbacks, and no official made a questionable call. Not everyone, however, felt as excited, thrilled and ready to watch the game beforehand as I did. First, I stocked the refrigerator with cold cuts, plenty of good drink, and I purchased lots of chips and dips. The game itself didn't start until 4:30, so I had time to gather all my clippings about the opposing teams; I enjoyed this almost as much as I did watching the game and my friends. Armed with statistics, and I was relieved by the odds, and hoping for a real showdown, I sat down to watch the best Super Bowl ever. I wasn't disappointed.

General Strategies for Editing Sentences

Now that we have reviewed some of the most common types of sentence structure errors and provided strategies for identifying and correcting them, we will conclude with several more general editing strategies. You will find that these strategies will help you become more proficient at both identifying and correcting the kinds of sentence errors that you commit.

Strategy: To locate errors in sentence structure, read your text out loud.

The best way to catch sentence structure errors is to read your text out loud and *listen* to it. Mark any sentence that sounds suspicious with pencilled brackets ([ ]). You may also wish to place a check ($\sqrt{}$) in the left margin next to each marked sentence. When you have completed your reading, give each of the marked sentences your attention. Reread every one out loud. If possible, ask a friend or roommate to listen to your questionable sentences, too.

A variation of this technique is to read an essay out loud *backwards*. This disassociates sentences from the context in which they occur. As a result, each sentence is heard and perceived as a *separate* entity; the textual context in which the sentence occurs cannot obscure the writer's perception of its intelligibility.

Strategy: To locate errors in sentence structure, be familiar with the sorts of sentence errors that you commit and learn to look for clues that will help you locate specific errors.

You will find it useful to know the sorts of sentence errors you tend to produce. For example, if you write sentence fragments like "*Although the data were inconclusive. The* researchers formulated some tentative hypotheses" you should be careful to examine sentences that contain connecting words such as "although," "because," and "if." And certainly, if a "suspicious" sentence contains a structure that starts with one of these connecting words, you have two pieces of evidence that there is something wrong— your own intuition and the presence of a word that appears in a problem structure.

Although writers commit a variety of errors in sentence structure, these errors tend to form patterns, to resemble one another. For example, most inappropriate sentence fragments that inexperienced writers produce are of several commonly produced types. Here are specific clues that accompany some of the most commonly produced sentence structure errors:

1. *-ING words:* If you produce dangling modifiers, misplaced modifiers, or sentence fragments, examine structures and sentences that contain words that end in *-ing*. Here are examples of common sentences structure errors that contain *-ing* words:

DANGLING MODIFIERS:

Examining the data, errors were found.

Lying on the beach, the sun felt hot.

The air conditioner sounded loud, *studying in the room next to it.*

MISPLACED MODIFIERS:

We saw the White House *walking down Pennsylvania Avenue.*

Licking her toes, Lucretia gave the kitty some milk.

FRAGMENTS:

Waking the babies with his hysterical yells. Bob ran through the yard.

The president stayed in his office. *Expecting his assistant to appear with important information.*

2.   *Connecting words such as "after," "although," "as," "because," "before," "if," "since," "unless," "until," "when," "whenever," "where," "wherever," "while":* If you produce fragmented modifiers, examine structures that begin with these connecting words. Even if a structure that begins with one of these words contains a subject and a verb, it may be a modifying fragment.

FRAGMENT:

Although the above list contains ideas that might be effective in my paper. I would like to generate more after I've been to the library.

Transitions are important both within and between paragraphs. *Because they help a paper move from one point to another in a logical manner.*

3.   *Connecting words such as "that," "what," "which," "who," "whoever," "whom," "whomever," "whose":* Connecting words such as "that" or "what" may be associated with two commonly occurring types of sentence fragments, fragmented modifiers and fragmented word groups that are modified. Here are some examples of both kinds of fragments that contain these connecting words.

FRAGMENTED MODIFIERS:

Most of the students have enrolled in introductory chemistry courses. *Which meet twice a week, on Tuesdays and Thursdays.*

After the pep rally, the president awarded the trophy to Don Collins. *Who is a senior in engineering and who is president of the Honor Society.*

FRAGMENTED WORD OR WORD GROUP + MODIFIER:
The unedited version of the manuscript, which is on display in the Rare Book room of the library. It is fascinating.
The new, exciting actor who refused to attend the Awards Ceremony. I think he is a jerk.

4. *Commas (,):* Although commas are commonly used punctuation, examining them may help you locate comma splices and/or dangling modifiers.

Commas may be used with particular connecting words, such as "and," "but," or "for," to join two complete sentences. However, commas may *not* be used by themselves to join two or more sentences. A comma splice is a sentence error that results when two sentences are joined with just a comma. If you write comma splices, you should carefully examine the structures that precede and follow *each* comma. If you locate a comma that is both preceded and followed by a sentence, you have located a comma splice.

COMMA SPLICES:
The flowers looked beautiful in the crystal vase, they were a gift from Joanne and Suzanne.
After the renovation, the room was painted bright red, no one liked it.

Commas are also used to separate an introductory or final word-group modifier from the rest of the sentence it precedes or follows. Since dangling modifiers most often precede or follow sentences, if you write sentences that contain dangling modifiers you should examine *every* word group that is separated from a sentence by a comma, whether the word group precedes or follows the sentence. If the word-group is acting as a modifier, be certain that the *actual* word(s) being modified is/are in the sentence.

DANGLING MODIFIERS:
Terminating his contract, no reasons were given.
Understanding the difficulty caused by the misunderstanding, every effort was taken to be conciliatory.
There were a variety of options available to consumers, *determined to attract new customers.*

As you become increasingly proficient at using various strategies for locating and correcting the types of sentence errors that you normally commit, you will become more skilled at identifying and rewriting poorly structured sentences that are anomalous or unusual for you. Even though you may eradicate most of the ill-formed sentences you write by learning to recognize and to correct *your* particular errors when you edit, some of the poorly constructed sentences you write will, invariably, be unique; they will fit no pattern. Editing such sentence errors is challenging because there are no clear-cut procedures to follow with regard to them. A writer need not be reduced to pure trial and error, however. To *locate* anomalous or unusual sentence errors, you should of course read your essay out loud, sentence by sentence, as already suggested. Here is a strategy for *revising* such sentences.

> **Strategy: To revise an ill-formed sentence, write what you intended to say on a separate sheet of paper, using as many sentences as you wish. The resulting sentences should then be combined to form a new sentence or sentences, which are reinserted into the text.**

If you use this strategy to rework a troublesome sentence, you need to be concerned about two problems that may arise:

1.   As you attempt to recombine the sentences that you jotted on a separate sheet of paper, you may find that you cannot reasonably incorporate them into one sentence. In such instances, you may produce two or more sentences in place of the *one* you are trying to revise. Be sure to examine these sentences carefully to determine whether you need to insert a connective word or expression between them, since the new sentences were derived from what was originally one sentence.
2.   The new sentence or sentences that you produce using this method may be quite different in structure from the original. You need to be certain, therefore, that the new sentence(s) fit into the text when you reinsert them. Read a good portion of what precedes and what follows the revised sentence(s) to make this determination.

Here is an illustration of this revision procedure.

UNIQUE AWKWARD SENTENCE:
After all the other reasons for school influencing an individual, by making friends or having new experiences, is the value of the education itself that was received.

SENTENCES THAT DESCRIBE WHAT I WAS TRYING TO SAY:
College is important for many reasons.

It gives you the opportunity to make new friends, for example.

It also gives you the opportunity to experience things you've never before experienced—like dorm parties.

Most of all at college you can get an education. (academic)

NEW COMBINED SENTENCE:
College is important for many reasons, the most important of which is that it provides students with the opportunity to get an education. College is valuable for other reasons too; most students make new friends, with roommates or classmates, for example, and many students experience what they've never had an opportunity to experience before.

The two new sentences are inserted into the space in the text where the original "unique awkward sentence" resided. Then a substantial portion of the text that comes before and after the inserted sentences is read aloud, *with the new sentences in place.* If the new sentences do not fit exactly, some connective devices may be required before the new sentences, after the new sentences, or before *and* after the new sentences.

Exercise 24

Read the following text. Locate and correct any sentence errors that you find by using the editing strategies you have learned in this chapter.

Some Musings About Context

Last week, a colleague of mine put a cartoon in my mailbox. A recent episode of *Hi and Lois*, which is a fairly popular husband and wife cartoon series. The cartoon consists of two frames. In frame one, Lois says to Hi: "You're not going to wear THAT tie, are you?" (Hi responds with a rather tepid, "Er . . . I guess not.") Frame two contains a "closeup" of Hi rummaging through the closet mumbling, "It's funny how wives can make a question sound like an order."

My first response to this little cartoon was to be irritated. I'm not certain that very many wives habitually make questions sound like orders. In fact, there is some evidence to the contrary. One linguist has discovered that women frequently make statements "sound" like questions. So as not to sound too assertive, domineering, or like a bossy person. Here is an example of this: Hubby gets home from work and asks, "Honey Cakes, when will dinner be ready?" The wife responds with a wimpy, "Six o'clock?" rather than with an assertive, "Six o'clock." (Presumably, to set dinner at six o'clock is an *executive decision,* which wives should not make.)

My next response to the cartoon was less emotional, it was also important, though. Thinking about the cartoon, the importance of context again became apparent. All language occurs in a particular context. Spoken language involves an exchange between a speaker (or speakers) and a listener (or listeners), who exist in a particular space (a classroom in an elementary school in Muncie, Indiana) and time (9:05 in the morning of the second Monday of November, which is the day before election day; it is also the Monday after the Muncie Eagles have met resounding defeat at the hands of the Peoria Tigers; it is also the first day of the school's "sell-pizzas-for-a-school-computer drive"). The speaker (Miss Dart, first grade teacher) and the listeners (twenty-seven first graders) are engaged in a particular activity (Miss Dart is trying to get her charges to stay seated so that she can take attendance). Miss Dart may select one of the following utterances:

1.   Young ladies and gentlemen, may I request the courtesy of your attention so that I can take role. This will enable me to proceed with my planned schedule, the contents of which—if executed—will entertain and edify you.

2.   If you children don't settle down immediately, I will begin handing out demerits (That means *you,* Eddie!). *Sit down.*

OR

3.   You miserable little savages, you disgusting monsters, if you don't park your bottoms immediately, I am going to hack you to pieces with my machete.

Clearly, each response is grammatical; the rules of grammar don't provide much help. Context, then, must be the determining factor: What does Miss Dart wish to accomplish; what *doesn't* Miss Dart wish to accomplish? Who is Miss Dart's audience, where is the communication occurring?

Context is even more crucial with regard to writing than speaking. Normally, speech *naturally* occurs within a context. The audience, speaker, environment, motivation for speaking are provided—automatically. Writing is another matter altogether. It is, for the most part, a solitary activity. The creation of a context for writing (Who am I writing to? Under what circumstances am I writing? Why am I writing? What do I hope to accomplish?) is largely the responsibility of the writer—as if she didn't have *enough* to do already.

My fit of peevishness (as if she didn't have *enough* to do already) interrupted my reverie about context. I looked again at the cartoon. This time I felt sorry for Hi, who was being ordered about by his snappish wife the poor thing.

I guess the context in which I read the cartoon had changed.

Exercise 25

Examine pieces of writing that you have written and that have been evaluated and returned to you. On the basis of this examination, list the kinds of sentence structure errors you tend to commit. Provide examples from your papers of each sort of error. Describe or identify the specific type of error in each sentence.

INAPPROPRIATE SENTENCE FRAGMENTS

1. _____

_____

2. _____

_____

3. _____

_____

4. _____

_____

INCORRECTLY CONNECTED SENTENCES: FUSED, COMMA SPLICES, EXCESSIVELY COORDINATED

1. _____

_____

2. _____

_____

3. _____

_____

4. _____

_____

SENTENCES WITH MODIFICATION PROBLEMS: MISPLACED AND DANGLING MODIFIERS

1. _____

_____

2. _____

_____

3. _____

_____

4. _____

_____

MISUSED PASSIVES

1. _____

_____

2. _____

_____

3. _____

_____

4. _____

_____

SENTENCES WITH FAULTY PARALLELISM

1. _____

_____

2. _____

_____

3. _____

_____

4. _____

_____

12 *Word Choice*

English, a language rich in vocabulary, provides users with a multitude of choices. However, this very richness can sometimes contribute to word selection problems, since there are so many options available from which to choose. Written language especially demands precision because the writer is usually not available to provide clarification if a reader has trouble understanding a text. Each writer must therefore take care to select the word or words that will convey exactly what he means. Incorrect or inexact or inconsistent choices result in ambiguity or misunderstanding for the reader.

Problems in word choice can affect a reader's understanding of a text in several ways. Inconsistent word choice can affect an entire text, causing the reader to be uncertain about the writer's intention. For example, if concepts or key terms seem to shift in meaning or tone, a reader may wonder about the stance the writer has chosen: Is the text meant to be taken at face value or is it meant to be ironic? Sometimes inaccurate or vague word choice can make it difficult for a reader to understand what the writer means in a certain portion of a text. If, for instance, a reader encounters a phrase such as "last summer I got into tennis," *he* must determine what the writer meant: Did the writer play tennis for the first time last summer? Had the writer played tennis before but started to play regularly, particularly enjoying it last summer? Or what? Sometimes word choice problems do not interfere with a reader's understanding of a text, but instead affect the reader's attitude toward it and/or his willingness to read it. It is not unusual for minor word choice problems, such as unnecessary repetition, to accumulate and together weaken the effect of an otherwise well-written piece by creating unnecessary "noise" or "static" that wears on and annoys a reader.

Part Three of *Roughdrafts* is devoted to editing, which we have defined as the final stage of the writing process, and the emphasis in Chapter 12 is on techniques the writer may use to detect and eliminate *occasional lapses* in word choice and/or to *refine* his choice of words one last time before presenting his text to a reader. To that end, we have elected to cover the most common word choice problems that routinely occur in largely finished, reader-based texts.

Chapter 12 is divided into five sections:

☐   Formality and Word Choice
☐   Using Words Accurately
☐   Avoiding Vague Words
☐   Eliminating Wordiness
☐   Editing Word Choice Problems

Formality and Word Choice

It is socially inappropriate for a person to wear a sweatshirt and tennis shoes to a banquet; it is also inappropriate to wear high-heeled shoes, a strapless evening gown, and a diamond necklace to a picnic. The formality of dress is often dictated by the nature of a particular event: "formal dress: tuxedoes and black ties"; "dress casually and comfortably." Language, too, should reflect a level of formality appropriate to its context. For an illustration of this, examine the following examples. Which of them seems more appropriate?

> From one customer of Joe's Corner Hamburger Joint to another:
>
> "Excuse me; could you pass the ketchup?"
>
> "Might I have your attention please? I detest encumbering you with my difficulty; however, I am in need of ketchup for my hamburger sandwich and, therefore, request that you hand it to me."
>
> From the President of the Undergraduate Student

Organization to the President of the University, at a public meeting:

"Hey prez. Let's face it. You really screwed up this time."

"Mr. President, many students, myself included, think that you did not handle the situation as well as you might have."

These rather exaggerated examples illustrate the importance of appropriate formality in speech. Appropriate formality is equally important in writing. Of course, the writer will have determined the level of formality long before editing begins, taking into account the nature of the audience, the relationship between the audience and the writer, and the writer's intention. Nevertheless, careful editing for words and expressions that are inappropriately formal or inappropriately informal is important. No matter how careful you may have been to select and maintain an appropriate level of formality, inappropriate words and/or expressions can slip by unnoticed, undermining an otherwise effective text by creating inconsistencies in voice, stance, and/ or tone that may cause the reader to wonder about your intention.

Words That Are Too Informal

Colloquial language, or "everyday" spoken language, is often too informal for semiformal or formal writing. The use of inappropriately informal language can cause a variety of problems. It can annoy or anger a reader ("That's *Mrs.* Jones to you!"). It can cause a reader to make a negative judgment about the writer's level of education or intelligence. It can create vagueness or make a reader uncertain of a writer's intention, since, under normal circumstances, informal language is used by those who know one another well and who share information about one another. Therefore, unless you mean to recreate a direct, informal "conversation" with an audience, colloquial words or expressions should be avoided:

> COLLOQUIAL:
> The LSAT is a *dumb* test.
>
> PREFERABLE:
> The LSAT is an *unreasonable* test.
> *or*
> The LSAT is an *invalid* test.
> *or*
> The LSAT is an *unfair* test.

Colloquial:

The newly built civic center is a *neat* building.

Preferable:

The newly built civic center is an *unusual* building.

or

The newly built civic center is an *attractive* building.

or

The newly built civic center is a *remarkable* building.

Colloquial:

All of the students *got* what Professor Lart was saying.

Preferable:

All of the students *understood* what Professor Lart was saying.

or

All of the students *followed* what Professor Lart was saying.

Exercise 1

Read the following sentences and replace colloquial words and/or expressions with more formal ones. Assume that all the sentences have been taken from pieces of writing that are intended to be semi-formal or formal in style.

Example:

I really got mad at Professor Heath when he made me retake the midterm.

Revised:

Professor Heath angered me when he made me retake the midterm.

1. After Mr. Deacon croaked, his family decided to put up a monument in his honor.

2. In response to many beefs from employees, a special service telephone number will be made available.

3. This service will be there for people who want it, starting at 8:00 A.M. on January 16th.

4. All of the guys on the loading dock were dissatisfied with the new arrangements.

5. Too many employees have been goofing off, so more stringent measures are needed.

6. The newscasters have been reporting lousy weather lately, which has made area viewers real cranky.

Slang is another common source of words and expressions that are too informal. As with other inappropriately informal words and expressions, slang can negatively bias or confuse a reader, since it is language peculiar to a particular group of speakers—adolescents, for example—and since it is short-lived.

Exercise 2

Replace the slang in the following sentences with more precise and more formal words or expressions.

> EXAMPLE:
> Professor Nielson was trashed out by his students' attitude.
>
> REVISED:
> Professor Nielson was upset because of his students' attitude.

1. Jella's new haircut is far out.
2. Nola is thrilled to the max about her room.
3. The undergraduates were uptight about their final.
4. The citizenry think that Mayor Largess is a heavy dude.
5. The renovation committee ran out of bread.

Words That Are Too Formal

Although writing is generally more formal than speech, it is dangerous to assume that inappropriately formal word choice cannot cause serious problems. Unexpected lapses into formality can confuse a reader. Also, the use of inappropriately formal words may annoy readers and perhaps cause them to make negative judgments. Excessive formality can result from the use of inappropriate words and expressions, or it can result from the inappropriate use or overuse of figurative language.

Inappropriate words and expressions contribute to inflated, pretentious writing. When you write, therefore, it is wise to avoid a word such as "masticate" if "chew" will do. Notice the difference between the two sentences that follow:

EXAMPLE:
Enclosure 2B has been provided to aid in the facilitation of data recording. The original form plus two reproductions should be forwarded to Bookkeeping.

REVISED:
Form 2B has been provided to help make record-keeping easier. The original and two copies should be sent to Bookkeeping.

An ordinary word, such as "think," is generally preferable to a fancy word, such as "deem." Select a word such as "deem" only if it is exactly the right one. If, as you are editing, you discover words such as "deem" or "apprise" or "terminate," you should examine the context in which they are used. Replace such words with more commonly used synonyms, such as "think" or "inform" or "end," unless they were chosen specifically for that context.

Exercise 3

Replace overly formal words in the following sentences with more appropriate ones.

EXAMPLE:
The decision of the committee is contingent upon the outcome of the election.

REVISED:
The decision of the committee will *depend* upon the outcome of the election.

1. The company will terminate that option soon unless consumers complain.

2. Each person masticated his pie carefully and imbibed his wine thoughtfully.

3. The utilization of those forms is inappropriate and it will not facilitate matters, either.

4. I have been apprised of the situation and will initiate action prior to the next senate meeting.

5.   The students gained admittance to the laboratory by means of a side door.

6.   The new mayor was observed leaving her domicile subsequent to her consumption of breakfast.

7.   The members of the Conciliation Team are cognizant of the fact that their charge is to facilitate a meeting between the appellant and the respondent.

Figurative Language

Fiction writers and poets often use language in unusual and imaginative ways. They use imagery, vivid language that produces mental pictures. They use similes and metaphors, which are comparisons of two dissimilar things. Of course, the use of unusual, imaginative language—figurative language—is not and should not be limited to poets and fiction writers. However, it is not easy to create effective figurative language. Nor is it easy to determine when it should be used or how often. Inexperienced writers, in an attempt to "wax poetic," can sometimes create inflated, pretentious—even silly—passages:

> My heart pounded as I entered the classroom—that large and ghostly repository of the souls of lost students. It banged against the branches of my rib cage like a tattered-winged moth, trying frantically to escape, but already mortally injured.

Figurative language can enhance a text, but it should arise out of a particular context. Figurative language should not be "put into" your writing so that it will sound "creative." Be sure to eliminate unnecessary or inappropriate figurative language while editing.

Exercise 4

Read each of the following sentences and eliminate any figurative language that you think is unnecessary. Be prepared to defend your decisions.

> EXAMPLE:
> The last voter entered the booth, clutching her ballot as if it were a winning lottery ticket. She had waited in line for two hours in order to vote.

REVISED:
The last voter entered the booth anxiously, having waited in
line two hours in order to vote.

1. Professor Beans checked his watch again; his students had five more
minutes to complete their exams. Then he would rip the papers from their
hands, rending flesh and bone.

2. Over the small town of Sidney the sun set like a Greek Goddess dipping
into the sea at nightfall—partaking of her evening toilette.

3. The members of the Ladies' Guild hovered around the salad bar, now
approaching now receding, hummingbirds of varied hues.

4. The siren wailed, a high pitched, greedy sound: "My. Me. My. Me.
More. More. More. More."

5. The joggers approached the bend in the road, panting and whistling
like locomotives, their legs giant pistoning wheels.

Exercise 5

Read the following excerpt. Replace words or expressions that are inappropriately informal or formal for this kind of text.

Crate-Training Puppies

Many urban dog lovers are not dog owners—although they desire to
become such. This is because they have determined that they do not have
sufficient yard space in which to build a dog run. Dog runs are useful for
a variety of purposes, one of the most vital of which is an aid in housebreaking
puppies. Since puppies learn most easily if they are not given an opportunity
to blow it, dog runs come in handy because Puppy can be put in the run
when "Mommy" and "Daddy" get tired of watching him for signs of "having
to go." Housebreaking with the aid of a run is far superior to paper training,
which—in fact—teaches a dog to do something ("go" on newspaper) which
he must, subsequently, unlearn.

Potential dog owners who do not possess sufficient back yard space for
a run need not rend their garments in abject despair, however. There *is* an
alternative to paper training: crate training. Crate training merely requires
a proper size puppy crate—which can easily be acquired at a local pet
establishment or at a large variety store that sells pet supplies—and two
days of careful attention to Fido.

First a word of encouragement and assurance to persons who wish to use the crate-training method. Puppy will not mind being put in his crate for periods of time during the first couple of weeks at his new home. He likes it in his crate; he feels OK: it's sort of like a cave. (It is important, however, to never place Puppy in his crate as punishment. Otherwise, every time he gets put in it, he'll think Master is mad at him.)

Crate training is really very simple: it merely involves paying close attention to everything Puppy does when he is not in his crate. Puppy is put in his crate whenever no one is around to romp with him and/or watch him. Puppy sleeps in his crate at night, therefore. He also spends time in the crate when no one is home. For the first two or three days after Puppy is brought to his new domicile, Mom or Dad removes him from the crate frequently, watching him like a bald eagle in search of prey. Each time puppy starts to sniff or scratch—up he goes, out to the yard. There, if he does "go," he is rewarded with a big deal response: "Good puppy. Precious puppy." Repeatedly, for an interval of two or three days, Pup is only given the opportunity to succeed: he soon learns that outside is where he does his duty. Incidentally, Little Fido won't soil his crate if it is the right size for him because the crate is his "nest" and he instinctively knows not to mess it.

Well, potential dog owners, who have been yearning for a precious ball of fluff and fur to warm the coldness of their souls that are yearning for warmth and understanding in the concrete canyons of American cities, now know what to do. Charge. Head for the pet store or the Humane Society. The spectre of paper training no longer looms.

Using Words Accurately

Synonyms

Synonyms are often defined as words with similar meanings; for example, "small" and "little" are synonyms. This definition is true enough, but it can be misleading: because of it, some individuals think that synonyms are interchangeable. In fact, no two words are completely interchangeable. Some synonyms are more interchangeable than others. "Large" and "big" may be interchanged in a great many contexts:

Her feet are *large*.   Her feet are *big*.
Her house is *large*.   Her house is *big*.
She made a *large* meal.   She made a *big* meal.
I bought a *large* bottle of wine.   I bought a *big* bottle of wine.
Large earlobes are best.   *Big* earlobes are best.
I got him a *large* box of candy.   I got him a *big* box of candy.

However, sometimes even these close synonyms cannot be used interchangeably:

> She has a *big* mouth. (Most often "big" would imply that she
> is talkative or a gossip.)
> She has a *large* mouth. (Most often "large" would imply that
> her anatomy [the mouth] is oversized.)

If a synonym for a word is *not* appropriate for the sentence into which it is inserted, the result may be a strange-sounding, unclear sentence:

> Maria had a great deal of change in her pocket.
> Maria *possessed* a great deal of change in her pocket.

> I gather that you are upset.
> I *grasp* that you are upset.

Sometimes a synonym may be inappropriate for a particular context because of commonly held feelings and attitudes associated with it. For example, although "thin," "slim," "scrawny," "skinny," and "slender" are all synonyms, it would be highly inappropriate to name a diet product "Carnation Instant Skinny." Also, the sentence "Marcia dieted so that she could be *scrawny*" seems ridiculous, but the sentence "Marcia dieted so that she could be *thin*" is perfectly acceptable.

When you edit your text, be certain that every word you use fits in the sentence and context in which you put it. Never pick an unfamiliar word from a list of synonyms (from a thesaurus, for example) and insert it into a sentence "for variety." If you find that you have repeated the same word too many times, replace it with a synonym with which you are familiar. If you must use a new word, look it up in the dictionary first. For example, suppose you need a substitute for the word "hideous," and the word "monstrous" is one of the listed synonyms. Find the dictionary entry for the word "monstrous" and read it carefully. Sometimes the dictionary will not only provide definitions for a word, it will also provide examples of how the word is used:

> *flavor*   1. Distinctive taste; savor: *a flavor of smoke in bacon.*

Such examples are usually very helpful, and you should read them carefully when they are provided.

Exercise 6

One sentence in each of the following sets contains an error in word choice. Locate each error, then correct the sentence by replacing the incorrect word with a suitable one.

> EXAMPLE:
> a. Josie told us about her experiences at the bus depot—a bizarre story.
> b. Every town, no matter how small, has one or two eccentric individuals.
> c. We were disturbed by the eccentric story we heard during dinner.
>
> We were disturbed by the *strange* story we heard during dinner.

1. a. The mutations in the tissue culture were unexpected.
    b. Dr. Morton could observe mutations in the children's behavior.
    c. The changes in Reva's attitude towards children were startling.
2. a. The bacteria were strange because they could reside in a culture with few nutriments.
    b. Martin has resided in Haskins for most of his life.
    c. These animals live in the foothills of the mountains despite the hostile environment.
3. a. The carpenter acquired a cold after he visited the hospital.
    b. Didn't the university acquire a great deal of oil-producing land?
    c. I got an eye infection and it's quite painful.
4. a. The students found that they could remember information better if they copied over their notes immediately after class.

    b. Because of her experience, Marlene located that she was really quite fortunate.

    c. We will locate the exact place if we're patient.

Exercise 7

Read the following sentences. From the accompanying pair of words, select the one that would be more appropriate in most contexts. Explain your choices.

    EXAMPLE:
    All last year I ate less so that I could be (<u>thinner</u>, skinnier).

"Skinnier" has an inappropriately negative connotation here.

    1. I (obliterated, destroyed) all of my old notes, since they weren't very legible.

    2. The mailman (left, vanished) soon after the party began because he needed to get home early.

    3. I (cut, sliced) my toenails after I took a bath.

    4. The president of the Etiquette Society (sipped, slurped) her tea.

    5. Mrs. Bostdork (tiptoed, slunk) across the room so as not to attract the attention of her students, who were taking a test.

    6. "And so we urge you to vote for John Meez, a (politician, statesman) who possesses vision and the will to act upon it."

    7. "We don't have any problems that can't be solved with cooperation and respect," (asserted, shouted) President Manley.

    8. The (international students, foreign students) from Barley University visited Chicago, Illinois, for the first time.

    9. The real estate ad lists a small (cottage, shack), available immediately, for sale or for rent.

    10. "The funeral will be held on Sunday afternoon, after which there will be a small gathering at the home of Mrs. Cargor, sister of the (dead person, deceased)."

Exercise 8

Read the following text and rewrite it, making any changes in *word choice* that are necessary.

The emphasis in this earth-shattering little volume is on practicality and applicability. Although it is apparent that Nimean is familiar with recent research in writing, most of the news is presented in the form of level-headed, unspeculative strategies and guidelines for writing instructors. Chapter 1's inception is devoted to a discussion of "what to do on the first day of class."

Then the chapter proceeds with exhaustive discussions of prewriting strategies and rough draft workshops. Other chapters deal with natural topics, such as paragraph construction, word choice, and sentence structure. Most of the exercises will validate useful—even for old composition teachers.

Too often, textbooks that paint themselves as resource books lack structure; the teacher must provide continuity. Fortunately, this book is odd: it is unified and comprehensive. I wholeheartedly sanction its use.

Words Spelled Similarly

Another common cause of inappropriately used words is confusing one word for another that resembles it closely. In English there are many pairs of words with similar spellings. These words often sound alike, and since many persons encounter them in speech rather than in writing, they may easily be confused for one another. If such a confusion is carried into writing, this sort of error in word usage can occur:

Maybelle felt *prosecuted* by her roommate, Lynnette.

In the above example, "prosecute," which means to conduct legal action against someone, has been mistakenly substituted for "persecute," which means to severely torment or harass someone.

Here is a list of words that are frequently confused for one another in college writing. Notice that some of the words, such as "accept" and "except," are pronounced in the same way by many speakers of English.

accept/except   incidence/incident
access/excess   lessen/lesson
affect/effect   minor/miner
allude/elude   moral/morale
allusion/illusion   persecute/prosecute
censor/censure   personal/personnel
complement/compliment   precede/proceed

conscience/conscious   predominant/predominate
credible/creditable   principal/principle
dominant/dominate   propose/purpose
eminent/imminent/immanent   respectful/respective
formerly/formally   sensuous/sensual
human/humane   stationary/stationery

If you sometimes confuse similar words for one another, it is probably wise to keep a list of the words that you have used incorrectly. That way, you can look for problems with those particular words as you are editing. In addition, if you are not familiar with *both* words in a pair of similar words, it is wise to look up in the dictionary every such word that you encounter while editing. You can then be sure that you are using the word correctly in the particular sentence in which you have used it and that you have spelled it properly.

Exercise 9

Choose five pairs of words from the list in this section and use each word in a sentence.

Exercise 10

Read the following sentences. Locate and correct any word choice problems you find.

> EXAMPLE:
> Senate voted not to *censor* the immoral colleague.
>
> REVISED:
> Senate voted not to *censure* the immoral colleague.

1. The members of Congress voted to censor Representative Marble-hedmer because of his involvement with foreign agents.

2. Marlena violated her principals as she became more involved with the local political machine.

3. Joe Finderlar tried to allude Professor Blancher's attempts to talk to him after class.

4. "Class, if you will please precede to page 342, we will resume our discussion."

5. Dr. Betsy Zenn, formally assistant director of the regional office, will be our guest speaker next Saturday.

6. All of the precedes from the car wash are going to be donated to the United Cancer Research fund.

7. I was made suspicious by Dieter's copious and exaggerated complements, especially since I knew he was applying for a job in my office.

8. Many of the local citizens were angry about the X-rated film, which seemed to present a disturbing morale: persons ought to seek gratification however and whenever they can.

9. After Dr. Todd was denied a security clearance, he was excepted from the list of those allowed excess to the computer facility.

10. The predominate characteristic of Zefferelli's films is the setting, which is almost always surreal.

Avoiding Vague Words

Even if a writer does not use words inaccurately or incorrectly, she may still make it difficult for the reader to understand what she means if she is not careful to use words precisely. There are several common sources of vague word choice, all of which should be detected and eliminated while editing.

Specific Words vs. General Words

Sometimes vague diction is the result of using a general word rather than a specific word. In everyday speech we often do not take the time to select specific words, which is why so many of our conversations are peppered with such expressions as "You know what I mean." Then, too, the way human speech is structured, it is often clear to the speaker when the other party does *not* know what is meant. If you wish dramatic proof that this is so, next time you are engaged in a conversation, determine what it is you do at regular intervals to let the other person know that you are following her. You probably say something like "uhuh" or "yeah," or you nod your head slightly, or a combination. At some point in the conversation, stop providing your nods or your "uhuh's" and watch what happens. Your partner will, almost immediately, respond with something like, "Do you understand?" or "Are you with me?" or "Are you listening?" Under normal circumstances, therefore, paying close attention to our selection of words in everyday conversation is not crucial.

Joyce: So what did you do then? I mean after, you know, when you got back.

Nadia: It was incredible. We talked for about two hours. About everything. You know, *everything*. Then I said I had to get back because of work.

Joyce: You mean you had to work Saturday? You didn't tell me.

Nadia: No. No. It's that paper I have due for comp. Remember? I read over my notes and looked at some books but I still haven't figured out what to do. I think I'm gonna go to the library, but it doesn't matter; whatever I do, he won't like it. Every English teacher wants you to do something different so you've gotta keep unlearning everything and relearning stuff each time. I wish they'd get their act together; it's really boring. You know what I mean? (During this part of the conversation, Joyce has been nodding or "umhumming.")

Joyce: Yeah.

Clearly, Joyce and Nadia share a great deal of information about one another. Joyce knows what Nadia means by "incredible." And she knows what Nadia means by "everything." When she experiences a misunderstanding, about Nadia having to work on Saturday, the context of the conversation gives her an opportunity to seek clarification.

The contexts in which most writing occurs are quite different from conversational contexts. Most readers would not be able to supply specific information about the meaning of "incredible" or "everything." Fortunately, the English language provides the writer with a dazzling array of choices so that she can replace vague, general words or expressions with more specific ones. Here are some illustrations of this, using the words "bad" and "great":

I had a *bad* day.   I had a *frustrating* day.

I had a *depressing* day.

I had a *worthless* day.

I had a *brutal* day.

The baby had a *bad* dream.	The baby had a *frightening* dream.
The car has *bad* brakes.	The car has *dangerous* brakes.
	The car has *defective* brakes.
	The car has *squeaking* brakes.
	The car has *slow* brakes.
	The car has *difficult to operate* brakes.
That was a *great* party.	That was an *exciting* party.
	That was an *interesting* party.
The designers had a *great* idea.	The designers had an *innovative* idea.
	The designers had a *profitable* idea.
	The designers had a *unique* idea.
Evelyn is a *great* person.	Evelyn is a *kind* person.
	Evelyn is a *sympathetic* person.
	Evelyn is a *sincere* person.
	Evelyn is a *charming* person.

Remember also that some words designate large, general groups of entities, whereas other words designate specific members of these groups. Specific words will often help you convey your intended meaning to a reader more precisely.

animal→dog→retriever→Labrador retriever

EXAMPLE:
I have a *dog*.
I have a *Labrador retriever*.

plant→flower→lilac→pink lilac

EXAMPLE:
The *flowers* were beautiful.
The *pink lilacs* were beautiful.

food→dessert→cake→torte→Bavarian torte→Bavarian chocolate-mocha torte

EXAMPLE:
The *food* was outstanding.
The *Bavarian chocolate-mocha torte* was outstanding.

When a writer edits a text, sometimes she cannot eliminate vagueness or convey precisely what she means or what has happened merely by substituting one word for another. Under these circumstances, it is preferable to reword a sentence, adding specific detail that will clarify the meaning.

EXAMPLE	REVISED
Elton is *very sick*.	Elton *has terminal lung cancer*.
I *relax in different ways* on weeknights.	On weeknights I usually *read science fiction novels, unless I'm too tired, in which case I lie in front of the television set*.
Professor Knox *became angry*.	*Screaming at the top of his lungs,* Professor Knox *flew out of the room, slamming the door behind him*.
The exam was *unfair*.	The exam *tested us on material that wasn't presented in the textbook or in the lectures*.
	or
	The exam *required us to write five essays in response to five complex questions in forty-five minutes*.

Writers differ with regard to how they tackle a writing task; therefore, it is difficult to prescribe specifically *when* you should be concerned with precise word choice. Obviously, if you first write—rapidly—for yourself, concerning yourself with word choice as you are producing a first draft would be needlessly distracting. On the other hand, you may be the kind of writer who finds word choice crucial in the early stages of writing: for you, selecting the *right* word or wording may be a necessary part of your inventing and planning process. Regardless of when you become concerned with the selection of precise words, you need to edit carefully for vagueness at the final stage of your writing process, since vague words are easily overlooked.

Exercise 11

Eliminate the vagueness in each of the following sentences. Assume that the contexts from which they were drawn do not clarify them adequately.

EXAMPLE:

Dave's car is *run down*.

REVISED:

Dave's car needs *a paint job and a new muffler*.

1. Many citizens were angry.
2. The meal at La Gregiare was fine.
3. That place sells dogs.
4. Evan said an odd thing.
5. The library guild recommended the novel because it thought it was good.
6. Mrs. Rhodes said that Josh needed to improve in his work.
7. Most of the proposals that were submitted were good.
8. Many of the watches were cheap.
9. The textbook was difficult, so most of the students became upset.
10. That television show is stupid, even if lots of people watch it.

Exercise 12

Eliminate vagueness in the following text by substituting words and/or rewording sentences where necessary.

The graduate program of the Department of Biology sometimes gets requests from the Graduate College for information. Every now and then the Graduate College requests information regarding the number of persons who finish various programs as opposed to the number of persons who leave. The Graduate College also is interested in employment patterns of people. Most of this data is requested for a span of time and must be presented in particular ways.

Currently, when we receive these requests, we must hand compile the data, which we get from student files. It would be great if the student information could be moved from student files to computer disks. Then, if we had the right kind of computer program, we could "ask" the computer to generate information for us in various ways.

The department can use two VT 100 terminals and an Apple IIe. Also, we have two printers, a Printmaster F10 and an Epson MX 100 dot-matrix

467

printer. In addition, we are trying to get a Shadow terminal, but we may not get it.

We appreciate your help. Let us know if we can do anything.

Clichés

Clichés are words or expressions that have become tired, drained of their original forcefulness, through overuse:

Bonita: Well, what do you think about Darla?

Edie: *Out of the frying pan and into the fire.* Boy, she *fell for it hook, line, and sinker,* didn't she?

Bonita: Shouldn't we say something to her? After all, we've *been around the block* a few times. We weren't *born yesterday,* you know.

Edie: No. I don't think so. Listen, she's *made her bed. Let her lie in it.* Besides, she'll *get over it.* After a while, it'll be *water over the dam.*

Bonita: I know. A person ought to *bite the bullet now and then.* Still, whenever I think about it, *it makes my blood boil.*

Although clichés are commonly used in casual conversation, they tend to weaken most texts, draining them of forcefulness and originality. Clichés can also cause vagueness, since they are widely used in a great many contexts, and are therefore quite general in meaning.

Exercise 13

Eliminate clichés from the following sentences.

EXAMPLE:
President Olfbun frequently gives lip service to the rights of students, but he never puts his money where his mouth is.

REVISION:
President Olfbun makes a pretense of caring about student rights but rarely acts on students' behalf.

1. Dr. Printo is a good therapist who can relate to a patient's problems.
2. The chief executive vetoed the selection of Rod Ravenhill as leading man because he considered Rod to be an over-the-hill has-been.
3. Now that she has recovered from surgery, June is the very picture of health.
4. Congressman Pickerell was as cool as a cucumber at the press conference even though the reporters were out to get him.
5. As a result of his conduct, the reporters considered the congressman to be an honest voice of the people, who shot straight from the hip.
6. Bella's eyes twinkled like stars as she ripped open her present.
7. Cindy's kiss took Benjamin to a place he'd never been to before, so he decided to go with the flow.

Jargon

Jargon is a term that has several meanings. It can refer to the specialized vocabulary used by members of a particular group or profession. For example, "software," "modem," "bits," "user-friendly," and "interface" are terms used by persons who have some familiarity with computers. The term is also used to describe language that is deliberately misleading: "He used a lot of jargon to cover up the fact that he didn't know the answer to our question."

Specialized vocabulary is absolutely essential in some contexts:

Dr. Binzer to Dr. Jort: Our patient has a localized swelling that is filled with blood. This swelling is located beneath the membrane that covers the brain and the spinal cord.
Dr. Jort to Dr. Binzer: Oh, a subdural hematoma.

Bob Zane to Ella Shone: Mrs. Shone, the part of your engine, which is required in the case of gasoline engines to produce an efficient explosive vapor of fuel mixed with air, needs repair.
Ella Shone to Bob Zane: So, how much will it cost to fix my carburetor?

However, the inappropriate use of specialized vocabulary can confuse readers, and make the meaning of a text vague or unclear. Sometimes writers use specialized words to impress their readers, to sound "intelligent," as if they "know what they're talking about." And although some readers are impressed when they do not understand what they are reading, other readers react negatively. Instead of thinking, "Gee, this must be deep. I don't understand a word of it" or "Gosh, Dr. Obscure must be brilliant. I can't follow what he's saying," they may decide that the writer is pretentious or pompous or, worse, dishonest: "This person is using all these technical terms to cover up the fact that he doesn't know what he's talking about."

As always, you must consider your audience and your purpose for writing in determining when and if you should use jargon. Careful editing for such terms is essential because use of jargon can be a flaw in an otherwise well-constructed text. As you edit, examine each technical or specialized term or expression that you use. If the term or expression is unnecessary, replace it with a more commonly used word or expression. If the term is necessary, be sure that your audience is familiar with it; if not, you should provide a definition or an explanation.

> The frequency counts were standardized according to the number of T-units, which are defined as main clauses plus any attached or embedded structures, in each essay.
>
> *or*
>
> The frequency counts were standardized according to the number of T-units in each essay. (A T-unit is one main clause plus any structure, clausal or nonclausal, that is attached to or embedded within it.)
>
> *or*
>
> The frequency counts were standardized according to the number of T-units[1] in each essay. (The definition of T-unit is placed in a footnote.)

Exercise 14

Assume that the jargon in each of the following sentences is unnecessary. Rewrite each sentence so that the meaning is clear.

EXAMPLE:
This computer is *user-friendly.*

REVISION:
This computer can even be used by novices.

1. Your familiarity with Part One of this Data Report Sheet will help expedite any track responses to your call.

2. These procedures will help library personnel interface with members of academic departments.

3. Dr. Meek has been instrumental in facilitating coexistence between the disputing parties.

4. The discussion of eligibility requirements generated a great deal of affect among the subjects.

5. B. Principus has argued that *Gone With the Wind* succeeds as a novel because the denouement occurs simultaneously with the climax.

Exercise 15

Eliminate unnecessary jargon from the following text.

The Board of Trustees approved on June 9, 1982, the attached retirement program, effective September 1, 1982. Seminal aspects of this package were derived from the recommendations of the Faculty Retirement Committee, chaired by Dr. Bill Blast.

The program is a responsive, integrated system which will allow for functional institutional involvement on the part of prospective retirees. Furthermore, its implementation is cost effective, involving modest expenditures, which will be absorbed by existing agencies and vehicles within the institution. A corollary benefit of the program is that it will increase faculty mobility options, providing individuals with the opportunity to seek expansion in compatible or parallel fields of interest, without the risk of financial debilitation.

Please note relevant eligibility provisions, specifically the inception of the policy that requires aspirants to submit a letter of intent to participate in the program to the appropriate contracting officer at least one year prior to his/her projected involvement.

Eliminating Wordiness

Wordiness is a common diction problem, and although it may not necessarily cause a reader to have difficulty understanding a text, it can tire him and thus weaken the effect of an otherwise well-written piece. A tightly constructed text with no excess words is best suited for any reader. Wordiness most often results from one of two major sources: (1) The use of several words when fewer or even one will do, and (2) the use of two or more words or word groups to express, unnecessarily, the same thing (redundancy).

More Words Than Necessary

Some persons require more words to express themselves than other persons do. This is fine. It does not necessarily make a style of writing or of speaking better or worse. However, general, cultural attitudes regarding what is good writing—or good art, good music, etc.—change. (If you want to see a good example of this, read something written by a fiction writer of the last century, such as Dickens, and compare it with a piece of contemporary fiction.) Currently, the consensus among many writers and teachers of writing seems to be that a concise, spare, make-every-word-count style is best, at least for nonfiction prose. Excess wordiness is often associated with artlessness, lack of skill, "nothing-to-sayism," and—worst of all—dishonesty.

Of course, the answer to the question, "would fewer words have been better?" is often debatable. For this reason, wordiness that is a result of "too many words" is often difficult to define and, therefore, difficult to locate and edit away. However, stylists and writing experts rather commonly agree on some sources of this kind of wordiness. Here are a few of these:

1. Commonly used phrases that can be replaced by one word:

for the reason that
due to the fact that   These expressions can be replaced
owing to the fact that   with the word "because."
because of the fact that
in light of the fact that

> EXAMPLE:
> I was upset *due to the fact that* I got a D.
> I was upset *because* I got a D.

2. Phrases that can be compressed into a verb or an adjective:

create pollution in   pollute
cause aging in   age

forward a recommendation	recommend
put forth a demand	demand
make an effort	try
make a motion	move
of a peculiar sort	peculiar
very unique	unique
puzzling in nature	puzzling
of an odd kind	odd
of a strange appearance	strange

EXAMPLE:

The worms found near the warm water vents were *of a peculiar sort.*

REVISED:

The worms found near the warm water vents were *peculiar.*

EXAMPLE:

The students *put forth a recommendation* that they should be allowed to use their meal coupons at the Soup and Salad Bar.

REVISED:

The students *recommended* that they should be allowed to use their meal coupons at the Soup and Salad Bar.

3. Adjectives that are expanded with "type" or "type of":

vegetarian-type	vegetarian
split-level-type	split-level
executive-type	executive
violent type of	violent
nourishing type of	nourishing

EXAMPLE:

Josie served a *vegetarian-type* meal.

Josie served a *vegetarian type of* meal.

REVISED:

Josie served a *vegetarian* meal.

Sometimes inexperienced writers use more words than necessary because they do not have extensive vocabularies or because they do not know how to create new words. For example, a writer who does not know the word "phrase" must use several words to express the concept: "a group of words that functions as if it were one word." A writer who does not feel comfortable compounding words is more likely to produce the sentence "They found lots of ore that contained bauxite" than to produce "They found lots of bauxite-bearing ore."

Overcoming wordiness is not easy. It requires willingness to be concerned with the finer points of a text. It requires trial and error. And it requires a sensitivity to written language. The easiest and most pleasurable way to develop this is to read widely.

Exercise 16

Revise the following sentences to eliminate wordiness.

> EXAMPLE:
> *At this present time,* he has no plans to reassess the project.
>
> REVISED:
> He has no plans to reassess the project *now.*

1. Joleen was perturbed by the fact that her father donated her coat to the church bazaar without asking for her permission.
2. The new restaurant that is located near Southlake Mall serves Chinese and Japanese type food.
3. Teachers always remind their students to read over their essays after they've written them for the purpose of finding errors in sentence structure, spelling, word choice, grammar punctuation, and other errors that occur at the sentence or word level as opposed to the text level.
4. The members of the psychology department, who had been instructed to bloc-vote, made a motion to table the amendment.
5. The Internal Revenue Service representative made an attempt to see where there were errors in the tax return.
6. Near the end of the campaign, both candidates accused one another of calling each other bad, insulting names.
7. The frightening fairy tale was about a dragon who breathed fire.
8. Everyone put forth an effort so that Zelda could attend the conference.
9. Mark is a person of an odd kind.

10. After evaluating the results of the survey, the company executive made a bold type of decision.

Redundancy

Redundancy refers to unnecessary repetition. Word pairs consisting of a word and a synonym are redundant. These pairs often *sound* quite grand: "each and every," "first and foremost," "one and only," "hopes and desires"—

> "And if elected I promise that *each and every* citizen of
> Muncie, Indiana . . ."

Unfortunately, many of these word pairs are so common that they often trivialize writing. Repetition is an important stylistic tool, but it should be original—dictated by the context.

   Redundancy also results from the use of unnecessarily repetitive modifiers. Here are some examples:

modern . . . of today or today's modern	visible to the eye
small in size	red in color
square in shape	wastefully squandered
short in length	organically without chemicals
period in time	important essentials
odd in manner	end result
audible to the ear	past memories
	future plans

   Whenever you write, repetition should be a result of a conscious decision—not an accident. Redundancy does not add anything of value to a text; therefore, you should eliminate it when you edit.

Exercise 17

Revise the following sentences to eliminate redundancy.

   EXAMPLE:
   The *end results* of the new merit policy will soon be apparent.

REVISED:
The *results* of the new merit policy will soon be apparent.

1.   Voter responsiveness is vital to each and every citizen in our contemporary, modern world of today.

2.   The hopes and desires of each and every student were voiced by Council President Hepworth as she discussed future plans for greatly increased student involvement.

3.   Our new deck is rectangular in shape, constructed and made of wood, which is brown in color, and entirely covered with small flecks of mica.

4.   In my opinion, I think the next exam will be of great importance.

5.   The important essentials for future meetings over the next several weeks are being determined.

Exercise 18

Revise the following sentences to eliminate wordiness.

1.   Repair that is done on one's home may take place during any part of the summer season.

2.   The first and foremost important topic for discussion this evening has to do with attendance, which has been low in amount, lately.

3.   On Tuesday at 9:00 a.m. in the morning, the first of three sessions devoted to review of recruitment programs will be presented in a lecture type format.

4.   The purpose of the meeting will be to discuss fully both policies and procedures regarding admission, advisement, and degree requirements that students are expected to fulfill before graduation.

5.   For all intents and purposes, President Bore has alienated the members of his commission that he established by not listening to their recommendations that he has received from them.

6.   All reports that are taken during the period of time from January 16 to January 23 should be submitted to the Provost so that his office staff will be able to evaluate and assess the information for the purpose of determining a final outcome.

7.   Endive's dress, which was a shocking orange in color, outraged Mark, who objected to the fact that it was low-cut in design.

8. The members of the teachers' union put forth a demand that they receive monetary wages for overtime, extra work performed in a professional type capacity.

Editing Word Choice Problems

As with sentence structure problems, a good strategy for locating word choice problems is to read your finished text out loud and listen to it. As you read, you should mark with pencil any words or expressions that make you stumble or that cause even a slight alarm to sound. When you have finished reading your piece out loud, examine each word or word group separately. In addition, keep a list of words that you commonly misuse and try to get a *general* sense of the sorts of word-use problems that you commit. Do you tend to be wordy? Do you tend to misuse words?

Exercise 19

Check the word choice problems that you commit most frequently.

I. Wordiness
   _____ I frequently use more words than are necessary.
   _____ I tend to repeat myself.
   _____ I often use two or more words that say the same thing.
   _____ Sometimes I use inflated, pompous words.

II. Incorrect Word Choice
   _____ I have trouble using the appropriate synonym in a particular context.
   _____ I sometimes use words incorrectly because I confuse similarly spelled or pronounced words.

III. Vague Word Choice
   _____ I use clichés too often.
   _____ I use jargon too often.
   _____ I use general words and expressions quite often.

IV. Improper Formality
   _____ I am often too formal when formality is inappropriate.
   _____ I am often too informal, even if informality is not appropriate.
   _____ I mix formal and informal words together.
   _____ I use slang too often.

Once you locate portions of your text that are problematic, you may select one of three revision strategies: (1) You may delete unnecessary words. (2) You may substitute a more suitable word or expression for a problematic one. (3) You may rewrite the sentence that contains the word or expression.

1. Delete unnecessary words:

   The $15 million dollars in funding currently available will be used to support qualified projects in research at this time.

   REVISED:
   The 15 million dollars will be used to support qualified research projects.

2. Substitute one word or expression for another:

   Bill's horrendous obfuscations enraged his siblings.

   REVISED:
   Bill's terrible lies made his brothers and sisters angry.

3. Reword the sentence:

   Anelida's male parent deemed that Dilworth was not a suitably affluent prospective candidate for his daughter, matrimonial-wise.

   REVISED:
   Anelida's father did not think that Dilworth was wealthy enough to marry his daughter.

Exercise 20

Edit the following text for word choice problems.

Tim Brent is eight years old. He likes to perform a variety of activities. For example, he adores watching good old television; he also is addicted obsessively to video games. And, of course, it goes without saying that he likes to engage in assorted playful activities. Tim is also an ace reader, but this wasn't always the case. Here is Tim's story.

Tim used to have trouble with his reading. His teacher had informed Tim's parents that although Tim was responding positively to mathematical instruction, he was sort of a zero in terms of reading. Tim's parents freaked out when they heard this. They wondered what would happen to Tim if he fell behind in reading. They agonized over whether Tim would be able to cope in this modern, technological world of today. They also worried that Tim's self-image might also be negatively effected: What if Tim became dejected and depressed; what if he started to think that he wasn't up to snuff, vis-a-vis the other kids. Then a miracle happened.

One day, Tim and his folks were strolling casually yet purposefully through some part of a store, and guess what? Some kid was at a computer doing educational stuff, but it was all kind of like a game. Well, Tim's mom got really agitative. She dashed over to the nearby sales representative and presented him with a query as to whether there were fun yet educational tapes for reading. As it turned out, there were a multitude of such tapes, a whole host of them. Tim's folks bought out the store that day. They got a computer and a whole lot of neat reading tapes.

That night was the first of many nights in a long succession of nights that Tim spent, spellbound, at the computer. He was practicing his reading, but—hey—he *liked* it. Far out, right?

Well, you guessed it. Our little story has a happy ending. Tim now reads as well as all the other children of his grade at school. Not only that, he loves to read. Each and every book he reads is something special. Each is a journey into the enchanted land of the imagination wherein dwell enchanted castles and trips to the moon. Because Tim's parents were responsive to his needs, because they synchronized his personal requirements with a functional, systematized, integrated instructional delivery system geared to provide him with optimum educational technology, Tim is okay today. Tim uses a computer. Don't you wish everybody did?

Grammar, Usage, 13
and Mechanics

The terms "grammar," "mechanics," and "usage" most often refer to matters having to do with: (1) the proper forms of nouns and pronouns, verbs, adjectives, or adverbs; (2) agreement between subjects and verbs or between pronouns and antecedents; (3) punctuation, capitalization, and manuscript form; and (4) spelling.

Editing for errors in grammar, usage, and mechanics is similar in many ways to editing for errors in word choice or sentence structure. General guidelines, such as reading with knowledge of the specific errors you often make in mind or reading out loud and listening to what you have written, are applicable. However, there are a few differences you should keep in mind as you edit for errors in grammar, usage, and mechanics.

Since many errors in grammar or mechanics may be very small, often involving one letter or one punctuation mark, they are easy to overlook. Consequently, some writing specialists advocate rather specialized techniques, such as reading backwards, to locate particular errors. We will present these techniques, where applicable. Another difference between editing for errors in grammar, usage, and mechanics and editing for errors in sentence structure and word choice is that this type of editing provides less room for choice. Usually there is only *one* way to spell a word, for example. Many writers, therefore, do not find this type of editing particularly stressful—there are no earthshaking decisions to be made. Unfortunately, as a result, this type of editing may become tedious. Here is, potentially, an explosive mixture: tedium + easy to overlook mistakes = many overlooked mistakes.

Numerous mistakes in spelling, punctuation, and the like can seriously affect even a fine, well-constructed text because a pattern of errors calls attention to itself, creating the impression that the writer does not care about communicating his intention to the reader. Therefore, it is important that you take editing seriously, allowing yourself sufficient time to edit carefully, following a cooling-off period after the completion of your final draft. Often, a writer devotes a tremendous amount of time to a piece; he thinks, plans, thinks some more, researches, plans again, produces a draft, and revises it, often several times. At last he is finished with the majority of the work. But the paper is due at 11:00 a.m., and he has been up half the night working with his text. He collapses, exhausted, at 5:00 a.m. and gets up at 9:45 to be on time for a 10:00 class. At 10:50 he edits hastily (while he is half dead) and finds, not surprisingly, very few errors. Unfortunately, the teacher finds quite a few: confusions between "there," "their," and "they're"; misspelled words, such as "recieved"; subject-verb agreement problems; pronoun-antecedent agreement problems. All of these problems could have been avoided if the writer had given himself enough time to disengage—"unplug himself"—from his text and if he had been alert when he performed his last reading.

Remember: It is unfair to you and to your writing to devote time and effort to creating a fine text, then fail to edit for small matters. The finished product may seem sloppy and poorly constructed as a result—rather like a well-designed, well-constructed tool shed onto which paint has been slopped, leaving bare patches, streaks, drips, and wavy lines. Your time and your thoughts are valuable. Give your writing, which has required an expenditure of your time and which contains your thoughts, all the attention it deserves.

Chapter 13 is divided into four major sections:

☐ The Difference Between Grammar and Usage
☐ Errors in Grammar and Usage
☐ Errors in Mechanics
☐ Spelling

Within these major sections, subsections address specific problems with nouns, pronouns, verbs, punctuation, etc. Consult the Table of Contents or Index to locate readily a problem you may need to work on.

The Difference Between Grammar and Usage

When linguists use the term "grammar," they generally use it in one of two senses. A linguistic description of a particular language, a set of statements or rules that explain how the language works, is called a "grammar" of that language. The set of rules that each human acquires, which enables him to speak and to comprehend his own language, is also called a "grammar." Each child acquires a grammar of his or her own language, in part, by hearing adults speak that language. And since no two children, even siblings, hear adults say exactly the same things, each child acquires a unique grammar. Put another way, no two individuals possess *exactly* the same grammar for their own language. However, although each person possesses a unique grammar of his or her own language, each grammar is very similar to every other in most respects. If this were not so, speakers of the same language would not be able to understand one another.

In what way *do* individual grammars differ from one another, then? You already know the answer to this question. Do you have a friend from another part of the United States who uses a different word than you do to describe something? For example, if you are from Ohio, perhaps you use the word "pop" to describe any flavored, carbonated beverage: "I love pop even though I know it's bad for me." Your friend from New York City uses "soda" to designate this sort of carbonated beverage, however. Who is wrong? Who is right? Neither of you. You and your friend speak different dialects or variations of English. Your English grammar specifies the word "pop" for such beverages; your friend's grammar specifies the word "soda."

From a linguistic standpoint, an expression is *grammatical* for a person if it follows the rules of his grammar. All speakers of English would agree that this string of words is ungrammatical: "House the boy dog in on." People would disagree, however, about an expression such as this: "I seen him do it." Some English speakers have acquired rules that permit the form "seen" as an appropriate past tense; other English speakers have acquired rules that permit only "saw" as a past tense form. Therefore, the sentence "I seen him do it" is grammatical for some speakers of English, but not for others.

Quite often, claims that such utterances as "I seen him do it" or "I done that already" are ungrammatical are not entirely accurate. It is more accurate to label such expressions as *inappropriate for a particular context*. For example, if every person in your home town uses the form "done" as a past tense form ("I done that") in casual conversation, it is both grammatical and appropriate for them to do so. And you are going to make many people angry if you come home after a year or two at college and correct their speech. On the other hand, it is inappropriate—and, for many of your readers, ungrammatical—to use "done" as a past tense form in writing, unless you are corresponding with a close friend. This is because writing is usually more formal than speaking; in many writing situations you are not at all acquainted with your audience.

If linguists use the term "grammatical" to describe any structure that conforms to an individual's own grammar, they use the term "usage" to refer to the *acceptability* of particular forms and structures among various groups of individuals and with regard to various contexts. Most of the writing you are required to do in college and most of the writing you may do after you graduate occurs or will occur in semiformal or formal contexts. The readers in the audiences you will be addressing will often be other professionals and/or other educated individuals. Therefore, when writing, you should usually use those structures that the majority of the members of the "educated middle class" consider grammatical. Taken together, these structures are referred to, collectively, as Standard English Usage or Edited American English Usage. Although the verb, noun/pronoun, adjective, and adverb forms we will present in the next section are grammatical, they are not the *only* grammatical forms. They are merely the forms that are both grammatical and acceptable in most contexts in which writing occurs. We will entitle the next section "Grammar and Usage" to reflect this; "Grammar and Usage" is really shorthand for "Grammatical forms and structures that are appropriate in most semiformal or formal written contexts."

Errors in Grammar and Usage

Noun Forms

NOUN PLURALS

Nouns change form to reflect plurality or to reflect possession. Most regular English nouns appear in their plain, uninflected form if they are singular. If a regular noun is plural, it will carry an "s" ending (inflection):

Singular	Plural
boy	boys
house	houses
bar	bars
infant	infants
fact	facts

The spelling of some regular nouns must be modified when a plural "s" ending is added: leaf/leaves; lady/ladies. If you are uncertain about how to spell the plural form of a regular noun, consult a dictionary or a handbook.

Irregular nouns do not form plurals by adding an "s" ending. These nouns, of which there are fortunately few, form plurals in a variety of ways: child/children; mouse/mice; goose/geese; deer/deer. Some nouns are commonly used in just one form, whether they are singular or plural. "Data," for example, is really a plural form, although it agrees with both singular and plural verbs. The singular form, "datum," is rarely used. The proper singular and plural forms of nouns such as "data" are usually not required, except in the most formal contexts. If you are in doubt as to the proper form of an irregular noun, consult a dictionary or handbook. These reference works will also indicate when and/or whether a little-used form, such as "datum," is required.

POSSESSIVE NOUNS

Nouns can be made to show possession by adding an apostrophe plus an "s" ('s) or by adding an apostrophe (').

Singular nouns that do not end in "s" take an apostrophe plus an "s":

That is the *girl's dog*.
Fred's behavior was odd.
We removed the *bird's food*.

Singular nouns that already end in "s" may take either an apostrophe or an apostrophe plus an "s":

Mr. Edwards' house is nice.   or   *Mr. Edwards's house* is nice.
The *lioness' coat* was beautiful.   or   The *lioness's coat* was beautiful.

Regular plural nouns already end in "s"; therefore, only an apostrophe is added:

The *boys' attendance* was poor.   boy + s + ' = boys'
The *girls' attendance* was poor.   girl + s + ' = girls'

Since irregular plural nouns do not take an "s" ending, an apostrophe plus an "s" is added:

The *children's attendance* was poor.   child + ren + 's = children's
The *men's attendance* was poor.   man + en + 's = men's
The *women's attendance* was poor.   woman + en + 's = women's

There are a number of special circumstances that can occur with regard to possessive noun forms. For example, compound nouns can be made possessive, according to a particular rule: mother-in-law's car.

"A" AND "AN" WITH NOUNS

Often singular nouns are preceded by "a" or "an"; for example, "a house," "a problem," "an answer." The rule is as follows: Use "a" before words that begin with a consonant *sound;* use "an" before words that begin with a vowel *sound:* "*an* hour," but "*a* heavy load." Note that the words "hour" and "heavy" both begin with the letter *h.* However, the *h* in the word "hour" is silent, so the word *sounds* like "our," which begins with a vowel sound: "*an* hour." On the other hand, the *h* in the word "heavy" makes a consonant sound; thus "*a* heavy load."

Exercise 1

Edit the following sentences for noun errors.

1. During the most recent meeting of the evaluation committee, Chair Benz distributed datum which summarize undergraduate grade point averages' according to students majors.

2. The graphs, which place the department slightly above the average, also reveal that the typical major registers for an heavy load.

3. Since there were several important issue on the agenda, program directors distributed their reports instead of reading them.

4.   Madeline Parre, representing the Environmental Safety Committee, reported that exposed asbestos insulations has been found in several areas on both the first and second floor's of Hayes Hall.

5.   Chair Benz will report the Committees' concerns to Bill Vogle, Acting Director of Personnel, after an investigation of the cited areas.

6.   Two proposal for the Professional Travel Fund, totalling $560.00, were discussed and then approved.

7.   Since a eight-month budget cycle is currently under consideration, a new means of program plannings and review must be established and implemented.

8.   Benz will schedule a meeting for all department personnel to discuss peoples' ideas regarding an eight-years plan.

9.   In preparations for this meeting, Gravit volunteered to read several proposal that have been submitted by other units' affected by the new policy.

10.   The Committee next meeting will be Wednesday at 3:30 in the Barth Annex.

Pronoun Forms

Pronouns are words that substitute for nouns (plus their modifiers) or for groups of words that act as nouns: *Faye's new car* broke. *It* broke. *What you did* was nice. *It* was nice. The form of a pronoun reflects its function in a particular sentence; the form also shows agreement between the pronoun and the noun for which it stands, which is called its *antecedent*.

PRONOUN FORM AND FUNCTION

Since pronouns are words that substitute for nouns or groups of words that act as nouns, they may function in all the ways in which nouns function: as subjects, objects, indirect objects, complements, and objects of prepositions. Unlike nouns, pronouns change in form to reflect their function:

Except as possessives, nouns do not change form to reflect their function:

SUBJECT	DIRECT OBJECT
The car broke down.	She kicked *the car*.

Pronouns can change form to reflect their function:

SUBJECT   DIRECT OBJECT
He became upset.   The dog bit *him.*

Pronouns have three forms that indicate their function: the *subject* form, the *object* form, and the *possessive* form.

1. *Subject Form:* I, we, he, she, they
The subject form is used for pronouns that function as subjects and subject complements.

SUBJECT   SUBJECT COMPLEMENT
We know that boy.   The authors of the play are Bruce
                                         and *I.*

2. *Object Form:* me, us, him, her, them
The object form is used for direct and indirect objects and for objects of prepositions.

DIRECT OBJECT   INDIRECT OBJECT   OBJECT OF
                                                PREPOSITION

The noise bothered   She gave *him* a kiss.   I drink to *us.*
  them.

There are some other less common uses of the object form; for example,

> "Annoying *them* was fun." ["Them" is the object of the verbal (gerund) "annoying."]

3. *Possessive Form:* my/mine, our/ours, his, her/hers, their/theirs
The possessive form is used to indicate a possessive relationship; "my," "our," "his," "her," and "their" replace only the possessive noun, whereas "mine," "ours," "his," "hers," and "their" replace both the possessive noun and its object.

> That is *Mary's* house.
> That is *her* house. (replaces possessive noun "Mary's")
> That is *hers.* (replaces possessive noun + object "house")

> *John's* car never breaks down.

> *His* car never breaks down. (replaces possessive noun "John's")
>
> *His* never breaks down. (replaces possessive noun + object "car")

There are also some other less common uses of the possessive form; for example, "His singing was awful." "His" is the subject of the verbal (gerund) "singing."

Pronoun forms often vary in casual conversation. It is not at all unusual to hear sentences such as these:

> "*Him* and *me* went shopping."
>
> "They gave Mary and *I* a hard time."
>
> "Who is it?" "It's *me*."

The forms of the italicized pronouns in the above sentences are grammatical for many speakers of English, but they may not be appropriate for some written contexts. Be sure to use the appropriate pronoun forms if you are writing in a semiformal or formal context. Also pay special attention to compound constructions, since they often confound a writer's sense of what sounds right. "She likes I" will sound strange to most writers, whereas "She likes Jane and I" may not sound strange. "I" is incorrect in both sentences.

VARIETIES OF PRONOUNS

The most commonly used pronouns, the forms of which were presented in the preceding section, are often called *personal pronouns*. There are also other types of pronouns, such as *demonstrative* pronouns; however, most writers rarely have problems with these, with two exceptions: The pronouns "who" and "whom" sometimes cause writers difficulty, and -self pronouns, especially "myself," can also be troublesome.

The form "who" should be used if the pronoun functions as a subject or subject complement. The form "whom" should be used in all other instances, except to show possession, in which case "whose" is used.

SUBJECT	OBJECT OF A PREPOSITION
Who is it?	To *whom* was she speaking?

If "who" or "whom" is in a clause, its form is determined by its function in that clause.

The man [*who* won the lottery] was delighted. (subject of the clause "*who* won the lottery.")

The woman [*whom* we elected] was delighted. (object of the clause "we elected *whom*.")

-Self pronouns contain the syllable "self" or "selves": "myself," "himself," "herself," "yourself," "themselves," etc. They should be used when the subject and the object or complement of a verb are the same. In such instances, these pronouns are called *reflexive pronouns*.

Joe hates *himself.*
I hurt *myself.*
Sheila cut *herself.*
She is not *herself* these days.

We exhausted *ourselves.*
You'll hurt *yourself.*
They drove *themselves* crazy.
I have not been *myself* since the accident.

-Self pronouns may also be used to emphasize another word in the sentence. In such instances, -self pronouns are called *intensive pronouns*.

The chairman *himself* handled the grade appeal.

The president *herself* awarded the trophy.

Neither reflexive nor intensive pronouns should be used unnecessarily. Specifically, "myself" should not be substituted for "me" in semiformal or formal writing:

CONVERSATIONAL
They chased my dog and *myself.*
My mother wants the best for *myself.*

FOR WRITING
They chased my dog and *me.*
My mother wants the best for *me.*

Exercise 2

Edit the following sentences for pronoun errors.

1. Microwaves may seem an unnecessary extravagance to some, but John and me consider ours' to be indispensable.
2. The primary benefit for myself is that meal preparation time can be reduced considerably.

3.   No one can say who microwaves most benefit; they seem to offer advantages to a variety of individuals.

4.   Last summer when my parents bought a microwave, I teased my mother, explaining that a microwave was unnecessary for she and my dad.

5.   Now I'm not certain that my opinion was correct, especially when dinner isn't ready until 8:30 because John and me got home from work late.

6.   Television commercials that advertise different kinds of microwaves, many of whom are reasonably priced, are quite convincing to John and I.

7.   Recently I have begun to wonder whether our friends will give John and I a hard time if we purchase a microwave—after we have paid off the balance we owe on the dishwasher.

8.   Whose to say? Maybe many friends and acquaintances will purchase ovens of their' own.

9.   I am a person whom, John says, is never able to make up my mind without conducting a public opinion poll.

10.   I don't agree with John; I think it's important to decide issues for one's self, but the opinions of others are always useful.

UNCLEAR REFERENTS

A pronoun must clearly indicate the word or word group for which it stands. When it does not, the pronoun is said to have an unclear antecedent or an unclear referent. As you recall, use of a great many pronouns with unclear referents may indicate *writer-based prose*. By the time you are editing, therefore, you should *not* discover lots of pronouns with unclear referents. If you do, you should reevaluate your text; perhaps it is not yet finished. You may need to do some more inventing, planning, or rewriting.

A nearly finished text may contain a few pronouns with unclear referents, however. Here are some general guidelines with regard to pronoun reference:

1.   Be certain that the reader does not have to guess which of two "nearby" nouns is the referent for a pronoun.

> Those errors as well as Joni's ideas for correcting them were
> unusual. Everyone was fascinated by *them*. (Does "them"
> refer to the errors, to Joni's ideas, or to both?)

CORRECTED:
Those errors were unusual, so everyone was fascinated with Joni's ideas for correcting them.

2.   Do not use a pronoun in the first sentence of a paragraph if the reader must look in an earlier paragraph for the referent.

Another *benefit* is that *they* don't require as much care as animals or fish do.

CORRECTED:
Another benefit with regard to plants is that they don't require as much care as animals or fish do.
or
Another benefit of raising plants is that they don't require as much care as animals or fish do.

3.   Try to avoid using pronouns that refer to words or ideas that are implied but not expressed.

Members of the Writing Lab staff distributed several worksheets about common writing problems. *This* helped Joe avoid writing sentence fragments. ("This" does not refer to an explicit word or idea in the preceding sentence.)

CORRECTED:
Members of the Writing Lab staff distributed several worksheets about common writing problems. The worksheet on sentence fragments helped Joe avoid writing fragments.

4.   "It" can sometimes function as a linguistic placeholder: "It is stupid to diet on Thanksgiving." (The sentence is a variation of "To diet on Thanksgiving is stupid.") Try to avoid placing a pronoun "it" close by a placeholder "it."

It is difficult to diet on Thanksgiving, but sometimes *it's* a good idea. (The first "it" is a placeholder; the second "it" stands for "to diet on Thanksgiving.")

CORRECTED:
Dieting on Thanksgiving is difficult, but sometimes it's a good idea.

Exercise 3

Edit the following text for pronouns with unclear referents.

   Next Thursday night from 7 until 9, members of the Writing Laboratory Staff will present a workshop for all students enrolled in Freshman Writing. The workshop will be devoted to a discussion of common sentence structure problems, such as faulty parallelism, and how to avoid them. During the course of the evening, worksheets with explanations and exercises will be employed, and it will give the participants practice and immediate feedback. Since enrollment for the Workshop will be limited, sufficient Writing Lab staff will be available to help students on an individual basis. Last year's participants found this feature of the workshop to be especially valuable. For this reason, all who wish to attend should sign up as soon as possible, either by mailing in the enclosed form or by stopping by the lab for it.

   Students who attend the workshop should bring a dictionary, a handbook, paper, and a pen or pencil. They should also bring several samples of their writing, preferably papers that have been evaluated by an instructor. This will enable a Lab staff person to offer personalized instruction.

PRONOUNS AND SHIFTS IN POINT OF VIEW

Illogical, unnecessary point of view shifts usually indicate a problem in the relationship among the writer, the audience, and the subject matter:

> Jogging is dangerous for *a person's* health if *that person* is over thirty. This danger may not yet be documented, but it soon will be. *A person* over thirty should engage in light exercise: reading, watching television, bath-taking, eating, and so forth. If *you* really want to "get *your* blood moving," perhaps *you* might engage in a more strenuous form of exercise such as walking (to the refrigerator; or to the television to change the channel).

Notice that the writer began with third person ("a person's"; "a person") and switched to second person ("you"). This sort of unnecessary shift in point of view can occur when an apprentice writer uses "you" to mean "people in general."

   Frequent, unnecessary point of view shifts indicate that a text needs more work, that it is not yet ready for editing. However, an occasional shift may slip by unnoticed. You should examine pronouns for consistency, because improper use can cause point of view shifts. Whenever you notice a shift in pronouns, from first person ("I," "we") to second person ("you") to third person ("he," "she," "it," "one") or from any singular pronoun ("he") to any plural pronoun ("they"), be certain that the shift is one that you intended:

> Jogging is dangerous for a person's health if that person is over thirty.
> *I* have determined that this is so through personal experience.

Here the shift from third person ("person") to first person ("I") is justified, since a general statement ("Jogging is dangerous . . .") is followed by a statement of personal experience ("I have . . .").

Exercise 4

Edit the following text for pronoun shifts in point of view.

The Search for a New Vice President
Bill Hayes, Student Representative on the Search Committee

Currently, the nationwide search for a new vice president for public relations is drawing to an end. The VPPR will be responsible for relations between the University and the community. Specific areas of responsibility will include fund raising, publications, alumni relations, and press releases. The new VPPR will also work closely with the business community in Barclay, towards the development of additional employment and recreation opportunities for you. As you can see, he or she will fill a vital role.

Last May, the Search Committee, chaired by Dr. Mary Misfell, selected six outstanding applicants from among the many talented and qualified individuals who applied. Each of the six finalists have since visited the campus and attended numerous interviews with us, the President, the other Vice Presidents, and all College Deans, as well as various faculty and student groups. Our response to all of the finalists has been positive, even enthusiastic. The members of the Search Committee will therefore have a difficult time as we narrow the group of six individuals to three. However, their challenge will not have ended there, since the three finalists must also be ranked before their names are submitted to the President, who is responsible for selecting the new VPPR.

If you have any preferences or opinions, it's not too late for students to make their recommendations to the Committee. But haste is important since President Kleber vows that he will present the members of the Board of Trustees with his choice for the new VPPR at the Board meeting next month, and Committee members are hurrying to accommodate him. The campus and local community all eagerly await the President's choice. I am sure that you will support whomever he chooses.

Verb Forms

Verbs change their form to show tense and to show agreement with a subject. The nature of a helping verb, or auxiliary, that precedes a verb, may also determine its form; for example, if a verb is preceded by a form of the helping verb "have," it must take a special form called the past participle: "I have *sung* a song." "She has *gone* home." "They had *eaten* already."

PAST TENSE

Verbs in English are either regular or irregular. Regular verbs form the past tense through the addition of an *-ed* ending: "walked," "talked," "kissed," "laughed." There are two problems commonly associated with the past tense of regular verbs. Sometimes writers may delete the *-ed* ending in writing, especially if it is deleted in speech: "Marcia walk home alone last night." Although such deletions may be appropriate in speech, written contexts require the past tense ending: "Marcia walk*ed* home alone last night."

The spelling of verbs to which the *ed* ending is added is not entirely consistent. For example, if a verb already ends in the letter *e*, only the letter *d* is added: "I loved his performance" (love/loved). If a verb ends in the letter *y,* the spelling varies; if the *y* is preceded by a vowel, *-ed* is added: "We annoy*ed* him" (annoy/annoyed). If the *y* is preceded by a consonant, it is changed to *i* and *-ed* is added: "She read*ied* herself for the test" (ready/readied). Verbs to which *ed* is added may or may not double a final consonant: "They conceal*ed* the evidence" (conceal/concealed) or "He plan*ned* a party for them" (plan/planned). Although there are a variety of exceptions regarding the spelling of verbs that end in *-ed*, each exception can be accounted for by a rule, such as that involving verbs that end with the letter *y*. If you are uncertain about a particular rule, a handbook will provide you with it. Always look up the spelling of the past tense of a verb in a dictionary if you are not sure of it.

Irregular verbs do not form the past tense by adding *ed*. In fact, irregular verbs most often change form, rather than take an ending, to form the past tense: "sing/sang," "buy/bought," "go/went," "see/saw." Some irregular verbs do not change their forms at all to form the past tense, although this is unusual: "cut/cut," "set/set." Many handbooks list most of the commonly used irregular verbs grouped according to their past tense forms; those verbs that change forms in similar ways are listed together ("sing/sang," "ring/rang," etc.). This makes it easier for a person to familiarize himself with forms he may not use frequently. It is not necessary, nor advisable, for you to memorize all the forms of every irregular verb, however. A good dictionary or handbook will give you this information.

PAST AND PRESENT PARTICIPLES

The past participle form of a verb is used following the helping verb "have" or following the helping verb "be" if the sentence is passive. Regular verbs form the past participle the same way they form the past tense—by the adding an *-ed* ending: "I walk*ed* to school. I have walk*ed* to school for ten years." Irregular verbs form the past participle by changing their form: "I *sang* that song last week. I have *sung* that song for ten years." Here are some more examples of sentences that contain verbs in their past participle form:

PAST PARTICIPLES WITH *HAVE*

I *have* bought a stereo.	She *has* jogged for several years.
The children *have* destroyed the plant	We *had* gotten nowhere fast.
The young man *has* gone.	I *have* always loved your cooking.

PAST PARTICIPLES WITH *BE*—PASSIVE

The dog was *kicked* by the horse.	The house was *bought* by the Halls.
I am often *burned* by the sun.	The song was *sung* by Martha.

Writers can find the past participle form troublesome for a variety of reasons. Both of the problems commonly associated with the past tense of regular verbs are also problems with regard to past participles for regular verbs. Writers may leave the *-ed* off a past participle as well as a past tense verb; for example, "I have walk to school for ten years." In written contexts, this is inappropriate and deleted *-ed* endings should be added where they are required: "I have walk*ed* to school for ten years." In addition, spelling irregularities regarding the addition of the *-ed* ending are the same, whether the *-ed* is a past tense ending or a past participle ending.

Another common problem with regard to past participles is that individuals' grammars vary with regard to past tense and participle forms. That is, for a great many persons it may be grammatical to say *either* "I did that" *or* "I done that." Or it may be grammatical for a person to say *either* "I have done that" *or* "I have did that." If your grammar specifies past tense or past participle forms that are different from the ones listed in dictionaries or handbooks, be certain that you use the appropriate forms in semiformal or formal written contexts. Sometimes it is *not* a good idea to rely on what sounds right as you are proofreading, since the forms you use in speech are the forms that will, logically, sound right. Under these circumstances, your best strategy for editing past tense and past participle forms is to anticipate, by examining other, earlier pieces of your writing, the sorts of inappropriate (for semiformal or formal written contexts) forms you might use and to look carefully for those forms.

Here is one last word of caution with regard to the past participles of regular verbs. As you remember, participles are a member of a class of words called verbals. As such, past participles can function as modifiers:

VERB	VERB MODIFIER
I *have frozen* some brownies.	John ate some *frozen* brownies.
I have *furnished* my apartment.	I rented a *furnished* apartment.

Persons who leave *ed* endings off the past tense and past participle forms of regular verbs will also leave the *ed* ending off past participles functioning as adjectives: "I rent a *furnish* apartment." "Martha is *prejudice* against me." "The jury heard *bias* testimony." If you leave off *ed* endings when you write, be sure to examine adjectives that might be past participles so that you can edit these forms as well: "I rent a furnish*ed* apartment." "Martha is prejudic*ed* against me." "The jury heard bias*ed* testimony."

The present participle form of the verb is used following the helping verb *be*, except with passives: "She *is* running." The present participle form is the same for all verbs: the ending *ing* is added to the verb. The spelling of the *ing* form of verbs is quite regular, although a final consonant may or may not be doubled: conceal/conceal*ing*; plan/pla*nn*ing. In addition, if a verb ends in the letter *e*, the *e* is dropped before the *ing* is added: dance/dancing. Finally, a present participle *cannot* function as a verb unless it is preceded by a form of *be*.

HELPING OR AUXILIARY VERBS

Helping verbs, also known as auxiliary verbs, function with other verbs to form complete verb phrases. In English, not many verbs can function as helping verbs. "Do," "have," and "be" may function as helping verbs:

> I *have done* my homework.
> I *am singing* a new tune.
> I *did make* my bed.

Modals—"may," "might," "can," "could," "shall," "should," "will," "would," "must"—also function as helping verbs:

> I *might study* tonight.
> They *might arrive* early.
> Mr. Jones *must leave* immediately.

Most writers do not have too much difficulty with helping verbs; however, it is important to know which helping verbs change form and under what circumstances. Modals *never* change form: "I might study." "They might study." However, "do," "be," and "have," as helping verbs, do change form to show agreement:

Joe *was* eating.	Mr. and Mrs. Jones *were* eating.
I *have* been tired.	He *has* been tired.
They *do* want to stay.	He *does* want to stay.

The form of "be" (as a helping verb) can also be influenced by the helping verb that precedes it. If "be" is preceded by the helping verb "have," it must be in its past participle form, which is "been."

I might *be* studying.	I have *been* studying.
They will *be* leaving.	They might have *been* leaving.

Exercise 5

Edit the following sentences for verb errors.

1. WLRZ, the local television station, has successfully conclude this year's membership drive.

2.   According to Pat Klima, station manager, additional funds were desperately needed because the cost of renting popular television series has rose drastically in recent years.

3.   Viewers were approach by a variety of methods, including mass mailings.

4.   Station personnel attribute the success of this year's drive, in part, to the increase size of the public segment interested in WLRZ's programming.

5.   In addition, individual families seemed to have being more willing to enroll in monthly installment payment plans, which has enable them to make large contributions.

6.   To quote Bill Maron, Assistant Station Manager, "The wonderful support we have got this year will inspire us all to work twice as hard to bring top quality programming to our viewers."

7.   In an unbias report, the local newspaper recently applaude WLRZ's fund raising effort.

8.   This year's success has inspire a careful examination of the fund raising techniques that were employed.

9.   Since there's "no arguing with success," most are of the opinion that next year's effort ought to resembled this year's as much as possible.

10.   The $156,000 that was raise will provide financial support for a variety of programming and services.

VERBS AS CARRIERS OF TENSE

Many persons confuse "tense" with "time," although they are not the same. Tense is a grammatical concept that has to do with the *form* of a verb. Time, however, has to do with *meaning*. Here is a simple illustration of this:

> Tomorrow I go to Chicago.

The verb "go" in the sentence is in the present tense, or form; the time of the sentence is clearly future—the action is to take place "tomorrow." In English, unlike many other languages, there is not strict tense-time correspondence. In English, adverbs and helping verbs, rather than the form of the main verb, often indicate "time."

You may find the distinction between tense and time useful; it may help you locate and correct another kind of point of view shift, called a "tense shift." As with pronoun point of view shifts, such shifts—if they are illogical or unnecessary—indicate a problem with regard to the relationship of the audience, the writer, and the subject matter. Numerous shifts indicate that a text may need work, that it is not yet ready for editing. Occasional illogical, unnecessary shifts, however, should be edited out of the text.

Sometimes tense shifts are illogical. For example, if you begin an essay by describing what you *would* do if you ever visited Paris ("I would eat at Maxim's. . . . I would visit the Left Bank.") and then you switch, for no apparent reason to the past tense ("And then I took a boat across the channel."), your readers will wonder whether or not you have ever been to Paris, and this in turn will cause them to wonder what your intention is for writing—to explain why you'd like to go to Paris? to explain what you did in Paris? to explain why you'd like to visit Paris again? In circumstances such as this, a change in tense has resulted in a change in time.

On other occasions, tense shifts are merely unnecessary and, therefore, intrusive. To describe actions that were performed habitually in the past, the simple past tense may be used with appropriate adverbs: "Every morning I got up and listened to the birds. . . . I went down to the beach and took an early swim." Habitual past action may also be indicated by the use of the modal "would" plus the present tense form of a verb: "Every morning I would get up and listen to the birds. . . . I would go down to the beach and take an early swim." Notice that two different tenses can be used to express the same "time." The use of simple past is preferable, since it is less wordy to say "ran" than "would run." Whenever more than one tense can be used to express the same "time," there is always the danger of inadvertant switches back and forth between these tenses. This can be intrusive, possibly confusing:

> ". . . Every morning I *got* up and *would listen* to the birds. This always *delighted* me and so I *would become* excited and energized. Surprisingly, I *didn't* have much of an appetite and so I usually *ate* a light breakfast. Soon I *would be* ready for my morning exercise. Always before it *would become* warm I *went* down to the beach and *took* an early swim. . . ."

Be certain that you edit carefully for inadvertant, unintended tense shifts. Reading your essay out loud may help you to locate these.

Exercise 6

Edit the following text for verb tense point of view shifts.

Bill Varney to Receive Award

Evelyn Johnson, staff reporter

Many of you have experienced the same thrills as I have as you watched Bill Varney on the ice at Blass Arena. Even before he leaves Arbor State to compete in national and international contests, we know there was something special about Bill. Maybe it's his energy; maybe it's his precision of execution; or maybe it's the joy skating so obviously inspired in him.

Now we see him only occasionally, when he returns to Arbor to dazzle new fans or to pay tribute to old ones. Bill has many "old" fans: Josh Brown, who has joined the hockey team three years ago because he was inspired by Bill's skating. Marla Torvish, four years ago a freshman, this year herself headed for national testing grounds. All of us consider Bill to be our own. Never mind that he now trains in Colorado; never mind that he lives in California. His home is in Arbor because that is where his most devoted fans lived.

This year Bill has (again) won the gold metal in the Championship. We know that he would. His skating, if anything, gets better this year. It will probably continue to improve, although watching him now, we find that difficult to believe. How can he improve? He's already perfect.

Yes, Bill Varney is a gold metalist again this year. But to his fans in Arbor he will *always* be a champion, win or lose.

VERB CONTRACTIONS

Often endings and/or punctuation do double duty in English. The apostrophe is used with nouns to show possession: "That is Mary's house." The apostrophe can also be used with a verb or a verb plus "not" to show that sounds and, thus, letters have been omitted:

I'm not tired.	The ' replaces *a:* I *a*m not tired.
She'll leave.	The ' replaces *wi:* She *wi*ll leave.
He didn't know.	The ' replaces *o:* He did n*o*t know.

Contractions usually reflect speech and are, therefore, considered inappropriate for formal written contexts, although they may be acceptable in some less formal written contexts. A few commonly spoken contractions may also be misunderstood and, therefore, misspelled: "I would *of* left early." "Would of" is a misapprehension of "would have," which has been shortened, or contracted, in speech to "would've."

Agreement

In English, one word may correspond with another in form to show a relationship between them. Subjects show agreement with their verbs; pronouns show agreement with their antecedents.

SUBJECT-VERB AGREEMENT

A verb in the present tense shows agreement with its subject. If the subject is "he," "she," "it," or any *singular* noun, an *s* is added to the plain, uninflected form of the verb, unless the verb is "be."

> The dog barks all the time.
> The building looks impressive.
> Cooking a gourmet dinner involves a great deal of expense.
> A stitch in time saves nine.
> He looks impressive.
> She runs five miles every day.
> It causes problems for everyone.
> The dog *has* a cold. (note the slight irregularity with the verb "have")
> Mary *does* her work. (note the slight irregularity with the verb "do")
>
> TO BE:
> The dog *is* tired.
> She *is* tired.
> It *is* tired.

If the subject is "I," "you," "we," "they," or any *plural* noun, the present tense of the verb does not take an ending or change form. Again, "be" is an exception:

> The dogs *bark* all of the time.
> The buildings *look* impressive.
> Gourmet dinners *involve* a great deal of expense.
> I *look* impressive.
> You *look* impressive.
> We *run* five miles every day.

They *cause* problems for everyone.

The dogs *have* colds.

The women *do* their work.

To Be:

I *am* tired.

We *are* tired.

You *are* tired.

The children *are* tired.

They *are* tired.

With the exception of the verb "be," verbs in the past tense do not change form to agree with their subjects:

To Be:

The dog *was* happy.

The dogs *were* happy.

I *was* happy.

We *were* happy.

All Other Verbs:

The dog *barked*.

The dogs *barked*.

I *screamed*.

He *screamed*.

You *screamed*.

We *screamed*.

They *screamed*.

When a verb takes a helping verb or verbs, the helping verb agrees with the subject, unless it is a modal ("will," "would," "may," "might," "must," "shall," "should," etc.): "The boy *has* eaten dinner." "The boys *have* eaten dinner." "The boy *is* eating dinner." "The boys *are* eating dinner." But "The boy *might* eat dinner." "The boys *might* eat dinner." If a verb takes more than one helping verb, the *first* helping verb, unless it is a modal, agrees with the subject: "The boy *has* been eating." "The boys *have* been eating."

Subject-verb agreement can cause a variety of problems for writers. As with other endings, the addition of the agreement *s* affects the spelling of words. However, the spelling rules that govern the addition of the plural *s* ending to nouns also apply when the agreement *s* ending is added to verbs.

Another common problem with subject-verb agreement is that although the *s* ending is used on verbs with *singular* subjects, it is also used to make nouns plural. Make sure that you edit carefully for "reversals" if you sometimes get confused about the "s" ending: for example, an *s* on a verb with a plural subject, such as "The dogs barks."

Some speakers of English do not say the *s* on verbs when they speak— "John walk to school every morning"—and this may affect their writing. Written contexts, however, require the use of an *s* ending: "John walks to school every morning." If you leave out *s* endings in your writing, you should edit your texts carefully, inserting the endings where they are required.

Other agreement problems result from the nature of particular sentences. Although the general rule that governs subject-verb agreement is fairly simple, it is not always easy to make subjects and verbs agree, for several reasons:

1. Sometimes it is not easy to determine whether a subject should be considered singular or plural. For example, compound subjects joined with "and" are treated as if they were plural, but compound subjects joined with "or" and with "either . . . or" and "neither . . . nor" may or may not be treated as if they were plural: "*John and Joe* bake pies." "Betty or Mary arranges the flowers." But "Betty or her children *arrange* the flowers." Certain pronouns, such as "everyone" and "everybody," *look* plural, yet they are treated as if they were singular: "Everyone wants a chance." Collective nouns may be treated as either singular or plural, depending upon how they are used: "The *number* of absences increases every year." But "A number of students *read* French."

2. Sometimes the structure of a sentence obscures the relationship between a subject and a verb or makes it difficult to determine what the subject is and/or whether the subject is singular or plural. A modifying phrase that contains one or more nouns, which may potentially be mistaken for the subject, may be located between a subject and a verb: "*Eddie Johnson,* together with his son and two of his daughters, *jogs* every morning. "The *cost* of apples and bananas *seems* outrageous." Inverted word order may make it difficult to locate a subject: "There *were* many moths in the room." ("Many moths were in the room.") "There *was* an apple on the table." ("An apple was on the table.") "Out the window *fly* the birds." ("The birds

fly out the window.") The form of a relative pronoun does not indicate whether it is singular or plural, so its antecedent must be located in order to determine the correct form of the verb: "The person [*who studies*] passes exams." But "The people [*who study*] pass exams."

As you can see, there are a great many circumstances in which the "simple" rule for subject-verb agreement is not so simple. You do not need to memorize all the separate rules that govern subject-verb agreement under these and other circumstances. However, you *should* be aware of these circumstances, so that you know *when* to consult your handbook. A periodic, brief review of the subject-verb agreement section in your handbook should enable you to remember most of the unusual circumstances regarding subject-verb agreement. Then, when you are editing, each time you come upon one or more such "special" circumstances, you will know that you need to consult your handbook—unless you have memorized the appropriate rule and/or exceptions.

PRONOUN-ANTECEDENT AGREEMENT

A pronoun agrees in number and gender with the word it refers to (its antecedent). If a pronoun's antecedent is singular and male, the pronoun should be singular and male in gender: "John drove me nuts. *He* forgot to put out the garbage." Plural pronouns do not show gender, and so they agree with their antecedents in number only: "The women watched the show. *They* liked it."

There are a few unusual circumstances involving pronoun-antecedent agreement, for example, whether collective nouns such as "group" are treated as singular or as plural antecedents. These instances and the attendant rules can be found in a handbook.

The most common problem involving pronoun-antecedent agreement occurs with such commonly used pronouns as "everyone" and "everybody." In speech, many persons use these pronouns as if they were plural: "Everyone wants *their* meal." "Everybody owns *their* own car." This is appropriate in most spoken contexts and in some written contexts. However, it is probably wise to treat such pronouns as *singular* forms in semiformal or formal written contexts: "Everyone wants *his* meal." "Everybody owns *her* own car." Writers who do not wish to use the male gender "his," but who find "his or her" to be cumbersome, should probably replace singular antecedents with plural ones wherever possible: "The students want *their* meals." "Most people own *their* own cars."

Many people commonly use the pronoun "their" as an "all-purpose" pronoun in a variety of informal, spoken contexts: "Every student wants *their* own car." "A person shouldn't buy *their* clothes at the local department store." This use of "their," while grammatical and appropriate for informal, spoken contexts, is not appropriate for semiformal or formal written contexts.

Exercise 7

Edit the following sentences for errors in agreement.

1. A portion of the analysis will be devoted to a discussion of the fees a student must pay before enrolling in their classes.
2. The cost of maintaining office machines have risen steadily this year.
3. Orders for commencement robes and caps are now due; any graduating senior should place their order with the Bookstore by Friday.
4. Several word processing software packages are now available for use with microcomputers; interested personnel should contact Computer Services if one is interested.
5. Wayne Leever and Bill Marsh, both 30-year veterans of Operations and Maintenance, was honored at a retirement party last Thursday.
6. The concert at the Arena was a success in spite of the fact that fans became restless when the soloist, Joe Bolder, arrived late for their performance.
7. The lecture on poisonous snakes of Northwest Ohio were poorly attended, especially since it was rumored that the speaker would pass around live specimens.
8. The local Bloodmobile will be in front of the Student Union on Friday; each donor should arrive as early as they possibly can.
9. Everyone was excited about the arrival of the Vice President and left their classes early to be sure of getting a good seat.
10. A video presentation of speeches by Arnold Needer and Donna Hough, candidates for Mayor, were shown on Public Television last night.

Adjective and Adverb Form

Adjectives and adverbs do not change form, except to show comparison. One-syllable adjectives and adverbs can show two different degrees of comparison with the addition of an *er* ending or an *est* ending. When two items are being compared, the *er* ending is used: "I am tall*er* than Jan." "I'll take the small*er* piece." "He runs fast*er* than Ed does." When three or more items are being compared, the *est* ending is used: "I am the tall*est* in the building." "I'll take the small*est* of the three." "Joe runs the fast*est*."

When an adjective or adverb has two or more syllables, the words "more" or "less" and "most" or "least" may be used to show comparison: "Eddie is more handsome than Brad." "However, John is the most handsome." "The filly, Dasher, ran the race more quickly than the other filly, Tortoise." "But Macon's Wish ran the most quickly."

A few adjectives and adverbs have irregular forms: "good/well, better, best" and "bad/badly, worse, worst." In informal speech it may be appropriate to say, "This is the most silliest movie I've seen in a long time." But in written contexts, either *er/est* or "more," "less," "most," or "least" should be used, not both together.

Editing for Errors in Grammar and Usage

Here are some general strategies for editing for errors in grammar and usage:

1. *Always* put some time, preferably at least 24 hours, between the completion of your text and your proofreading of it.

2. Be willing to spend the necessary time to do more than edit if you find some major problems with your text.

3. Read slowly. If you rush, you will not find all the errors in your text.

4. Try to become aware of your own pattern of errors: Do you have difficulty with verbs? If so, with regard to what? Do you leave off *ed* endings? Do you sometimes interchange past tense forms with past participle forms? Does the type of error you commit sometimes involve a spelling problem, such as the addition of an *-ed* ending? The best way to learn your own error profile is to keep a cumulative record of your grammar and usage errors. Arrange the errors in categories, and keep a tally; your instructor can help you with this. This will give you an idea of the errors you commit and the frequency with which you commit them.

5. Edit *separately* for each error you commit often. That is, if you tend to produce a variety of errors in grammar and usage, proofread separately for each major error. Here is an example: Suppose, when you write, that you occasionally fail to make your subjects and verbs agree, you frequently omit past tense *-ed* endings, you occasionally misplace the apostrophe in possessives, and you frequently use pronouns that do not agree with their

antecedents. Here is what you should do. Proofread separately for *-ed* endings; make sure you examine both past tense and past participle verbs and past participles functioning as adjectives for left-off *-ed* endings. Also, proofread separately for pronoun-antecedent agreement, paying special attention to "their" whenever you find it. Finally, do another proofreading for misplaced apostrophes and subject-verb agreement errors. Remember, your short-term memory is limited; it can hold only seven bits of information. If you try to edit for too many errors at the same time, you will not be effective in locating them. Be certain to use your dictionary and your handbook when you are correcting the errors that you have located.

6. If you read aloud to locate errors in grammar and usage, read slowly and be careful that your speech habits do not cause you to read past errors. If you normally use a particular, inappropriate form when you speak, a quick reading will very likely not help you locate instances of that form. In addition, it is common for persons to translate an incorrect form into a correct one while reading. In other words, the form "walk" may be written in the text, but the writer *reads* it as "walked." When this happens, the writer does not notice or correct the error. For these reasons, reading aloud is generally more helpful in locating problems in sentence structure and word choice than in locating grammar and usage errors.

7. Use spatial strategies to help you locate grammar and usage errors. For example, if you have a problem with word endings, pay particular attention to the ends of words. You might even practice discriminating for endings by selecting a short passage—approximately 100 words—of text from a magazine or book and circling or underlining every word ending of a particular sort—say *ed, ing,* and *s*—that you find. If you have problems with word forms, focus on the shapes of whole words, rather than on the ends of words. Some persons like to hold a ruler under each line as they proofread because they feel it helps them train their eyes on the appropriate portion of text. Some persons like to use their hands to block out preceding and following words or to point to each word as they proofread. Try these strategies; they may help you.

8. Keep your reference tools (dictionary and handbook) handy; otherwise, you may not bother to get up and use them.

Exercise 8

Begin to inventory the grammar and usage errors that you commit. Gather information by looking through some texts that you have already written.

Look for these categories of errors:

A. Nouns
    1. Plural form (*-s*)
    2. Possessive form (*-s*)
    3. Spelling with plurals and possessives
    4. A/An with nouns
    5. Other
B. Pronouns
    1. Case forms
    2. Unclear referents
    3. Point of view shifts
    4. Other
C. Verbs
    1. Past tense form (*-ed*)
    2. Past tense forms (irregular)
    3. Past participle form (*-ed*)
    4. Past participle as adjective forms (*-ed*)
    5. Past participle forms (irregular)
    6. Spelling of regular past tense and past participle forms
    7. Spelling of present participle form
    8. Contractions
    9. Tense shifts
    10. Other
D. Helping Verbs
    1. Spelling
    2. Form
    3. Agreement
    4. Other
E. Agreement
    1. Subject-verb
    2. Pronoun-antecedent
F. Adjectives/Adverbs

Exercise 9

Edit the following text for errors in grammar and usage. Good luck!

MEMORANDUM

To: Faculty and Staff
From: Dean R. Important, Provost
Re: Contractual Intent and Budget

Approximately two-thirds of the University's operateing budget comes from state instructional subsidys. As a result, each years budget planning is highly dependent upon the actions of the State Legislature. In recent months, I have reported to the Faculty Senate, to the Planning Committee, and to other group the many uncertainties regarding this years budget. Although the current appropriations bill, if passed, would increased our subsidies by 5%, it is not at all certain that the bill will receive the number of necessary votes in the House.

Currently, therefore, I can make few forecasts about this. In fact, it is clear that the Board of Trustees will not have sufficient financial information before the end of the Spring Semester to complete the annual budget. This means that it will not be possible for continuing employees to be issue contracts. The University would have no alternative other than to issue letters of intent: such letters will serve to notify everyone that they will receive contracts for employment at a later date. The letters of intent will not make references to salary increase because the amount of money available for such increases are not known.

Nevertheless, I have requested all departments and units to continue to engage in its regular personnel evaluation process. These are mandate by the Academic Charter and a continue postponement of such evaluations will eliminate the opportunities for merit increments when the budget is approved by the Board of Trustees.

These delays in awarding contracts are troublesome; we appreciate the difficulty that they have caused you. However, the efforts of the State Legislature has not yet resulted in a budget, which—in turn—allow our Board of Trustees to approve it. For the immediate future, therefore, we will continue our contingency planning so that we'll be prepared—as much as we are able—for whatever budget we receive. In addition, I will keep personnel informed of any development, should they arise.

I am grateful for your patience and your cooperation. It is greatly appreciated.

Errors in Mechanics

There are many rules that govern *mechanics*, by which we mean matters having to do with manuscript form, punctuation, capitalization, abbreviation, etc. For this reason, we will merely highlight some of the more common rules involving mechanics, especially those related to often-committed errors.

Finding errors in mechanics can be difficult, since the eye must attend to rather tiny features in a text, such as the omission of a comma or the inadvertent substitution of a colon (:) for a semicolon (;). On the other hand, correcting mechanical errors is not difficult because punctuation, capitalization, and abbreviation conform to rules. However, we must make a distinction between *editing* for errors in punctuation and *deciding upon* punctuation, which are distinctly different matters. As a writer writes, he must make many decisions, some of which involve the use of punctuation. For example, a writer may be faced with a decision like this:

"Which option should I choose?"

OPTION ONE:
The delegates were willing to negotiate, but they were not ready to make a decision.

OPTION TWO:
The delegates were willing to negotiate. But they were not ready to make a decision.

Clearly, this writer's decision involves the use of either a comma (,) or a period and a capital letter (. B). But the decision cannot be based on a *rule* for comma or period use; it must be based on such contextual matters as whether and to what extent the writer wishes to separate and to emphasize the fact that the delegates "were not ready to make a decision." Indeed, if the writer chooses to emphasize that idea, he might choose to separate the second sentence *and* to capitalize the word not: "But they were NOT ready to make a decision." Decisions such as these are a part of the writing and rewriting process; they are not a part of editing. By the time a writer is editing his text, he should have made most such decisions.

Manuscript Form

Unless you are typing—in which case you must follow various rules governing margin size, spacing, etc.—the only rule regarding manuscript form that you need to follow is the rule that requires you to indent the beginning of each new paragraph. Of course, you may decide, after you have finished a text, that headings would help the reader move through it more easily. And, if you have produced a research report, the manner in which you document information in your footnotes and bibliography and/or present data is important. There is no universal set of rules governing documentation; each discipline prescribes its own. Not only that, journals, funding agencies, companies, and the like often have additional regulations regarding format and/or documentation. Therefore, it is a good idea to find out in advance any rules governing manuscript form, whether these rules are prescribed by a person, such as your instructor, an agency, a discipline, or a profession.

Punctuation

PUNCTUATION AT THE END OF SENTENCES

Three different punctuation marks may appear at the end of a sentence: a period (.), a question mark (?), or an exclamation point (!). While you are editing, make certain that your periods are distinct and recognizable. If you occasionally write comma splices, be certain that your periods do not resemble commas; if they do, your reader may read them as such. Be certain to eradicate all double or multiple final punctuation, since, in most instances, your readers are likely to consider repeated terminal punctuation either informal or immature, or both: "Wasn't the committee interested in the report of the Student Senate???????" Finally, use the exclamation point sparingly. If you like to use the exclamation point a great deal, examine each instance of use carefully, and eliminate all but the most essential. Overuse of the exclamation point will diminish its effectiveness.

PUNCTUATION WITHIN SENTENCES: SEMICOLON, COMMA, COLON, DASH

Four types of punctuation are commonly used within sentences: the semicolon (;), the comma (,), the colon (:), and the dash (—).

The Semicolon   The semicolon is most often used for one of three reasons. First, it is used to join two related independent clauses. (An independent clause is a clause that can "stand alone" as a sentence.) Here are some examples:

> I got tired. I went to bed.
>
> JOINED:
> I got tired; I went to bed.

They raided the compound. It was deserted.

JOINED:
They raided the compound; it was deserted.

The electricity went out during the storm. It was not restored until the following morning.

JOINED:
The electricity went out during the storm; it was not restored until the following morning.

Second, semicolons are also required when two independent clauses are joined with one of these connecting words, called "conjunctive adverbs": "accordingly," "also," "besides," "consequently," "furthermore," "however," "moreover," "nevertheless," "otherwise," "then," "therefore," "thus," "still." Here are some examples:

I ate too much. I became ill.

JOINED WITH "THEREFORE":
I ate too much; therefore, I became ill.

The mayor endorsed the changes in zoning regulations proposed by the commissioner. The changes were defeated when the city council voted on them.

JOINED WITH "NEVERTHELESS":
The mayor endorsed the changes in zoning regulations proposed by the commissioner; nevertheless, the changes were defeated when the city council voted on them.

Less frequently, semicolons are used to separate lengthy items in a series, especially if the items contain commas. Here is an illustration of this use of the semicolon:

Each of the participants was given a questionnaire, a survey of their interests and of their preferences; a booklet of instructions, some of which were to be ignored; and a marking pencil containing specially prepared graphite.

Each of the participants was given a questionnaire, a survey of their interests and of their preferences, a booklet of instructions, some of which were to be ignored, and a marking pencil containing specially prepared graphite.

Notice that the punctuation in the second sentence gives the reader no clue to the major and minor divisions within the sentence. In fact, if sentence two is read first, it is easy to mistake "a survey" as another item given to the participants. The use of the semicolon in the first sentence, however, makes it clear that each participant was given three items: a questionnaire, a booklet, and a pencil.

There are two common errors involving semicolons. Sometimes semicolons used with connecting words such as "therefore" or "moreover" are misplaced: "The argument was a common one however; the means of presentation was unusual." The semicolon always precedes a connecting word that is being used to join two sentences: "The argument was a common one; however, the means of presentation was unusual."

Sometimes semicolons are mistakenly used to separate portions of a sentence that are not independent clauses or items in a series: "Having determined that he would not receive his refund as promised; Mr. Bell wrote a letter to the president of the company." "The children left behind a series of messes; clots of food, spilled pop, and broken toys." Semicolons used in this way should be replaced with proper punctuation: "Having determined that he would not receive his refund as promised, Mr. Bell wrote a letter to the president of the company." "The children left behind a series of messes: clots of food, spilled pop, and broken toys."

Exercise 10

Read the following sentences carefully and edit them for semicolon errors. Some sentences may be correct.

1. The delay was inexcusable; therefore the two parties agreed to sever the partnership.
2. As a consequence of their actions; the team was disqualified.
3. The play closed early; nevertheless the actors were paid in full.
4. He couldn't make a down payment; unless he got a raise.
5. The commissioner vetoed the changes; nevertheless, the city council remained firm in its resolve.

The Comma   There are many rules governing comma use, some of which are applied more uniformly than others. For example, the rule that requires a comma between the name of a city and a state is uniformly applied: "Toledo, Ohio." Others might be described as optional to preferable, for example, the rule that requires a comma following an introductory element: "After the long night, Marcia decided to go home." Quite often, a decision to use or not use a comma is governed by the context and, therefore, is not a matter of editing.

We will not reproduce the numerous comma rules here; that would be needlessly redundant, since your handbook already contains them. However, here are some general strategies regarding comma use that you may find helpful.

1. Use commas to indicate that a modifier is *not* in its usual place, especially if the modifier is long. Adverbs usually modify verbs, which are most often located near the ends of sentences; word-group adverbs that appear at the beginning of the sentence are *not* in their "usual" place, therefore, and should be separated from the sentence with a comma:

> EXAMPLES:
> *Because they finished the test,* the students left the room.
> *After many hours of careful stalking,* the lion finally chased the deer.
> *In spite of his many assurances*, we didn't feel comfortable.

Single-word adjectives usually precede the noun they modify; word-group adjectives usually follow the noun they modify. Adjectives placed elsewhere with regard to the nouns they modify should be set off by commas:

> EXAMPLES:
> The children, *tired and cranky*, whined all day long.
> *Watching the sea gulls glide over the water*, Daisy couldn't remember the last time she felt so relaxed.
> The new math instructor arrived early, *anticipating questions*.

2. Use a comma if its omission would cause the reader difficulty. Although too many commas in a sentence can be distracting, sometimes it is essential to provide the reader with a comma. Here are a few sets of sentences; notice that without a comma the reader must stop and reread in order to interpret the sentence properly.

In the spring time seems to race by.
In the spring, time seems to race by.

As the weather changed attitudes towards work seemed to improve.
As the weather changed, attitudes towards work seemed to improve.

But while the water dripped off came the paint.
But while the water dripped, off came the paint.

3.   Do not use commas to separate subjects from predicates or verbs from objects or complements, even if the subjects, objects, or complements consist of word groups:

INCORRECT:
What she did, was to write a letter of complaint. ("What she did" is the subject of the sentence.)

CORRECT:
What she did was to write a letter of complaint.

INCORRECT:
They wondered all night, whether the issue would pass. ("Whether the issue would pass" is the object of the verb "wondered.")

CORRECT:
They wondered all night whether the issue would pass.

INCORRECT:
Joni's idea was that, each person would receive extra vacation time for any additional work. ("Each person . . ." is the complement of the verb "was.")

CORRECT:
Joni's idea was that each person would receive extra vacation time for any additional work.

4.   Do not separate a two-part compound element with a comma, even if the element consists of a word group:

INCORRECT:
What we expected, and what we found were quite different.
("What we expected" and "what we found" are the two parts
of a compound subject.)

CORRECT:
What we expected and what we found were quite different.

INCORRECT:
I wondered what to do, and where to go. ("What to do" and
"where to go" are the two parts of a compound object.)

CORRECT:
I wondered what to do and where to go.

INCORRECT:
The members of the executive board examined the proposal
with care, and with caution. ("With care" and "with caution"
are the two parts of a compound modifier.)

CORRECT:
The members of the executive board examined the proposal
with care and with caution.

Comma problems are more often a result of too many commas than of
too few commas. When you are editing for comma problems, therefore,
you should probably examine your text for unnecessary commas. Again,
you should become familiar with the sorts of comma errors that you tend
to commit. For example, if you separate two-part compound elements with
a comma, you must examine every "and" preceded by a comma *very*
carefully to determine whether the "and" connects two parts of a compound
element. If it does, you should remove the comma. Here is an example:

SENTENCE ONE:
The students objected to the display in the union, and they
complained to the Director. ("And" precedes an independent
clause, "they complained to the Director." Therefore, the
comma is appropriate.)

SENTENCE TWO:
The students objected to the display in the union, and
complained to the Director. ("And" precedes the second half

of a compound predicate, "complained to the Director."
Therefore, the comma is not correct.)

Edited:
The students objected to the display in the union and
complained to the Director.

The preceding example illustrates another useful strategy for editing for
errors involving commas: Whenever possible, pay close attention to the
structure of sentences that contain punctuation about which you are uncertain. Most punctuation rules, including those for commas, depend on
sentence structure. For example, in order to apply the rule regarding the
punctuation of introductory modifiers, or to determine whether you have
misapplied it, you must be able to locate the subject of a sentence; otherwise,
you will not be able to determine whether or not a sentence contains an
introductory modifier. An introductory modifier is a modifier that precedes
the subject of a sentence: "*After polishing the car for hours,* Marcia was
tired."

When you are editing for comma errors, do *not* make decisions about
whether to add or delete a comma by reading out loud and "listening for
pauses" *unless* you are certain that you know how to read out loud well.
A person who is not skilled at reading out loud well may read and insert
unnecessary pauses. Here are some of the places in which an unskilled
reader might insert pauses when reading out loud the first sentence in
this paragraph:

> When you are editing / for comma errors / do not make decisions
> about whether to add / or delete a comma / by reading out loud
> and / listening for pauses / unless you are certain / that you
> know how to read out loud well.

Of course, the result of inserting commas in all or most of these places
would be a sentence that many readers would find difficult to process:

> When you are editing, for comma errors, do not make decisions
> about whether to add, or delete a comma, by reading out loud,
> and listening for pauses, unless you are certain, that you know
> how to read out loud well.

If you do not know how well you read out loud, ask your instructor for
guidance.

Finally, in order to edit for commas and other matters involving punctuation, you must be fresh and alert. Be sure to allow a reasonable period of time between the completion of any major work on your text and the beginning of your proofreading for mechanics. In addition, if you know that you make a great many grammar and usage errors, edit for errors in punctuation separately—preferably after allowing some time to elapse following your editing for errors in grammar and usage. Errors in comma use may seem small and trivial, but a great many of them, especially a great many unnecessary, incorrectly used commas, may seriously affect the reader's perception of the quality of your text.

Exercise 11

Edit the following sentences for comma problems.

1. What she said, was cancel the book orders.
2. They feared all night, whether the storm would cease.
3. But as the submarine sank crewmen said their prayers.
4. In spite of the good weather no one seemed particularly happy.
5. Belinda's conception of the problem was that, too many of us are trying to become the head of the group.
6. What we had heard, and what we actually saw were quite two different things.
7. The friends said goodbye in the foyer, and wished each other a happy voyage.
8. Be certain that, when you get home you call the cleaners.
9. Nobody was really certain whether the event was cancelled, or scheduled as usual.
10. What had happened last night was that, they simply got tired and went home.

The Colon   When it is used within a sentence, the colon is often used as a sort of punctuational equal sign (=). Used in this capacity, the colon indicates that something equivalent is to follow:

> Her needs were simple: a small living space, transportation to
> and from work, a modest stipend for food. ("needs" = "a
> small living space, transportation," etc.)

One thing is clear: the committee members must reach an agreement before the end of the week. (The "thing that is clear" = "the committee members must reach an agreement. . . .")

The rules that govern language can be subdivided into three subsystems: phonological, semantic, and syntactic. ("three subsystems" = "phonological, semantic, syntactic")

A colon may also be used in place of a comma before a long quotation. A colon is more effective than a comma in calling the reader's attention to a quotation:

COMMA:
In his opening day speech, President Bilge said, "We must all work together to create a working environment that encourages each person to develop his or her potential."

COLON:
In his opening day speech, President Bilge said: "We must all work together to create a working environment that encourages each person to develop his or her potential."

Colons are often used to indicate that an example or explanation is to follow:

PRECEDING AN EXAMPLE:
"A sentence fragment may result from the separation of a modifier from the sentence of which it is a part: *Opening the present with zeal.* Josh tore the paper to shreds."

PRECEDING AN EXPLANATION:
"The situation is difficult: neither of the parties is willing to compromise."

The main error that writers commit when they use colons within sentences is to interrupt a sentence by separating an important part of it from the rest of the sentence. Here are some examples:

INCORRECT:
The women at the day care center decided to make two policy changes: to raise tuition and to stop providing breakfast

because they needed to economize. (The colon and its phrase,
": to raise tuition and to stop providing breakfast," separate
the reason for the policy change, "because they needed to
economize," from the rest of the sentence.)

CORRECT:
Because they needed to economize, the women at the day
care center decided to make two policy changes: to raise
tuition and to stop providing breakfast.

INCORRECT:
The leaders of the group: the president, the provost, and the
treasurer, left the conference early. [The colon and its phrase,
": the president, the provost, and the treasurer," separate the
subject of the sentence, "the leaders of the group," from the
predicate, "left the conference early."]

CORRECT:
The leaders of the group, the president, the provost, and the
treasurer, left the conference early.

or

Some members of the conference left early: the president, the
provost, and the treasurer.

INCORRECT:
The main portion of the letter, which explained the reasons
for their dissatisfaction: inequitable treatment and low pay,
was deleted.

CORRECT:
The main portion of the letter, which explained the reasons
for their dissatisfaction, inequitable treatment and low pay,
was deleted.

or

The newspaper didn't print the main portion of the letter,
which explained the reasons for their dissatisfaction:
inequitable treatment and low pay.

As you can see, there are two means of editing errors in colon use. You
can replace the colon with another, more suitable punctuation mark, often
a comma. Or you can rework the sentence so that the colon and the
structure that follows it come at the end of the sentence.

Exercise 12

Edit the following sentences for errors in colon use.

1. The issue became complicated for two reasons: no one knew who had authored the memo and all of us were ashamed because the memo had been lost.

2. The panel members: Larry, Justin, Joan, and Betty, called for a referendum to halt the sale of liquor.

3. Forget the soda: Jack has brought fifteen cases and none of us can drink that much after the last party.

4. Each of them: the mayor, the treasurer, and the county supervisor were indicted.

5. All of their thoughts were centered on: winning the game.

The Dash   Dashes are used rather infrequently—especially since one of their major functions is to emphasize a part of a sentence by setting it off. Overuse of the dash may diminish its effectiveness as a means of emphasis. Here are some examples of sentences in which the dash is used to provide emphasis:

> The members of the study group decided to report their findings immediately—to the president of the institution.

> The evaluation precipitated a remarkable response—a deluge of protests.

> Tabitha decided to quit her job—immediately.

Sometimes a dash can be used in place of a comma if a sentence already contains a great many commas. In such instances, the dash, since it is a different kind of punctuation, helps the reader determine the important structures within a sentence:

> Comma:
> The residents of the building, especially those who had lived there for more than five years, were determined to prevent it from being sold to an agency that would, very likely, convert the apartments into condominiums, expensive condominiums.

> Dash:
> The residents of the building, especially those who had lived there for more than five years, were determined to prevent it

from being sold to an agency that would, very likely, convert
the apartments into condominiums—expensive
condominiums.

When you are proofreading, try to edit out unnecessary dashes, especially
if you know that you tend to overuse them. However, you should also look
for sentences in which there seem to be a great many *necessary* commas;
if none of the commas can be eliminated, perhaps one can be replaced by
a dash, especially if this will emphasize an important element within the
sentence.

PUNCTUATION IN PAIRS

Often punctuation marks work in pairs (or, as with commas, in series) to
set off or separate structures within sentences. This is especially true if
the structures are nonrestrictive and/or movable or if they seem to be
interjected or inserted into a sentence. Here are some examples of sentences
with nonrestrictive and/or movable structures set off by commas:

The students, eager to be home on time for vacation,
arranged rides well in advance.

The organizers, considering the needs of all the workers at
the company, proposed a variety of workshops and
information sessions.

All of the children, especially those with weak reading skills,
were encouraged to attend.

The young woman, with the brown hair long enough for her
to sit on, played the flute solo at the concert.

Here are some examples of sentences with interjected structures set off
by dashes:

The attitude of the majority of the students—at least the
majority of those polled—was negative.

Each of the enclosures was helpful—we thought—in assisting
members of the fifth ward.

Marcia was angry—in fact furious—about the results of her
exam.

Three kinds of punctuation, the comma, the dash, and the parenthesis, occur in pairs. (Parentheses, of course, always occur in pairs.) There are a variety of rules governing the use of this punctuation. In some instances, however, the use of *any* of these three sorts of punctuation would be grammatical. In such instances, the decision to use commas, dashes, or parentheses is related to the context: how much separation is intended; how important is the structure to be set off; how much does or should the structure disrupt the normal flow of the sentence:

> The documents, which were highly inflammatory, were distributed at the beginning of the meeting.

> The documents—which were highly inflammatory—were distributed at the beginning of the meeting.

> The documents (which were highly inflammatory) were distributed at the beginning of the meeting.

The punctuation of the structure "which were highly inflammatory" is correct in each of the three example sentences. But notice how the different punctuation affects the meaning of the sentences. Although you probably make many—if not most—such decisions regarding punctuation as you draft your text, you may wish to review these decisions as you are editing and alter them if you think it is appropriate to do so.

You should also be careful to edit for *both* elements in a punctuation pair, especially with commas. If you mean to set off a structure within a sentence, *one* piece of punctuation will only delineate either the beginning or the end of the structure; this will not help your reader identify the structure at all. In fact, it may cause difficulty:

> INCORRECT:
> After the movie, the children, who had been quite well-behaved became unmanageable. [Because the comma at the end of the modifier "who had been quite well-behaved" has been deleted, the phrase "the children" appears to be set off. This is confusing for the reader because "the children" is the subject of the sentence; subjects of sentences are not set off with commas.]

> CORRECT:
> After the movie, the children, who had been quite well-behaved, became unmanageable. [The other comma of the

comma pair has been inserted, setting off the modifier, "who had been quite well-behaved."]

Exercise 13

Edit the following text for errors in punctuation pairs.

After the first showing of the movie, the church group, already tired from the picnic decided not to stay for the second feature. The movie was—after all the least interesting part of the conference activities. (No one felt the courage to tell Bob, the conference director that, of course. The younger kids, eager to toast marshmallows (and hear ghost stories rushed off to the river bank ahead of the chaperones. In the end, most of us felt—not without some weariness, mind you—that the weekend had, more or less been a success.

PUNCTUATION ASSOCIATED WITH WORDS: APOSTROPHE, HYPHEN

Two punctuation marks are commonly used within words: the apostrophe (') and the hyphen (-).

The Apostrophe   As explained in the grammar and usage portion of this chapter, the apostrophe is used with nouns to show possession:

> The women's ideas were very good.
> Before the day was over, Joshua's toys were put away.
> The boys' team was very skilled.
> Wondering about the results of the survey, Mr. Morgan asked his son's opinion.

The apostrophe is also used in contractions to indicate omissions:

> We'll be leaving this Thursday.
> Before the weekend arrives, let's finish this work.
> I'm not going to finish on schedule.
> There's going to be a debate about this.

Other, less common uses for the apostrophe are described in a handbook.

Editing for apostrophes may not be simple. The apostrophe is a tiny mark. And it is used to delineate two quite different matters. If you do not leave out apostrophes, you merely need to train your eye to attend to this rather small "squiggle" located near the "top" of a letter or word rather than near the bottom, and make certain that your placement is accurate. If you leave out apostrophes associated with possessives, then you need to proofread for possessive nouns, making certain that the noun has an apostrophe as well as an *s*. Again, attend to placement. If you are not good at spotting apostrophe problems, eye-training practice may be useful. You might choose a passage from a text and circle the apostrophes that you find. Finally, if a text is intended to be formal, it should not contain any contractions; you need, therefore, to proofread carefully for contractions and edit out any that you find.

The Hyphen   Hyphens are most often used in compound words that have not been in use long enough to be spelled as one word. Many commonly used words in English are compound words that are spelled as one word; "greenhouse" and "football" are examples. Other compound words, although in common use, are spelled in the dictionary with hyphens, such as "snail-paced" or "spaced-out." Sometimes hyphens are used in words with prefixes or suffixes, such as "ex-husband." The best strategy for determining whether you should or should not use a hyphen is to look up the word in the dictionary. The dictionary will show your word spelled as one word, with a hyphen, or as two separate words. If you cannot find a word in the dictionary, but you intend to use it as a word, spell it with a hyphen: "The *pre-freshmen* arrived last week." If you use a word that is made up of several words, use hyphens between them: "The foul-cursing politician" or "The hurry-up-and-finish-it essay." Since hyphens are probably left out more often than they are put where they are not needed, you should look for instances in which you might have deleted a necessary hyphen. Also, make certain that you edit for switched hyphens and dashes; they function very differently, and you do not want to confuse them. Typed dashes consist of two lines (--); typed hyphens consist of one (-). Longhand dashes may merely be drawn longer than hyphens (—), but we recommend that you use two lines for a dash, regardless. In that way, your reader will always recognize a dash and be able to distinguish it from a hyphen.

Capitalization

Editing for capitalization more often involves locating and correcting words that *should* be capitalized but are not, rather than vice versa. Although there are far too many capitalization rules for you to memorize, you need to be familiar with the range of rules so that you have a general sense of what needs to be capitalized. The best way to become familiar with the range of capitalization rules is to read through the section on capitalization in your handbook more than once. If you frequently make capitalization errors, you should also determine whether there is a pattern; for example, do you have difficulty knowing when and when not to capitalize academic disciplines, such as economics, chemistry, English, physics, Spanish? Once you discover your particular pattern of capitalization problems, you should edit with specific structures in mind.

Exercise 14

Edit the following sentences for apostrophe, hyphen, and capitalization errors.

1. The boys clothes were thrown all over the living room.
2. The green-house prices were exorbitant but we paid them anyway.
3. The spanish teachers' car was undamaged by the tornado.
4. The frequent mis-use of the word "regard-less" is a product of poor Schooling in Midwestern States.
5. Although I dont always agree with Hank, he seems to have his head on straight.
6. The porter family from new Mexico doesnt have a new phone number yet.
7. Our newspaper, the business times-Herald, just announced that it was hiring ten new employees.
8. Theres no reason why the committee cant meet tuesday instead of Monday.
9. Frankly, I dont mind if the children sing Rudolph the rednosed reindeer again this year.
10. Something's always going to happen when Sheila drives the cadillac to work.

Quotation Conventions

A writer may choose to quote someone directly (direct discourse): John said, "I am sorry." Or he may choose to quote someone indirectly (indirect discourse): John said that he was sorry. Punctuation is not the only matter affected by the choice of direct or indirect discourse. The structure of the sentences that reflect direct or indirect discourse are different:

DIRECT DISCOURSE:
The students shouted, "We're not leaving!"
The president asserted, "The university must go forward."
Mary asked, "Can I leave class early today?"

INDIRECT DISCOURSE:
The students shouted that they were not leaving.
The president asserted that the university must go forward.
Mary asked if she could leave class early.

Editing for quotation errors, then, is not just a matter of examining punctuation. You must examine each instance in order to determine whether you are quoting *exactly* or whether you are reporting what was said. Some writers mix direct and indirect discourse: Mary wondered "whether I should leave." Such mixtures create problems with sentence structure as well as with punctuation. When you edit, make certain that the structure of your sentence reflects what you intend it to reflect. If you are quoting directly, and if your sentence is structured properly, you must examine your quotations for proper punctuation and capitalization. The quotation should be enclosed in quotation marks, the first letter of the quotation should be capitalized, and a comma or colon should precede the first quotation marks:

Lorna asked her instructor, "Do I need to retype my entire essay
or may I cut and paste portions of it?"

Placement of punctuation is also important; in general, terminal punctuation (such as a period) is placed before the final quotation mark. There are a variety of circumstances under which quotations may be incorporated within a sentence, and many of these circumstances are governed by rules.

Exercise 15

Edit the following text for errors in quotation conventions.

When the evening began Laura nervously asked if "she could leave her purse on the counter near the door."
"I don't mind, but you'd better leave your jewelry in the safe, I told her."

Then it became apparent that she wasn't the only one who was somewhat distressed by the guest list. Why did Charlie come, Theresa quizzed. What was I supposed to say: "He came because I wanted to make everyone uneasy?"

Charlie himself wasn't too pleased with the turn of events. "Can't you see it was a mistake, Nell"? I shouldn't have come, he confided. But there was no use prolonging the suspense. All of my friends needed to know that he was out of prison and heading for a new life. The rest of them asserted that it was not "possible" for a thief to turn over a new leaf.

Charlie would prove them wrong, I thought to myself.

Editing for Errors in Mechanics

Our treatment of mechanics has by no means been exhaustive. We have presented some commonly used rules of mechanics, omitting a great deal— for example, rules that govern underlining and rules that govern abbreviation. We have also omitted a great many uses of items that we did cover—for example, uses of quotation marks other than direct quotation. We presented the matters we did discuss within the context of editing: how does a writer edit for errors in mechanics? Here, collectively, are the strategies we recommend for editing for errors in mechanics.

1. Edit for errors in mechanics when you are alert and well rested.
2. Allow sufficient time to elapse after the completion of major work on your text before you begin to edit.
3. If you have many difficulties with grammar and usage, you should edit separately—preferably at another time—for errors in mechanics.
4. Determine the nature of the mechanical errors that you commit. Edit for these particular errors; develop strategies that will help you locate them.
5. Always have a handbook nearby when editing for mechanics.
6. Read very slowly. Use a ruler, or your hands, or a piece of paper to help you focus your eyes on the text as you read.
7. Scan your text to determine whether a particular punctuation mark, such as the dash, appears to be overused.

Exercise 16

Begin to determine your own pattern of errors. Examine your essays and indicate the sorts of errors you commit. Look for these categories of errors:

A. End Punctuation
    1. Periods
    2. Exclamation points
    3. Question marks
    4. Other
B. Punctuation Within Sentences
    1. Semicolons (describe the nature of the errors)
    2. Commas (describe the nature of the errors)
    3. Colons
    4. Dashes
    5. Other
C. Punctuation Pairs
    1. Commas (describe the nature of the errors)
    2. Dashes
    3. Parentheses
    4. Other
D. Word Punctuation
    1. Apostrophe with possessives
    2. Apostrophe with Contractions
    3. Hyphen
    4. Other
E. Capitalization (describe the nature of the errors)
F. Quotation Marks
    1. Direct quotations (describe the nature of the errors)
    2. Other
G. Underlining, Abbreviations, Numbers, Other (describe the nature of the errors)

Exercise 17

Edit the following text for errors in mechanics.

Dear Mr. Baker:

   Approximately two weeks ago we sent letters to a select group of undergraduate students primarily seniors inviting each one to attend a day long workshop on the topic "The search for Excellence in Undergraduate Curriculum." At that time, we asked each of the students to submit the names of two individuals who would also be invited to attend. We told students that they should nominate persons who would benefit from the workshop, and who'd contribute significantly. You have been nominated and, thus we are extending an invitation to you to attend the workshop. It will last from 9:00 a.m. to 4:00 p.m. on Saturday May 24.

The main speaker at the workshop will be Dr. Maybelle Mayloff, Senior Curriculum Analyst and Specialist from the state department of education, she will deliver a talk about the "ideal curriculum design and means of implementing it. We are fortunate to have Dr. Mayloff as our featured speaker, since she has been a major force with regard to several reforms: increased foreign language requirements; changes in language arts curriculum; increased science and math requirements, recently instituted by the state.

Following Dr. Mayloffs talk, a panel of educators: Dr. Mark Feeno, Dr. Evelyn Teebe, Dr. David Yentle, and Dr. Bonita Marquez will respond with reactions, and with commentary. The workshop participants will, then form small study groups each group assigned a specific task.

If you are interested in attending what promises to be an exciting important workshop please complete the attached form, and send it immediately to the center for the study of education 200 Abel Hall. It is important that we receive your response by the end of the week—since we have a packet of materials and background readings that we wish to send each participant!

This Workshop on "The search for excellence in undergraduate curriculum is being co-sponsored by Able Vine Zeedly foundation and by the Center for the study of Education. We all hope that you'll attend, and help make our conference a success.

Spelling

A dictionary is an essential reference work for a writer. One should be accessible throughout the writing process. Some writers wish to be able to determine the spelling of particular words as they are writing; other writers need to determine the exact meaning of particular words as they are writing. Many writers merely use a mark of some sort to indicate words that they intend to look up in the dictionary later, as they are editing. The detection and correction of spelling errors can be done at any time during the writing process; however, spelling errors can easily slip by until a text is nearly completed and should, therefore, be attended to—again—during final editing.

As with other errors, you can locate and correct spelling errors much more easily if you are conscious of the kinds of errors you make. You can then attend to certain words and certain letter combinations, which is much simpler than scrutinizing each and every word for a potential spelling error of some sort. What follows is a discussion of some common sources of spelling problems and some strategies for locating and correcting them.

Unfamiliar Words

Everyone constantly encounters new words by reading them and/or hearing them spoken. Encountering an unfamiliar word in speech rather than in writing presents several problems: the context in which it is heard is not "fixed"; it is not written down so that it and the unfamiliar word within it can be examined carefully. As a result, a listener's sense of the meaning of an unfamiliar word may not be entirely accurate. Additionally, the visual shape of a word encountered in speech cannot be recorded.

Most people do not remember how or when they acquire particular words, whether in spoken contexts or written contexts. It is, therefore, a good strategy to look up *every* word that is unfamiliar, rarely encountered or used, in a dictionary. If you find it distracting to look up words in a dictionary while you are writing, you should keep a pencil handy; circle (or check or underline) any word that you are not entirely confident about. You can look up these words later, after you have completed most of your work, erasing each circle as you verify each word.

Pronunciation

Although the spelling of a word may reflect the way it sounds, this is often not the case; "en*ough*" is an example. The letters in the English alphabet do correspond with sounds, but there are only 26 letters in the alphabet and far more than 26 sounds. Consequently, the same letter often represents more than one sound: *a*bout; *c*at; *f*ather. Also, English spelling is not regular with regard to sound-letter correspondences, and so the same sound may be represented by several different letters or letter combinations: *f*ather; enou*gh*; *ph*ylum. To further complicate matters, every speaker of English possesses a unique grammar. Therefore, not all speakers of English pronounce words in the same way.

Because of the many differences in sound-letter correspondences, relying on the way a word sounds as the sole means of determining how it is spelled is not always a good idea. One of our students was aware of this when he announced that he needed to look up the spelling of "Tennessee." His teacher was surprised: "But Joe, you're wearing a hat with the name of the state spelled on it." And Joe said, "No. I mean how do you spell 'tennessee' as in 'he has a tennessee to do something.'" Joe did not use "tendency" frequently, and he knew that he needed to look it up.

Of course, uncommon or infrequently used words are not the only ones that are not spelled the way they sound. And it may not occur to an inexperienced writer to look up a word that he uses often in speaking. An inexperienced writer, therefore, may assume, on the basis of pronunciation, a spelling that proves to be incorrect. "Would of" is a good example of such an error. In speech, the contraction of "would have" is "would've," which many people pronounce "would of"—thus the spelling "would of."

Since there is no special way to determine which commonly used words you should look up in a dictionary and which you should not, begin immediately to keep a list of words that you misspell. Try to determine which ones, if any, you misspell because of the way you pronounce them. Then either memorize the spelling of these words or remember that you should look them up: "I know I never spell 'separate' right; I've got to look it up."

Endings

As you recall, nouns, verbs, and adjectives regularly take endings. Nouns become plural by adding an *-s* ending. Regular verbs show the past tense or past participle form by means of an *-ed* ending. All verbs form the present participle by means of an *-ing* ending. Adjectives show degrees of comparison by means of *-er*, and *-est* endings or by the addition of the words "more," "less," "most," and "least."

There are a number of spelling rules associated with the addition of these endings, all of which are contained in your handbook. You should be familiar with these rules, or you should be familiar with the circumstances under which they are required. In the latter case, you will need to look up the rule in your handbook, or you will need to look up the word in your dictionary. Otherwise, when you add endings to nouns, verbs, or adjectives, you may misspell a word. For example, suppose you need to write the plural form of the word "city." You need to know *either* of the following: (1) "City" ends in a *y* that is preceded by a vowel; therefore, the spelling is slightly irregular—I can't just add an *s* (citys). I need to look up the rule in my handbook. Or I need to look up the spelling of the plural form of "city" in my dictionary. (2) "City" ends in y. The rule is that if a word ends in a y that is preceded by a consonant, the y changes to i and *es* is added: "cities."

One of the common processes by which new words are formed in English is through the addition of prefixes ("large"—"enlarge") and/or suffixes ("teach"—"teacher"); this process is called *derivation*. Words formed through the process of derivation are often difficult to spell. This occurs because many commonly used suffixes are pronounced in the same way but spelled differently: "ance/ence"; "tion/sion." Sometimes the spelling of an ending reflects the grammatical function of that ending. The endings of the words "typist" and "happiest" are pronounced the same; the different spelling reflects the fact that they do not function in the same way. The ending on "typist" is a suffix, which has been added to create a new word: "type"—"typist." The ending on "happiest" is the superlative (a degree of comparison) ending, which has been added to show that three or more entities have been compared, and one of them is the "most" happy. Often letters at the end of a word are dropped or doubled when a suffix is added: "combine/combination"; "occur/occurrence." Many of the spelling rules that govern the addition of a suffix are the same as the rules that operate when regularly used endings, such as *s*, *ed*, *ing*, *er*, or *est*, are added. If you are not certain how a word with a prefix or suffix is spelled, you should look it up in your dictionary, unless you know the appropriate spelling rule.

Words That Sound Alike

Some words that sound alike but that have different spellings and different meanings are frequently confused with one another. Scanning a list of such words prior to editing is sometimes a good means of recognizing them.

CONTRACTIONS AND POSSESSIVE PRONOUNS

The apostrophe (') is commonly used under two circumstances: with nouns to indicate possession, as in "Mary's house," "the boys' dog," "a child's rights," and in contractions to indicate omissions: "I'll go soon," "She's tired." Pronouns do not show possession by means of the addition of an apostrophe plus an *s;* they change form to indicate possession. Here are the possessive forms for pronouns: "my/mine"; "your/yours"; "his/his"; "her/hers"; "its"; "our/ours"; "their/theirs"; "whose." Since pronouns change form to show possession, an apostrophe associated with a pronoun indicates a contraction: "I'm" = "I am"; "you're" = "you are"; "we're" = "we are"; "it's" = "it is"; etc.

Here are some contractions and possessive pronouns that are commonly confused because they sound similar:

its/it's	The group made *its* contribution. (possessive) John says *it's* time for dinner. (contraction = it is)
your/you're	I like *your* style. (possessive) *You're* on the team. (contraction = you are)
their/they're	*Their* goose is cooked. (possessive) *They're* losing. (contraction = they are) Note: "Their" and "they're" are also confused with the word "there," which can also be contracted with "are": "*There* are six children in the family"; "*There're* six children in the family."
whose/who's	*Whose* gloves are these? (possessive) *Who's* leaving? (contraction = who is)

Edit carefully for confusions between contractions and possessive pronouns. If you are not certain which form is correct, you can always "uncontract" the contraction and see whether the resulting sentence makes sense: "Their/they're laughter was contagious." Uncontract the contraction: "They are laughter was contagious." The sentence does not make sense; therefore, "their" is the correct form: "Their laughter was contagious."

OTHER FREQUENTLY CONFUSED WORDS THAT SOUND ALIKE

Here is another list of words that have different meanings and are spelled differently, yet are pronounced similarly:

accept/except
advise/advice
affect/effect
all ready/already
all together/altogether
all ways/always

capital/capitol
cite/sight/site
cloth/clothe
coarse/course
complement/compliment
conscience/conscious

allude/elude   council/counsel
allusion/illusion   descent/dissent
ascent/assent   desert/dessert
assistance/assistants   devise/device
bare/bear   elicit/illicit
board/bored   fair/fare
brake/break   formally/formerly
breath/breathe   forth/fourth
by/buy   holy/wholly
human/humane   presence/presents
later/latter   principle/principal
lead/led   respectfully/respectively
lessen/lesson   right/rite/write
lose/loose   stationary/stationery
maybe/may be   supposed to/suppose
moral/morale   to/too/two
past/passed   than/then
patience/patients   through/thorough
peace/piece   waist/waste
personal/personnel   weather/whether
precede/proceed   were/where/wear

Editing for Errors in Spelling

Once you have located them, spelling problems are easy to correct if you know how to use a dictionary. However, misspelled words may be difficult to find, since they often "look" correct. Some strategies will increase your ability to locate misspelled words; however, if you frequently overlook a great many misspelled words, then you need to develop strategies that will help you improve your ability to spell. In this case, we recommend that you purchase a "programmed" spelling review for adults; such a text will review for you, lesson by lesson, the important spelling rules and principles. A programmed text is written to be used by a person without the aid of an instructor; thus, you will be able to review spelling rules on your own and at your own pace.

Here are some methods for editing for errors in spelling. Once you have located potential spelling errors, you need to look up each word in a dictionary—unless you are certain that you know how to spell it.

1.   Allow sufficient time to pass after you complete major work on a text and before you edit.

2.   If you tend to overlook misspelled words regularly, you should edit separately for spelling errors. Do not edit for all errors in grammar and usage, mechanics, and spelling at one time *unless* you rarely make errors of these sorts.

3.   If you are a poor speller, keep an up-to-date list of the words that you misspell. The list should be alphabetized, and you should update it each time you receive an evaluated piece of writing that contains spelling errors that you overlooked. Scan your list immediately before you edit. You should also work with a list of frequently misspelled words, such as the one in your handbook; select a few words at a time and learn the correct spelling for each word.

4.   Become familiar with the types of spelling errors that you make and learn any appropriate rules.

5.   Keep a pencil handy when you are drafting so that you can circle words that you think may be misspelled. In this way you will not have to interrupt your writing to look up words in the dictionary.

6.   Keep a dictionary close by *at all times*. Otherwise, you may be tempted not to bother looking up a word because it is too much trouble.

7.   Develop memory "tricks" that will help you remember how to spell words that cause you difficulty; for example, "separate has 'a rat' in it: sep*arat*e."

8.   Sometimes it is easier to locate misspelled words if your text is typed rather than handwritten. Try typing a draft *before* you edit for spelling, even if a typed draft is not required.

9.   Reading out loud may not be helpful, since pronunciations of words vary. However, if you do read your text out loud to spot spelling errors, be certain that you read slowly. Try to isolate each word, since normal speech is rapid and tends to combine words into pronunciation groups that do not reflect how the words within those groups are spelled. For example, in normal, rapid speech "Did you go?" is pronounced as one word: "didjugo?"

10.   Increase your precision in attending to written words by doing discrimination exercises: select a passage of text and have a friend misspell many of the words and then recopy or retype the passage for you. You should find and correct every error. Check your results with the original passage: Did you locate every error?

Exercise 18

Begin to collect and categorize the types of spelling errors that you make. Examine your essays and indicate the sorts of errors that you commit.

A. Unfamiliar Words (list in alphabetical order)
B. Words That Take Endings
    1. Regularly added endings (list the words): *-ed, -s, -ing, -er, -est*
    2. Other endings (list the words): *-ant/-ent, -ance/-ence, -nce/-nts, -tion/-sion,* other
C. Pronunciation Differs from the Spelling (list in alphabetical order)
D. Words That Sound Alike but Are not Spelled Alike (list in alphabetical order)
E. Words with Letters That You Misorder (list in alphabetical order): *ie/ ei,* other

Exercise 19

Edit the spelling errors in the following sentences.

1. I would of examined the documents more carefuly, but I didn't sleep well last night and that seems to have effected my performance.
2. Please seperate the completed applacations from the incomplete ones.
3. The occurances of last evening must not be repeated; otherwise, we might loose our lisence.
4. The assistence I was given by they're Costumer Relations Officer wasn't particularly helpful; infact, I probly could of done better by myself.
5. Evan bought some new cloths after he lost fourty pounds; everyone has been complementing him because he looks terific.
6. The students are becomming bored with the current recreation program and there moral is getting low.
7. I have already refered several of my freinds to the Writing Lab because its in thier best interest to learn how to revise thier own papers.
8. Occassionaly I study for an exam several nights in a row, but I usualy find its suficent to prepare the night before.
9. Responsable citizens should participate in their own governence and exersise their right to caste a vote.

10. We will precede through the remaining chapters at an accelarated pace since the end of the semester is loomming before us.

Exercise 20

Edit the spelling errors in the following text.

Dear Sir or Madam:

I have recently discovered that there is an opening on St. Anselm's hospital staff for a laboratory technition. I am presently a senior at Fanshaw State University, majoring in biology; I plan to graduate in June with a degree in microbiology.

Early in my college career, I became interested in pathology and so I have taken courses in licology, virology, and parisitology. All biology majors are required to take a two semester sequence in chemistry, which I completed my sophmore year. I also took additional courses in chemistry, specificly, qualitative analysys, quantatative analysis, and organic chemistry. For the past two years I have arranged my course work so that I could develope my skills in the detection and identification of diseases, especially those caused by bacteria.

Both my biology classes and my chemistry classes have given me the oppotunity to develope my laboratory skills: I have extensive experience in titration, in developing appropriate growth media, and in the growing as well as the maintenance of bacterial cultures. My work with bacterial cultures has also included the identification of particular cultures as well as the separation and maintenance of one culture from a media that contains a vareity of cultures. I have also worked extensively with the microscope and I have experience with various staining techniques and with using an oil imersion lense.

Last spring semester, I completed the internship required of microbiology majors. I choose to do my internship in the laboratory at Mercy General Hospital in West Lamington. I can, if required, provide you with the evaluation of my performance; I also received a letter of commendation from Mary Briggs, who is one of the Lab Directors.

I have already been offered a job as a lab technition at Mercy General, but I have lived in Newark all of my life; most of my family lives in Greater Newark. I am familiar with the city and I would prefer to work in the vicinity.

If you desire any additional information, such as letters of recommendation or my university transcript, please let me know; I will see to it that you recieve these immediatley. I would also be pleesed to interview with any members of your hospital staff at their convenience.

Sincerely,

Exercise 21

Edit the following text for errors in grammar and usage, mechanics, and spelling.

Dear Dr. Delcrow:

I am writing in regard to your anticipated opening for an English teacher. I am a senior at Bostwick State University; I will graduate this June with a Comprehensive English Education major. My file which includes my Official transcript, and letters of reccommendation is availible from the University Placement Office.

My qualifications for these job are unique: I am compatent to teach grammar, reading, writing, and literature, not only that my comprehensive major will certify me to teach speech classes as well as English classes. I am currently student-teaching a rewarding experience indeed.

Allow me to tell you more about my academic preperation: For almost four years I have been studying to teach English, although I did begin my academic career as a Mathematics and Economics major. I have taken many literature courses: poetry, fiction, and drama, that I have enjoyed and profitted from. I have also enrolled in speech courses and in Creative Writing courses. Last semester I did a senior tutorial which has enabled me to explore fully the relationship between the poetry of John Donne and computer technology.

My experience is as extensive as my course work. I have since my sophomore year, been tutering students' in writing. I am also a member of various organizations such as The National Caucus of Students Preparing to be English Teachers. As I have said, I am currently student teaching under the supervision of Mrs. Joyce Karter who has been assigning me numerous tasks. I haven't as yet been allowed to teach class, but I am confident that this might ocur in a matter of weeks.

Before I close, I would like to tell you about one other qualification that I possess, I am able and willing to coach a number of sports: football, swimming, hockey, baseball, basketball, tennis and track. During highschool I was a member of each of these teams; receiving a varsity letter for all of them. I was also voted most valuabel player on the football, swimming, hockey, and track team my senior year. While at collage, I have not participated formerly on any of these teams but I am confident that my highschool experience, and my physical skills will enable me to coach them if needed.

If you are interested in more information about me or if you would like to set up an interview please contact me. I am most eager to hear from you.

Sincerely,

INDEX